AFRICAN & AMERICAN

NATION OF NATIONS: Immigrant History as American History

GENERAL EDITORS: Rachel Buff, Matthew Jacobson, and Werner Sollors

African & American

West Africans in Post–Civil Rights America

Marilyn Halter and Violet Showers Johnson

NEW YORK UNIVERSITY PRESS

New York and London

NEW YORK UNIVERSITY PRESS
New York and London
www.nyupress.org

References to Internet websites (URLs) were accurate at the time of writing.
Neither the author nor New York University Press is responsible for URLs that
may have expired or changed since the manuscript was prepared.

Library of Congress Cataloging-in-Publication Data
Halter, Marilyn.
African & American : West Africans in post-civil rights America /
Marilyn Halter and Violet Showers Johnson.
pages cm. — (Nation of nations: immigrant history as American history)
Includes bibliographical references and index.
ISBN 978-0-8147-6058-1 (cl : alk. paper) — ISBN 978-0-8147-6070-3 (pb : alk. paper)
1. West Africans—United States—Social conditions. 2. West Africans—United States—
Ethnic identity. 3. United States—Emigration and immigration. 4. Africa, West—
Emigration and immigration. I. Johnson, Violet Showers. II. Title.
E184.A24H35 2014
305.896'6073—dc23 2014011581

New York University Press books are printed on acid-free paper,
and their binding materials are chosen for strength and durability.
We strive to use environmentally responsible suppliers and materials
to the greatest extent possible in publishing our books.

Manufactured in the United States of America

10 9 8 7 6 5 4 3 2 1

Also available as an ebook

To the Memory of Amanda Houston and Lawrence H. Fuchs

CONTENTS

PREFACE: GRIOTS FROM DIFFERENT SHORES

In West Africa, the *griot* is a staple in the preservation and presentation of the history of the region and the people. Griots, also known as wandering musicians, move extensively within their communities and beyond. In the process they expand their outlook and collect numerous diverse experiences that shape their craft. Although, fundamentally, griots' expertise is endogamous, as it is handed from one generation to another, they are also known to move beyond traditional familial and social borders. Their journeys take them to new locations where they may meet others like them with whom they join forces to develop and recount stories of a particular people.

In many ways we see ourselves as such collaborating griots who have broken from the ingrown dictates of the craft and who have brought together the experiences of our travels to tell the stories of West Africans in the United States. We are daughters of two diasporas who have embarked from different shores: Violet from West Africa—from Lagos to Kaduna to Freetown. While she was being introduced to civil rights history by a white Peace Corps volunteer, who shared his *Ebony* magazine with the neighborhood kids, Marilyn was moving from her tiny Jewish community in northern Minnesota to New England to experience the civil rights and social justice movements as a college student. As Violet was leaving Africa for the first time and launching her transnational travels within Canada and England before finally coming to the United States, Marilyn had found her way to New Bedford, Massachusetts, and Cape Verdean Americans. Several years later, our paths crossed intellectually and the wandering griots finally met to begin our own intricate collaboration. Our partnership is very much representative of this West African genre as we continue to move within the society we study and in how we have shaped this project. Whether watching the World Cup with Ghanaians at a restaurant in Chicago (in a remarkable stroke of luck, the match was between Ghana's Black Stars and the U.S. team), attending an evening of celebrating Nigerian fashion in Houston, visiting a West African tropical food store in Maryland before breaking bread with a Sierra Leonean family, or observing the complex transnational diasporic existence of West Africans and Afro-Caribbeans in South London, Peckham, Brixton, and Bermondsey, England, as participant-observers, much like the West African griots we have wandered within these communities, gathering our lyrics for the stories we recount and analyze in this book.

Using selective sampling to conduct qualitative, in-depth interviews, we have carried out our ethnographic investigations in a range of locations where West African immigrants are aggregated. Although ours is a nonrandom sample, we have been mindful of selecting key respondents to include a gender balance and diverse representations of a wide variety of ethnic, nationality, religious, age, social class, and occupational groups. Thus, we have conducted field work and collected oral histories from those of all walks of life among especially Nigerians in the Houston and Atlanta metropolitan areas; Ghanaians in Chicago and the Washington, D.C.-Maryland-Virginia corridor; Sierra Leoneans in greater Atlanta, the D.C. area, London, and Sierra Leone; Liberians in Providence and Minneapolis-St. Paul; and Cape Verdeans in cities and towns throughout Massachusetts, Rhode Island, California, New Jersey, and the Cape Verde Islands. With regard to the Francophone West African community, although we conducted some interviews in the New York metropolitan area, we have relied more heavily on the excellent existing studies in this field, especially works by Zain Abdullah, Cheikh Anta Babou, Manthia Diawara, Sylviane Diouf-Kamara, Ousmane Oumar Kane, and Paul Stoller.

Our journeys were much enhanced by the skilled graduate and undergraduate research assistance we received along the way. We thank Elisa Vitalo, Estelle Pae, Shelly Habecker, Marcy DePina, Yolanda Curtis, Afua Agyeman, Osei Agyeman-Badu, Sandra Enimil, Veronica McComb, and Annie Wilson. We are enormously grateful to Boston University's Institute on Culture, Religion and World Affairs, especially the dedicated support for this project that former director Peter L. Berger gave us from its inception. As we embarked on this endeavor, we also benefited from the collegiality of Jill H. Wilson of the Brookings Institution, who shared some of her demographic findings on African immigration. We have had the opportunity to present pieces of this research at the University of Minnesota, George Washington University, the University of Massachusetts Boston, the University of Massachusetts Dartmouth, the University of Maryland, the University of Michigan, Agnes Scott College, Boston University, Texas A&M University, the Russell Sage Foundation, and the Massachusetts Historical Society's Immigration and Urban History Seminar Series. The feedback we received at these presentations invariably helped to sharpen our analysis and stimulate our thinking. We also thank our editor at NYU Press, Eric Zinner, as well as Nation of Nations series editors Rachel Buff, Matthew Jacobson, and Werner Sollors. We remain particularly indebted to Matt, who read the manuscript with such incisive engagement and, much to our delight, at every stage conveyed his affirmation of its value with scintillating gusto!

Marilyn is particularly grateful to two giants in the field of immigration studies for setting her on the path to this project. In separate conversations more than a decade ago, both David Reimers and the late Lawrence Fuchs emphasized the dearth of scholarship on recent immigrants from Africa and pushed her to build on her earlier research on the history of the Cape Verdean diaspora to explore this broader topic. She has also been fortunate to be part of a small community of women, her "work and play" group, that has been meeting in various iterations for nearly thirty years to shepherd each other through the challenges of leading meaningful professional lives with joy and lightness. She so appreciates the precious connections and loving guidance of Peggy Bacon, Bettina Borders, Kathy Condon, Janet Freedman, Donna Huse, and Sandee Krupp. Marilyn also especially cherishes her friendship with Doris Friedensohn, first kindled at an American Studies Association convention many years ago. Doris has been not only a keen reader of portions of this manuscript but also a dazzling companion in the dissections of American culture and politics. Finally, Marilyn dedicates this book to her mother, Marcella Halter, who during the years that Marilyn was working on it, reinvented what it means to be eighty-something and now ninety-something as an age of stunning vibrancy; to her husband, Jonathan DePina, whose incandescent love and unswerving support are simply immeasurable; and to their sparkling and accomplished children—Conor, Marcy, and Portia—as well as their grandson, Bowen, each of whom combines thoroughly American experiences with deep links to continental Africa, past, present, and, most gratefully, future.

Violet owes much of the inspiration, knowledge, and understanding for her input in this joint project to entire West African immigrant communities, especially the Sierra Leonean community of metropolitan Atlanta. She is most grateful to members of these communities for their gracious accommodation of her sometimes intruding presence and their courteousness as they journeyed with her through changing and conflicting insider (fellow immigrant)/outsider (detached scholar) phases of interactions. Many members of the Nigerian and Sierra Leonean communities became her *ebi* and *fambul* (relatives). Their support and enthusiasm for this project clearly conveyed the African adage, "it takes a village." Violet cannot name every member of this village of supporters, so she will simply say *eshé* and *tenki* to all. However, she would like to acknowledge by name three people to whom she dedicates this book: her mother, Edna Taiwo Showers, whose transnational life continues to shape Violet's; and her husband, Percy Ayomi Johnson, and her son, PJ, for their love, dedication, and willingness to understand that the many Sierra Leonean and other West African immigrant functions they attended as a family were never simple cultural socialization, but potentially vital sources of material for *African & American*.

Introduction

The Newest African Americans?

There is a new breed of internationally mobile, young people
of African descent making their mark on the world. They are
neither Africans nor Americans or Europeans for that matter but children of many worlds, Afropolitans they are.
—Taiye Tuakli-Wosornu, "I Am an Afropolitan"

In her memoir, *My Heart Will Cross This Ocean*, Kadiatou Diallo,
mother of Amadou Diallo, the unarmed immigrant from Guinea who
in 1999 was killed by four New York City police officers, discusses her
response to how her son was described in the media:

> None of this hurt me as much as *unarmed West African street vendor*.
> This label stole his story. To call him West African revealed nothing. He
> had lived in three different West African countries, in five different towns
> or cities in Africa, with subtleties that made each one distinct. He lived
> in two different cities in Asia, had studied in the best schools in these
> places, and had been part of a neighborhood in New York for nearly two
> and a half years, selling, buying, eating, rooting for teams, kicking a ball
> in the playgrounds, going to the movies. Didn't that give him even the
> slightest claim to being not just a West African but a New Yorker too?[1]

Kadiatou Diallo's lament speaks directly to the central aims of this
study, a project that probes such questions as these: Just who was Amadou Diallo? What is the meaning of West African identity, and what
are the claims of West African newcomers to the United States? Will
these overwhelmingly nonwhite African migrants who come from
such wide-ranging cultural backgrounds ever become New Yorkers

or Texans or Minnesotans, too? In short, will they become the newest African Americans? Bridging the fields of immigration, ethnic, and African American studies, this volume explores issues of cultural identity formation and socioeconomic incorporation among immigrants and refugees from West Africa during the past forty years.

The recent influx of West Africans to the United States is part of a much wider postcolonial phenomenon, evident in a modern-day dispersal of sub-Saharan Africans within and outside the continent. Consequently, a vibrant new African diaspora has been unfolding in diverse ways, and the United States has been pivotal to this development. As scholars have remarked about the African diaspora in general, it is characterized by heterogeneity and hybridity. Change, transformation, or, as Paul Gilroy describes it in his seminal work, *The Black Atlantic*, "transfiguration" underscores the diasporic experience, even as the participants struggle to transplant their pasts and "repeat the unrepeatable."[2] The term "West African" connotes a pan-ethnic conglomerate with color as well as some aspects of shared regional and historical

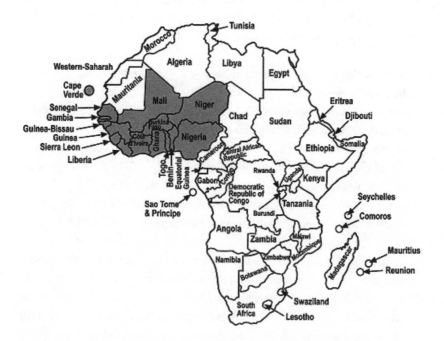

Western Africa. Source: The World Bank, http://go.worldbank.org/0EV05NZQo1.

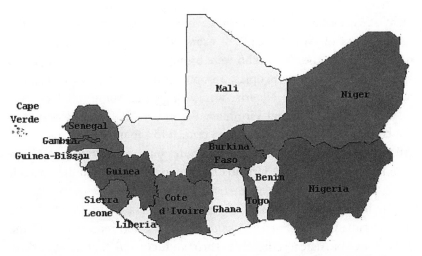

The Economic Community of West African States (ECOWAS). Source: Marcon International, Inc., http://www.marcon.com/marcon2c.cfm?SectionGroupsID=51&PageID=356.

experience in common. The nations included under this rubric—Benin, Burkina Faso, Cape Verde, Côte d'Ivoire, Gambia, Ghana, Guinea, Guinea-Bissau, Liberia, Mali, Mauritania, Niger, Nigeria, Senegal, Sierra Leone, and Togo (Saint Helena, a British overseas territory in the southern Atlantic, is also included on some lists of countries in West Africa)—represent the legacy of colonial intervention that coerced peoples of a wide variety of traditions, cultures, languages, religions, and worldviews who otherwise would not have necessarily grouped themselves in this way. Nonetheless, since this was the part of Africa where much of the transatlantic slave trade was conducted, the region signifies a cultural geography that represents continuity between long-standing African Americans who are the descendants of slavery in the United States and the newest arrivals from the continent. The linkage stretches back to well before the nation was formed. Though brought to the New World in chains, Africans were among the first Americans, while today they constitute a notable segment of the country's most recent settlers.

Indeed, the ancestors of most black Americans today would most certainly be linked back to the areas of the continent that constitute the nations of West Africa since the majority of those who were forced into slavery and who ended up on America's shores from the colonial period right down to the abolition of the slave trade in the United States were captured out of West Africa.[3] For example, throughout the eighteenth century, among the slaves who were brought to toil in the Chesapeake, the proportion of Igbo peoples, a population that originated from the area that later became Nigeria, was so high that some scholars have begun to refer to colonial Virginia as "Igbo Land."[4] Thus, the region of the continent of Africa that was so crucial to the initial making of the Atlantic World during these many decades past is continuing to play a significant role in refashioning the contemporary black Atlantic through the establishment of new West African immigrant communities.

The increased presence of African newcomers to the United States has prompted native-born blacks to become much more aware of the specificities of African ethnicities through increased contact with their continental counterparts. A related factor in the shifting dynamics of this newest iteration of the global black Atlantic has been the craze to trace and discover one's origins via the advanced technologies that DNA testing now makes possible. As the Nigerian-born NBC television correspondent, Michael Okwu, put it in the opening line of a 2005 feature on the *Today* show about the Genographic Project, a collaboration between National Geographic and IBM to collect DNA samples, "The search for our ancestors is a national pastime—the second most popular hobby after gardening."[5] In the meantime, taking advantage of these new sequencing methods and an ever-expanding database, flawed as these investigative tools have been shown to be, Oprah Winfrey has learned that she is descended from the Kpele people who lived in the Guinea Highlands of what is now central Liberia; the celebrity minister T. D. Jakes was able to track his ancestry to the Igbos of Nigeria, as was Academy Award–winner Forest Whitaker, while Whoopi Goldberg found out that her lineage comes from the Papel and Bayote tribes that clustered in modern-day Guinea-Bissau. Taking it a step further, the actor Isaiah Washington became the first African American to gain Sierra Leonean citizenship based on DNA matches. Ever since, he has dedicated much of his time and donated significant resources to the country he now counts as his homeland, including setting up a village school in southern Sierra Leone. Over and over again, as the ability to determine distinctive ethnicities and pinpoint tribal origins becomes more sophisticated, the native-born African American population is discovering that the transatlantic ties to their forebears most often weave back to the region of West Africa.

While some with the means and an adventurous outlook do make the trip to West Africa to cultivate their newfound ancestral identities, the majority do not actually physically travel to the continent to pursue such connections. Instead, they rely on the surrogate West African communities already transplanted to this side of the Atlantic to nurture the link. For example, Stella Stinson, whose DNA testing traced her ancestry to the Mendes of Sierra Leone, found in the vibrant Sierra Leonean immigrant community in Atlanta a tangible base from which to learn about, affirm, and project this newly discovered ethnic identity. As if to publicly illustrate this affiliation, in April 2008, when the musical group Sierra Leone Refugee Stars visited Atlanta, she not only joined "other" members of the local Sierra Leonean community at the preperformance dinner and backstage events but also proudly held up her DNA Certificate of Heritage in every photograph in which she appeared. The heightened awareness fostered by the increased visibility of West Africans in the neighborhoods, churches, *masjids* (mosques), schools, and shopping centers of areas where long-standing descendents of slavery also reside in combination with the much publicized discoveries by high-profile celebrities of their antecedents in West Africa that have triggered the more widespread interest in pursuing these potential bonds mark a new phase in the remaking of the Atlantic World.

But it is not just the linkage of the American-born with the West African–born that has been legitimized. Those who compose the recent Caribbean diaspora in the United States are also pinpointing their roots and ascertaining the role of West Africa in their family histories. And as with their African American neighbors, they, too, alongside the few who decide to participate in organized heritage tours to West Africa itself, have been turning to surrogate West African enclaves in the United States to facilitate and confirm these ancestral connections. Atlanta resident Owen Powell originally from Jamaica, followed up his report of his DNA results with a trip to the Mende villages of Sierra Leone. Upon his return, he was excited to display his pictures with chiefs, elders, and other villagers at a fund-raising event for MUSAC House of Caring, a local Atlanta Sierra Leonean immigrant organization. Like Stinson, this descendant of the historical diaspora was eager to share proof of his authentic membership in the American West African collective that represents a share of the new diaspora.

Thus, from West Africa to the West Indies to destinations like metropolitan Atlanta, significant segments of black America are forging new meanings and interpretive frameworks for understanding the paradigm of the Atlantic World. It is this transfiguration in the diversity and complexity of the role of the new West African diaspora in the recent history of the black Atlantic that our study describes, explains, and interrogates. We explore the intricate patterns of adaptation and incorporation among the immigrants and their children, the evolution of new forms of transnational ties with Africa and Europe as well as translocal connections among the numerous enclaves in the United States, and the impact of the recent postcolonial and voluntary immigration of West Africans on the changing meanings of "African Americanness."

American African or African American?

Because people of African descent typically have not been counted as part of America's migratory tradition, as a subject of social scientific inquiry, immigration from Africa has thus far lacked a primary academic address. With the exception of the recent burgeoning scholarship on the Caribbean influx, the research on these populations has fallen between the cracks of traditional disciplinary boundaries. The focus in African American studies has been on the coerced migrations of the transatlantic slave trade era or the legacy of that movement, while the historiography of immigration scholarship has concentrated on voluntary migratory flows, first almost exclusively on generations of European settlers and more recently on arrivals from Asia and Latin America to the United States. What keeps being overlooked in this polarized framework is the systematic investigation of the voluntary African immigrant experience. As the editors of a collection of black immigrant self-ethnographies, Percy Claude Hintzen and Jean Muteba Rahier, point out in their introduction to the volume, even when black diversity has been the very subject of treatments of representations of blackness in the United States, as was the case with two well-regarded documentaries, Marlon Riggs's Black Is . . . Black Ain't (1994) and Henry Louis Gates's Two Nations of Black America (1998), foreign-born blacks were never mentioned and remained outside their purview.[6]

In 2005, however, in a truly redefining moment that has contributed to finally shifting this disciplinary divide, New York's distinguished Schomburg Center for Research in Black Culture launched a groundbreaking new exhibition, "In Motion: The African American Migration Experience," an initiative that represented a major reconceptualization of African American history by putting migration at the very heart of the narrative. In addition to a comprehensive tracing of the transatlantic slave trade, the project documents the great migrations, the Caribbean and Haitian flows, as well as voluntary African immigration.[7] And it could not have been more timely since in just the past four decades, more Africans have come to the United States of their own volition than were forcibly brought in bondage to the shores of the Americas during the more than three centuries of international commerce in human slavery subsequent to European contact. Indeed, if the authors of the recent sweeping history of global migration *Exceptional People: How Migration Shaped Our World and Will Define Our Future* and other demographers are correct in their predictions, Africa will supply the next big wave of immigrants, outpacing even those from East Asia.[8] In the near future, as the levels of poverty recede on the African continent, more and more people will be able to obtain the necessary resources to make international migration an option for them. Thus, new and complicated chapters are being added to the African narratives of migration, an arc that had been dominated by the bitter history of slavery and later the internal migrations from the rural south to the industrial centers of the midwestern United States; yet these subsequent episodes represent equally compelling stories in the unfolding of a dynamic new African diaspora.

Prior to the late 1970s, with few exceptions, not only was immigration scholarship synonymous with research concerning voluntary arrivals from Europe, but within that framework, European newcomers were assumed to have ethnic identities. Issues of racial identity, however, belonged exclusively to the domain of African American history. Just as immigration scholars overlooked race and the forced migrations of African Americans in the past, African American scholars concentrating on the slave trade, in turn, ignored immigration; somehow the migration experience and the scholarship related to it were not considered to be a part of the relocations of slavery. Thus, immigration history and African American history followed two separate trajectories, with ethnicity the province of immigration studies and race the subject of African American history. This was a black and white world, where Asians, Latinos, and Caribbeans rarely appeared on the scholarly radar. Furthermore, on both sides of this gulf, questions of identity itself were peripheral. Among immigration historians, ethnicity figured much more prominently within discussions of assimilation or nativism than in analysis of distinctive cultural practices and the performance of ethnic identities, while scholars of African America were preoccupied with the subjects of slavery, segregation, and discrimination, not the nuances of race and culture, topics that did not begin to receive serious attention until the late 1980s.

While enhancing our knowledge of the African-born population carries undeniable value, understanding the experience of this little-known slice of contemporary American society takes us yet another step further as it unsettles accepted narratives of black identity and the meaning of race in the United States. Most recently, Eugene Robinson, the Pulitzer Prize–winning journalist for the *Washington Post*, named this challenge to received ideas about race *Disintegration*, the title of his 2010 book on the fragmentation of black America. Key to his analysis is the significance of "the stunning increase in the flow of immigrants from the African continent," a population he is quick to point out ranks as "the best-educated immigrant group in America, with more advanced degrees than the Asians, the Europeans, you name it."[9] Robinson argues convincingly that along with the influx of Caribbean newcomers and increasing numbers of those with mixed-raced ancestry, new Africans constitute a key "emergent" cohort in the development of dramatic, contemporary redefinitions of blackness in the United States.

Such a repositioning was exemplified when, in the spring of 2011, President Barack Obama made his first trip back to Harlem since being elected to the White House to hold a fund-raiser in this historic black neighborhood. But rather than hosting the dinner at the usual venue for such occasions, the well-known Sylvia's, where Sylvia Woods, dubbed the "Queen of Soul Food," had famously welcomed dignitaries from Bill Clinton to Nelson Mandela, the president held the event at a new neighborhood restaurant, The Red Rooster, opened a few months earlier by celebrity chef Marcus Samuelsson. President Obama's choice was noteworthy, signifying the diversity of the new African America, since although Samuelsson now calls Harlem his home, he is African-born and is the author of *The Soul of a New Cuisine: The Discovery of the Foods and Flavors of Africa.*

Susan Greenbaum acknowledges that she is oversimplifying, but the research that she conducted covering over a century of Afro-Cuban presence in Tampa, Florida, led her to sum up the difference in the concepts of race and ethnicity in this way: "Race is a uniform you wear, and ethnicity is a team on which you play. We all have both race and ethnicity, a color-coded phenotypic identity and membership in some historically defined natal community."[10] However, the vast majority of West African immigrants feel that while they are compelled to wear a uniform, nobody recognizes the team they represent. In his self-ethnography, Nigerian novelist Olúfémi Táíwò coined the term "newly-minted blacks" to refer to immigrants from Africa and the Caribbean who discover the salience—and the chokehold—of blackness only upon settlement in the United States. Of his own experience, he poignantly explains,

All my life in Nigeria, I lived as a Yorùbá, a Nigerian, an African, and human being. I occupied, by turns, several different roles. I was a hugely successful Boy Scout. I was a well-read African cultural nationalist. I was a member of the Nigerian province of the worldwide communion of the Church of England. . . . I was a student leader of national repute . . . an aspiring revolutionary . . . a frustrated journalist who, to his eternal regret, could not resist the call of the teaching profession. . . . I was an ardent football player of limited talent. . . . I was a budding spiritualist. . . . Meanwhile, each one of these roles that I filled at those times was itself a complex of associations, expectations, and responsibility, which all together made for a complex, rich, multidimensional and, I dare say, very *human* life.

As soon as I arrived in the United States of America [in 1990], I underwent a singular transformation, the consequences of which have circumscribed my life ever since: I BECAME BLACK! . . . *The difference is that as soon as I entered the United States, my otherwise complex, multidimensional, and rich human identity became completely reduced to a simple, one-dimensional, and impoverished nonhuman identity. I am saying, in* other words, that to become "black" in the United States is to enter a sphere where there is no differentiation, no distinction, and no variation. It is one under which you are meant to live one way and one way only, regardless of what choices you wish to make.[11]

Similarly, acclaimed Nigerian writer Chimamanda Ngozi Adichie, who migrated to the United States in 1996 at age nineteen, recalls how she felt about becoming newly minted:

> I was annoyed the first time an African American man called me "sister." It was in a Brooklyn store, and I had recently arrived from Nigeria, a country where, thanks to the mosquitoes that kept British colonizers from settling, my skin color did not determine my identity, did not limit my dreams or my confidence. And so, although I grew up reading books about the baffling places where black people were treated badly for being black, race remained an exotic abstraction: It was Kunta Kinte.
>
> Until that day in Brooklyn. To be called "sister" was to be black, and blackness was the very bottom of America's pecking order.[12]

Many years later, Adichie revisited these confounding dynamics in her novel of the Nigerian diaspora, *Americanah*. The central female character, Ifemele, had immigrated to the United States from Nigeria as a young adult and becomes so utterly disturbed by the convoluted racialized environment that she starts to identify herself with a new category, as "Non-American Black," posting a popular blog where she airs provocative rants on the subject, including this admonition: "Dear Non-American Black, when you make the choice to come to America, you become black. Stop arguing Stop saying I'm Jamaican or I'm Ghanaian. America doesn't care. So what if you weren't 'black' in your country. You're in America now. We all have our moments of initiation into the Society of Former Negroes."[13]

Even though the great majority (83 percent) of West Africans in the United States racially self-identify as black Africans, that does not automatically or necessarily translate into identifying as African American.[14] Yet, blackness remains a fundamental factor in shaping their immigrant experience. In spite of the well-documented ethnic conflicts in the region, West Africans, coming from societies with diverse populations, already possess certain multicultural competencies. The question is whether these are the right skills for the distinct permutations of American pluralism. Since race and color hold little relevance at home, many of the newcomers, even the most educated, arrive without a clear grasp of the workings of racism and the black experience in the United States.

The overarching focus on native-born African Americans and its resultant eclipse of the new African diaspora have wide-ranging implications and place unnecessary limitations on interpretations of many facets of American society. As the organizers of the Black Alliance for Just Immigration, a group of African Americans and black immigrants in Oakland, California, who came together in 2006 to advocate for immigrant rights, framed it,

> Even with the clear evidence of African restaurants, arts and crafts shops and hair braiders that spring up nearly every month, Africans as a community remain invisible and not integrated into the traditional black institutions, churches, schools and political organizations. When the word "immigrant" is used among all communities, the one image that is least considered is a black face of an African immigrant.[15]

Thus, because of these entrenched suppositions, African immigrant religious communities, for example, typically go unseen in mainstream American life. As Jacob Olupona, the leading scholar in this fledgling academic field, has pointed out, when these groups are recognized, they are incorrectly considered to fall under studies of the "black church." Yet, this is a label that specifically refers to African American Christian communities, leaving no room for inquiry into the religious experiences of immigrant blacks, including those from Africa; nor does it acknowledge the role of foreign-born religious leaders in establishing particular African immigrant congregations.[16] Similarly, the historiography of black politics has been hampered by a narrow assumption of homogeneity among black political constituencies. The variegated forms of socialization and divergent associational networks exhibited by African immigrants have led political scientist Yvette Alex-Assensoh to argue for a newly emergent twenty-first-century black *ethnic* politics that challenges received ideas about unified black political behavior in America. As recent African immigrants bring more transnational, heterogeneous, and contested perspectives to racial politics in the United States, the prevailing analysis of a uniform black political positioning historically so intrinsic to the scholarship has become outmoded, insufficient to explain the intricacies of current ethnoracial patterns.[17]

It remains to be seen just how pliable notions of African American identity structures and their attendant cultural signifiers will be with regard to incorporation of the contributions of the new African diaspora. If African immigrants truly become African American, in the words of African Studies scholar Msia Kibona Clark, "does it mean that room will be made on soul food menus for fufu [West African] and ugali [East African],"—signature African dishes?[18] Yet another leading Africanist, Ali Mazrui, has suggested turning the category "African American" on its head to better reflect the postcolonial diaspora and instead referring to them as "American African."[19]

Thus, in the realms of religion, politics, and culture, as well as other crucial arenas of socioeconomic life, though still largely invisible to the wider society, the new African diaspora, from coast to coast, joins the mass migrations of people from Asia, Latin America, and the Caribbean who are radically reshaping contemporary America. Along with this far-reaching transformation, the false dichotomy between immigrants and racial minorities has been upended. Inclusion of the booming multiracial population of recent years, both immigrant and second generation, further confounds questions of racial and ethnic identity, mandating not only fresh perspectives on contemporary demographics but also a reexamination of how these populations were categorized, classified, and labeled in the past. Indeed, this volume finally brings the experience of those of recent African ancestry from the periphery to the center of current debates in the field of immigration studies, especially regarding issues of cultural and economic adaptation in a global and transnational context.

The New West African Diaspora

What is this West Africa? Geographically in the west of the continent, it is made up of modern nations that emerged from centuries of European imperial intervention. Zain Abdullah divides West African immigration to the United States into three stages: the first is the period of the transatlantic slave trade spanning the sixteenth to the early nineteenth centuries; the second begins in 1808 when the Act to Prohibit the Importation of Slaves first took effect and continues until passage of the Hart-Celler Bill in 1965, liberalizing immigration policy in the United States; and the last phase, still ongoing, is the post-1965 era.[20] The bulk of West African newcomers, having migrated from the former colonies of Britain, are English-speaking. Smaller numbers hail from Francophone Africa, while those from the Republic of Cape Verde speak Portuguese. With very few exceptions, the new Americans arriving from West Africa are black. Not since the era of the forced migration of half a million Africans in the slave trade have so many newcomers from the region settled in the United States. However, this time, rather than being coerced, they are migrating of their own volition, although it should be acknowledged that characterizing this flow as "voluntary" can be problematic. Increasingly, scholars from various disciplines are insisting that the movement of various African groups as a result of war, political instability, natural disaster, and extreme poverty should be considered as akin to forced migration. Nonetheless, while West Africans of the first diaspora were captured and brought to American shores in chains, in recent years the reverse has been the case, as a considerable number of the latest influx entered as refugees seeking a path to freedom.

Beginning in the late nineteenth century, initially pulled by the labor needs of the American whaling industry, immigrants from the Cape Verde Islands left their drought-stricken archipelago located off the west coast of Senegal, islands that had long been colonized by Portugal, to make southeastern New England their new home. These Afro-Portuguese settlers are particularly noteworthy as they represent the first voluntary mass migration from Africa to the United States in American history. The Cape Verdeans are still making the transatlantic journey, but especially over the past four decades they have been accompanied by a broad range of newcomers of diverse ethnic and national origins from the other major West African sending countries of Nigeria, Ghana, Liberia, Sierra Leone, and Senegal, as well as smaller numbers of arrivals hailing from the other countries of the region. Taken together this movement represents a kaleidoscopic variety of ethnic, linguistic, and religious groups that are transforming the ethnoracial landscape of American society.

Overall African immigration has grown dramatically in recent years. By 2007 one of every three black immigrants hailed from the continent of Africa.[21] Between 1960 and 2009, the African foreign-born population in the United States leaped fortyfold, from 35,355, a figure that represented 0.4 percent of all immigrants, to nearly 1.5 million, totaling 3.9 percent of all immigrants, with much of the growth occurring in just the past two decades. Indeed, more than three-quarters of the African foreign-born have arrived since 1990.[22] In the decade of the 1990s, sub-Saharan Africa became the fastest growing region of origin of all foreign-born residents in the United States, nearly tripling in size, and continues to increase apace today with a nearly 100 percent growth rate during the 2000s. Not even the downturn in the economy that began in late 2007 appears to have slowed down this population.[23] Although among the cohort of black immigrants taken as a whole those from the Caribbean have consistently outpaced newcomers from Africa, the Caribbean flow has been decreasing in recent years. This trend in combination with the swelling of African arrivals has led some demographers to predict that by 2020, continental Africans will surpass Caribbeans as the largest group of black immigrants in the United States.[24] Moreover, in contrast to the African sojourners of the pre-1975 period, these more recent arrivals are in the United States for the duration; 75 percent of those interviewed in a national study stated their intention to settle permanently in their new adopted land.[25]

Of the million and a half foreign-born from continental Africa in the United States today, over a third (36.3 percent) are from the region of West Africa.[26] Meanwhile, the number of West African newcomers has continued to increase into the second decade of the twenty-first century. Those hailing from Nigeria compose the largest population of West Africans currently living in the United States, followed by arrivals from Ghana, Liberia, Cape Verde, and Sierra Leone.[27] Data from the 1980 Census forward show that together newcomers from Nigeria and Ghana have dominated the flow, accounting for approximately 65 percent of the population from the region.[28] As of 2009, African immigrant men overall (53.6 percent) outnumbered women (46.4 percent). However, in three of the West African groups, females exceeded males—among Liberians (53.1 percent female, 46.9 percent male), Sierra

Leoneans (50.6 percent female, 49.4 percent male), and Cape Verdeans (50.2 percent female, 49.8 percent male).[29]

As for age upon emigration, West Africans mirror the general immigrant population where the most typical newcomers relocate in the decade of their thirties, with an average age of thirty-four years old (although Cape Verdeans average about five years older than the other West African populations).[30] According to the 2000 U.S. census, for the first time in census history, immigrant children were the fastest growing segment of the U.S. population, and furthermore, currently one out of five children in the United States is the offspring of an immigrant. Africans are no exception to this trend. In 2005, the population of children with at least one parent who was born in Africa reached approximately four hundred thousand.[31] Not surprisingly, given the extent of the war-related deaths, political chaos, and rampant disease resulting from the nearly fifteen years of civil conflict in Liberia that ended only in 2003, the foreign-born from Liberia, many of whom came with refugee status, count the highest percentage (20 percent) among West Africans of those nineteen years of age or under in their immigrant group. Furthermore, adoptions of Liberian children by American parents are on the rise. While Americans have adopted Ethiopian children for years, the number of adoptions from Liberia greatly expanded after 2003 and the end of the war. Some of the recent upsurge in interest in international adoptions in general has been sparked by high-profile celebrity cases, most notably those of Angelina Jolie and Madonna, but prospective parents are attracted to Liberia in particular because of its simpler regulations and more hospitable environment. Instead of a typical delay of two years or more to adopt in many countries, the average waiting period in Liberia is only eight months; moreover, it is a country in which U.S. agencies are permitted to operate, thereby facilitating what is always a daunting and complicated process.[32]

Push and Pull: Immigrants and Refugees

During the span of the twentieth century the flow of West African migration shifted course from a pattern of relocation to Western European destinations based on long-standing associations with the former colonial powers of Britain and France to the United States instead.

Immigration policy in Europe that became increasingly more restrictive in part to discourage migration from its former colonies in Africa, such as the passage of legislation in France in 1974, ending legal immigration from the continent, coincided with more liberalized and equitable policies on this side of the Atlantic, especially in the areas of family reunification, skill-based provisions, and the criteria to claim refugee status.

Two specific pieces of legislation especially contributed to the increased flow. The 1986 Immigration and Control Act made it possible for undocumented migrants to gain legitimacy, and under its provisions amnesty was granted to approximately thirty-five thousand Africans. The 1986 measure also introduced the lottery system that became part of the 1990 Immigration Act, the other significant legislative pull factor. This law increased the allotment of skilled newcomers, and thus separated the number of employment visas from those admitted through family reunification stipulations, and, even more significantly, included a Diversity Visa Program (more commonly known as "the lottery") meant to broaden the nations of origin of new immigrants to incorporate underrepresented regions of the world by allotting fifty-five thousand randomly selected visas a year. The program initially begun as a pilot project to bring in more Irish immigrants as well as those from Eastern Europe, but sub-Saharan Africans have ended up heavily benefiting from this plan. Although they account for fewer than 4 percent of the foreign-born in the United States, they have garnered over 40 percent of the new lottery visas. Between 1995 (when the program was first implemented in its current form) and 2010, over three hundred thousand African newcomers have been able to take advantage of this initiative, winning in the process the much-coveted permanent residence credential (the Green Card). By the end of the 2000s, nearly half of all immigrants who obtained legal permanent residence through this channel were African-born (49 percent in 2009 and 48 percent in 2010). Since implementation of the DV Program, approximately 40 percent of Africans who have won the lottery hailed from West African countries, with those from Nigeria and Ghana representing the top numbers of recipients from the region.[33] Once in the United States, lottery winners are then eligible to apply for family members to join them.

Moreover, in recent years Africans have increasingly been granted refugee status as their means of legitimate settlement in the United

States. Whereas after passage of the Refugee Act in 1980 the bulk of those who were resettled were from Vietnam and Russia, with the end of the Cold War combined with pressure from the Congressional Black Caucus (CBC), the plight of African refugees became more widely recognized. In 2000, revisions to the Refugee Act significantly raised the ceiling for Africans overall from seven thousand to eighteen thousand a year, so that by 2007 a third of all refugees and asylees came from African countries.[34] In addition, some who entered on short-term visas found that circumstances in their home countries had grown even more untenable in the time they were away and became eligible for amnesty programs. Others were able to provisionally legalize their standing through a measure established by Congress as part of the 1990 Immigration Act known as temporary protected status (TPS), granted to entire countries and meant to harbor those who cannot return home safely because of war, natural disaster, or other overwhelming temporary conditions for periods of up to eighteen months. The Liberian diaspora particularly benefited from this program, which was extended even beyond the end of the civil war in Liberia and the successful 2005 election of President Ellen Johnson Sirleaf because the high levels of unemployment and lack of immediate resources to rebuild the country would have made it nearly impossible to absorb all at once the numbers of would-be returnees from the United States. In 2007 when TPS effectively ended for Liberians, a new provision of temporary legal status under presidential directive, known as deferred enforced departure (DED), was implemented to enable Liberian refugees to continue to live and work in the United States without fear of forced removal. In August 2011, President Obama gave authorization to extend DED status for Liberians until September 30, 2014.

Such policies have resulted in vibrant ethnic communities in select metropolitan areas. For example, since the 1990s refugees from Liberia who have been resettled in Philadelphia outnumber all other refugee populations in a city that since the early 1980s has proactively welcomed over thirty-five thousand refugees from diverse origins.[35] Although qualifying for refugee status was a significant migration channel for select West African countries in the first decade of the twenty-first century, since 2009 because of improved conditions in their homelands, the nations of West Africa have not been among the top ten origin countries for refugees to the United States.

Finally, a crucial factor in redirecting the African diaspora was the prolonged recession in Europe in the decades of the 1970s and 1980s while the United States was experiencing economic growth.[36] Until the mid-1970s African arrivals constituted a very small proportion of the foreign black population in the United States. Those who did migrate from the African continent in the mid-twentieth century came primarily from South Africa and Egypt and were mainly white, although included among this cohort were Asian Africans, those descendents of Indians who had been recruited to East Africa in the nineteenth century as laborers primarily to help build the railway system. Since the 1930s but especially after 1960 and the overthrow of colonial rule, those West Africans who were leaving the region came primarily to obtain a higher education and were almost all speakers of English rather than other European languages. Following long established colonial links, most of the young Africans who left the continent to study in the first three-quarters of the twentieth century went to European institutions of higher learning. However, a growing African interest in American education was sparked by the role of historically black colleges and universities (HBCUs) established well before the 1960s civil rights reforms—some date to the mid-nineteenth century—in attracting the earliest wave of African students and providing a milieu for young African American and African immigrants to interact. Nonetheless, those who matriculated at HBCUs, like Nnamdi Azikiwe, who arrived in 1925 and was to become the first president of Nigeria, and Kwame Nkrumah, who came to the United States a decade later and went on to become the first prime minister of Ghana, tended to return home after their studies.

In the 1970s, developments in Europe, Africa, and America prompted the beginning of a permanent and more visible black African presence. As Britain and other European nations were closing their doors to their former colonials, the United States, recently transformed by the civil rights struggle, was implementing more inclusive immigration laws. In the United States, the CBC was formed in 1971, when the election of nine African American members made the House of Representatives more racially integrated. The extent of the protracted battle for racial equality in the United States and, in particular, the role that the

CBC played in spearheading the legislative reforms that allowed for an increase in African newcomers are, unfortunately, often overlooked by the immigrants.

A few short weeks after passage of the pivotal Voting Rights Act of 1965, the Immigration Reform Bill, also known as the Hart-Celler Act, was quietly signed into law, ending the preferential quotas of the 1924 National Origins legislation, a policy that had been the crowning culmination of the early twentieth-century anti-immigrant crusade to restrict the flow of immigrants only to those of Western and Northern European descent and keep everyone else out. Initially, when the Hart-Celler measure was passed, it was largely ignored by activists in the civil rights movement whose focus was on the immediacy of addressing long-standing racial injustices in America. Indeed, not even the framers of the legislation itself recognized what a transformative impact the new policy would have on the racial and ethnic composition of American society. Congressman Emanuel Celler, the cosponsor of the bill, himself declared, "There will not be, comparatively, many Asians or Africans entering the country . . . since the people of Africa and Asia have very few relatives here, comparatively few could immigrate from those countries because they have no family ties to the U.S."[37]

But, of course, the framers were wrong. Here was legislation that, in the years since its approval, has led to sweeping demographic changes and a complete shake-up of the country's ethnoracial landscape. Furthermore, between the civil rights legislation of 1964 and 1965 that enabled African Americans to fully participate in the electoral process and the Immigration Reform Bill of 1965 that opened the doors to immigrants of African descent from all over the world who had previously been excluded, the measures that President Lyndon Johnson signed into law resulted in policies that had a profound impact on the contours of African America. And if the rhetoric of racial equality so critical to the push for civil rights in the post–World War II era influenced the political rationale for rescinding an immigration policy in the United States based on a racialized national origins quota system, in a symbiotic relationship the leaders of the civil rights movement were, at the very same time, inspired by what they were hearing about the courageous struggles on the African continent in these years to overthrow

European colonial rule, establish national sovereignty, and exert a Pan-Africanist ideology.

It was not until the formation of the CBC, itself the result of the 1960s civil rights suffrage reforms that made the election of enough black congressmen to constitute such a quorum, however, that the direct links between African American advocacy and measures that would benefit potential immigrants from Africa (and the Caribbean) were made. Once elected, African American members of Congress served on committees that sponsored pivotal reforms of existing immigrant and refugee policy that led, for example, to an increase in the ceiling for African refugee admittances under the terms of the Refugee Act of 1980. Furthermore, the CBC endorsed the controversial provisions under the 1986 Immigration Reform and Control Act (IRCA), also known as the Simpson-Mazzoli Act, that permitted undocumented immigrants who had lived in the United States since 1982 to regularize their status, a policy change that was crucial to making it possible for many hundreds of African immigrants to remain permanently in the country. This measure was especially beneficial to the small wave of undocumented newcomers from Senegal who in the 1970s began to arrive in New York City, where they sold their wares on street corners to passersby eager to purchase everything from watches to baseball caps at cheap prices. In subsequent years, African American legislators continued to lobby on behalf of African settlers for the implementation and extension of TPS to Liberians and Sierra Leoneans.[38] Thus, in very real terms, the fruits of the civil rights movement have been a critical link in the establishment of the recent African diaspora community in the United States and could arguably be added to the list of salient pull factors in the context of their transnational migration.

At the same time, the unrelenting cycles of political conflict and internal corruption in West Africa in recent decades, resulting in toppled governments and repressive military dictatorships, have pushed many residents to relocate on a more permanent basis. Oftentimes rising fertility rates, ecological disasters, and displacement from the land have led to massive population pressures and such dense and rapid urbanization that endemic poverty and economic collapse have accompanied the civic unrest to create crisis conditions that further impel the migrants to uproot. They come to the United States in search of better economic and educational opportunities, to seek asylum, as well as to reunify families. Given the income gap between the United States and the countries of this region—a 2005 study, for example, found that the per capita income of American citizens was more than twenty times higher than per capita income in Ghana and Senegal[39]—it is no surprise that economic motivation has been a strong driver of this flow. Indeed, in its examination of reasons to emigrate, this same survey concluded that while women may have attached less importance to financial gain than their male counterparts since they also gave salience to family reunification, overall for both men and women the hope of significant improvement in their financial circumstances was by far the primary motivating factor in giving serious consideration to leaving their home-lands for the United States.[40]

Among those migrating as refugees, the earliest group was Nigeri-ans escaping the 1960s Biafran War. However, more recently, it has been Liberians and Sierra Leoneans who have gained refugee status, fleeing escalating levels of political oppression and persecution. Of the 19,070 refugee arrivals from Africa in 2001, for example, 18 percent were from Liberia and 11 percent from Sierra Leone. With the end of civil war and the restoration of peace in both countries, the number of refugees has dropped dramatically over the past several years. In 2008, out of a total African refugee population of 8,943, fewer than 1,000 were Liberians and a trickle of 99 individuals came from Sierra Leone.[41] Particularly for refugees but also those with voluntary immigrant status, the journey to the United States is not always direct and can often be the last step in an experience of multiple dispersals. Prior to the transatlantic move, many new immigrants and refugees had been involved in transborder migrations within West Africa and, in some cases, to other regions of the continent.

Demographic Trends and Patterns of Settlement

The immigrant-student tradition begun in the early part of the twenti-eth century persists to this day, facilitated by academic awards like those from the African Graduate Fellowship Program (AFGRAD), estab-lished in 1963, as well as Fulbright scholarships that have enabled prom-ising candidates to benefit from an American education. This vanguard, however, has expanded in the twenty-first century to include sizeable numbers of newcomers from the region who arrive already highly educated and professionally trained. In fact, recent trends show that the United States, along with Canada and Australia, have been attracting the more highly educated African newcomers, while the European countries such as England and France tend to draw those who are less well trained.[42]

Levels of development in their home countries in both the public and private sectors simply have not been able to keep up with the number of young West Africans who have obtained secondary and post-secondary degrees and are seeking employment commensurate with their qualifications. Consequently, they look for such job prospects abroad, and thus the brain drain is often a concomitant theme of the new African diaspora. Particularly given the number of physicians and nurses among the highly trained professionals who end up emigrating to both the United States and Europe, some have voiced serious concern that the outflow of talent from the continent has robbed many African nations of the best of their homegrown human resources.[43] Yet others on the brain gain side of the equation contend that these skilled migrants can do more to benefit their homeland economies by landing decent jobs in the United States and sending significant earnings back to relatives who have stayed behind. To be sure, some estimates put the level of remittances to African countries in recent years at close to $40 billion annually, more than four times the 1990 total of $9.1 billion, and remittances are second only to direct foreign investments in generating financial inflows. In 2010, Nigeria alone, the country with the largest numbers living abroad, received half of all remittances to the continent.[44]

A 2009 national marketing survey of African consumers revealed that the most prevalent reason given by the newcomers for why they migrated to the United States was for educational opportunity.[45] Evidence from the qualitative interviews in this study confirms this aim. Indeed, according to U.S. Census Bureau findings, the educational attainment of Africans, both first and second generations, was higher than that of any other group, native- or foreign-born. Of African-born adults age twenty-five and older who resided in the United States in 2009, 41.7 percent held a bachelor's degree or higher.[46] This figure is slightly higher than that of Asian immigrants and well above the 26.8 percent level of the total population of the foreign-born and the 28 percent of native-born adults.[47] Among West African groups, Nigerians have the highest level of attainment of a bachelor's degree or higher, at 60 percent. As one noted scholar of African American studies put it, "The irony cannot escape anyone: Africa, the least educated and most underdeveloped continent in the world has the most educated population in the world's most developed country."[48]

By the 1990s, the first wave of West African settlers, whether arriving as students, refugees, or lottery holders or through other means, was starting to become naturalized and as American citizens could begin to develop a network that would facilitate further immigration by sponsoring immediate family members, including spouses, children, and parents, under the standard provisions of family reunification. Furthermore, among the foreign-born overall, Africans are less likely to be unauthorized, so that as legal residents a higher percentage of the population has been eligible to take advantage of these channels. Consequently, in addition to increases that had been driven by the initial quest for financial and educational gains, the pull of the Diversity Visa Program, and the movements of refugees, by the twenty-first century, it has been the migration of immediate relatives that has been the most significant in expanding the recent flow. As early as 2001, more than half of all African newcomers entered the country in this way. And because those from the Anglophone nations of the region as well as those from Cape Verde have resided in the United States for the longest period of time, they are more likely to have attained the necessary legal status to sponsor the migration of their kin than other African immigrants. Thus, in 2010, for example, as the oldest source country among African nations, Cape Verde had a 98 percent share of its immigrants who were admitted through family reunification. Furthermore, of the six countries that had the highest proportion of immigrants who came via the provisions for family sponsorship (at two-thirds or more)— Cape Verde, Malawi, Senegal, Gambia, Nigeria, and Ghana—all except Malawi are in West Africa.[49] Yet while the African-origin population, like all the other foreign-born in recent years, relies on family reunification as their primary channel to the United States, the reason they are such a fast-growing cohort compared to other immigrant groups is due to the additional numbers among them who qualify for either the Diversity Visa Program or for refugee status.[50]

Although the West African immigrant pool has diversified considerably with regard to socioeconomic factors when compared to the much smaller and more elite group who came before the 1980s, and despite the greater numbers of refugees in the mix of the past two decades, this is still a population that overall arrives with significant training and skills. A 2011 World Bank study classified the majority of the immigrants from Nigeria and Ghana, the two largest source countries, as highly skilled: 59 percent of Nigerian and 47 percent of Ghanaian newcomers.[51] Another earlier survey based on the 2000 U.S. census determined that Africans were arriving with training in technical and scientific fields that fit occupational areas where there was still demand. For example, of those African immigrants who listed their occupations, 44 percent could be categorized as holding professional, managerial, and technical (PMT) positions, as compared to 34 percent of immigrants overall employed in PMT jobs.[52] The advantage the immigrants have over native-born blacks and others can, in part, be accounted for by the selectivity of their premigration educational and income levels. Those who are eligible to make the most of professional and academic opportunities in the United States and those who can afford the costs of transcontinental relocation are, by and large, individuals who have had significantly higher educational and financial resources in their home countries from the start. Even applicants for the Diversity Visa Program must meet certain qualifications, including at least a high school diploma or a recent job that required two years or more of training, to gain entry. Moreover, studies show that legal immigrants tend to be more highly educated than the unauthorized, and Africans have a low percentage of undocumented arrivals among them.[53] Finally, with the exception of those from Cape Verde and Senegal, West African immigrants rank high in English proficiency, which gives them another advantage in the workforce.[54]

A recurrent theme in the accounts of this and other research on the recent African diaspora, however, reveals that the premigration emphasis on education has become even sharper in the migrants' new home, where the newcomers are known for their perseverance in procuring still more advanced educational training after relocating. According to census numbers, African immigrants have a 96 percent high school graduation rate nationwide, a total that is 12 percent higher than the national average, while a disproportionate percentage of students at top universities are children of African immigrants.[55]

Over three-quarters of African immigrants were adults of working age in 2007, but census findings confirm that higher levels of education and English proficiency for African newcomers have not necessarily produced comparable levels of income. A 2008 study of skilled immigrants showed that among the highly educated, Africans (and Latin Americans) do much worse in the job market than do Europeans and Asians and also that Africans have the highest unemployment rates among all foreign-born populations, including Latin Americans.[56] Furthermore, according to data from 2009, overall the African-born were more likely to live below the federal poverty line than both other immigrant populations and the native-born. There were striking differences among origin countries regarding poverty levels, however. Those from selected nations of West Africa, especially Nigeria, Sierra Leone, and Ghana, were much less likely than newcomers from countries like Somalia and Sudan, who have arrived in such large numbers as refugees, to live below the poverty line.[57] Nonetheless, with the exception of Nigerians, who make more than the average U.S. resident, West African immigrants as a whole have a slightly lower median household income than the overall population ($50,424 versus $52,029).[58]

Both African men and women were more likely to be employed in the civilian labor force than immigrants in general, but many members of the contemporary influx work in the service economy—in hospitality services, in the health care industry, where they work as nurses, nursing assistants, orderlies, or respiratory and lab assistants, or in transportation-related jobs such as taxi drivers and airport porters—with the men also working in construction and extraction. For example, in 2008, 35 percent of Liberians could be found working in the service sector.[59] Since the early 1980s, black immigrants have filled the lower-level positions of the health care support sector especially in the cities of the Northeast such as Boston and New York. Initially this group was mainly migrants of African descent hailing from the West Indies. More recently, however, West African arrivals have become more visible in this occupational sphere, challenging the dominance of the Caribbean presence. As of 2009, compared to both the male and female immigrant populations overall, African men and women workers were more likely to report holding jobs as health care practitioners and in other health care support occupations. Indeed, fully a third of African women were working in health care jobs.[60]

Their high rate of participation as health care practitioners reflects another common occupational trend. Confronted with structural barriers and other practical considerations, many West African men and women, both immigrants and refugees, take jobs that are, in many ways, radically different from what they did back at home and are not necessarily commiserate with their higher levels of professional training. Thus, in addition to technical, sales, or administrative positions, new arrivals work in construction, in landscaping, at food processing plants, and in other low-level, custodial service jobs such as security guards, parking lot attendants, busboys, and housekeepers. Nonetheless, as of 2008 over half of Nigerians (54 percent) reported that they were employed in managerial or professional occupations.[61]

No matter what the job, however, the immigrants are more likely to be employed than native-born blacks. Data correlating levels of employment with race and ethnicity demonstrate the foreign-born from Africa positioned right in the middle of the rankings, below non-Hispanic whites and Asians but above Latinos and African Americans.[62] Finally, as has been the case for many new immigrant groups before them, rather than joining the secondary labor force, some West Africans have gone into business for themselves as their strategy for making it in America, with Cape Verdeans having the highest rate of self-employment among this population.[63]

These enterprises are almost always located in urban areas, where the vast majority of West African immigrants reside.[64] Even members of refugee groups who with the help of their sponsor organizations have initially settled in rural districts eventually relocate to the cities, especially those places with sizable coethnic populations. Whether living in urban, suburban, or small town locales, however, they are more likely to be settled in the Northeast or South, with 75 percent of West Africans, almost equally divided, residing in these two regions of the country.[65] In all the top metropolitan areas settled by African immigrants, the growth rate in the past decade exceeded 100 percent: in

Washington, D.C.Maryland-Virginia, 148.9 percent; New York City, 134.2 percent; Atlanta, 284.6 percent, Minneapolis-St. Paul, 628.4 percent; Houston, 129.1 percent; and Philadelphia-New Jersey, 220.6 percent. New York City is the largest single destination for those born in West African countries, and within the metropolis, the borough of the Bronx hosts the greatest numbers of West African residents. The other urban centers where West Africans constitute the most populous group of African settlers include Houston and Minneapolis (both 61 percent), Boston (60 percent), Chicago (58 percent), Philadelphia and the greater Washington, D.C., area (both 53 percent), and Atlanta (48 percent).[66]

With the exceptions of New York's "Little Senegal" in West Harlem, "Fuuta Town," a district in Brooklyn where Pulaar-speaking migrants from northern Senegal are aggregated and a burgeoning concentration of Ghanaians dwelling in what is becoming known as "Little Accra" in the Bronx, as well as particular neighborhoods where Cape Verdean immigrants congregate in selected cities of southeastern New England such as Brockton, Massachusetts, and Pawtucket, Rhode Island, West Africans do not, for the most part, inhabit visible ethnic enclaves. However, such geospatial clustering is always in flux. While predominantly inhabited by Senegalese, even Le Petit Sénégal is ethnically diverse. Not only do other Francophone West Africans, such as those from Côte d'Ivoire and Mali, reside there, but the neighborhood's bustling business sector draws West African immigrant consumers who are residing throughout the New York metropolitan area and who partake of the products and services that the district offers as well as its vibrant social life. Souleymane Dembele, a cab driver who emigrated from Mali in 1992, lives in the Bronx, but that does not stop him from trekking at least twice a week to Les Ambassades, a Senegalese-owned café in Harlem; on Sundays he has a standing date with his West African compatriots that he says goes a long way to quelling his homesickness. The proprietor, Gorgoi "Abe" Ndoi, who opened the bistro in 2003, calls his establishment "a West African concept," and it has become just that—a popular gathering spot for transplanted Africans.[67] Increasingly, as well, the clientele frequenting the neighborhood shops and restaurants are as likely to come from English-speaking as French-speaking countries.

The incremental shift from a national to a more regional local identity has led some to begin to refer to the area as Little West Africa instead. Indeed, in a 2010 radio interview reporting on the musical tastes of chef Samuelsson, he cited the particular influence of West African musicians in his neighborhood:

> Where I live in Harlem is called "Little West Africa." If you are in Harlem on a Saturday or Sunday, on the West side, you'll see big tall Senegalese—West African men, from Mali, Ghana and they come from the mosque and they'll come eat, talk and converse. And out of their cars, you hear . . . West African music, you can buy West African films, CDs, you can buy ginger juice . . . it's truly a whole subculture.[68]

Because so many of those who live and work in the district are followers of Islam, you are also likely to catch the sound of the muezzin's call to prayer ringing out five times daily, as is the religious custom. In another neighborhood of metropolitan New York, the South Bronx, where West Africans are also increasingly concentrated, the Francophone owner of a popular restaurant, in a clever twist that reinforces a broader regional identity, named his establishment Café de C.E.D.E.A.O., which is the French acronym for Economic Community of West African States (ECOWAS), the official coalition of West African nations. Meanwhile, in the true definition of an ethnic enclave, since the early 1990s, when the contours of Little Senegal first began taking shape, a majority of the owners of the local businesses have also chosen to take up residence in that part of the city. Some community leaders have even credited West Africans with reinvigorating the neighborhood, as their industriousness and entrepreneurship have caught the attention of many observers, including city officials and religious leaders.[69]

Nonetheless, despite these few examples of residential aggregation in major urban areas, for the most part West African newcomers are more dispersed, living in districts where other recent immigrant groups, including other African, Caribbean, Latino, and Asian populations, are located, as well as in established African American neighborhoods. In metropolitan New York, for example, West Africans can often be found living in the areas of Harlem, Brooklyn, and the Bronx that are predominantly populated by African Americans.[70] Across the country, however, in Portland, Oregon, a very different geographic pattern has emerged. Recent census estimates show Portland's population of U.S.-born

African Americans has declined slightly since 2000 but its African-born population increased nearly 90 percent from 2000 to 2007 and now makes up about 12 percent of the black population. Of course, no matter what region of the country, African immigrants of the earlier, pioneering generation who arrived when the restrictive residential covenants of institutionalized racial segregation were still in place, such as the practice of redlining, had no choice but to live in black neighborhoods. Moving to the white suburbs simply was not an option.

Increasingly, nonetheless, like many other new Americans of the last two decades, West Africans are acquiring the resources and have the choice to move to suburban neighborhoods; some migrate directly to settle in middle-class suburbs, bypassing congested and impoverished inner-city districts altogether, in a departure from the traditional urban ethnic succession model.[71] What is noteworthy about their residential patterns is that they do not necessarily adhere to the long-standing racialized and segregated mappings of the American metropolis. Rather African immigrants are as likely to reside in affluent zip codes where non-Hispanic whites live as in disadvantaged areas where blacks and other nonwhites are the majority. For example, studies of metropolitan Washington show that the vast majority (90 percent) of African immigrants live in suburban locales, and while concentrations of the African foreign-born can be found in the more run-down neighborhoods east of the city such as Prince George's County, Maryland, an area with a large black population, they are just as likely to be living in predominantly white and wealthier Montgomery County, Maryland, or Fairfax County, Virginia.[72]

Research that compared African immigrant with African American residential trends in the northeastern, southern, and midwestern regions of the United States confirmed the pattern of metropolitan Washington. The findings showed that African immigrants tend to live in neighborhoods with other residents who are also highly educated and who share a similar socioeconomic status regardless of racial background, while native-born blacks reside in locations where fewer than 20 percent of their neighbors hold a college degree. Furthermore, the African diaspora population typically lives in parts of the city that are likely to be highly segregated from African Americans. African immigrant segregation from African Americans in major metropolitan areas has hovered between 60 and 70 percent during the past two decades.[73] The new African diaspora is thus scattered residentially across a broad socioeconomic and ethnoracial residential spectrum, unsettling the historically normative geography of racial divide that for decades has characterized the housing market in so many of America's big cities.

Wherever they may reside, their religious participation is extensive, whether the affiliation is Christian, Muslim, indigenous African, or some combination of these faiths; there are simply very few nonbelievers among this population. While African services in the American setting may be associated with mainline religions such as the Methodists and Roman Catholics, the most rapid expansion has come from evangelical Christianity, which has experienced an ongoing and unprecedented surge in Africa and in other parts of the developing world. Thus, African migrants are following the trajectories of their Latino and African American counterparts, fueling a vibrant evangelical movement. West Africans, especially those from Nigeria and Ghana, are at the forefront of the new African church movement in the United States. Many of the founders were brought up in the Anglican, Methodist, and Orthodox churches but have branched out to Pentecostal, storefront congregations. Paradoxically, for decades the United States dispatched missionaries to West Africa to establish start-up churches, but today the reverse is taking place. Many of the independent and indigenous churches of West Africa are routinely sending missionaries from the region to America to minister to new immigrant communities and to recruit additional members to their congregations. This is a phenomenon that illustrates well the complexity of the transcontinental interpenetration and cross-fertilization of culture. African congregations in the United States typically maintain close links to churches in their countries of origin where local practices have been incorporated, sending pastors for training and exchanging clergy, hymnals, and prayer books.

Meanwhile, denominations have been multiplying at an explosive rate. While many of the leaders of the new African church movement have been active in their homeland congregations, increasingly many "American-made" pastors have emerged. Retaining their day jobs, as it were, such people of the new breed of men and women of the cloth are ministers on Sundays and designated weekday bible study days and accountants, nurses, or professors during the rest of the week. Their congregations are heavily West African. Often, the dominant group in the membership reflects the national or even ethnic affiliation of the pastor and the leaders. Yet the rapid expansion of venues for religious worship has not just been confined to the Protestant sects. For example, in response to the arrival of growing numbers of Ghanaian Catholics, the Diocese of Brooklyn and Queens added an apostolate in which Mass is conducted in Ashante and Fante, two main dialects of Ghana. Furthermore, like the Pentecostal Christians, the West African Muslim migrants, most of whom come from French-speaking countries, have developed their own storefront mosques while others regularly worship together in the homes of the Imams. They have also organized their own religious hubs, like the Senegalese Islamic Center in New York. As has been the case with so many other diaspora populations in the United States, past and present, West African churches and mosques have reshaped traditional practices in their new setting, establishing a theology of relevance whereby religious institutions function as organs for faith-based community development tailored to the specific needs of the immigrants.

Practicing West Africanness

As a diasporic identity, the designation of "West African" is an evolving concept, embraced by some and much less relevant to others of the various populations who are categorized under this grouping. Initially more imposed from the outside than self-selected, the term was first most widely used by the media to signify the Francophone, mainly Senegalese, residents of New York City, especially with regard to headline-grabbing incidents like the Amadou Diallo case or when West African street vendors made news in the 1990s as they battled real estate mogul Donald Trump and then mayor Rudolph Giuliani to protect their ability to hawk their wares on the sidewalks of Manhattan. By then the traders were a more diversified population, comprising the newly arrived from Mali, Côte d'Ivoire, Ghana, and Niger who had joined the newcomers from Senegal, and thus the label "West African" served as even more convenient shorthand.[74]

Outside of New York City and the large West African community that resides there, in other metropolitan areas where West Africans are highly concentrated such as Houston and Minneapolis, they are much less likely to self-identify as West African. Rather, more commonly, the immigrants prefer to use more distinctive ethnic labels such as Yoruba or Mende or more precise national identities such as Cape Verdean or Liberian. Indeed, it is not surprising, given how recently in the grand scheme of world history national independence was achieved in the region of West Africa—beginning in the 1950s and ongoing until 1975— that many in the diaspora still wish to identify themselves in ethnic terms while others insist on a national identity given that as a people they held the status of colonials for so long, all the while yearning to fully possess their identity as a nation.

Nonetheless, in practice and as they settle into the various communities across the United States, the newcomers have developed what can be characterized as a West African collective sensibility. In other words, while they do not describe their ethnicity as West African, they still manage tropical food stores that cater to people from an array of West African countries, carrying Nollywood films and Ghanaian Highlife DVDs even if the owners are neither Nigerian nor Ghanaian themselves; they belong to congregations and masjids composed of people from diverse West African origins; and they support each other by attending functions sponsored by a variety of nationalities, even when the occasion does not specifically represent their particular homeland affiliation.

Still, like Kadiatou Diallo's objection to how her son was tagged in the press coverage of his killing when she protested that "to call him West African revealed nothing," most of the people who actually compose the new West African diaspora find the term lacking. Similarly in the aftermath of the 2011 scandal involving sexual assault charges against former IMF chief Dominique Strauss-Kahn by Nafissatou Diallo (no relation to Kadiatou and Amadou), a hotel chambermaid from Guinea, when a group of Sierra Leonean women in Atlanta discussed the dynamics, they too felt that the way the media described the accuser was insufficient. They resented the use of "West African" because they saw it as obscuring the victim's Guinean nationality and, even worse, her specific ethnic background of Wolof, Fullah, or Mandingo. In this way, West Africans are no different from their South Asian, Central American, or Caribbean counterparts. In general, regional labels or even more broadly construed pan-ethnic terminology such as "Latino," "Asian," or "West Indian," while often preferable at the institutional level and in the marketplace due to their economy and convenience, have not been embraced by individual members of their respective groups as they find such umbrella categories imprecise, artificial, and without personal meaning. As one first-generation Sierra Leonean woman perceptively phrased it,

> In Sierra Leone we are not West Africans, even though we do the West African School Certificate; our country is a member of ECOWAS; we have relatives in several West African countries; and we have a common "West African pidgin English." I guess in Sierra Leone we took our regional identity for granted. Now in the United States we are being asked to see the significance of what it means to be part of the regional collectivity that shaped us and continues to influence us. We don't like that it is being imposed on us. But in reality what is happening is that we practice West Africanness but we are not "West Africans."[75]

No matter what the ethnic or nationality group, such blanket terms do not account for the diversity and complexities of the cultures that fall under such broadly based taxonomies, and the inadequacies and ambiguities of these labels have become increasingly more apparent. Even so, over time, designations such as "Hispanic" and "Middle Eastern" and the category of "West African" under consideration here, despite their oversimplifications, become more widely utilized and accepted by insiders and outsiders alike.

1

West Africa and West Africans

Imagined Communities in Africa and the Diaspora

I cannot realize I have actually left West Africa. . . . What is
its spell? I cannot tell you, nor wherein lies its strange and
unfathomable charm. It lays its hand upon you, and, having
once felt its compelling touch you never can forget it or be
wholly free from it.
—Princess Marie Louise, daughter of Britain's Queen
Victoria, *Letters from the Gold Coast*

West Africa has laid its hand on the immigrants, refugees, naturalized
Americans, and undocumented aliens of this study. Even their children,
who migrated at an early age or were born in the United States, are not
wholly free from it. As the premigration milieu, it was responsible for
much of their formative experiences and continues to influence settlement and adaptation patterns in the United States. While European
official languages, Western educational systems, religious denominations, and ethnic affiliations underscore significant differences among
the nations, there has always been a West African regionalism that
binds the inhabitants. In December 1944, the newly crafted pamphlet of
the London-based West African National Secretariat declared, "WEST
AFRICA IS ONE COUNTRY: PEOPLES OF WEST AFRICA UNITE!"[1]
The authors—Kwame Nkrumah from the Gold Coast, Wallace Johnson from Sierra Leone, and Bankole Akpata from Nigeria—knew that
technically West Africa was never "one country." But they understood
firsthand the potency of the historical and ongoing experiences that
fostered a regional identity and destiny that then enabled them to mobilize abroad. This regional vibrancy continues to be salient after independence and offers a compelling objective for examining postcolonial

immigrants from that region under the rubric of West Africans. Centuries of internal and external trade, European colonization, and postcolonial advancement and challenges provided common ground even as these factors proved to be divisive. Unending in- and outflows of people, commodities, ideas, and cultures shaped and reshaped ethnicities, religions, traditions, and relationships. To better grasp the trajectory of the West African immigrant experience in the United States, the complexities of this population's premigration history also need to be understood.

Precolonial Beginnings of Regionalism

As far back as the seventh century, the Arabs of the Maghreb (region north of the Sahara) dubbed the region south of theirs *bilad al sudan*, land of the blacks. Ironically, then, one of the first collective identities imposed on West African inhabitants was a racial one, which centuries later they were to encounter in complex and perplexing ways in the United States. The racial implications aside, the term was used more for geographic demarcation. By 1500, West Africa was made up roughly of three main regions: western Sudan, central Sudan, and the forest region. The histories of the great Sudanic empires of Ghana (650/700–early 1200s), Mali (1220s–1490s), and Songhai (1420s–1591) clearly exemplify the interconnected existence of the peoples of the western Sudan even before the arrival of their Arab neighbors who came with the introduction of Islam and the beginning of the trans-Saharan trade.[2] Through complex and sophisticated networks of clans, villages, occupational specialization groupings, and ethnic affiliations, the inhabitants interacted with each other on various levels, from extended family units all the way to centralized political organizations. When the Soninke people founded the Ghana Empire, they had just become the dominant group among other ethnicities that included the Malinke (also known as Mandinka and Mandingo) and Mossi. The Malinke emerged victorious among other groups, including the Sosso, to establish the Mali Empire. And the Sosso dominated still other ethnic groups, including the Malinke and Tuareg Berbers, to form the Songhai Empire around the bend of the Niger River.

Similar developments shaped the central Sudan. The Kanuri people, who are now citizens of present-day Nigeria, Chad, and Niger, created the Kanem-Bornu Empire, which was influenced by many of the same factors that created and sustained the much older western Sudanic empires: the trans-Saharan trade, Islam, and friendly and hostile commercial and cultural exchanges between the diverse clans and ethnic groups. One major group they interacted with was the Hausa, also of the central Sudan. Although the Hausa city-states (*Hausa Bakwai*), which emerged around the late 900s, did not unite in a centralized polity like the empires to the west, they developed a vibrant history shaped by interactions among them and with other groups in the central Sudan and beyond. As participants in the trans-Saharan trade, they established long-lasting relationships with the Kanuri people of Bornu, the Berbers of the Sahel, and the Arabs of the Maghreb. By 1800, Hausa leather, a commodity in much demand, had found its way to Spain, where it was erroneously labeled "Moroccan leather," a misnomer that acknowledged not the Hausa producers of the sub-Saharan region, but the lighter-skinned Arab middlemen of the Maghreb. This disservice belies the significance of the Hausa in the region prior to the nineteenth century. As producers and itinerant traders, they penetrated vast areas of the western and central Sudan and the forest region, exchanging not just commercial goods, but also language, music, and dress. As Mahdi Adamu concludes from his extensive research of the Hausa in a regional context, no cultural and economic history of precolonial West Africa can properly be written without consideration of the Hausa factor.[3]

The Islamic Revolution or jihads of the nineteenth century was one of the most influential developments that shaped and illustrated the interconnectedness of the peoples of West Africa. At the center of this history were the Fulbe/Fulani/Fula, an ethnic group ubiquitous in the entire region. The jihad in Hausa land, which started in 1804, was led by Fulani Muslim teacher Usman Dan Fodio, even though the Fulani were an ethnic minority among the indigenous Hausas. The other major jihad of the revolution was led by another Fulbe, Al-hajj Umar. His jihad brought many changes among the Mandingo, Wolof, Bambara, and other peoples of Futa Jallon and Futa Toro (present-day Mali, Guinea, Senegal, and Gambia) at a time when the French were beginning to penetrate the region. Umar's jihad brought many of the clans and ethnicities together under the Tukolor Empire. Also of importance, Umar introduced the Tijaniyya Brotherhood and a stronger footing for

Islam, which up to that point was largely a nominal religion, embraced more practically by only the Fula. This Islamic grounding was later to be an asset for the people in their encounter with the French, as demonstrated by the rise of Amadou Bamba and the Murid, a brotherhood that was to play an instrumental role in the lives of some of the immigrants of this study in both Senegal and the United States.[4]

Dan Fodio's jihad had a profound impact on large parts of what came to be Nigeria: it established Islam as a formidable religion practiced by other groups besides the Fulani; elevated the Quadiriyya to prominence as the leading brotherhood; ensured the ascendancy of the Fulani, formerly a minority group persecuted by Hausa leaders; and created the Sokoto Caliphate, which not only succeeded in uniting the disparate Hausa states, but also incorporated other groups, including the Gwarri, Nupe, Tiv, and even small portions of the Yoruba, another large group of the region.[5] Long before the jihad, the Hausa, famous for itinerant trading, had established commercial relations with the Yoruba, their neighbors in the southern savanna and the forest region. The Yoruba are united by a creation account that has them descending from a single ancestor, Oduduwa, who is believed to have been lowered from the heavens by *Olorun* (God). Ile Ife, in present-day Osun State in southwestern Nigeria, where Oduduwa landed, is still considered the spiritual home of the Yoruba. At the time of the jihads, Oyo, a Yoruba political entity, was one of the thriving kingdoms of the forest region. Through aggressive expansionist campaigns, it brought together various Yoruba entities and incorporated non-Yoruba peoples, including the Aja and Fon of Dahomey, the present-day Republic of Benin.[6]

Like the Yoruba, Hausa, and Fulani, the Akan people of the forest region registered a vibrant precolonial history that demonstrates the interconnectedness of the peoples of West Africa. Original inhabitants of present-day Ghana, Togo, Burkina Faso, and Côte d'Ivoire, the Akans carved centralized polities and thriving economies. By 1650 a group of Akan clans had developed a sophisticated political organization, the Asante Empire, with Kumasi as the seat of government. Spiritually united by the revered Golden Stool, they bulldozed their way through the region, garnering tributary states and controlling vital trade routes. Only the Fantes stood in their way. Under the Fante Confederation, this group of Akan clans put up a formidable resistance to the Asante from the early eighteenth century until the British conquest of the area in the nineteenth century. Incessant conflict did not prevent progress. The warring forest region societies developed sustainable economies (based on natural resources like gold and fish, and effective contacts with trading partners) and rich cultural systems that included diverse Akan dialects, religious and spiritual beliefs and traditions, and structured systems of chieftaincy and royal succession.[7]

The foregoing is a mere sample of the peoples who lived in the West African region before the colonial era and how they interacted with each other and began to carve the characteristics of the region. Their complex historical development through trade, politics, religion, and culture ensured that their identities and physical location would transcend the artificial boundaries that followed official European colonization. Although languages and other cultural features distinctly defined the many ethnic groupings, they coexisted in ways that led to the birth of a regionalism that would become even more complex with the arrival and interference of different groups of Europeans.

Transcolonial Ethnicity

"He [the white man] has put a knife on the things that held us together and we have fallen apart." These famous words, uttered by Obierika to Okonkwo, Chinua Achebe's protagonist in *Things Fall Apart*,[8] were perhaps the quote most remembered and recited by students studying for the West African School Certificate O-levels in the 1970s. Indeed, Obierika was partly right: European colonialism caused upheavals that resulted in disarray.[9] However, as Africans and Europeans adapted and reacted to their complex encounters, new and modified political, economic, and cultural systems refashioned demography and ethnicity, making it impossible for things to *completely* fall apart.

Merely going by the official landmark of the Berlin Conference of 1884–1885, which partitioned Africa, the colonial era would seem a mere episode in a long history: the period from the Berlin Conference to Ghana's independence in 1957 is, after all, only seventy-plus years. Although practically speaking this is what is known as the official era of colonization, European imperialism in the region, which was to profoundly shape Africa and Africans, actually began centuries before

Berlin—with the arrival of Portuguese merchant explorers in the mid-fifteenth century at the uninhabited archipelago of Cape Verde, located approximately 350 miles off the west coast of present-day Senegal. For over five hundred years, until 1975, when the islands became an independent nation, the inhabitants lived under Portuguese colonial rule. Almost from the very beginning of settlement, West African slaves were being brought to the islands initially to labor on sugar and cotton plantations, but the parched climate prevented truly successful commercial cultivation of the land. What soon became more important to the Portuguese than agricultural production was the strategic location of the archipelago as a crossroads in the expanding slave trade. Situated near the Guinea coast and on the trade winds route to Brazil, the islands served as an entrepôt for the distribution of goods, for supplying foreign vessels with needed supplies and salt, and for transporting slaves to the New World.[10]

No one studies European imperialism in Africa without considering the Atlantic slave trade, and no study fails to acknowledge the centrality of West Africa in this poignant historical saga. So prominent was this region in the trade that from the sixteenth to the early nineteenth centuries the West African coast, known as the Guinea coast, was also often referred to as the Slave Coast. Europeans encountered, traded with, and sold members of the ethnic groups already established in this area: Hausa, Yoruba, Igbo, Wolof, Mandingo, Fulani, Bambara, Temne, Ga, and Akan. Along with some groups from central Africa (notably Angola), but still predominant in number, these West African groups contributed the most to the foundation of African America.[11] Given this place in African American history, it is not surprising that at the beginning of the twenty-first century, with the rise of ancestry tracing through DNA, African Americans, including celebrities like actor Isaiah Washington, are making connections and finding their way to West Africa.[12]

Simultaneously as Europeans devastated whole communities in pursuit of profit through the diabolical trade in humans, they forged entities that foreshadowed the modern nations. By the end of the slave trade in the early nineteenth century, and long before the Berlin Conference, European nations had begun to exert control in what were practically colonies but often referred to euphemistically as "spheres of influence."

The historic "scramble for Africa" in the 1870s and 1880s accelerated the quest for more definitive boundaries and resulted in official partition that was validated in Berlin. The consequences for West Africans were profound and continue to account for many of the fundamental characteristics still evident in the twenty-first century. The European appendages of British, French, and Portuguese began to be defined and applied in the colonial era. To illustrate with the case of the Mandingos—and there are many similar examples—by the nineteenth century not only were some inhabitants of the Futa Jallon region ethnically Mandingo, but also other mitigating factors such as the influence of language were now beginning to confer markers of French on them. Similarly, relatives of the Futa Jallon Mandingos, but who found themselves physically in the British sphere of influence in areas of present-day Sierra Leone, began to deal with British cultural markers. Thus, with European colonization West African ethnicities, though still firmly established, were being nuanced in significant ways that reflected where they were located within the Europeans' spheres of influence.

Some of the foremost historians of African history have emphasized the vitality of the European heritage.[13] As deep-rooted as ethnicity had become by the time of European intrusion, one's ethnicity—Yorubaness, Hausaness, Akaness, and so on—was also affected by one's exposure to and function within a specific "Europe-in-Africa" milieu. Ali Mazrui tackles the differing outcomes of European colonial construction of African political entities. He concludes that there is a potent distinction between British and French imperialism in the overriding consequence of the interplay between "imperial ethnicity" and "African ethnicity." While the result for the French colonies was the construction of "nations," for the British colonies "states" were the outcome.[14] David Robinson offers a similar assessment in colonial comparative history showing French flexibility, in certain areas like religion, that contrasted with the British approach that led to a more rigid configuration, which, as noted above, Mazrui calls "state." According to Robinson, the French were guided by a religious-cum-political ethnography that served as a road map: "At no time would one think of France as an Islamic Power. But by the early twentieth century, French authorities were actively discussing and evaluating their policies as *puissance musulmane*, by which they meant an imperial power with Muslim subjects."[15] Demarcation

along European national lines/approaches went beyond European officials and policy makers. The Africans took sides too, showing their
increasing affiliation with their specific European heritage. Whole
groups of people with long ethnic, linguistic, religious, and other cultural ties clashed over what was the best modern system of government,
education, culture, and overall influence.

On the threshold of decolonization, two eminent West African men
vividly illustrated this division that stemmed from European affiliations. Felix Houphouet-Boigny, who led the Ivory Coast to independence, engaged in a heated debate with Kwame Nkrumah of the Gold
Coast. Houphouet-Boigny stood firm on his vision for a Franco-African
community, as Nkrumah, shaped by his experiences in the Anglophone
world—the Gold Coast colony, the United States, and Britain—refused
to back down from his own idea of a post-European West Africa. Ultimately, on April 6, 1957, exactly one month after Ghana attained independence, the two leaders bet on their stands, agreeing that they would
reassess the outcomes in exactly ten years time to see who was right.[16]
Perhaps the most intriguing fact about these two men, as they played
out the trappings of their imperial nationality, was that in terms of their
African ethnicity, they were both Akans. Houphouet-Boigny was a
Baoule Akan and Nkrumah was an Nzima Akan, born in Nkroful, an
Akan village in British territory but right on the border of the British
Gold Coast and French Ivory Coast.

This interplay, and sometimes outright collision, between European
imperial nationality and African ethnicity is a critical factor in the history of West Africa and West Africans and key to understanding some
of the subsequent developments in the diaspora. While the Houphouet-
Boigny-Nkrumah encounter became political legend and was well publicized, most of the equally illuminating exchanges and encounters that
transcended colonial boundaries and influences occurred daily among
more ordinary folk. And migration was the catalyst. As Brian Catcho-
pole and I. A. Akinjogbin point out in their School Certificate O-levels
survey of West Africa, in fascinating ways, alongside a West African
heterogeneity is an essential cultural homogeneity. Importantly, these
scholars emphasize that this complex homogeneity has been continuously shaped by extensive migration sagas which they call "minglings
[sic] of people."[17] This mingling began well before the colonial period, as

illustrated by the examples given of the migrations of the Fulbe, Hausa, and Yorubas. But without a doubt, West African migrations increased immensely during the colonial era, an inevitable outcome of colonial policies and changes.

Through capitalist exploitation, colonialism resulted in massive scales of urbanization that in turn triggered similar scales of migration that transcended colonial boundaries and affiliations and affected the region in ways that continue to be central to the lives of West Africans, even in the diaspora. As Adu Boahen and many other Africanist historians have emphasized, most of the "development" in Africa during the colonial era occurred as defaults on the path to European development through colonization.[18] With the introduction of cash crops, European currencies, monetary taxation, and export-import systems, by the 1890s some bustling areas, nerve centers of the new colonial economy, had developed into bustling towns and cities. Some towns like Kumasi (in present-day Ghana), which had been the capitals of precolonial African states, developed into modern centers for communications and collecting points for locally produced commodities such as cocoa, groundnuts, and palm kernel. Mining was a significant stimulus of urbanization. Enugu in Igboland (present-day Nigeria) grew in response to the exploitation of coalfields in its vicinity; and Port Harcourt was established in turn as a terminus for a railway bringing coal from Enugu to the coast. Jos in Hausa land developed as a major town around tin mining, as did Kono (present-day Sierra Leone) around the excavation of diamonds. Similarly, cash crops, which undergirded the colonial export economy, served as agents for the development of important urban concentrations: Kano (Hausa land), which gained popularity for its awesome groundnut pyramids, grew as a town around that crop. Groundnut was also a key stimulus for the growth of Bathurst (now Banjul in present-day Gambia) and Dakar and Rufisque (present-day Senegal). Kaduna (present-day Nigeria) witnessed a similar development around the cultivation of cotton.[19]

With urbanization came the lures of the city. Besides the obvious draw of employment, migrants from rural areas were attracted to the vibrancy of the infrastructure, the physical landmarks of modernity and Westernization: banks, office buildings, schools, clinics and hospitals, churches and mosques, and roads and streets that dwarfed the footpaths of the villages. Just after independence, when the first censuses of the new nations were done, the magnitude of migration into the burgeoning cities was revealed. As demographers discovered, by independence, the average proportion of the native-born in West African cities was 42 percent.[20] Some of the statistics for individual towns were astounding. The 1960 Ghana census reported that only 25 percent of the population of Takoradi, 40 percent of Sekondi, 37 percent of Kumasi, and 47 percent of the population in Accra were of local origin. A 1960 Ivory Coast special study estimated that only 29 percent of the population of the country's largest city, Abijan, had actually been born there. A similar survey undertaken in Kaduna in 1965 reported that at least 70 percent of the inhabitants were migrants.[21] Another crucial point the statistics confirmed was the extent of the diversity of the urban populations. They reflected "mingling" at its zenith. Towns, which on the surface were known by their "ethnic" labels, were in reality agglomerations of West African ethnicities. By independence, Accra, Ghana, which was known as a Ga-Adangme area, was not a city of Ga people. The 1960 census reported that it contained representations of eighty different ethnic groups. Lagos, a Yoruba town of Eko Yorubas, had seen mass migrations of other Yorubas—Ijebu, Egba, Ijesha, Ekiti, and so on—and non-Yorubas, like their Edo (Benin) neighbors and Igbos and Hausas. By Nigerian independence in 1960, Kaduna, a "Muslim, Gwari-Hausa-Fulani town," had developed as the cosmopolitan capital of northern Nigeria with, according to a 1965 survey, an adult population that was "one-third Hausa, one-fifth Igbo, with substantial numbers of Yoruba and other northern and midwestern [Edo] peoples present."[22]

Yet another notable demographic pattern was that the migrations and heterogeneity of urban populations were transcolonial. West Africa, a protagonist in the worldwide African diaspora, can speak of its own regional diasporas. Almost every major ethnic group has a history of significant migration waves. The Mandingos provide some of the best insights into this development. Over centuries, prosperous traders and zealous Islamic clerics from their original home west of the Niger (in territories that were part of the ancient states of Ghana, Mali, and Songhai) spread out throughout West Africa, forming large concentrations in areas of what are now present-day Senegal, Guinea, and Sierra Leone. They can also be found in significant numbers in Burkina

Faso, Guinea-Bissau, Gambia, Ivory Coast, and Liberia. The stigma of "outsider" has plagued whole Mandingo populations beyond their original homes of present-day Mali and Mauritania. For example, in Sierra Leone, the Temne and Limba people with whom they share parts of the northern region view them as "outside invaders." It is remarkable then that in spite of the discrimination and marginalization, this group succeeded so well in commerce, served in prominent government positions, and in 1996 made history when one of them, Alhaji Ahmad Tejan Kabbah, was elected president of Sierra Leone.

In neighboring Liberia, although Mandingos have registered similar success, especially in business, their marginalization, according to scholars, has been quite severe. There have been serious cases of physical persecution and blatant denial of civil rights to the Liberian Mandingos.[23] Much like the Mandingo, the Hausa, Yoruba, Fula, and Igbo populations are dispersed in urban centers throughout West Africa. As with the Mandigos, the Hausas spread out as long-distance traders and Islamic teachers. Significant "outsider-citizen" Hausa communities have been established by migrants and their children, notably in Ghana, Niger, and Burkina Faso. Smaller Hausa migrant communities can be found in Sierra Leone, Guinea, and Ivory Coast. In the nineteenth century, the Yoruba extended beyond their homeland in present-day western Nigeria to other areas in the Savanna and forest region. The nineteenth-century Yoruba civil wars (1817–1830s) were very instrumental in this extension of a Yoruba presence into Dahomey (present-day Republic of Benin) and Togo. In language, dress, music, and distinct Yoruba names, the Yoruba presence has been pronounced in these countries. Although the civil wars did not affect a big part of what is now Ghana, they did reach the northern parts, mainly through trade as the Yorubas established a permanent and highly visible presence in the Gold Coast, which later became Ghana.[24]

Throughout the colonial era, as the imperial European powers drew the boundaries of their spheres of influence, West African ethnic groups continued a tradition of mingling through trade, religion, intermarriage, and other cultural exchanges. Thus, for example, the reality in British Bathurst was the aggregation of diverse groups of Wolof, Mandingo, and Fula. Some of the Mandingo had come to Gambia from Portuguese Guinea-Bissau as well as French Mali and Mauritania. The Ewe also transcended colonial boundaries, going beyond their homeland in the southeastern British Gold Coast to the southern areas of neighboring French colonies of Dahomey and Togo. Almost as if to "Africanize" the European-created city, migrants and indigenous inhabitants coexisted and interacted in ways that evoked traditional African culture and traditions. By the end of the colonial era, as the outgoing colonial powers solidified the European languages as official languages for modern African democracies, cities clearly reflected their versatility in African languages: in Kaduna, although the prevalent language was Hausa, Igbo and Yoruba were also widely spoken; in Accra, Ga, Twi, Yoruba, and Hausa were all spoken; and in Rufisque, Wolof, Mandingo, and Fula expressed the African multilinguistic character of a Senegalese French colonial city.

While European-inspired urbanization fostered migration, there is no denying the African agency in the shaping of migration movements and their consequences. However, there is evidence that European colonial policies directly dictated migration, even if some of the consequences were unanticipated. For example, in the British colony of Nigeria, the Igbos were considered the most Westernized; they had adopted Christianity, had a high rate of Western education, and were economically industrious. Therefore, the colonial government used them to sustain the administration. They were the predominant group as far as their representation in the civil service throughout the colony, and they were encouraged by the government to go to other areas as teachers and traders. The Igbo diaspora in Nigeria is therefore partly the outcome of official British colonial policy. By independence, Igbo ubiquity in the colony was underscored by their conspicuous prosperity in almost every facet in almost every region. They were resented for this, especially in the north, a situation that was played out most clearly in the late 1960s riots (*araba*) that preceded the Nigerian civil war.[25]

Moreover, no other group exemplified the European hand in the diaspora in West Africa than the Creoles of Sierra Leone. In the colonial era, the British happily labeled this unique West African ethnic group "Black Englishmen." In some respects, the Creoles were a British creation, emerging as they did from the creolized outcome of decades of interactions among the various groups settled in the Sierra Leone Peninsular under British auspices: the Black Poor (blacks repatriated from Britain in 1787), Nova Scotians (former black loyalists of the American Revolution who were first settled in Canada and repatriated to Sierra Leone in 1792), Jamaican Maroons (slave rebels who after a truce with the British colonial government put down their arms and agreed to be resettled in Sierra Leone in 1800), and Liberated Africans or Recaptives (West African slaves bound for the New World who were "recaptured" after the 1807 abolition of the slave trade and settled in Sierra Leone from that time to the 1830s). By the middle of the nineteenth century, the lines distinctly dividing the various groups had blurred and it was clear that a new African ethnicity, the Creoles, had emerged.[26] British paternalism and Creole ambition propelled this group to elitist heights, a consequence that created tension between the Creoles of the coast and the indigenous groups, which by independence had been labeled *upline* people.[27] By the 1880s, with British support, the Creoles had become "firsts" in the whole of sub-Saharan Africa in almost every aspect of Western modernity: the first lawyer, the first doctor, the first secondary schools for boys and girls, and the first institution of higher learning. Fourah Bay College, still touted as the first university in Africa south of the Sahara, though founded in 1827 as a colony-wide institution, was seen as an integral part of Creole culture because of the predominance of Creole students.

The British, as if to benefit from their labor, used the Creoles to sustain British administration, missionary work, and culture not just in Sierra Leone but throughout the West African region. This was the genesis of the Creole diaspora in West Africa. Creole men, who were recruited to work in other colonies, usually took their families with them or started new families that were consciously formed as "Creole families" within the colony host society. It was common practice for the men to go back to Sierra Leone to take Creole wives. It was this pattern that Samuel Dandeson Showers followed when in 1947 he left Kaduna, where he had settled, to go to Freetown, Sierra Leone, to marry Edna Taiwo Johnson, a fellow Creole, who like Samuel had been born in Nigeria to Creole expatriates but had gone to Sierra Leone, when her parents finished their "tour of duty" in Nigeria. Nigeria, which was the most frequent destination in the West African Creole diaspora, exemplifies the history of Creoles abroad. The Creole communities formed by the migrants, who were called *Saros*, were recognizable throughout Nigeria, from Lagos to Hausa land, Igbo Land, and the delta region.[28]

The delta region of Nigeria was one of the nerve centers of the Creole diaspora in West Africa from the late nineteenth century to the end of the colonial era. The individual most responsible for the settlement of Saros in this region was Samuel Ajayi Crowther, who, though strictly speaking was not Creole, shaped and illustrated the history of the Creole diaspora and, indeed, the crucial point of porous colonial boundaries. Crowther was an Egba Yoruba from Abeokuta who was rescued as a teenager (maybe thirteen) from a slave ship and resettled in Freetown in the colony of Sierra Leone in 1822. He became the first student of Fourah Bay College and later the first black Anglican bishop in colonial Africa. The Church Missionary Society (CMS) used him for their work in Nigeria, the colony of his birth, and Sierra Leone, the colony of his liberation. He founded the Niger Mission in 1857 with an all-African staff, most of whom were Saros.

Crowther, through his legacy, was truly a "West African." The students of Fourah Bay College, who, by independence in 1961, were drawn from all over West Africa, are known as "Crowther's Children." His "real," biological children are just as exemplary of the West African collective. His daughter, Abigail, married a Nigerian-Saro, and their son, Herbert Macauley, is an icon in Nigerian history as one of the fiery nationalists who fought the British for self-government. Another daughter, Susan, married G. C. Nicol, a Creole who worked for the British in Bathurst, Gambia, and was influential in the Creole "Aku" community of that city. Thus, in Nigeria, Sierra Leone, Gambia, and other parts of Anglophone West Africa, Ajayi Crowther and his children epitomized the movement of people, a signature staple of West African colonial history.[29]

Even as Crowther's historians continue to disagree on the extent of his role as an instrument of European imperialism, they hardly differ on the vitality of his insistence that his work for the British and his fellow Africans must connect the urban and the rural, the town and the village. Crowther perceptively grasped a vital aspect of West African migrations in his time—the enduring connection between the origin of migration and the new home. Strong ties between migrants and relatives in the rural areas were seldom broken. As one of the first demographers to study West African regional migrations emphasized, reciprocal visits were instrumental in blurring the gap between countryside and town. According to M. P. Banton, "In West Africa, there is often less difference, sociologically speaking, between towns and countryside. Many people who come to reside in the urban centers are already acquainted with town ways."[30] No matter how successful the move to the city turned out to be, the majority of the migrants consciously did not want to break away from their places of origin. The hometown is where one has kinship connections and where one is inextricably united with the land because that is where one's umbilical chord is buried. Migrants often went to the hometown to participate in traditional rituals and festivals like naming ceremonies, engagements and marriages, funerals, rites of passage, chieftaincy installation ceremonies and other hometown civic celebrations.

The migrants' loyalty often went beyond recreation. Many actually continued to contribute in practical ways to the hometown economy. For example, they went to take part in cultivation, mostly during harvest. Lillian Trager discusses these enduring ties between city and countryside in her study of the Ijesha Yoruba. She notes that no matter where the Ijesha migrated, the hometown remained central in their lives because that is where their "kinship" (*egbe*) physically and spiritually resides: "A person who does not have an egbe is not properly adjusted."[31] This quest for continued community belonging also led the migrants to develop "hometown associations" in the cities. For example, the Yorubas replicated hometown by establishing kinship institutions wherever they settled. By the end of the colonial era, the British Gold Coast as well as French Dahomey and Ivory Coast had well established egbes, founded by Yoruba migrants, who continued ties with Yorubaland, a pattern that was ongoing after independence and extended to Yoruba immigrant communities in America and Europe.

Another useful example is the Krus, who like the Yoruba, Igbo, Hausa, and Mandingo can speak of their own diaspora within and outside West Africa. The Krus are one of the primary original ethnic groups of present-day Liberia. A seafaring people, they had by the end of the nineteenth century established migrant communities in various coastal areas of West Africa and even in Europe, particularly Liverpool, England. One of the biggest Kru communities in West Africa is in Freetown, where, through their work with English shipping companies like Elder Dempster, they were able to establish a presence in that city known for its natural harbor, the finest in West Africa. In 1816, the British colonial government developed a "reservation" for the Kru maritime workers and their families. By the twentieth century, this British creation had become Kru-Town, with the Krus in control of their ethnic enclave and its institutions. Through these institutions, they reconstructed their Liberian hometown, as underscored by their language (spoken fluently by generations born in Freetown), churches, ethnic businesses, and even their own judicial system, regulated in their "Kru courts by their Kru chiefs, who settled palavers and other legal issues."[32]

One noteworthy characteristic of Kru immigrant communities in West Africa is the high visibility of women. Because the men were often away at sea for long periods, fundamentally the sustenance of the community fell to the women, who raised the children almost as single parents, were active in church, even though the head pastors were always male, formed and headed benevolent and recreational associations, and regulated reciprocal visits and other contacts with the Liberian homeland. While the absence of Kru men made the role of women more easily recognizable, the tremendous impact of women in migration and urban living in West Africa during the colonial era is a feature that holds true for all the groups throughout the region. As Kathleen Sheldon emphasizes, West Africa was centuries ahead of other parts of the continent in the establishment of cities and in reflecting the vital roles of women in sustaining these cities and connecting them with the rural areas.[33]

In the colonial era, women migrated in significant numbers, although, due mainly to the new economic institution of migrant labor, males predominated. As Catherine Coles explains in her study of Hausa women in Kaduna, even Muslim Hausa-Fulani women, traditionally secluded and thought to be less mobile, were significant players in the demographic shifts that engulfed Hausa Land in the twentieth century.[34] Many of the Hausa women moved with their husbands and their families, just like the Creole women who accompanied their husbands who relocated to other colonies as British civil servants. However, there is ample evidence that women, even those who accompanied their spouses, migrated in the colonial era for the same economic reasons as those of the men—expectations for urban opportunities. One of the literary classics of the 1960s illustrates this pattern. In the acclaimed novel

Jagua Nana, another West African Certificate O-levels favorite, Nigerian author Cyprian Ekwensi traces the story of an ambitious young Igbo woman who left her hometown to seek a better life in Lagos.[35] Although Jagua Nana, the protagonist, is a complex character, having to resort at times to prostitution to make her way, the novel gives insights into the resilience of women as "breadwinners" in their own right in the burgeoning colonial urban centers. Many worked out of the home as domestics, teachers and nurses. But perhaps in no other arena did they make their mark in urban economic development as much as in entrepreneurship, specifically as the now ubiquitous West African market woman.

The market was one of the most distinguishing features of the region's evolving urban settlements. Vibrant commercial centers, many markets were huge, occupying numerous acres. By the beginning of the twentieth century, it was clear that women were the movers and shakers of the markets, from Makola in Accra to Sangada in Dakar, and Dove Court in Freetown. As D. F. McCall observed in a study undertaken right after independence, in West Africa the market had become a women's world. Marketing was easily combined with domestic duties, especially child care. The social atmosphere added to the economic benefits: "Women plait (braid) each other's hair while waiting for customers to buy their goods; they gossip or nurse their small children; and cut vegetables and undertake other preparations for the family's main meal."[36] It is this social atmosphere that has led some scholars to emphasize that many West African women in the colonial era did not regard trading in the market as an occupation. For example, Kenneth Little, agreeing with McCall, noted, "This is particularly the case for Yoruba women for whom attending a market is part of their way of life. Petty trading . . . is a pleasure and a necessity, as well as a skill, the 'essence of social life' . . . and not all women in the market are interested in material gain."[37] This did not mean that the women were ignorant of their economic value and responsibilities. Gracia Clark, writing decades after scholars like McCall and Little, who stressed the casualness of the market, explains the situation more accurately. In her study of Ghanaian women, she concluded that "far from venturing into male-identified spaces or shirking their maternal duties, women traders follow the most common occupation for urban Ghanaian women in markets considered stereotypically female spaces."[38] Therefore, what seems closer to the reality is that African women were perceptive enough to recognize a gendered occupational, economic niche, one that they have inhabited since the colonial era.

As effective regulators of this critical economic institution, these women have demonstrated their cognizance of the centrality of the market in the economic well-being of their societies. Throughout West Africa, the women formed financial market associations known variously as *egbe* among the Yorubas and *nanemei akpee* among Ga women, to name two examples. These associations established and regulated market systems, from stall allocation based on commodity specification to imposing and collecting market dues and providing capital. Misty Bastian provides a good case study of the effectiveness of these associations in her research on Igbo market women and their standoff with colonial authority.[39] Whether as a gendered social/cultural/recreational institution or a formidable economic organ, the markets were central in the lives of West African women and girls. They shaped their outlook and experiences, even of those not directly involved as vendors or children of vendors. And, importantly, they provided the contexts for some of the roles the women would eventually play in the development of West African immigrant communities in America.

By independence, markets reflected what West Africa had become, representing the peoples, commodities, traditions, and processes that were changing the region. At markets whites (known variously as *Oyinbo* in Yoruba land, *Bature* in Hausa land, *John Bull* in the Sierra Leone colony, *Bruni* in the Gold Coast, and *Toubab* in Gambia) made conspicuous appearances as consumers; diverse West Africans haggled passionately, using several languages and gestures that projected their African ethnicities and European colonial origins; and migrants and visiting hometown relatives offloaded merchandise from the countryside even as they stocked up on a variety of goods from the city in preparation for traditional festivals and other celebrations that affirmed the vitality of traditional Africa in the midst of European colonialism. Indeed, the white man's knife had been felt and circumstances had changed. Yet in the throes of colonial domination, African agency held its own, so that by the time the new nations were declared, it was clear that, alas, things had not fallen completely apart.

Nationality, Citizenship, Ethnicity, and
Postcolonial Regionalism

As one independence celebration followed another (Ghana 1957; Guinea 1958; Nigeria, Senegal, Togo, Mali, and Ivory Coast 1960; Sierra Leone 1961; Guinea-Bissau 1974; Cape Verde 1975; etc.), the painstakingly crafted flags, coat of arms, and national anthems signified the awesome reality of modern nationhood. European statecraft, with varying degrees of African input, had succeeded simultaneously in bringing together and separating ethnic and religious groups. Former colonial officials, independence activists, historians, and political scientists have written and continue to analyze the fascinating, in some cases promethean, ways in which the Africans moved toward developing a sense of nationhood and citizenship through political parties, constitutions, and parliamentary democracies that had to take into consideration centuries of diverse and complex traditional African political and cultural systems.[40] The feat of nationhood is not covered here, but suffice it to emphasize that the artificiality of West African nation-states was clear from the onset and sparked problems, some of which exploded, shaking the very foundations of the state.

Even before the British, French and Portuguese flags were lowered to make way for the colorful new ones, the phenomenon of "tribalism" had begun to show potentially disruptive signs: political parties for the most part were formed along ethnic lines; newspapers and radio stations openly displayed ethnic affiliations; government positions were distributed via ethnic loyalties; and even the newly formed "national" armies emerged with ethnic cracks. Consequently, from the onset, nationhood/nationality had to contend with ethnicity. By independence, ethnicity was firmly in the core, with each ethnic group "a distinct category of society, self-consciously united around shared histories, traditions, beliefs, cultures, and values which mobilize its membership for common political, economic and social purposes."[41] As Donald Rothchild and Victor Olorunsola explain in their study of state versus ethnicity, the situation was one of nationalism versus subnationalism, the ethnic groups, being "subnational" entities. Thus, nations were born with a dilemma, well articulated by Rothchild and Olorunsola: "How can independent African states preserve and enhance their coherence while at the same time accommodate the legitimate demands advanced on the part of ethnic groups for autonomy and particular interests?"[42]

Nigeria was the first of the new nations to confront this question in a most catastrophic way. In May 1967, after a military coup the previous year and a series of pogroms, *araba* (Hausa for divide), against Igbos who had settled in the north, the Igbos of eastern Nigeria announced that they were seceding from Nigeria to form their own Republic of Biafra. The bloody Nigerian Civil or Biafra War that ensued (1967–1970) is still the most poignant chapter in the history of that country. Although the nation was mended and the Igbos were brought back into the federation of Nigeria, the "Biafra factor" lingered and is still being addressed in Nigeria and the diaspora, including among communities covered in this study.[43] Although a whole nation was engulfed in the crisis, the Nigeria-Biafra conflict grew mainly out of the collision of two "majority" ethnic groups in a hegemonic encounter. This was merely one aspect of the "ethnic problem" or "tribalism." There were also the "minority" ethnic groups that also negotiated and fought for their place within the nation-state. Since the beginning, scholars, including Westerners like pioneer historian of modern Africa Scottish John D. Hargreaves, have put the blame for the creation of "minority" ethnic groups on colonialism. According to Hargreaves, "So many so-called minority problems in contemporary Africa derive from changes introduced by the creation of colonial states, rather than from some exotic African malady called 'tribalism.'"[44]

Writing much later, historians, who now include many Africans, have continued to examine the issue of minority ethnic groups and its threat to the nation-state. Cyril I. Obi and E. Osaghae have studied the Ogoni people of the Nigerian Delta region who offer some of the most illuminating examples of how minority ethnic groups emerged and where they stand in present-day West Africa.[45] Dubbed "oil minorities" for their territorial homeland that is squarely situated in the richest oil fields, the Ogoni people have suffered indignities and persecution in their own homeland at the hands of transnational companies, specifically Shell Oil, and a repressive Nigerian government.[46] Obi and Osaghae, using the Ogoni case, are among contemporary scholars who continue to reiterate the charge of Hargreaves and others before them that European powers and their colonial policies were most responsible

for the creation of the African minority tribe crisis. While scholars continue to debate the extent of European culpability in the creation and
repression of minority ethnic groups, the situation is clear—whether as
"subnational" groups or ethnic minorities, in postcolonial West Africa,
ethnicity continues to challenge the nation-state. And more important
for this study, the dynamics of the hierarchy of ethnic groups have had
an impact in varying ways on the West Africans in the United States
and continue to shape aspects of their experience as immigrants.

In spite of the continuing threat to the nation, however, West African
countries have basically remained within the rubrics of their original
European construction. West Africans, even in the heat of "in-house"
fighting, mark their independence from Europe, display their flags and
other patriotic symbols, and when they travel abroad, including their
migration to the United States, do so on their nation's clearly designated
passport. The determination to remain modern nations along Euro-
pean-drawn borders is conscious, official policy.

European influence is also responsible for amalgamations or collec-
tives that transcend the nation state. Indeed, the very nations were born
out of collaborative struggles that brought activists of different colonies
together: advocates of independence from various British colonies were
able to come together in the National Congress of British West Africa;
workers from Bamako (Mali) to Conakry (Guinea) united the French
West African colonies and ushered in the period of nationalist struggle
with the railway strike of 1947 to 1948; and Guinea-Bissau and Cape
Verde fought together for independence from Portugal.[47] The regional
lines depicting specific European legacies continued after independence. French-speaking West Africans continued ties beyond the
obvious official language. For example, the CFA, commonly referred
to as the West African franc, is a daily reminder of the "French heritage," which continues to define and bind the people who use it as their
currency.

After independence, the former British territories of West Africa,
like other former British territories elsewhere, elected to join the British Commonwealth. In spite of strong national and ethnic identities,
this membership in the British Commonwealth went beyond diplomatic maneuvers at the top between African leaders and the British
government and monarchy. Individuals were directly affected by the

implication of this international membership. Perhaps nowhere else was this more exemplified than in the passports of the African nations. Up to the 1980s, the passports indicated that the holder was a citizen of both his or her particular African nation and the British Commonwealth. Many of the people studied in this work were admitted into the United States with such a passport. As C. W. Newbury had predicted as early as the beginning of this union, "West Africa, like the rest of the Commonwealth is part of a regional complex with extra-Commonwealth relations. The hard facts of economic geography and the emotional appeal of pan-Africanism to some extent compete with Commonwealth loyalties."[48] Indeed, the tensions between British Commonwealth and West African Regionalism surfaced early, explaining why, for example, a Sierra Leonean Muslim Mandingo would continue to feel a stronger bond with a Senegalese Muslim Mandingo he or she meets and interacts with in the context of the United States than with a "fellow Commonwealth" Christian Ga from Ghana.

Britain's discriminatory application of the terms of this union contributed to the reduction in the reality of belonging. West Africans had no illusions of their being transformed from British colonial subjects to British postcolonial citizens. By the 1980s, it was becoming increasingly clear that the Commonwealth was tier-based and, more disturbing, regulated with racial and racist considerations. For example, unlike Canadian and Australian citizens, West Africans were required to apply for visas to enter the United Kingdom. In some respects, the subsequent regional cooperation forged among independent states was a negation of paternalistic, flimsy European-dictated regionalism. On May 28, 1975, the Economic Community of West African States (with no European interference or guidance) was formed to achieve "collective self-sufficiency" for the West African nations and their peoples. By the last decade of the twentieth century it had become quite clear that various conflicts stood in the way of self-sufficiency. The regional response to this reality came in 1990 in the creation of the Economic Community of West African States Monitoring Group (ECOMOG), a West African multilateral armed force for the protection of the region and the enforcement of peace and stability. The timeliness of this regional army was undisputed: armed conflicts, the so-called civil wars, were beginning to ravage West Africa. The most serious ones, which came to define ECOMOG's controversial role in the region, were the Liberian and Sierra Leonean conflicts.[49]

Whether through officially regulated activities of ECOWAS and ECOMOG, European legacies of languages and educational systems, or centuries-old ethnic and cultural affiliations, West Africans abroad are cognizant of various expressions of their regional and collective identity as West Africans. A recent meeting of the Methodist Boys High School and Methodist Girls High School (Freetown, Sierra Leone) Alumni Association in Georgia at the home of one of the members illustrates well the continued centrality of regionalism in the lives of immigrants in the United States. As they socialized before their monthly gathering, two new faces began to tell the group who they were. One was a Mandingo born in Liberia who had grown up in Liberia, Gambia, and Sierra Leone. In Sierra Leone, he had attended the Methodist Boys High School, which was the reason he had come that day to join the alumni association. The other new person did not attend either of the schools but was there because he had given a ride to one of the members participating in the meeting. He explained that he was a Hausa Ghanaian and had grown up in Ghana and Nigeria. He mentioned that in Nigeria, he lived mostly in Kaduna. Immediately, a member of the association started speaking Hausa to him, and the two heartily began to reminisce about Kaduna before the civil war. It turned out that the member who now engaged this visitor about life in Kaduna was born and raised in a Saro community in Nigeria and later moved to Sierra Leone, where she attended the Methodist Girls High School. Soon the group broke into a series of conversations about backgrounds and experiences across West African national boundaries. Looking at his watch, the president of the organization interrupted the animated exchanges: "We have work to do for this association and our schools in Freetown, so we cannot spend more time talking about what is so fundamental in our lives. We all know that had it not been for all the meddling by Europeans, we would all be one country."[50] Over half a century later, much like Nkrumah, Akpata, and Wallace Johnson in England, a group of West Africans in the diaspora, this time across the Atlantic in the United States, recognized its interconnectedness through history and migration.

This episode in a living room in metro Atlanta and the descriptions and assessment of this chapter demonstrate how West Africans

fundamentally exist in a "world in motion." Complex processes of mingling and intermingling have shaped centuries of their history, from the
precolonial empires to the European demarcation of colonies and states
to postcolonial national vicissitudes and regional cooperation. In short,
the subjects of this study are no strangers to hybrid spaces.

Going Overseas: To the "Mother Countries"

As intraregional migration shaped West Africa and West Africans,
movement out of the region and the continent was also making its
mark. Of course, the involuntary migration of the trans-Saharan and
Atlantic slave trades took West Africans to the Islamic/Arab world as
well as to Europe and the New World, respectively. But this chapter
now turns to migration beyond the shackles of captivity. As Europeans colonized Africa, they extended their professed "civilizing" mission
to include encouragement of African travel to European metropolises.
European benefactors concentrated on the elite, arranging for the children, especially males, to attend European educational institutions. By
the first decades of the twentieth century, small African student-émigré
communities could be found in almost every major Western European
metropolis—London, Paris, Lisbon, and Berlin. Furthermore, a diasporic mingling had begun to occur in these European cities among the
West Africans and between them and their counterpart colonials from
the Caribbean. It was within this context that Sierra Leonean, Ghanaian, Gambian, and Nigerian students in London got together in 1925 to
form the West African Students' Association. In Paris in the 1930s, Senegalese Léopold Sédar Senghor, Martinican Aimé Césaire, and French
Guyanese Léon Damas developed negritude, a lasting literary and ideo-
logical phenomenon that continues to influence black nationalism.[51]

  Besides in regard to a few cases like that of the Kru maritime workers, pursuit of Western education came to define West African immigration to Europe before 1940. This changed after 1945. As European labor
became increasingly expensive, African labor, which was exploited
mostly within African colonial boundaries, began to be sought and
recruited for European economies. While Britain satisfied this need
mainly by enlisting labor from its Caribbean colonies, France recruited
massively from Africa. By independence, West African migrant

communities, made up of people from Senegal, Mali, and Mauritania, had become visible enclaves in French cities like Paris and Marseilles. From independence until 1974, France ensured the continuation of this labor supply by granting "favored nation" status to its former colonies and reaching agreements on labor migration with the new African governments.[52] This outlet for emigration was serendipitous. Ironically, with independence came an initial tightening of national boundaries, a postcolonial outcome that curbed the once fluid intraregional mobility. Suddenly, Western-type papers and documents (passports and visas) were required to enter and visit or work in nations other than one's own. Postindependence nationalism and the strict border enforcement that came with it led to a series of expulsion and deportation campaigns. Senegal expelled Guineans in 1967; Sierra Leone, Guinea, and Ivory Coast expelled Ghanaian fishermen in 1968; Ghana expelled all non-Ghanaian West Africans without resident permits in 1969; Ghana and Ivory Coast expelled Togolese farmers in 1979; and the largest mass expulsion occurred in 1983 when Nigeria hunted and deported nearly 1.5 million illegal West African migrant workers.[53] Even after the creation of ECOWAS in 1975, as some of the examples above underscore, the deportations and expulsions continued. And when, by 2000, the various governments decided to work through ECOWAS and other regional protocols to "recreate a borderless West Africa," extraregional international immigration had reached phenomenal scales and now included the United States in a major way.

By the mid-1970s, conditions in Europe forced a revision of immigration policies, altering migration patterns grounded in decades of imperial ties. In Britain, the increasing "menacing black presence" had become a source of concern. In 1958, clashes between West Indian immigrants and whites led to what were labeled "race riots." In 1962 Britain passed the Commonwealth Immigration Act, designed to curb immigration from its former colonies. This policy was revised as more limitations were added from 1962 to 1974. By the revision in 1974, the rationale for restriction had become bolder in its emphasis on ancestry and heritage. It was clear that the more stringent immigration policy targeted not the more favored Commonwealth members—Canada, Australia, and New Zealand—but the "other" members from Asia, Africa, and the Caribbean. Although conservatives were more vocal

and assertive about restriction, both the Labour and Conservative Parties were united in their conclusion that "excessive" immigration from
the Caribbean especially was creating unwanted competition for jobs
and housing. Although West Indians were the "black faces" of immigration restriction from the 1950s to 1970s, Britain's strict new policy
drastically curtailed immigration from Commonwealth West African
nations as well.[54]

France, too, had begun to see the downside of its generous postwar,
postcolonial immigration policy. By the end of the 1960s the baby boom
generation was maturing and the entrance of large numbers of women
into the labor force reduced the need for foreign labor. The global oil
crisis of 1973 and the recession it sparked gave France the opportunity
and validation to revise its immigration legislation. In 1974, France
passed the labor immigration ban, which, although initially temporary, was made permanent in 1977. The Ministry of State for Immigrant
Workers offered *l'aide au retour*, monetary support to facilitate immigrants' return and resettlement in their home country. While Spanish
and Portuguese immigrants (happy to return after the Franco and Salazar dictatorships, respectively) accepted the offer, Africans, the real target, did not.[55] Instead, some decided to relocate and encourage prospective migrants in West Africa to move to other areas in Europe that were
unconventional destinations where they had no linguistic, cultural, or
colonial ties. Consequently, from the late 1960s, West African migrants
in France and Britain began a regional move within Europe that took
them to countries like Spain and Italy.[56] Importantly, at the same time,
West Africans at home began the remarkable shift to setting their sights
on the United States.

Significantly, however, the severe immigration restrictions from the
1960s to 1980s did not mean a halt to West African entry into Europe.
Thus, the flow to the European continent did not remain static while
the movement to America grew. In reality, West African students,
workers, and families continued to migrate to Europe, although in
reduced numbers. Then by the 1990s, with a revision of immigration
laws designed especially to accommodate refugees, there was a resurgence of mass relocations to Europe. The statistics reveal that in some
cases admission of West Africans into Europe was very close in scale to
the numbers admitted into the United States. In fact, if the individual

receiving countries are grouped collectively as Europe, the total numbers do surpass those of the United States. For example, the United Nations High Commission for Refugees (UNHCR) estimated that in the decade of 1995 to 2005, 13,863 Nigerians were admitted as refugees to the United States, 11,749 to the United Kingdom, 10,406 to Germany, and 6,510 to France.[57] The continuing significance of Europe as a destination for West Africans is perhaps most reflected in the first decade of the twenty-first century by the magnitude of the "transit-country problem." Determined to get to Europe via North Africa, hundreds of job-seeking men and women from mostly Nigeria, Ghana, Mali, and Senegal have risked their lives to be smuggled into Europe. The smugglers, known as *Tchagga*, have developed a sophisticated network that, according to authorities in Europe and North Africa, has ensured an endless flow of successful and unsuccessful illegal border crossings into Europe through Libya, Algeria, and Morocco. Some of the migrants have been stranded in these transit countries for years, during which time they remain destitute and often abused, while they wait for their luck to change and eventually set foot on European soil. In 2008, Nigeria's Ministry of Foreign Affairs reported that at least fifty-nine thousand Nigerians without valid traveling documents were in North Africa seeking to migrate to Western Europe.[58]

By the 1990s, West Africans' world in motion had become much more complex. Not only did intraregional migration continue, mass migrations were occurring to America, South Africa, Europe, Australia, and the Gulf States, especially Saudi Arabia. Therefore, it is imperative that postcolonial West African American immigration history be studied, described, and understood within the context of what many scholars have rightly dubbed "the new African Diaspora."[59]

Coming to America

The 1960s and 1970s were decades of significant transformations in global migrations. Among the most noteworthy was the new West African migration to the United States. As the 1960s ushered in African modern nationhood, Africans (especially the nonelite, nonactivist) began to really learn about America and Americans. Historian Cyril Patrick Foray noted, "As closely related as West Africans are to blacks

in America, those Africans not enslaved were kept out of the migration and settlement which formed black America. With the exception
of Liberia [and Cape Verde, whose migrants to America had developed
transnational connections], most West Africans were socialized to see
America as a 'distant, foreign land,' and, instead, encouraged to concentrate on forging relations with the European colonizers, who were made
out to be their kin of sorts."[60] In 1969, African American missionary
Daisie Whaley felt this disconnect from her West African kindred. She
explained her first encounter with the people of Ivory Coast in this way:
"The African residents stared at me. This was their first time seeing
an African-American person. They touched their nose, then touched
my nose. They touched their hair, then touched my hair. They touched
their hand, then touched my hand. They said, 'she looks just like us,
we wonder if she will love us.'"[61] This situation was drastically altered
as the American presence in West Africa significantly increased after
independence. One crucial conduit for this shift was the new Kennedy
administration program, the Peace Corps, founded in 1961. Peace Corps
volunteers made inroads into a cross-section of West African society,
providing firsthand information about the United States, its peoples,
and its culture.

This was not the first time that Americans interacted with "non-Libe-
rian" West Africans, especially in the Anglophone territories, however.
During the colonial era, both white and black American churches and
secular institutions extended their activities to West Africa, as underscored by the American Presbyterian churches and schools in Ghana
and those of the African Methodist Episcopal, Evangelical United
Brethren, and the United Brethren in Christ in Sierra Leone. Facing
stiff competition from the "official," colonial missions and institutions,
preindependence American religious and secular philanthropic groups,
though successful, were not able to connect West Africa to the United
States as strongly as their European counterparts were doing for West
African–European relations. Many Africans who came to the United
States for education prior to the 1960s were assisted by these American
groups to study in private and public, mostly predominantly black, colleges and universities. Recruitment was not easy as they had to struggle
against the European propaganda alleging the inferiority of American
education. For example, when in 1947 Angela Tuboku-Metzger, who

was to become a long-standing leader of the Sierra Leonean community in Atlanta, first decided to pursue a degree in higher education by coming to the United States, she noted that the reaction of some of her relatives was far less enthusiastic than it normally would have been. Similarly, in Nigeria some British colonial officials were known to claim that a master's degree from the United States was equivalent to a bachelor's from a British university. And in Sierra Leone in 1943, the Board of Governors of Freetown's Methodist Girls' High School refused to consider an American-trained applicant for the position of principal of the school.[62]

It was under the gaze of skeptical critics and detractors that a small group of West African students came to the United States before independence including Nkrumah and Nnamdi Azikiwe. They, like many in their cohort, went back to Africa after their studies to join in the efforts for self-government, independence, and nation building. The high return rate of American-trained graduates played a part in dispelling some of the European-generated contempt for American education. The careers and achievements of prominent nationalists like Nkrumah and Azikiwe not only confirmed the high academic standards of advanced education in the United States, but also revealed the value of exposure to African American activism. Besides these celebrated nationalists, many other American graduates excelled in the civil service, private companies, and academe.[63] With diminishing direct contact with European officials, many of whom left after independence, West Africans were able to gain firsthand opportunities to assess American education through contact with American university graduates and observations from the increasing presence of Americans, from missionaries to Peace Corps volunteers and embassy staff. The Peace Corps in particular could make a long-lasting impact. When in 1996 Eddie Kamara Stanley successfully sought asylum to escape the brutality of the civil war that was raging in his homeland of Sierra Leone, he was already out of the country attending a conference in Vienna for journalists who were covering the war. Yet rather than seek refuge in Austria as the nuns there encouraged him to do, he made arrangements instead to get to the United States. He explained that since Sierra Leone was a former British colony, most of his compatriots growing up in Freetown in the 1970s had aspirations to be in London, but in those formative years, Eddie met a Peace Corps volunteer who sparked his desire to one day make his new home in the land of opportunity with its multiethnic population that she described to him. He remembered that she told him, "It's difficult to come here but if somebody comes here you have many chances for progress." And then he added, "I believe America is the best. It's the nation of nations. You see every nation in America."[64]

The role of American diplomatic missions must also be acknowledged in this account of increasing interest in the United States. As sovereign nations, now essentially in charge of their own foreign policy, the new African countries strengthened relations with the United States, as evidenced by expanded diplomatic/embassy initiatives and activities. The United States Information Services (USIS) was the foremost embassy unit to disseminate information about American society, including educational opportunities. Every USIS office had an educational officer who advised young people who were interested in studying in the United States. They made available an array of information and services, from providing and explaining university catalogues to making arrangements for the Test of English as a Foreign Language (TOEFL). USIS extended its services beyond the urban centers where the embassies were located into the rural areas. In his account of his impressions of the United States upon immigrating, Kofi Apraku expressed his amazement that the opportunity to compete for the International Scholarship Exchange Program extended to his "nonelite" school in Tweneboa in the outskirts of Kumasi, Ghana. He won this scholarship, which became his ticket to America in 1972.[65] Growing American presence extended to the primary and secondary schools. West Africans who attended school in the 1970s still reminisce (even in the diaspora) about the American lunch program. The American-based humanitarian organization CARE made lasting impressions on the African students, who still remember the CARE cornmeal and bulgur lunches.

The built environment of educational and other edifices also conveyed the increasing American presence in West Africa and the corollary message of prosperity in the United States. USAID sponsored the construction of roads, bridges, and schools. The Kennedy Building, complete with a replica of Apollo 11 in the entrance, became the tallest, most imposing structure on the Fourah Bay College campus and in the whole of Sierra Leone in the 1970s. And, crucially, at a time when former colonial powers were drastically cutting financial aid for education in Europe, the United States introduced government-sponsored scholarships like the African Graduate Fellowship Program, established in 1963, as well as the Fulbright program, established in 1946 and extended to Africa in 1950. While these government scholarships were important and are the ones often cited, by the 1980s the majority of West African students who came to the United States for higher education were sponsored by research/teaching graduate assistantships from state and private colleges and universities, as well as through scholarships from church and secular philanthropic organizations. Also, on the African end, many others were sponsored by government scholarships and private family funds. It is worth noting that the Soviet Union had also begun to offer study-abroad opportunities to West Africans, thus highlighting the extent to which these new U.S. aid initiatives must be viewed within the context of the Cold War.

Whether diffused through scholarships, buildings, or the contributions of Peace Corps volunteers, the message was clear by the 1970s that the United States offered an exciting alternative to Western Europe. Going to America meant going to "the Super Power." As Lawrence Okafor observes, "American education became even more popular when America landed a man on the moon in 1970 and to the youth in many African countries, America was now seen as the country with better technology and the place to go for university education." In Ghana as Apraku prepared his essay to compete for an American scholarship, he could not help comparing conditions in the United States with those in Africa and Europe: "The United States, on the other hand, seemed so full of life and hope, energy and purpose. The 1972 presidential campaign that pitted George McGovern against incumbent President Richard Nixon was well under way. The Vietnam War that had torn the country apart and appeared to have undermined the very fabric of the American society was coming to an end. In general there was a conspicuous air of hope and optimism that proved rather affective."[66]

Although the prospective emigrants did not know this, much of the sense of possibility about the United States was the result of the movement for civil rights and other forms of social activism in this period.

From the pathbreaking civil rights legislation of 1964 and 1965 and the formation of the Congressional Black Caucus in 1971 to the dramatic liberalization of immigration policy, most notably the 1965 Immigration Reform Bill, but also the subsequent 1980 Refugee Act, the 1986 Immigration Reform and Control Act, and the 1990 Immigration Reform Bill that included the Diversity Lottery, developments in America during these transformative years directly influenced the course of West African immigration history.[67]

The shift in U.S. immigration policy could not have come at a better time for what had now become a beleaguered region in a crisis-ridden continent. As Joseph Takougang emphasized in his essay "Contemporary African Immigrants to the United States," the story of postcolonial African migration to America is embedded in the "hopes-turned-disappointments" of independence with its legion of economic, political, and social calamities that dashed dreams and triggered mass migrations. West Africans throughout the region and across socioeconomic strata felt the dire economic woes from which it seemed no one could escape—what Takougang further has described as "economic paralysis and political suffocation."[68] In Senegal in the late 1970s and early 1980s, a severe drought exposed the government's lack of a viable agricultural policy and its inability to deal with a natural disaster at a time that the world price of peanuts fell drastically. A rural exodus from the Groundnut Basin to urban centers like Dakar confirmed the severity of the situation. But the movement continued beyond Dakar as inhabitants of the urban areas were also moving. SAPs, the dreaded structural adjustment programs of the International Monetary Fund and the World Bank, demanded currency devaluation and other austerity measures, penalties that brought almost every economic sector to its knees as the cost of living hit unimaginably high proportions. Abu Lo, an assistant manager of an insurance company in Dakar who moved to the United States in 1980, explained the extent of emigration: "The groundnut farmers were not the only ones to move; teachers, accountants, mechanics and managers all moved. As long as you have the opportunity, you moved." Lo's sentiments here are similar to those expressed to anthropologist Bruno Riccio during his research on emigration from rural Senegal. One of his informants said, "If someone does not emigrate, it is because he has no legs to do it."[69]

This desperate scenario of economically motivated migration played out, with nuanced details, in all the West African nations. J. Lomboko, a Ghanaian teacher, was forced to move first to Nigeria, then to Transkei (one of the so-called independent African Bantustans in apartheid South Africa) before moving to the United States in 1981. In his own words, "Structural Adjustment was killing us in Ghana. Even the price of a necessity like a tube of toothpaste was prohibitive. My wife saw women in Makola market count pepper and sell it one by one, instead of in small heaps, like they used to. I had no choice but to take my family and my certificates to look for a better life." And Y. Okegbu relates his story, demonstrating that even Nigeria, the region's giant, was not immune, especially after the end of the brief oil boom of the early 1980s:

> After studying in the United States, I went back home. Yes, to help build the nation, but also to carve out a good life for me and my family. For a while things were good, Nigeria had a growing oil economy. But things got progressively worse: no longer could we easily maintain the upper-middle class lifestyle that brought me back, complete with a nice car, a nice house and private schools for our children. So, I took my American- and Nigerian-born children and my black American wife and we returned to the United States.[70]

Indeed, this "return migration" is a vital but often overlooked pattern of movement. Evidence suggests that many West Africans who had studied in the United States in the 1970s and early 1980s, initially went back to their home countries but then returned to America as part of the late 1980s and 1990s migration waves. They did so through several different strategies including utilizing family reunification policy via their American-born children or spouses, as foreign students again on F or J visas, as workers on H-1 visas, or as tourists who later overstayed and ended up joining the ranks of the unauthorized in a country where they had once been documented.

Whether as return or first-time immigrants, the new diaspora in the United States was not monopolized by men desperate to fend for their families. In fact, pragmatic economic decisions altered the gender ratio as women began to arrive in unprecedented numbers, sometimes as single women, but often as "path breakers" of family migration. The

SAP devaluation crisis in Senegal offers a good illustration. Schomburg Center scholar Sylviane Diouf comments on how migration switched gender roles: "It was women's traditional role to stay at home and patiently wait for men [away as migrant laborers] to send money to feed the family. But in 1994, when 14 countries in Africa's 'franc zone' saw their common currency, the CFA franc, lose 50 percent of its value, the region's people were forced to look for economic opportunity elsewhere. The devaluation gave women no choice but to go out and make money on their own."[71]

From the early 1990s, a great number of West African emigrants were double fugitives—from economic woes and the atrocities of war. The refugee crisis of the last decade of the twentieth century and early twenty-first century created one of the most important backdrops for the new immigration. The small number of refugees who found their way to the United States in the late 1960s and early 1970s during the Biafra War is almost negligible when compared to the exodus thirty years later, this time predominantly from Liberia and Sierra Leone. The conditions and developments that led to war in these countries are huge and too complex to discuss in this overview.[72] It is enough to emphasize that the wars of specific nations resulted in a regional crisis. Underscoring the existence of an "arc of instability," a nongovernmental organization (NGO) refugee policy analyst explained, "The violence is interwoven. War in Liberia begat war in Sierra Leone, which in turn begat attacks in Guinea and prolonged the civil war in Côte d'Ivoire. The recognized borders don't mean anything to many of the hardcore combatants. When a country finally achieves a peace treaty, the guys who make a living through the barrel of their guns seep across the border to the next country."[73] Even though violence did not break out in every nation, all the nations were affected by the pressures of displacement. Under the auspices of individual West African states and the UNHCR, refugee camps were erected in Ghana, Nigeria, Gambia, Ivory Coast, and especially Guinea, which accommodated the largest number of refugees. Furthermore, ironically, Nigeria, whose high contribution of forces to ECOMOG gave it a leading role in the Liberian and Sierra Leonean crises, had its own refugees, many of whom were to contribute to the U.S. statistics on refugees from Africa. Since the early 1990s, Nigerians have fled from the Sani Abaca dictatorship, ethnic conflicts, and Islamic extremism and the implementation of the sharia, the sacred law of Islam, in some parts of the north.

Although their numbers are small, one important group of West African refugees that has typically been overlooked in the discussion of political and religious refugee resettlement is women fleeing patriarchal persecution, specifically the horrors of female genital mutilation (FGM). In 1996 the case of Fauziya Kassindja brought attention to these "unsung refugees." Kassindja had fled Togo in 1984, just hours before her scheduled circumcision. In the United States she faced deportation after her claim for asylum was rejected. After her case was publicized, in June 1996 a federal judge ruled that Kassindja's situation was grounds for asylum. Many similar cases involving women from West Africa and other regions where FGM is practiced have followed, a development that has sparked a debate not just among feminists and other groups in mainstream America but in the immigrant enclaves as well. West Africans in America are divided over the validity of FGM as grounds for asylum and the repercussions of all the publicity about the practice on the immigrants and their communities in the United States.[74]

No matter the circumstances of their flight, there are some crucial factors that must be considered when looking at refugees from West Africa. First, the history must be studied within the larger picture of refugee dispersal in the continent and multiple destinations around the world. With deep UN involvement through the UNHCR, "resettlement" was truly international. Refugees were resettled in receiving African countries as well as the United Kingdom, Germany, France, Ireland, Belgium, the Netherlands, Australia, Canada, and the United States. This worldwide refugee dispersal dispels the perception of "the American Burden"—America shouldering the West African refugee problem. Second, the "transit country," secondary and tertiary migration, multiple flight, and multiple migration phenomena must be addressed. Most of the refugees did not come directly to America. They settled in one or two other countries in West Africa before coming to the United States. Some stayed in the transit countries for a number of years before they were processed for resettlement. Grasping the complexity of multiple migrations is central to understanding adaptation in the United States, as noted by one Sierra Leonean woman who lived in French-speaking Guinea for three years before eventually being resettled in

English-speaking Minneapolis. "By the time I reached America I could speak some French and was behaving in some Guinean ways. But all the official people in the refugee assistance places who worked with me only took my Sierra Leonean nationality into consideration. But my Guinean experience, even if not as important as my Sierra Leonean nationality, is important."[75] Furthermore, some families are separated as a result of multiple flights, as family members may be dispersed to different camps in different West African countries. Some members may remain in the transit countries for years waiting to be reunited with relatives who have already made it to the States, as was the case of one Liberian man whose family was dispersed in camps in Ivory Coast, Ghana, and Guinea. Eventually he was relocated to America while his wife was still in the Ivory Coast and other family members were sent to Canada and Australia. And, third, the diversity of refugee groups should be understood and explained. Contrary to widely held perceptions of an undifferentiated mass of mostly rural, uneducated people, cohorts of West African refugees contain significant numbers who are members of the urban elite. Included are professionals and successful entrepreneurs whose lives were suddenly and severely disrupted by the upheavals or who, already frustrated by the political and economic conditions, were already poised to emigrate when war broke out.

Although refugee admittance is a major process of the new diaspora, as John Arthur stresses, of the hundreds of thousands of Africans who seek refuge and asylum status every year, only a small percentage, fewer than 5 percent, are allowed into the United States.[76] By 2000, therefore, "winning the lottery" had become a more hopeful, viable means of coming to America. As a Sierra Leonean online newspaper declared in 2010,

> Without a doubt, the surest way to come to the United States from Sierra Leone these days is through the Diversity Lottery Program (DV). Those who succeed and immigrate to the States do not have to go through what many who came on visitor's visas and overstayed go through. Once they arrive, they get the right to work and drive right away. After five years, they will become eligible for citizenship. Now that the war is over, Sierra Leoneans no longer qualify for resettlement programs that were popular during the war.[77]

"DV" has become a fixture in the lexicon of West Africans; the newspapers write about it, radio and television programs explain and discuss it, and even villagers in some of the most remote parts know about it. Transnational family and institutional networks have been created to facilitate the transmission of information and other assistance for participating in the program. For example, one of the most popular West African immigrant publications, *African Abroad*, found in most of the tropical food stores and other businesses in American cities, devotes attention to DV opportunities. Contributing attorneys Sheila Amaka Odiari and Joseph Rotimi Famuyide provide detailed information and advice about the program, from deadlines and entry procedures to qualifications and eligibility as well as fraud and scams. Even requests for divine intervention are a common aspect of the DV story on both sides of the Atlantic. Churches, especially the Pentecostals and Evangelicals, have devised special prayers and other forms of supplication for God's help in winning the lottery. In West Africa, in addition to special church prayers and fasting, traditional spiritual institutions are also consulted to invoke the hand of African deities in American immigration. Every West African nation has stories about its people and the American DV. Government and nongovernmental websites relate tales of misconceptions about the program and provide information to set the record straight about academic and occupational qualifications and entry deadlines and requirements. Some of these accounts deal with such obstacles as ignorance about the required high school or West African School Certificate O-levels qualification and the prohibitive nonrefundable application/entry fees of $755, not including additional costs for a medical exam, security clearance, and money for travel to the United States.[78]

As many of the electronic, print, and "word-of-mouth" DV "primers" warn, being selected in the lottery does not guarantee a DV visa. That is family members, especially those already living abroad, are continually implored for active involvement and assistance. Family members living abroad in the United States, as well as Britain, Canada, and other parts of the diaspora, are very much involved in the DV migration project. They send money because very often many of the applicants, even those who exceed the basic eligibility criteria and are university graduates who have worked longer than the required two years, cannot afford the more than thousand dollars involved. This much-needed financial assistance from abroad should not diminish the significance of assistance within the West African societies. There are local family and community networks that provide the monetary support needed for an individual or a group of people in their DV quests. And when a winner actually makes it to the United States, it is such a cause for celebration that families will even hold special "DV success" parties.

Whether via the DV or through other channels, simply achieving immigrant status—becoming a "been to"—carries much cachet. Thus the immigrant success story begins first with gaining the opportunity to actually make the move, and those who do are already admired and held in higher esteem at home, even before they have successfully settled in their new destinations. Such dynamics can heighten the pressures for the newly arrived who often are struggling with the challenges of relocation. Individual and collective assistance has been a constant in the immigration narrative. This is reflected mostly in that quintessential component of the immigrant experience—chain migration. American anthropologist Enid Schildkrout relates a signature chain migration story. In 1972 a Ghanaian, Ibrahim, whom Schildkrout had befriended during her fieldwork in Ghana, was now living in New York and asked her to help arrange for his wife Safiya to join him, which she did in 1973. Once on their feet, they took the responsibility of assisting other members of their extended family to move not just to the United States but to other points in the transnational diasporic world that had emerged by the end of the twentieth century. According to Schildkrout, "Over the years many other members of this family have come to New York for brief visits or long residences. In 2007, there were seven cousins from Ghana in New York, not to mention one in Germany, two in England, two in Spain, one in Italy, and one in Chad. One person lived in Saudi Arabia before coming to New York; another lived in Nigeria."[79] Moussa Magassa played a similar role as Ibrahim's for his Malian extended family and the community. Coming in the late 1970s with the first wave of Malian migration to the United States, Magassa came to be known as an early godfather of the small Malian community in New York for his contributions in bringing his fellow Malians and helping them settle. His brick townhouse near Yankee Stadium was known even in Mali as a beacon for new immigrants and a symbol of a Malian's success in America. When that house burned down in 2007, killing several members of his polygamous family, the tragedy was mourned equally in two countries in two continents.[80] Anthropologist Abdoulaye Kane has studied similar chain migration patterns among Haal Pulaar from Senegal, Mauritania, Mali, and Guinea who have developed close-knit communities in New York through chain migration.[81] These are only a few examples of a host of chain migrations that feature in the West African diaspora in the United States and elsewhere.

An overview of West African migration to the United States would be incomplete without some attention to the issue of brain drain. Although the West African immigrant pool has diversified considerably with regard to socioeconomic factors when compared to the much smaller and more elite group who came before the 1980s, and despite the greater numbers of refugees in the mix of the past two decades, this is still a population that overall arrives highly skilled with training in technical and scientific fields that fit occupational areas where there is still demand. The skilled and professional workers include the following categories: educators (teachers, from the primary to the tertiary levels), lawyers, computer scientists, accountants, engineers, architects, doctors, pharmacists, nurses, radiologists, and physiotherapists. Of all of these, no other groups are used to describe and discuss the brain drain as much as doctors and allied health care professionals, especially nurses. What by the 1990s had become an exodus of doctors and nurses can be explained simply by the deplorable health care infrastructure in Africa (ill-equipped facilities, low pay, no opportunities for professional growth, and misappropriation of foreign aid designated for health) and the growing opportunities in those fields in industrial/developed countries. Like health care professionals elsewhere, West African doctors and nurses migrate to further their careers and to improve their economic and social situation. By 2004, 2,697 West African–trained physicians were practicing in the United States—2,158 from Nigeria alone, and 478 from Ghana.[82]

As revealing as the figures are about the characteristics of the new West African migration to America, the influx of skilled and professional workers must be understood within the broader context of contemporary international labor migration, which John Arthur calls "the circulation of elites." To explain this circulatory migration, Arthur presents examples of physicians moving to multiple cities before eventually reaching the United States. Of African physicians in the United States, 40 percent had participated in varying degrees in multiple international migrations, especially to Britain, Canada, Saudi Arabia, and the former Soviet republics. Furthermore, many of these individuals had earlier participated in intra and interregional migrations within Africa, especially to Nigeria, South Africa, Libya, Botswana, Lesotho, and Swaziland.[83] Thus, like all other aspects of postcolonial West African immigration to the United States, this phenomenon of the brain drain must be studied within the contexts of the wider ongoing diaspora.

Whether as professional or skilled workers, returnee immigrants or refugees, by the end of the twentieth century, diverse groups of West Africans were living, working, and raising children in the United States. Writing about immigrants who came centuries before, historian Bernard Bailyn talks about "worlds in motion,"—the circulation of people throughout the British world, and he describes the waves of migration to North America in the early eighteenth century as "a spillover—an outgrowth, an extension—of these established patterns of mobility in England."[84] Considering the differences in epochs and origins and conventional emphases on distinctions between old and new immigrations, twentieth- and twenty-first-century black West Africans and white eighteenth-century English immigrants would not seem comparable. Yet they share fundamental characteristics in their patterns of migration. Like the Pilgrims and the Puritans, so associated with the foundations of the United States, West Africans' experiences in and contributions to America and the black diaspora are influenced in great measure by the "worlds in motion" from which they came.

2

Occupational Detour

New Paths to Making a Living

To a typical immigrant onboard a plane enroute to the United States, it's a dream of "success here I come." The story usually changes for many and they lose their dream in the cloud of uncertainty presented by a "begin again syndrome."
—Nigerian American entrepreneur Tajudeen Ajadi

Three and a half centuries before Tajudeen Ajadi's observation, when men, women, and children from West Africa were forcibly moved across the Atlantic to what later became the United States, they came not in planes but in the holds of slave vessels, where it was absolutely impossible, actually insane, to entertain dreams of success. Yet as streams of international labor migration, both the old and postcolonial diasporas share a common characteristic in the centrality of work. West African slaves were often calculatingly selected for their expertise, based on projections of what they would contribute to the plantation economy. A good example of this was the importation of skilled rice planters from what is now present-day Sierra Leone for rice cultivation, the backbone of the economy of the Sea Islands of Georgia and South Carolina, from the seventeenth to the nineteenth centuries.

Moving forward to the second half of the twentieth century, this time West Africans had instead been arriving with qualifications and experiences that, on the surface, appeared to be a good fit for an American society that had evolved by this time into a capitalist, postindustrial economy. Under these circumstances, the migrants found themselves in the position to actually evaluate their suitability and, as such, were able to deftly formulate their hopes and dreams of success. Their qualifications and preparedness have been widely acknowledged and their

accomplishments touted. But failure to probe the seemingly uncomplicated outcomes obscures a great part of the story of work and success in
the postcolonial diaspora.

Generally, the narrative is one of circuitous journeys—for those who
pursue practical routes into unintended work activities, as well as those
who engage in their planned livelihoods. More often than not, the positions they were trained for and held at home are not available options
for them in the United States. While at times the newcomers are simply transplanting the skills of their premigration experience as with the
Murids from Senegal who bring a time-honored legacy as traders and
merchants to selling their wares on the streets of New York, more often
the jobs that West Africans find themselves doing in their new settings
represent what we are calling an "occupational detour"—from banker
in Lagos, Nigeria, to security guard in metropolitan Atlanta, from secondary school teacher in Freetown, Sierra Leone, to nursing assistant in
an adult day care center in Houston, or, even more dramatically, from
honored chief of the Akwamu people of Ghana to taxicab driver in
New York City. Sometimes the adaptation is more nuanced—Senegalese women convert their hair-braiding prowess, part of the traditional
domestic socialization for young women in their homeland, into successful entrepreneurial activity in the United States. This chapter, therefore, is not merely an account of the kinds of occupations performed by
migrants from the recent West African diaspora in the United States.
Rather it also reveals the detours that undergird these patterns of work
and socioeconomic mobility among the newcomers, whose precursors'
labor helped shape America in centuries long passed.

Aspirations, Qualifications, and Accomplishments

Very few researchers of West Africans and their children in the late
twentieth- and early twenty-first-century United States have ignored
the compelling statistics about the educational and professional preparedness of this group of immigrants for the American labor market.
Since 1990, the U.S. Census Bureau, the Immigration and Naturalization Services, and the U.S. Citizenship and Immigration Services have
provided ample, widely disseminated records about the level of educational attainment of African immigrants in general. As mentioned in

chapter 1, continental Africans have the highest educational attainment rate of any group in the United States, native or foreign-born. Statistics that reveal more specific information about those from West African countries make the same point with decennial census and American Community Survey results from 1990 to 2010 ranking West African national groups, especially Nigerians and Ghanaians, at the very top. Beginning with tabulations of the 1990 census, sociologist Amadu J. Kaba noted that out of 158.9 million people in the United States aged twenty-five and over, 20.3 percent had bachelor's degrees or higher. For 52,388 Nigerians aged twenty-five and over, 52.9 percent had bachelor's degrees or higher, second only to another African group, Egyptians, with 60.4 percent. The 26.3 percent of Nigerians with graduate degrees was the highest rate among all sixty-eight ancestry groups listed.[1] High educational achievement remained a salient characteristic of West African immigrants throughout the first decade of the twenty-first century as well. Analyzing 2005 to 2009 data from the American Community Surveys of the U.S. Census Bureau, a Migration Policy Institute study offered useful statistics for specific West African groups in 2007. All the West African countries listed, with the exception of Cape Verde, where more than half the immigrants had just a high school degree or even less education, tied or exceeded the 18 percent rate of the native-born with bachelor's degrees: Nigeria 35 percent, Ghana 20 percent, Senegal 23 percent, Sierra Leone 19 percent, Guinea and Liberia 18 percent, Cape Verde 7 percent. Similar interpretations can be deduced from the figures for graduate and professional degrees: American-born 10 percent, Nigeria 27 percent, Ghana 14 percent, Senegal 10 percent, Sierra Leone 13 percent, Guinea 10 percent, Liberia 7 percent, Cape Verde 4 percent. Thus, for example, the proportion of Nigerian immigrants who held a bachelor's degree or better had risen from 52.9 percent in 1990 to over 60 percent by 2009.[2] Studies are also beginning to show that the sons and daughters of these immigrants are continuing this pattern of educational success in the United States, as their rates of entrance into particularly elite private colleges and Ivy League universities like Princeton and Harvard are higher than those of the native-born black population.[3]

Such findings have been widely reported and discussed since they first became available. In 1996, an article in the *Journal of Blacks in*

Higher Education began with the declaration, "Listen up those of you who believe that cognitive inferiority is hard-wired into the brains of black people. African-born immigrants who now reside in the United States are more highly educated than are U.S. whites."[4] This facet of black immigration, particularly the predominance of African-origin students enrolled in the country's most selective colleges, has been tackled in the public media as well, especially making news when at a Harvard alumni reunion in 2004, noted black public intellectuals Lani Guinier and Henry Louis Gates, Jr. raised the controversial issue of the implications that the educational attainment levels of Caribbean and African immigrants may have on affirmative action policies. They questioned whether the beneficiaries should be inclusive of all black applicants, whether native or foreign-born, or be limited solely to those who are the descendants of slaves in the United States.[5]

There is no denying the advantage of education as part of the human or social capital that West African immigrants possess and its importance for entry into managerial and professional positions in the American labor market. Such a correlation has not been lost on the immigrants themselves, as University of Wisconsin professor Festus Obiakor attested when he explained, "With an undergraduate education in Nigeria, I was excited when I was granted admission to pursue a graduate degree in the United States. My experiences as an African immigrant have been revealing, fascinating, frustrating, and intriguing. . . . I am a proud product of the American dream; and from my experiences one can see the good and the bad."[6] As Obiakor's statement begins to suggest, the mere possession of social capital does not make realization of the American dream, particularly entry into the skilled, professional, and managerial labor arenas, automatic or simple. Still, there are people like Obiakor whose success stories illustrate the interplay of education and occupation. From scientists, engineers, and computer specialists to doctors, lawyers, and architects, they epitomize the highly educated West African professional class (however small) in America.

Still adhering to premigration criteria for status ascription, many of the immigrant generation continue to view intellectuals and education practitioners as premium measures of occupational success. And by the beginning of the new century there were luminaries to demonstrate the strides made in registering the contributions of this group of West

Africans to American life and society. Consistently forging ahead in the academy, West Africans and other Africans have been identified as one major factor enhancing diversity in American higher education since the 1980s. They are visible, actually sometimes conspicuous, on college and university campuses and at professional conferences, academic meetings, and other such forums.[7]

These individuals illustrate an undisputed component of postcolonial West African American migration—distinguished, well-educated professionals who are engaged in occupations that require advanced degrees. Importantly, also, their accomplishments are earned in and recognized by the mainstream, a phenomenon that is embraced and celebrated in the immigrant communities. In 2007, this is how *African Abroad* reported the new appointment of one of the accomplished members of the Nigerian American (Naija American) community: "Kathy Daramola, Naija New Yorker, has been named to the top post of Assistant General Council at the New York City Department of Corrections. Kathy, a product of the famous University of Benin [in Nigeria], has since done a thanksgiving at her church and further celebration is still under wraps."[8] The same publication celebrated the socioeconomic mobility of the group, manifested in the steady growth of high-profile professionals and ownership of fancy cars. Highlighting the occupational standing of a selected few, part of an article, "Benzy [as in Mercedes Benz] Naija-New Yorkers List Grows," read as follows:

> It is no more a secret that Naija New Yorkers are now firmly established in the middle and upper class of the Big Apple. To celebrate their attainment of status as first generation immigrants, many are now showcasing their achievements. . . . Here is a sample list of who are the Benzy riders. God Bless America! Dr. Osho (MD) of Downstate Hospital, Brooklyn; Reverend (Dr) Adegoke Abraham Oyedeji—Pastor/Professor; Alex Kabba—Journalist; Chief Kwash Enekwechi Ozo Ochendu I, Chief Anthony Ukoli, Chinyere Okigwe—Civil Servants; Attorney Yinka Dansalami; Elder Tunji Ojekunle—Finance/Wall Street.[9]

Indeed, by the dawn of the twenty-first century, West Africans were prominently dispersed in professional occupations and throughout business districts from Madison Avenue to the Loop in Chicago to Peachtree Street in Atlanta.

But depictions of work and the West African immigrant experience must not end here, for numerous other first-generation immigrants either have not made it to the traditionally desirable occupations or are temporarily in other occupational spaces while attempting to make their way to the professions. Consequently, even for those who eventually become part of the "Benzy riders elite," it is useful to consider how they got there. The trajectory taken by Liberian dentist and Ohio resident Nicodemus Kortie is illustrative. Arriving in 1992 with a bachelor's degree in biochemistry from Cuttington University in Liberia, Kortie was convinced that entry into his field of training would be swift. Instead, as he put it, "it all ended up in the figment of my imagination. I had to leave behind the so called pedigree and start life all over again."[10] Like Kortie, many stories involve some kind of diversion or alternative activities. What are the factors that prompt such departures? What does veering off course entail? What kinds of permanent reactive, adaptive results emerge from such detours?

Twists and Turns, Jobs and Careers

Since the 1990 census, official records have affirmed that employment rates for black African immigrants are higher than for immigrants overall or for U.S.-born adults. In 2007, for example, 75 percent of African immigrants aged eighteen to sixty-four were employed, versus 71 percent of immigrants overall and 72 percent of U.S.-born adults.[11] Moreover, a 2009 study showed that the highest levels of labor force participation among the African-born were from the following West African countries: Nigerians 77.9 percent, Ghanaians 77.0 percent, and Gambians 76.1 percent.[12] It should also be noted that the strong level of participation in the civilian labor force pertains to women as well as men. Among the overall African immigrant population, women born in Ghana and those from Cape Verde in particular exhibited above-average employment rates.[13]

Such robust participation in the American labor force, as depicted by the figures, does not immediately reveal the intricate underlay—multifaceted occupational journeys marked variously by turbulence, stops, restarts, steady movement, alternative routes, and complex destinations. Atlanta taxi driver Ghanaian Moses Danquah described the reality succinctly: "Work in America can be an unanticipated journey. It is full of twists and turns in the road to jobs and careers."[14] Similarly, when Lawrence Okafor interviewed members of the West African diaspora for his study exploring the ingredients for success among this population, he emphasized just how difficult occupational adjustment can be, especially with regard to what he saw as the pursuit of "zigzag" qualifications in a variety of fields just to gain a foothold in the American wage economy. Most find that they must work multiple jobs or that they need to combine several part-time positions while also enrolled in classes to obtain the necessary additional educational credentials that will make them competitive for occupations that, in turn, will secure an improvement in their livelihoods. Either way, the need to put in extremely long hours, often including night jobs in order to support their family members, both in the United States and those still living in West Africa, can take its toll. Although some eventually settle in their new American careers, others end up frustrated, never really getting over what they perceive as a loss of social status even when they are able to earn a decent living.[15] Although the available data have not been broken down by specific national origin group, the level of underemployment of high-skilled African newcomers overall is alarming. In 2009, for example, over a third of those African immigrants who had been in the United States for fewer than ten years and arrived holding a college degree or higher were working in unskilled jobs.[16]

Ayobami Odeyemi perceptively portrayed the fits and starts in the occupational pathways to the American dream in "An Open Letter to My Brother in America." In the simulated correspondence between two brothers (one in Nigeria, the other in America), Odeyemi captures factual scenarios of employment detours. The brother in Nigeria writes,

> You narrated your experience on arriving there [America], how you had to toil day and night doing menial jobs to pay your bills. You did talk about your experience at McDonalds, Wal-Mart, Burger King and as a cab driver, even though you have an accounting degree and an MBA from one of the leading universities in Africa. . . . You worked two jobs, cleaning offices or doing night watch. . . . I thought you were with some

big companies like GE, Toyota, Ford, etc. . . . . "I sure was working with some big companies," you said, "not as a middle level manager but as a cleaner and door man."

Your story shattered my dream of America as a perfect entity in this imperfect existence. . . . America isn't paradise after all.[17]

Such occupational trajectories, with side trips and retoolings, have resulted in West Africans making forays into a variety of sectors of the U.S. labor force. They have pursued jobs in factories, as day laborers, and in service positions, especially as workers at big chain restaurants, housekeepers in hotels (from affluent, upscale hotels to budget motels), child care providers, hairdressers, nursing assistants and orderlies, home health care providers, security guards, airport workers, gas station and parking lot attendants, and taxi and long-distance truck drivers. They have even been spotted in a range of jobs in winter resorts, environments vastly different from the tropical climate from which they hail. Commenting on foreign workers in the Rocky Mountain ski slopes of Colorado, a *New York Times* article declared, "West Africans in the Rockies are part of the rapidly changing face of the ski resort work force as the classic American ski bum, immortalized in movies and magazine covers, becomes scarce."[18] A most revealing occupational detour arena, the ski slopes offer jobs—janitors, chambermaids, dish washers, waiters and other low-status positions—that the college-educated among the immigrants did not do in their homelands in any work environment, let alone in a workplace as alien to their original surroundings and accustomed climate as a ski lodge. Focused on their migration goals, however, they have been willing to put up with the dramatic changes in their occupational status as well as the harsh weather conditions. The antithesis of the ski bum, Fatou Toure, a twenty-year-old woman from Côte d'Ivoire, said "I'm here for a precise goal: to make money. I see all those people slipping around; that's not for me."[19] Similar sentiments were expressed by Mauritanian Sidy Ba, a cleaner during the day who worked at Wendy's at night: "We can't live the life of America. We can't go to nightclubs, go to restaurants, go to basketball games. We eat together. We send money home."[20]

Why did these resilient ski resort workers, and thousands of other West Africans in other parts of the United States, end up in jobs they had not planned on, in some cases far beneath their educational qualifications and premigration work experiences? Several answers pertain, starting with a fundamental deficiency—the lack of the required authorization to work in America for some in this cohort. With the exception of the DV lottery category, the visas under which West Africans typically arrive into the United States include specifications that do not afford them ready documentation to enter the labor market. Students (F and J visas) have rigidly limited work privileges, and visitors (B visas) who end up over-staying are absolutely prohibited from working. West Africans, unlike those from Mexico and some others from the Western Hemisphere or Asian immigrants, have not been regular beneficiaries of worker visas. Consequently, a great number of them initially confront legal handicaps in using their certificates and other documentation that would have enabled them to pursue jobs in their premigration occupations.

Many, who initially came on B visas relate stories of how they deliberately did not travel with their certificates or anything that would reveal their academic and professional credentials when entering as visitors. Possession of such documentation alerted immigration and customs officials to their intention to remain permanently. It is thus through the mail or other "unaccompanied" means that they get the documentation of academic and previous work experiences, sometimes several years after their arrival. Without the necessary employment authorization, they are forced to settle for "safe" jobs within the immigrant enclave economy or areas in the mainstream where they can get away with little or no scrutiny of their immigration status. Houston-based Nigerian filmmaker Nnaemeka Andrew Madueke accurately illustrates the tortuous trajectory of the B visa West African immigrant while in transition from visitor to permanent resident. In the movie *Mystery of Birds*, the protagonist, Vivian Ije Nwamadi, works in the hidden economy as a sales clerk in an African tropical food store and as a babysitter for a white American family, as she waits to get the proper employment documentation from her sham "Green Card" marriage to Gil, an American citizen. When Vivian gets her employment authorization, she quickly seeks and obtains the desk office job for which her Nigerian education and work experience had prepared her.[21]

The ambivalent attitude of American standard-bearers toward African education is another challenge that is responsible for the disparity between the immigrants' educational training and their new occupations. Many employers dismiss the premigration academic qualifications because of ignorance or arrogance. Admittedly, some Americans know very little about West African educational systems and are unable to properly determine their American equivalencies. However, frequently, they simply judge the credentials as inferior. Perceptions about the substandard quality of almost everything African have led some American employers to question the relevance of African educational and occupational training. Furthermore, some people believe that there is a high rate of fraud that in turn has jacked up the rate of West African (and African in general) educational attainment. Charges have been made that the certificates and other credentials are tainted by individuals and sometimes with the help of officials in their home country institutions or legal aids in their immigrant enclaves in America.[22] Such accusations increased tremendously when American mainstream media began to focus on corruption in West Africa, specifically the notorious Nigerian "419 scams."[23]

Contempt for and mistrust of African educational qualifications are a major employment challenge that the immigrants themselves constantly address. Approaches to surmounting such obstacles are not uniform. Some internalize the devaluation of their African credentials and decide to downplay or omit them, while some adamantly invoke them, taking pains to point out the "prestige" of their institutions. An article applauding the work of a prominent Nigerian attorney defiantly noted, "Who says foreign law experience cannot help you win a case in the United States? In the past one month, Attorney Rotimi Famuyide's legal practice experience abroad and his experience as a law lecturer in a law school abroad, helped win three difficult immigration cases—in Ohio, New Jersey and New York."[24]

Whether they omit, downplay, or affirm their premigration credentials, most West Africans in the United States are convinced of the efficacy of obtaining further education in the United States. For professionals, like doctors and lawyers, some form of U.S. accreditation is mandatory. Still, some go further (graduate degrees) beyond the required basic board or some other license certification. Nonprofessionals eagerly pursue U.S. higher education to enhance the chances of their entry into the skilled and professional occupational arenas. There are legions of accounts about the hard work and sacrifices made doing several low-status jobs at the same time that the migrants pursued the necessary recredentialing that would eventually enable them to enter their desired fields. By the 1990s, it had become commonplace to see West Africans in workers' break rooms in hotels, hospitals, nursing homes, security posts, and even in stationary taxis, reading and doing university assignments. A Ghanaian woman, a graduate of the University of Ghana, Legon, who pursued a master's in clinical psychology in the United States, echoed the sentiments of many of her fellow West Africans when, at her graduation bash, she declared, "This [her U.S. degree] is a big addition to what I brought with me from Ghana—a solid educational foundation. After much humiliation and sacrifice, now I am ready to go through doors, which must now open to me because I have proved that I can do it in two countries and two continents."[25]

For some, the motivation comes not in pursuit of furthering their own education but rather in the hope that their efforts will make it possible for their children to have the best schooling. When the college-educated Ebbie and Gladys Obukwelu emigrated from Nigeria in the 1980s, they knew they would likely have to take jobs beneath their levels of education in order to make ends meet in the United States. They settled in Brockton, Massachusetts, and indeed Gladys found work as a medical assistant while Ebbie drove a cab. Hardworking parents, they were determined that their five sons would get the best possible education and made whatever sacrifices were necessary to pay the tuition at a highly regarded private school in the area. As of 2012, their investment in the kids' education was already paying off. Three of their sons had attended college at Harvard—the oldest had graduated and was working as a New York investment banker; one son was a freshman at St. John's University; and the youngest was still doing well at Boston College High. The Obukwelus were willing to take an occupational detour themselves in order to make the climb back up the social ladder possible for their children.[26]

Nurses

The expansion of the service sector in postindustrial societies worldwide has facilitated the recruitment and incorporation of women into social reproductive and service occupations such as nursing and other caregiving jobs through new transnational and regional networks.

In the 1970s, Filipino and Afro-Caribbean women were the face of foreign workers in America's health care industry.[27] By the 1990s, even though these women were still prominent in the field, nurses, nursing assistants, and home health care aides from West Africa, most especially from the English-speaking nations of Nigeria, Ghana, Sierra Leone, and Liberia, had become very visible. Thus, by the end of the twentieth century, health care work, particularly nursing, had become one of the central markers of a population that was still gaining its footing and recognition as an American ethnic group. Simply put, nursing is a niche occupation. Earlier migrants, like the Caribbean and Filipino women, had captured that vocation but did not completely fill it. When West African immigrants began to arrive in significant numbers, plenty of room was still available in this arena, a field that had already established a reputation for recruitment of foreign workers.

Because hospitals and other health care facilities in the United States have been experiencing such a shortage of both trained nurses and physical therapists in recent years, beginning in 2005 these two occupations became the only exceptions to the Department of Labor's policy requiring proof that a foreign national is not taking a job from a U.S. citizen. Still the red tape for making such arrangements can be daunting and the procedures for the sponsoring employers are particularly challenging. Nonetheless, since becoming a physical therapist requires four years of schooling while pursuing a nursing career takes only two years, it has been more expeditious at their end for West Africans to prepare themselves for nursing jobs while continuing to work with potential employers to make their hiring possible.

As had been the pattern by century's end, trained nurses from various West African nations were wooed and recruited by U.S. governmental and other agencies like the American Hospital Association or found their way to the United States through their own individual or collective family arrangements. For example, in 2000 over five hundred nurses left Ghana for employment in industrialized countries, including the United States. This was twice the number of the graduates from nursing programs in the country that year.[28] In 2006, a transnational Ghanaian community newspaper headquartered in Marietta, Georgia, found that although there were a number of "decent, well-meaning government and private agencies, there were also very unethical ones whose recruiters went into African countries and recruited as much as 100 percent of a graduating class."[29] The report did acknowledge, though, that "the majority wanted to leave on their own accord." Therefore, evidently, many of the West Africans who initially filled this American occupational niche had premigration training. However, many more took up this line of work after migration. West Africans are confronted with structural barriers and other practical considerations, and the high levels of their participation in the health care sector, among both immigrants and refugees, reflect the trend of taking jobs that are, in many ways, radically different from what they did back at home. For example, women with first degrees, teacher certifications, and teaching positions in elementary and secondary schools in their countries of origin found themselves having to take an occupational detour when they came to the United States. First they retrained to become nursing assistants and then while working at that lower level job many continued to study to gain the credentials to then become licensed practical nurses and registered nurses.

Data from the 2009 census show that compared to female immigrants overall, African-born women were more likely to report working as registered nurses, as other nonphysician health care practitioners, and in health care support occupations. African male workers, too, were more heavily concentrated in health-care-related jobs, a trend that began at the close of the 1990s.[30] It is such departures from premigration employment patterns into a postmigration niche that is our main concern here. Why and how do West African women and men from diverse academic and professional backgrounds become nurses in America? And what are the financial, cultural, class, and gendered outcomes?

The demand for nurses in the United States is endless, and the potential for making money from this occupation is enormous. This was the message that rang clearly in West African enclaves around the United States and even found its way to the homelands in the last quarter of the twentieth century. A crucial appendage to this labor demand is the opportunity for immigrant status and a pathway to American citizenship. Since 1952, U.S. immigration laws have facilitated the admission of qualified foreign nurses as professionals under the temporary worker H-1 visa. Throughout the second half of the twentieth century and into the twenty-first century, health care employers continued to emphasize the unabated need for foreign nurses and their desire for special provisions ensuring their recruitment under any immigration reforms. Politicians and activists joined the call for uncomplicated immigration provisions to facilitate such recruitment. For example, in 2007 Senator Judd Gregg of New Hampshire urged his colleagues to support Senate Bill 1639, the Comprehensive Immigration Reform Bill, which would give higher consideration to qualified nurses seeking permanent residency in order to relieve a severe shortage in New Hampshire and nationwide. As he pleaded, "The shortage of nurses in our country is reaching crisis levels, and any effort to fix our broken immigration system should not worsen the problem. Rather, we should improve the immigration bill currently in the senate to ensure that hospitals can recruit qualified nurses and continue to provide quality care."[31]

That same year, closely following the progress of the debate on comprehensive immigration reform, leaders in West African immigrant communities across the nation spread the word that, as a newspaper headline declared, "Good News: Green Cards Now Available for Registered Nurses and Physical Therapists, Mad Rush Began July 1, 2007."[32] This close connection between nursing and immigration status had been well established by this time. Since the mid-1980s, advertisements like the following had become familiar to prospective immigrants in Africa as well as those already in the United States looking to regularize their status: "Wanted: African Nurses for US jobs. Company will provide USA Green Card for applicant and immediate family members. Salary from $30/hr to $60/hr."[33]

While recruitment of foreign nurses almost immediately points to searching abroad, in West African immigrant circles the opportunity is very much internal. One crucial facet of U.S. immigration laws, as they pertain to recruitment of foreign nurses, is the extension of their application to foreigners already in the United States who could fill the void. West African diaspora community leaders, at meetings, in columns in ethnic newspapers, and in other forums, urged nurses already in the United States and those out of status to avail themselves of the provisions of the immigration laws. Furthermore, and very important, these advocates also encouraged those who are not nurses or other health care practitioners to enter the field and get permanent residency. Wanting to stay permanently in the United States, some women and a few men readily made up their minds to pursue training in nursing. In other words, propelled by immigration status considerations, they made conscious and deliberate choices to abandon homeland occupations. Financial gains were also very much a part of the reorientation and detour. From recruiters and other sources, word spread in the enclaves that nursing is one of the most lucrative professions in the United States. Consequently, some looked forward to netting a twofold reward—their green card and a well-paying job. Still for some who already had legal status, they were lured by the prospect of making money and attaining the American dream more quickly through nursing than through the premigration employment that may have worked for them in the homeland.

Aspiring nurses have taken advantage of facilitators and incentives that enabled them to start their new occupational journeys. Through several networks in the community—church, associations, businesses, and ethnic newspapers—they learn about training institutions and funding. They became informed from flyers available in African businesses and distributed at community events, as well as from newspaper advertisements announcing training and work opportunities, like the one for a three-year program at the University of the District of Columbia for free tuition, free books, a $250 monthly stipend, and guaranteed job placement at Providence Hospital upon graduation.

Although a few women and some men attended nursing school full-time, the majority pursued their nursing degrees and other qualifications part-time. They kept their non-nursing jobs or nondegreed, lower level health care work like nursing assistantships, which they did during the week, mostly from Monday to Thursday. From Thursday to Saturday they trained to be nursing assistants (those who may want to use this as a stepping stone), licensed practicing nurses, and registered nurses at a number of institutions across the country. For some this involved out-of-state travel. For example, since the late 1990s, several Ghanaian, Nigerian, and Sierra Leonean women in Atlanta have studied for their nursing degrees in Alabama. Through effective networks, they have developed buddy clusters through which they carpool, study and prepare for exams, and share accommodations at extended stay hotels. Teresa Cesay, an Alabama nursing graduate, euphorically proclaimed at her graduation party, "The nursing training experience is a labor of love in sisterhood. We did it together and we are determined that this cooperation in our adopted land must continue. If you are interested in pursuing nursing or if you know any woman who is, come to me and I will show you how."[34]

The sheer pride, confidence, and elation engendered by nursing in America are themselves useful indices of the departures in perceptions and reception of an occupation previously widely underrated and maligned at home. In the various West African countries, nursing was viewed as women's work only a few notches above domestic labor. Typically, since the colonial era, women who went into nursing lived in hostels during their training. Hostel living became a contested issue by the period of national independence and into the postcolonial era. In reality, most of the nurse trainees saw hostels as avenues to assert their own personal independence; however, their student accommodations came to be branded in society as breeding grounds for promiscuity. As sociologist Fumilayo Showers details in her comparative study of nursing in the homelands and in the United States, mainly because of the gendered devaluation of nursing in the home countries, many women, especially from middle- and upper-middle-class backgrounds, shunned that work.[35] In the United States, however, admittedly, they became attracted to it by the immigration status benefits, but also by the educational and professional prestige this occupation potentially carried in their new home. As immigrants coming from European-patterned educational systems have observed, nursing education in the United States is unique in its provision of degrees as advanced as the doctorate level. In the countries from which West Africans hail, training in nursing is typically seen as vocational education. Being able to tag this occupational detour to a fundamental value—the quest for higher education— facilitated the journey. Rose, from Ghana, one of Showers' respondents, explained this simply but effectively: "I realized that nursing is not what everyone [back home] thinks. It is different here . . . you can do more. You can go further, you can do your masters, and even get a doctorate . . . you can do anything you wish to do."[36]

This conviction of almost limitless prospects is what propelled mostly women and some West African men to leave premigration occupations to pursue nursing. Personal stories abound that reveal this integral facet of the unfolding saga of the postslavery, postcolonial, post–civil rights West African American. Omolara of Houston had studied English and African literature at Ahmadu Bello University in Zaria, Nigeria, and had taught for two years at a secondary school in Kawo, Kaduna state, before emigrating. In America she decided to go into nursing to first regularize her status and that of her husband and children, and then to "pursue other material things afforded by the American dream, while charitably helping humanity."[37] Omolara, who attained a doctorate in nursing, became the head of a hospital unit and a part-time professor at a community college. Rosamond, who came to New Jersey with a permanent residence status through the lottery, did not need nursing for immigration legal processing, but she saw the educational, professional, and financial opportunities it afforded. Although she arrived in 2001 with a bachelor's of arts and secondary teaching diploma from the prestigious Fourah Bay College in Sierra Leone and with many years of secondary teaching and college administration experience, she decided to go back to school for her nursing degree. Through her work at nursing homes and hospitals, by 2012 she had advanced to manager of a small nursing home facility. In spite of this career success, she was also seriously exploring going back to school for her master's in nursing.[38] Ellen's detour was just as sharp. In Sierra Leone she also was a graduate of Fourah Bay College but with a bachelor's of science in economics. She had done remarkably well professionally and had risen to the position of manager of one of the branches of the premier bank in the country. This was quite an achievement for a woman. The Sierra Leonean civil war forced her family, which included her husband and two children, who were teenagers at the time, to move to Atlanta. Concluding that she would not be able to work in banking at the level and prestige she had just left behind, she decided to enter nursing, first as a nursing assistant and later as a trained and licensed nurse. As she herself marveled, "This occupation has taken me into a completely new life. I have done it all; I worked in nursing homes, hospitals and now, as a traveling nurse, I work around the country, which is not as hard to do as some might think, because I am already wired with the immigrant mentality of continuous mobility."[39]

Sharper still is the detour taken by the increasing number of Nigerian, Ghanaian, and Sierra Leonean men going into nursing and other health care occupations. In the mid-1990s, when the West African male nurse began to be a noticeable phenomenon, many of the African countries from which the immigrants originated did not even have male nurses or at the most could speak of only a handful of male nurses who stood out as an anomaly. The severity of the detour is further highlighted by the very obvious fact that even in their new home the presence of male nurses is still a rarity. In 2004, only 5.8 percent of the licensed registered nurses in America were men.[40] Into the second decade of a high-tech twenty-first century, male nurses were still openly ridiculed as an aberration. For example, in 2011 in an episode of *Glee*, a popular TV show, a lead character, Sue Sylvester, a cheerleading coach, remarked, "A female football coach, like a male nurse, is a sin against nature."[41] In challenging male nursing as "unnatural," very often it is a double assault on the men's gender and sexuality.[42] For men of African descent, their marginalization in the field is further exacerbated by their miniscule presence even when compared with the relatively small numbers of Caucasian and Hispanic male nurses. It was for this reason that the American Assembly for Men in Nursing, which launched a focused campaign in 2011 to increase the number of male nurses by 20 percent by 2020, decided to invest additional attention to the recruitment of black males.[43]

The contours of male nursing in the United States underscore the double front within which West African immigrant men are playing out their occupational detour: Not only are they breaking new ground within their ethnic economic subcultures, they are doing so within a larger arena fraught with conflicting notions of the rewards and challenges of this work. For the women who have transitioned into nursing as a new line of work, they were still entering a traditional ("natural") field, while for the men the new terrain is vastly alien in both their old and new homes.

Interestingly, many of the new African male nurses in America believe that their existence within their ethnic enclaves has served as social capital for entering into and coping with the still "feminine"-oriented occupation. More often than not their detour is a collective family decision guided by clear immigration goals. Like women, some men went into nursing to regularize their immigration status. Many have also admitted that they were lured by the financial rewards they observed their spouses, sisters, and other female relatives and members of their communities earn as nurses. Responding to the perceived threat of emasculation, many are reassured that the standards of the subculture are more attuned to the practical necessities of resorting to nursing to fulfill "macho" immigration objectives. As one Ghanaian male nurse in Chicago put it, "When I walk into a party or some other event, people respect me because they know how much money I have spent on them and the occasion. All that money comes from my work as a successful nurse. They must ask themselves, 'is that the earning capacity of a weak man?'"[44]

Furthermore, they have attempted to follow and conceptualize gender hierarchies based on nursing specialties. For example, Nigerian Ephraim Owusu and Sierra Leonean Joseph Freeman of Silver Spring, Maryland, learned from each other and from their colleagues at the hospital where they worked what "respectable" specialties to seek out. They concluded that the greater the shortage of workers in a particular specialty, the more difficult it must be and, therefore, the more masculine the perception of the skills involved. They zeroed in on two main areas—acute critical care and anesthesiology nursing. Indeed, the literature on labor shortages in nursing confirms that these specializations are chronically understaffed and minority nurses are poorly represented within them.[45]

As perceptive as the African men are about nursing in the United States and their ability to handle the challenges, a stampede into the field has not developed; nursing among West Africans in America is still very much women's work. Moreover, nursing has gained a reputation of being extremely lucrative. Depictions of the prosperous female nurse have spread widely in West African immigrant communities in the United States and across the Atlantic to homeland sites, even in some of the most remote villages. The message is that nurses are paid very well, own expensive cars, and can afford houses that are described as mansions. Sierra Leoneans in Bowie, Maryland, for example, usually point out to visitors the elegant houses of nurses in affluent parts of the suburb, and the "Society News" section of *African Abroad* frequently reports in illustrative accounts about nurses, invariably women, who throw spectacular housewarming parties to "present their mansions and give thanks for prosperity."[46] Similarly, homeland newspapers routinely have reported on nurses buying and building houses in America and for relatives at home. In 2008, *Awoko*, a Sierra Leonean daily, declared in one of its headlines, "The verdict is in; female nurses are the richest and most successful of our people in the USA."[47] In an electronic discussion forum in 2009, some Nigerians addressed the question, why are all Africans nurses in America? As these examples demonstrate, most of the comments alluded to the opportunity to make money: "There is this funny stereotype going on that 'all Africans are Nurses,' even bankers in Nigeria are into Nursing in America, men [too] are into Nursing. Why? I really really wish I had any other answer apart from this one I am about to give—nursing is MONEY"; "Most people say they are doing it because it's their passion, but the truth all ends up in the MONEY aspect."[48]

These representations of the successful West African nurse have elicited the wrath of some of the men who resent what they see as a drastic reevaluation of a premigration occupation. Even though some of the men are the ones who actually had arranged for or encouraged their wives to pursue nursing as a viable immigrant strategy, the reality or even suggestion that their wives earned more money than they did deeply bothered them. The implications and outcomes of nursing had gone beyond making a living and attaining their immigrant dreams. Nursing was molding the women into new women—African American women. A Nigerian movie released in 2006 depicts the gendered crisis emanating from women's work as nurses. In *My American Nurse*, the protagonist, Shehu, journeys home to Nigeria to find a wife who can be certified as a nurse in America and help make them some money. But as the plot summary explains, "When Shehu returns to the USA with a new wife . . . he didn't count on his woman, because of her new-found prestige as a nurse in America, learning the ways of the African American woman. Now his wife has embraced her new-found identity, and Shehu is stuck trying to figure it all out."[49]

Indeed, who is this new woman, fashioned from the independence that came with work and making a living? West African immigrant

communities are not unique on this issue. The experiences of Dominican women have been examined and used to illustrate the realign-
ment of gender relations as a consequence of women's work in America.[50] Sociologist Susan Pearce was definitely alluding to occupational
detours when she observed that immigrant women in present-day
America pursue a variety of jobs that may not match fields in which
they were trained in their home countries. She points out that some
find the U.S. labor market to be liberating, allowing them to move
into new professions in which there may have been few opportunities
in their home countries. Pearce uses historian Donna Gabaccia's term
"gender pioneers" to further illustrate the transformative consequences
of immigrant women's work. Gender pioneers, according to Gabaccia,
are women with professional training in nontraditional fields in their
home countries.[51] Interestingly, in the specific case of West African
female nurses in America, far from entering a nontraditional field, they
are transforming a traditional profession into a liberating occupation.

Besides the earning power African female nurses are said to wield, in
significant ways, they have made inroads as influential leaders of their
communities. They are equipped with knowledge and skills about a
crucial facet of life in America—health care. In West African diaspora
communities across the nation, the nurses are at the forefront, organizing and leading meetings, workshops, and other activities designed to
educate the immigrant and subsequent generations about sickness and
health in a foreign land and how to navigate the mind-boggling process
of accessing health care. They are well organized into state chapters and
nationwide associations along premigration ethnic and national lines—
Asante Nurses of Chicago, Nigerian Nurses of Connecticut, Nigerian
Nurses Association of USA. Through their organizations and vital contributions to their families and the larger community, they have become
a new breed of what Victor Greene calls "ethnic brokers."[52]

Resentment of the real and perceived growing clout of West African
nurses has led to brutal, sometimes deadly consequences. By the 1990s
domestic abuse of nurses had begun to be identified as one of the major
problems in several West African communities. Most alarming was
what seemed like a rash of murders of nurses by their husbands that
occurred in the last decade. Nigerian men, especially, were the culprits.
The headlines in the ethnic newspapers were horrifying: "Nigerian Man

in Tampa Beats Wife to Death with a Baseball Bat" (*African Abroad*, July 15, 2010), "Nigerian Man Shoots Wife in Atlanta" (*African Abroad*, February 28, 2011), and "West African Dallas Man Orders Drive-by Hit of a Wife Who Succeeded Too Much as a Nurse" (*Houston Punch*, January 17, 2010). Indeed, the majority of the murder victims were identified as hardworking, successful nurses. Even though many community leaders, some of whom were women, cautioned that the rate of domestic violence specifically targeting nurses may have been exaggerated, the confirmed incidents were distressing enough for Nigerian nurses to get together to tackle the problem. In 2007, the president of Nigerian Nurses of Connecticut convened a meeting of chapter presidents to address the mounting violence, including killing of nurses. The gathering led to the formation of the National Nigerian Nurses Association. The new national body came up with the following strategies to combat the problem: educate nurses to put God first, family second before their careers; educate nurses back home about the reality of being a nurse in America before they make the transition; reach out to the men and make them understand that nursing is a difficult career and they need to support their wives; finally, develop programs to help reduce stress as nursing is very stressful in America.[53]

Indeed, nursing in America has proved to be a strenuous detour. Increasingly, questions are being asked about whether the prosperity of the West African nurse is overblown. Do the nurses really make that much money? If they do, then at what cost? The women have to put in many hours and work nights and weekends to earn the kind of salaries they crave in order to buy the houses and cars, send their children to upscale private schools, and take care of their family in the homeland. Dr. Grace Ogiehon-Enoma, president of the Nigerian Nurses Association, USA, reiterates what many already know. Insisting that the men who killed their wives because they made too much money were ignorant, she insists, "For you to work as a nurse and have money, you have to do two to three jobs to make it, so I don't know why they think nurses make a lot of money."[54] The "suffering" of nurses is almost as prevalent a theme in the immigrant communities as their success and prosperity. It is common knowledge that nurses often have to skip many events or show up for only a short while because they have to work. Husbands conveying apologies for their absent wives has become an expected practice. The nurses themselves usually point to their selflessness and contributions to humanity. Essentially, this tendency is a carryover from the premigration image of nursing and, indeed, a universal representation of that profession. Nursing has often been seen as a calling often with religious or spiritual undertones in which nurses have been described as doing the will of God or some divine being in the pursuit of the welfare of humanity.

While, generally, this altruistic quality is upheld and articulated by West African nurses in America, a palpable friction has developed between the pre- and postmigration cohorts over who is truly representative of a moral pursuit of the profession. Those who practiced nursing before coming to the United States still invoke the sacrifices of practicing a woefully underpaid and blatantly denigrated job in the home countries. In her essay, aptly titled "We Are the Real Nurses, They Are Just Opportunists," Showers discusses how the nurses craft and manage their professional identities to expose the divide. Explaining what she calls "professional distancing," she demonstrates the discursive strategies employed by African (mostly West African) women to distinguish between those who view nursing as a moral calling versus those who entered into nursing upon migration, as a calculated opportunistic action to capitalize on an occupational niche.[55]

Whether premigration "selfless humanitarians" or postmigration "opportunistic capitalists," the many nurses from Nigeria, Ghana, Sierra Leone, Gambia, and Liberia who have now become such a recognizable feature in the landscape of American health care are in varying degrees pursuing paths that drastically diverge from their homeland experiences with regard to academic training, professional practice, and societal perceptions of their occupational value. Indeed, whichever way it is assessed, nursing as a niche for West African immigrants is an arena that glaringly demonstrates the intricate diversions in education, work, and group relations.

Cabbies

The 2000 census revealed not only that the number of taxi drivers in the United States had climbed to an all-time high by the twenty-first century, but also that the driver workforce had changed significantly.

While the majority continued to be U.S.-born, it was evident that the foreign-born had established a significant presence in this occupation.[56] The immigrant presence had become particularly noticeable in major metropolitan areas where foreign drivers constituted over 50 percent of taxi drivers. The nationwide percentage of foreign-born drivers was 38 percent.[57] Africa, broadly named, has been identified as one of the three major regions—including South Asia and the Caribbean—from where the drivers emigrated. While, as an entity, African taxi drivers represent a diverse group that includes those from other regions of the continent, West Africans constitute a significant portion of the African drivers. In cities like New York, Chicago, Dallas, Houston, Atlanta, Boston (increasingly), and the DC-Virginia-Maryland tristate area, Nigerians, Ghanaians, Senegalese, Gambians, Guineans, Liberians, and Sierra Leoneans had become recognizable "faces" of the taxi business even before the Census Bureau publicized its illuminating findings. Thus, West Africans are very much a part of changes within an occupation whose niche for foreign labor was expanding rapidly by the twenty-first century. Furthermore, almost all of the members of this new and growing segment of American taxi drivers had not been taxi drivers in their homelands, making this type of employment a vital strand of the occupational detour narrative.

Typically, taxi drivers toiling and surviving on the chaotic, traffic-jammed streets of Lagos, Enugu, Freetown, Accra, Kumasi, or Banjul do not emigrate to the United States. They are mostly uneducated, street-smart men, willing to confront the fast-paced, frenzied world of Africa's public transportation and not the kind of people who show up at American embassies seeking visas. Who are these West African taxi drivers in American cities? Like so many of the nurses, they are immigrants pursuing practical routes to success. They are mostly educated people who came to the United States aspiring to further their education and gain more skills that would equip them for "prestigious" occupations and professions nowhere close to cab driving. The "over-educated cab driver" has become a central theme in the narrative of the West African immigrant experience, recognized by commentators both within and outside the community. Lamenting in the ethnic press that driving a taxi has become the signature of underemployment among West African cabbies in Chicago, Dan Tham, the author of the article, introduces the example of Edwin Egbejimba. After finishing his O' and A'- level secondary education in Nigeria, Egbejimba came to the United States to study psychology at Chicago State University. While attending CSU, he drove cabs on a part-time basis. After graduation, he could not readily find a job in his field, and he did not (and could not afford to) interrupt his pursuit of making a living, so he converted his cab driving to full-time instead.[58]

Across major American metropolitan areas, similar stories of the educated African taxi driver can readily be found. Alan Sitomer, 2007 California teacher of the year, blogged about his encounter with one such individual. He recounted his conversation with a middle-aged driver who wore flip-flops, a weathered T-shirt and a pair of shorts, and who "did not look like a man with too many nickels in his pocket."[59] After a stimulating exchange in which the driver used sophisticated language and dissected almost every part of American society, Sitomer concluded, "A cab driver from West Africa. On the outside, I gotta say, he didn't look like much. On the inside, I wished he'd run for office. [He] spoke 5 languages, read, read, read all the time. . . . And to him, things are clear as a bell."[60] The taxi drivers, for their part, are desirous of this kind of recognition of the discrepancy between their intellectual savvy and their American employment. Like Sitomer's driver, they are known to divulge this sophistication through conversation, but often would also directly let their American fares know their premigration status. *Daily Northwestern* contributor Nisha Chandran related a similar encounter. She observed, "Dressed for office, though his cab sits behind Burger King waiting for his next call, Nigerian cab driver Pius Adejumobi spoke proudly of his educated background."[61] Adejumobi, a university graduate, had worked in several offices as a manager and banker in Africa before moving to Chicago. Proclaiming himself "an office guy," Adejumobi opened up to Chandran that "driving taxis and other odd jobs he has put himself through—including manual labor jobs such as tent making and laying, moving and gutter cleaning—are just temporary steps." He planned to eventually attend graduate school in communications and return to his preferred office lifestyle.[62] Sierra Leonean Alex Kabba, executive director of the Chicago-based United African Organization, a nonprofit group that oversees public policy work to empower African immigrants, seemed to be reciting a famous taxi driver's refrain when he noted, "We are talking about the crème de la crème of post-colonial African elites coming here."[63] This echoes a similar assertion by a Boston taxi driver in a conversation with his African American passenger. Emphasizing that driving a taxi belied his social standing, he explained that he hailed from a family that was well known as "the Kennedys of Sierra Leone."[64]

This thorny issue of diminishing status notwithstanding, paradoxically cab driving in the United States has presented opportunities for income and educational advancement. One of the most alluring aspects of the job is its flexibility, which translates to time (and space) for further education. Since most often drivers can set their own pace and hours, many are able to drive during the day and attend classes at night or vice versa. They may also drive taxis during the week and attend classes during the weekend or vice versa. Even at work, the nature of the occupation allows them to take "education breaks." Sometimes conspicuously, West African drivers sit in their taxis during slow periods and read, do assignments, and carry out other school-related learning tasks. In some instances, the education break is even taken collectively. Drivers, usually from the same ethnicities and nationalities but also across ethnic and national lines (especially if they attend the same colleges or pursue the same programs) gather to discuss their schoolwork while their taxis are lined up at a variety of sites, from airports to train and bus stations to hospitals and hotels. New York City cabbie George Asare accurately articulates this occupational advantage:

> Setting your own hours is one reason why so many Ghanaians get into this work. Many drivers take classes in their free time, trying to get more professional training. Many were doctors and engineers in Ghana. . . . Higher education will give them more opportunities, since most hope to return home one day and open their own businesses or enjoy retirement. . . . We expect it to take many years, perhaps over a decade, but picking up fares in New York City lets us invest in our future.[65]

While charting their futures in non-taxi-driving professions, many of the drivers do make money in their detour employment. Not unlike the popular portrayals of nurses, word has spread in the immigrant communities that taxi drivers can earn a lot of money, especially when they operate in vibrant, bustling metropolitan centers where taxi rides are integral to the transit and commuter culture. By 2010, stories about high-earning taxi drivers had become so widespread that a series of cyberspace conversations addressed the question: Are Nigerian Taxi Drivers Really Rich or Telling Fantastic Stories?[66] Many of the immigrants-turned-taxi-drivers are quick to emphasize that finding a consumer base in an amenable transport culture is one thing, being able to work long and strenuous hours is another, the latter being the more crucial factor. In discussions, many contributors pointed out that Nigerian and other West African drivers are known for working very hard. As one of them declared, "Knowing our people, we work hard as heck, so you might see a taxi driver working up to 15 hours out of the day and by the time he stops for that day he may have made as much as $700 after the fees he might have to pay for the car. Most of these guys also live with roommates [an advantage], which also helps save money."[67]

Whether questioning the accuracy of high pay in America or not, one thing is true: the earning potential for taxi driving is definitely a departure from homeland realities. In the homeland, it is not the taxi drivers who ply the streets who are the money makers. It is the businessmen and businesswomen who own the taxis (in some cases a fleet of taxis) who are the real beneficiaries of revenue. In the United States, most of the immigrants making money from the taxi industry are driving, loading and offloading luggage, and being courteous to an array of customers, some of whom, as one taxi driver put it, they would not even deal with if they had been working in their trained fields.[68]

Increasingly, many West African cabbies, like those of other immigrant groups, are pursuing more lucrative avenues of self-employment. Many start with a kind of subcontracting arrangement under the medallion system. Simply put, under this system drivers purchase a license from a medallion company—basically a franchise—to operate a taxi as their own. While many desire to own medallions, in some cities the licensing fees are exorbitant and the regulations and penalties for violations are prohibitive. It is for this reason that many West Africans joined the protest against the introduction of the medallion system in Washington, D.C., in 2011.[69] In cities like Chicago and New York where medallions are well established, West Africans have been able to use them to create more independence and ownership of their detour trade.

West African–owned taxi companies began to spring up in some cities, albeit slowly, by the 1990s. One of the first to be successful was the New Harlem Car Service, established by Senegalese Cheikh Amar and Mokhtr Diop. After driving taxis in New York for several years, they decided to pool their resources to create a venture that would capture African labor and the American market. In 1994, when they started up, there was already a steady presence of African men and a few women who wanted to drive taxis while they figured out how to make it big in America. Amar and Diop knew this from their own experiences and from living within their enclaves. They were convinced that it was time for Africans to own taxi companies, for several reasons: American-owned enterprises exploited foreigners; African novice drivers needed more empathetic businesses to put them through the checkered experiences of driving cabs in American cities; and finally, and very important, ownership of such endeavors signified economic growth, more financial independence, and increased social status. Capitalizing on the same existing opportunities and rationale, West African men have opened small cab companies in various cities.[70]

In 2011, the *New York Times* featured a taxi enterprise story that well illustrated several features that are common to the West African occupational trajectory. The piece described the successful taxi business of husband-and-wife team Isaac and Elizabeth Osei, owners of the fifty-car fleet company Napasei Taxi Management Corporation in Midtown Manhattan. Mr. Osei also happens to be an African chief—Nana Gyensare V—of five communities in Ghana's eastern region. The intrigue engendered by this fact was not lost on the *Times* article's author, who aptly titled her piece "An African Chief in Cabby's Clothing."[71] Isaac moved to New York in the early 1980s. In 1982, he started driving a cab, as so many of the newcomers do, as a transitional occupation. He acquired a medallion license and established his semi-independent taxi business, from which he was able to accrue enough capital to open a restaurant in Harlem. When the restaurant and his first marriage failed, he went back to driving a taxi. Elizabeth's path was even more checkered. She arrived in New York in 1986 and worked as a home health nurse, newspaper delivery woman, and taxi driver. The romantic relationship between Isaac and Elizabeth actually grew out of their airport taxi stand chats. In 1991, even before they got married, Elizabeth helped save Isaac's failing medallion affiliation. After their 1995 marriage, using their knowledge of the taxi business and their insider connections with the African immigrant community and its labor pool, they slowly built their business, which by 2011 had become, according to the report, "a small taxi empire in New York."[72]

Although their story represents the ideal attainment of the American dream that every West African who takes up taxi driving as a transitional occupation would like, the majority of cabbies do not end up owning companies. Almost simultaneously as the advantages of cab driving as a niche occupation are conveyed, caveats about the hurdles and perils are emphasized. The disadvantages are many. The demand for cab services can be seasonal, rendering income unreliable. Many taxi drivers, as independent workers, do not have health insurance. And most serious is the danger taxi drivers face from violent cab-jacking and robberies, some of which have ended in devastating loss of life and a chilling end to the occupational journey and the American dream.

Crimes against taxi drivers across America are not unique to immigrant drivers or West Africans. But whenever one of their own is assaulted or killed, the news is reported and received almost as if this group of foreign drivers is especially targeted. In fact in the late 1980s, word spread that criminals had declared war on the African immigrant taxi community in Harlem. Indeed, as law enforcement and newspaper reports in New York confirm, many African drivers were the victims of violent crimes between 1986 and 1999. In that period, at least sixty African drivers were murdered. Most of them were Francophone West Africans from Senegal, Guinea, and Côte d'Ivoire who spoke French as well as their West African languages—Wolof, Fulani, and Dioula. It was largely this language barrier that drove them to taxi driving, an occupation they could do without a high proficiency in English. This barrier was also in some instances their downfall. Dame Babou, a journalist and activist from Senegal, explains, "They became the laughingstock of Americans, especially African Americans, because they did not speak English well . . . they were easy ear marks for the passengers, who cheated them out of fares and for killers who lured them to dangerous places, all the while dominating them through their fluency in a language the drivers did not know."[73]

These drivers ended up in life-threatening situations not just because of their language deficiencies, however. Many of the drivers from English-speaking countries, like their French counterparts, encounter perilous circumstances because they are forced to fill the void left by medallion and more established taxi drivers who routinely refuse to work in certain neighborhoods. Like other groups, especially Latino and Caribbean immigrants, most West African drivers, particularly the newest arrivals, are gypsy cabbies. Many of them are forced into this option because in most metropolitan areas, rigid limits are imposed on the number of authorized medallions. Although earlier in the twentieth century gypsy cabs invariably denoted illegal taxis, by the time the West Africans became part of American transportation, gypsy cab drivers had become non-medallion, independent taxi drivers, very often using their own cars. Such drivers are usually affiliated with car service companies to which they pay standard fees so they will send them passengers and keep them busy. In spite of this arrangement, the gypsy drivers still randomly pick up fares without the assistance of the companies. Determined to capitalize on the vacuum in undesirable neighborhoods, they end up cruising some of the meanest and bleakest streets of American cities.[74] And they made it known that they would tackle any location where the Yellow Cab will not go. For example, Sy-Savane Alpha Oumar, a Guinean Harlem-based gypsy cabbie, flaunted on the side of his white Jeep Cherokee, "I'm Not Yellow. I Go Anywhere!" On December 11, 1999, this audacity cost him his life, as he was shot by an unknown assailant he picked up on his own, even though he also worked with the New Harlem Car Service.

Although the killing of cab drivers from West Africa is believed to have been at its highest in the mid-eighties to the early nineties, it continued into the twenty-first century to be a dangerously menacing problem. The various communities have been touched since the murdered drivers had come from throughout West Africa and worked in a range of U.S. cities. The ethnic and mainstream media told the stories with headlines like "Hardworking Ghanaian Cabbie Gunned Down in College Park (Suburb of Atlanta)," "Sierra Leonean Taxi Driver Brutally Murdered in Harlem," "Gambian Taxi Driver's American Dream Ends in Deadly Nightmare in Columbus Ohio," "Houston, TX: Nigerian Cab Driver Shot Dead Today," and "Ex-Con Killed Ghanaian Cab

Driver in Staten Island." In 2001, the assault on African taxi drivers (a lot of them West Africans) in Philadelphia had become so alarming to the immigrant community that the Philadelphia Taxi Association decided to organize a demonstration after a Senegalese driver, Mamadou Gackou, was killed that summer. Taxi drivers from across the country converged on the city, and although many of the drivers and their supporters were West Africans, the demonstrators were a diverse group of continental Africans, Haitians, and Latinos, mostly Dominicans. They expressed their sadness and frustration over the violence against cabbies and appealed to the city to investigate the problem, identify the real and likely assailants, and develop and implement protection strategies, including the installation of cameras in taxis. The protest was captured in a documentary by local Eritrean filmmaker Filmon Mebrahtu.[75]

The high rates of violent crimes against cabbies have taken West Africans into some of the most contested paths of their postmigration occupational journeys. Those avenues are fraught with complex issues about race and ethnic relations in America. The victims, their families, and their communities have had to confront the question: who are the real and likely culprits in these assaults? By the first decade of the twenty-first century, many of the immigrants, swayed by the statistics of solved cases, had begun to pin the problem on African Americans and Latinos, but especially on their fellow blacks. What is more, a lot of them did not see it as accidental. Instead, they believed that the victims were often specifically targeted by a violent, inherently crime-driven group. For example, Gambian driver Saime Cesay, recounting a 1993 cab-jacking at knife point by three African Americans, said, "They never asked for money. I had $80. . . . Maybe they wanted to kill me. I felt they were doing this because I am African."[76]

Whether they wanted to kill their targets merely for being African or to rob them, African Americans came to be the symbol of the ultimate peril of taxi driving as a niche occupation. Even African American leaders could not escape censure. Many cab drivers believed that black activists, who were so adept at championing causes for social justice, were not interested in the crisis-level assaults on African cabbies by mostly African American assailants. Dame Babou accused black leaders like Al Sharpton of becoming interested in injustice against Africans only if it gave them the kind of spotlight they got from the Amadou Diallo killing.[77]

By 2005, African Americans and West Africans had begun to dialogue about the rift caused by the taxi drivers' killing crisis. Some illuminating thoughts were shared on cyberspace in a series of blog discussions set up by journalists and activists in the immigrant communities. In one such conversation, an African American stated, "I hate to be apologetic but I often times find myself apologizing to African victims for crimes that were perputrated [sic] by other black people not because I feel that I am responsible . . . but also to let them know some of us care. . . . All of us aren't savage or cold hearted." To this another contributor responded, "Black on Black crime is unfortunately a phenomenon which occurs worldwide (including Africa). . . . African Americans have the stigma of being inherently criminal in nature. Making a mass apology . . . actually furthers our criminal image. . . . This is not a stigma or assumption we want to embrace knowingly or unknowingly."[78] In 2009, the conversations were still going on. In one of the cyber chat rooms, an African American contributor shared her husband's experiences with mostly African taxi drivers in Washington, D.C., who almost unfailingly reiterated stereotypes about African American traits of complacency, laziness, and violence. Responding to her husband's request for her opinion on why these Africans were doing this, she said the problem was a fundamental disconnect from the American past. As she put it, "The cab drivers have no perspective on American history and culture through which to view the citizens they hold in contempt. . . . And those new African immigrants would not have even wanted to come to this country without the civil rights movement in which many of the African American citizens gave their bodies, their freedom, and even their lives."[79] In fact, years before this post, a similar allusion to the disconnect from the past had been made by a contributor in a similar conversation series: "When I sit down with African immigrant cab drivers and talk to them about slavery, poverty, the broken family and how this government promotes violence through the media, most of them look at me like I'm making excuses, smile and keep going. But a few of them understand and want to hear more."[80]

The tensions caused by the misunderstandings and tragedies are often lost on outside observers who do not really see the ins and outs of taxi transportation within a range of intraracial contexts from the purviews of passenger and driver. Television magazine shows like ABC's *20/20* and *Primetime Live* have done exposés on the racism of white cab drivers in major American cities who refuse to serve people of African descent. African American activists and public intellectuals have also tackled the issue of white racist drivers who discriminate against African Americans and other minorities. For example, the late Manning Marable, who was a renowned African American historian, political scientist, and professor at Columbia University, used to relate an experience he stressed was common to African Americans across class: as recently as 2004, a total of six taxis driven by whites refused to pick him and his wife up on Broadway in New York.[81] African American scholar-activist Cornel West, in the preface to his classic *Race Matters*, recounted a similar scenario: hailing a cab on a corner in Manhattan's tony Upper East Side, no fewer than nine unoccupied taxis passed him by. When the tenth did not pull over for him but stopped for the white woman who had just stepped to the curb right next to him, he gave up and took a subway. Ironically, he was trying to get the ride in order to make it on time to the scheduled photo shoot for the very cover picture of the *Race Matters* volume![82]

These experiences, as with most of those talked about in the mainstream media and scholarship, are viewed within the context of white-on-black racism. But an examination of the West African experience reveals a complex, actually perplexing side to this facet of modern Jim Crow. African cab drivers themselves have admitted that, fearing for their safety, they often do not take black people whom they detect or even suspect are native-born blacks. Gambian Saime Cesay, though remorseful, admitted that when he was ripped off by two African Americans, in anger he said to them, "That is why the Spanish livery drivers don't take you."[83] African Americans know this side of "African racism," a practice that many in both black groups see as a troubling anomaly. The pain being conveyed by an African American blogger is palpable. He pronounced, "There is no greater challenge as a black man than to get an African immigrant driver to pick you up on the street."[84]

The intricacies in group relations were also played out with Latinos, another minority group highly represented in taxi transportation. In some cities, especially neighborhoods like the Bronx, Harlem, and

Brooklyn in New York, West Africans compete with Latinos, especially Dominicans and Ecuadorians. West Africans have sometimes complained that the Latinos disrespected them, often projecting African American stereotypes on them. In other words, the West African cabbies resent it when they are not acknowledged as "other blacks." The West African–Latino friction was prominently articulated in the aftermath of the killing of Ghanaian cabby Kwame Appeigyei on April 19, 2006, in Staten Island. Some African cabbies, frustrated by the slow pace of the investigation, accused the "White and Latino-controlled" New York Federation of Taxi Drivers of being just as apathetic to the issues plaguing African cabbies as the "White-controlled" New York Police. They pointed a finger at Dominican-born Fernando Mateo, president of the New York State Federation of Taxi Drivers, whom they felt was insensitive to African drivers, deciding that he reacted more assertively to the murders of his own people, the Latinos. Mateo's candid assessment of the circumstances of Appeigyei's killing did not help. He said that by picking up fares off the street or from the ferry terminal, Mr. Appeigyei violated regulations of the Taxi and Limousine Commission, which would have protected him. He tersely concluded, "It breaks my heart, but the truth of the matter is, if you don't take care of yourself, this is what happens."[85] Not all of the cab drivers or African activists felt that Mateo devalued Africans. Babou, for example, said he had worked closely with Mateo before and knew that he meant well for all drivers. And longtime Nigerian driver Olusegun Omowunmi believed that "a lot of the accusations flying around about Mateo and others are the result of pent up ethnic group tensions just ready to explode."[86]

Whether real or perceived, prejudice against them from other ethnic groups was instrumental in propelling African cab drivers to insist on tangible solidarity through associations that would look out for them specifically. By the 1990s, West African cab drivers had begun to do what cabbies from other regions were doing—they were launching local and national associations. Some of the most notable ones are the Ghanaian Taxi Drivers Association of New York, the Ghanaian Cab Drivers Association of Chicago, the Gold Coast (Ghana's colonial name) Taxi Association, and the Nigerian Taxi Association of Houston. These organizations are as much a welfare network as they are an organ for protest and activism. Detouring into the taxi business as they did from completely unrelated fields, new drivers are usually unaware of so many of the challenges. Managing their health is one of the biggest problems the drivers confront. Most of them work as self-employed operators but cannot afford to pay for health insurance. Some of those who drive cabs on a part-time basis get coverage through their other jobs. More commonly, West African taxi drivers with good health insurance get coverage from their spouses who are employed full-time in the wage economy. Besides grappling with health insurance, taxi drivers have to deal with the vulnerabilities of the job, for which they are often totally unprepared: notoriously dangerous neighborhoods; delicate, "American-style" etiquette of driver-customer relations; and law enforcement. The founders of the associations envisioned that, as intermediaries between the drivers and mainstream society, these organizations would assist the immigrants in their adaptation within arenas they never bargained for in their premigration settings. George Asare, one of the founders of the New York–based Ghana Taxi Drivers Association, articulated this function: "The association was formed a few years ago to promote the welfare of Ghanaian taxi drivers . . . [members] pay a few hundred dollars annual membership. In exchange they get help with business costs and compensation if something happens to them or their family. When you get sick for two weeks you get $500. . . . For a month you get $1,000."[87]

In addition to practical assistance rendered by the associations, their relevance is increasingly being demonstrated in their determination to boost the profile of the immigrant taxi driver in America and the homeland. Pointing to the reality that the American cab driver had become a fixture in West African immigrant communities, leaders of associations promote a reorientation in how that occupation is viewed. They hammered home the perspective that taxi driving is an endeavor that plays a significant role in their communities, even if it continues to be transient employment. Furthermore, some immigrants have been engaged in this "transient" work for over two decades. Such long-term cabbies have reminisced about how far taxi driving had come by the twenty-first century. They recall two decades earlier when taxi drivers were ashamed to let their fellow immigrants know exactly how they made their living. As Sierra Leonean Allieu Kamara recounts, "In the early 1980s we made every effort to avoid areas where we knew a lot of our own people lived. When we were not at work, we parked our cabs as far away from our homes and anywhere we knew our people would be gathered."[88] In contrast, by the end of the first decade of the twenty-first century, as a Ghanaian Atlanta-based cabby remarked in 2009, "Now you see a number of taxis and limos parked in apartment complexes where a lot of Ghanaians and other Africans live. Even at our parties and other festivities, cab drivers who come to these events briefly before or after work, actually drive their cabs there. So it is not unusual to see the cabs mingled among the Benz, Lexus and other luxurious cars so typical of our communities."[89] Moreover, some of these luxury cars are the taxi drivers' "other cars," driven to the events by their spouses and other relatives.

Importantly, formal taxi drivers' groups, which were increasing in numbers by 2000, were as much an indicator of the vital presence of the West African taxi driver as they were a means of increased acceptance and respect for the cabbies and their craft. The associations aimed at solidifying the presence of taxi driving as a vital and progressive occupation. Isaac Kwaku Duah, president of the Ghanaian Taxi Drivers Association of New York, declared that the association has come to stay and urged its members not to do anything that would mar the peace, love, respect, and unity that existed in the association.[90] This unfolding permanent presence has been clearly affirmed in Chicago, where the Ghanaian Cab Drivers Association, founded in 2000, became well known for its annual "high society" banquet. At the 2005 banquet, the president, John Henry Assabill, asserted that the association had moved "from sustenance to establishment."[91] Like its New York counterpart, it also was there for the duration. Assabill announced that immigrant taxi drivers had just begun a new page in "an ever progressive and technologically innovative business."[92]

This new page was reflected in the novel kinds of relationships being formed with the immigrant and homeland communities. The taxi associations became so successful at fund-raising that they have become one of the significant sources of financial support for individual and collective causes. Association records point to the various amounts disbursed to ethnic and other organizations in the immigrant communities for development in America and the home countries. This new role translated to a reassessment of taxi drivers at home and abroad. Assistance given out is clearly identified as coming from the efforts of taxi drivers. Their practical contributions and standing overall have garnered respect and validation, including official recognition. For example, in 2009, the outgoing consular general of the Ghana mission in New York, Mr. Joseph Ngminebayihi, remarked that he was extremely impressed with the work and stature of the Ghanaian Taxi Drivers Association of New York. He concluded that it was one of the biggest and best organized groups with which he had ever interacted and assured the members that he would take his observations home to the government and people of their home country.[93] As Ghanaian taxi driver David Sarpong explained,

> When the money is used to build a bridge or a community center in our hometowns, collectively we are recognized. The people can see what money from driving taxi in America can do. But this is just a collective recognition of the association that sent the money. Individually we still struggle about prestige, which is why we must study more and get moving to other jobs.[94]

Sarpong is perceptively accurate, for as individuals and associations are succeeding in elevating taxi driving as an enduring, respectable occupation, simultaneously the narrative of that job as underemployment—incongruent with educational and professional abilities—continues to be related in the United States and the homeland. A 2006 account in one of the community publications fully illustrated this clash of pathways. The report described how a Ghanaian driving his empty cab around the Port Authority Bus Terminal and Eighty-Sixth Street and Madison Avenue in New York, looking for fares on a slow day, hurt his back in an accident. Like so many cab drivers, this man did not have health insurance. His health deteriorated as he could not afford appropriate treatment. Eventually, he could not continue driving a taxi, which in the past had earned him a lot of money and allowed him to purchase a nice home in America and to build one back in Ghana. The notable point that the narrative aimed to convey was made clearly: The injured taxi driver had once told a young man studying at one of the New York colleges to quit school and go drive a cab, because that was where the money was. The student, not heeding the taxi driver's advice, finished college and, according to the report, went on to get "a pretty decent job." The account concluded, "Who is the richest among the two now? A cabby with a broken back who may never drive a cab again, or a student who has his Bachelor's degree and earning a comfortable living?"[95] This parable-style newspaper story is representative of the kind of conversations about taxi driving that persist in the immigrant communities. Although taxi drivers associations and other collective efforts are making headway in changing perceptions, West Africans who mostly enter the taxi industry as a temporary step in their educational and occupational journeys still view taxi driving as an ephemeral pursuit, which sometimes is best described as something else. As a Nigerian Dallas-based cabbie put it, "Often, both here and Nigeria, when I visit, I never mention taxi driving by name. I simply say I am self-employed; I am in business. Seems like I am bending the truth, but not really. Taxi driving is just a segue into another occupation, possibly, full-fledged business."[96]

Detour to Prosperity and Demise?

At a Sunday worship service in Stone Mountain, Georgia, Pastor Hezekiah Adeyemi from Nigeria lamented the dismal attendance: "Why is it that well brought up people, grounded back home in the fear of God, have now made work their master? The pews are empty today because our members are either at work or too tired from work to come to church."[97] Similarly, at the funeral of a fifty-four-year-old immigrant from Sierra Leone, Reverend Timity admonished the mourners, "Let us all learn from this sad event that life can be short. I say this especially for the growing number of you who now make work and money your master; the reality now is that your mortgage sleeps in your beds while you labor, sleep-deprived at work."[98] And Imam Abu King told a group of partygoers celebrating the successful treatment of a cancer victim now in remission that too much stress from work and making money in America played a vicious role in aggravating illnesses and diseases. He reminded his audience that "as we have been taught since back home when we began to study the *Quoran*, Allah, the merciful, the benevolent does not want us to put work and money above him and ourselves."[99]

These qualms and rebuke are echoed in secular circles with almost equal anxiety. The immigrants themselves debate the outcomes of their new paths to work and wealth. A 2011 article by Naija American journalist Rudolph Okonkwo effectively highlights many of the issues. With specific examples of Africans, but mostly West Africans, dying young across the United States, he discusses the insidious contributions of work to hypertension, heart attack, kidney failure, stroke, and other diseases that trigger premature death.[100] Although a detailed statistical investigation into the death rates of West African immigrants is not available, news and activities in the communities suggest a disturbing increase. Okonkwo notes that unlike in the 1990s, most Africans by the early twentieth century know someone who died in America. The many fund-raisers for resources to send corpses home or for burial in the United States are seen as a reliable index. As Okonkwo concludes, "For such people [those who lose their loved ones or who plan and execute the fund-raisers], they do not need a scientific study to affirm what they feel deep in their hearts: more of their people are dying in America."[101] He insists that this is not just because the increased presence of West Africans in America logically means more deaths, as some have emphasized. Okonkwo's concern represents a feeling rapidly growing in immigrant circles that overwork in pursuit of the American dream has caused Africans to neglect preventive and curative health. Even before Okonkwo's piece, in 2007 another Naija American journalist, Funmi Adepitan, had drawn attention to the destructive outcomes of overwork in the United States in his article "Lust for Dollar = Early Grave?"[102] Dr. Benjamin Nwosu, a Nigerian endocrinologist in Massachusetts, confirmed that new research had begun to show a higher prevalence of a stress-related disease like hypertension in people of African descent living in the United States compared to Caucasians or other Africans living in Africa. He stressed, however, that this situation and sudden death incidents are more complicated than a mere problem of working too hard: "The reasons for these differences are not known, but scientists believe that these may have to do with both genetic and socio-demographic factors such as dietary habits, poor socio-economic status, stress, and poor access to healthcare facilities in a foreign land."[103]

The more balanced medically informed assessments of commentators like Dr. Nwosu notwithstanding, ill health and other perils of overwork in America continue to be an issue in West African immigrant communities. In the same piece where Dr. Nwosu gives his medical opinion, another professional, Obeke Johnson, a Nigerian computer engineer from Lynn, Massachusetts, stuck to the point that too much work gets in the way of good health: "People are suffering in silence. African men are not taking care of themselves."[104] Adebayo Olusanya, who gave up her third job at a nursing home after a scare from a mild stroke, offered a comparison between the causes of premature death in West Africa and the United States: "Ironically, back home poor people die of poverty often caused by unemployment and lack of basic necessities and rich people die of cushy jobs and sedentary lifestyle; whilst here in the land of opportunity we die from too much work, or should I say 'overemployment,' which, though our jobs give us wealth and basic necessities, they challenge us and make us run around all the way to our graves."[105]

This chapter has not been concerned primarily with ascertaining exactly how overwork contributes to premature death among West African immigrants. Nevertheless, the conversations and debates around this issue are useful in underscoring our premise of detour as an integral element in researching, describing, and explaining occupational experiences among this group of immigrants. From pastors to imams and community leaders, the emphasis is on departure—from familiar work habits to new ones dictated by new employment pathways. For some the detour in work habits and overall lifestyle is perhaps even more drastic than the change in occupation itself. Whether the change in occupation is drastic or not, the total sum of the processes involved in making a living affords valuable insights into the different approaches and outcomes that shape the West African immigrant experience in America.

3

Capturing a Niche

The West African Enclave Economy

I did not even know that people from Ghana and Nigeria had moved into this area until I began to see their booths mushroom all around the market. And they are diehard traders, too.
—Atlanta African American flee market vendor Lakwana Payne

As has been the case for many new immigrant groups before them, rather than joining the secondary labor force, just like the aspiring cab drivers who have become owners of medallions, some West Africans have gone into business for themselves as their strategy for making it in America. Some may have been entrepreneurs in their home countries and arrived with enough capital to be able to readily open a similar type of enterprise shortly after immigrating, while others have had to work first in other jobs before acquiring the necessary funds and the wherewithal to become self-employed. With the additional support of cultural resources such as rotating credit pools, a rich communal associational life, and often the backing of local religious communities, West Africans have found that entrepreneurial initiatives can often provide the best pathway to economic stability. Pointing to the significance of business as a demographic gauge, the ethnic press also drew attention to the existence of a viable West African community in Atlanta by describing it in a 2008 article as having "at its heart the rise of African entrepreneurs who think big, are unafraid and play for keeps."[1] Similarly, Dominicans in the South Bronx mostly know about "los africanos," as they call the West Africans, through their businesses and business practices.

This Africanization of space through self-employment is the main subject of the most definitive study of West African entrepreneurship in America. In *Money Has No Smell*, anthropologist Paul Stoller shows how this population of primarily Senegalese merchants successfully transplanted centuries-long business patterns to neighborhoods of New York City. According to Stoller, the peddlers bartering trinkets on the sidewalks of New York had, indeed, often come from historic business communities and, in many cases, were also members of established shop-keeping families who were thus replicating the migratory commercial role that itinerant traders before them played in earlier generations.[2] Most of these street vendors, who have come to represent the face of West African business in New York and many other major American cities, are Muslims of the Muridiyya Brotherhood, a Sufi order that mandates entrepreneurial productivity for both material and spiritual development.[3] Stoller also points to the Hausas, another West African group known for its business history. The Hausas, whose ancestral homeland is in northern Nigeria, where they are concentrated, are dispersed all around West Africa precisely because of centuries of continuous trade migrations. Among Hausas, *kasua* (the market) is at the center of the community. Besides the Senegalese and Gambian Wolofs and Hausas, there are several other West African groups that have long been touted for their entrepreneurial adroitness: the Yorubas, Igbos, Fullahs, Mandingos, and Temnes, to name a few. In the various West African metropolises the marketplace and business are certainly integral features of everyday life.

Yet while entrepreneurship has arguably become the most conspicuous marker of the new African diaspora in America and many immigrants who have pursued this path had well established premigration patterns to emulate, operating a business, whether on the streets or in stores, markets, and agency offices, has been strikingly absent from the list of motivations in the decision to relocate. A 2009 national marketing survey of African consumers revealed that the most prevalent reason given by the newcomers for why they migrated to the United States was educational opportunity.[4] Evidence from the qualitative interviews in our own study confirms this aim. Thus, the discrepancy raises the central question of whether the prospective migrants planned (or even anticipated) replicating this distinctive entrepreneurial history in their new homeland. Did they set out to do business as their forebears did in Africa? Our findings suggest that this was rarely the case.

The overwhelming majority of postcolonial West Africans who have settled in the United States simply did not envision entrepreneurship as the channel to success. Most of them came first and foremost to pursue preplanned educational paths or determined to carve out their academic pursuits after arriving in the United States. Even migrants who hailed from successful entrepreneurial families did not come to extend the family business. Family resources earned from business in Africa, and possibly in Asia and the Middle East, have been used, instead, to plan and support further education in America. The most famous of the West African peddlers in New York, tragic murder victim Amadou Diallo, hailed from a reputable Guinean business family that paid his way to America where his goal was to be a computer specialist. Like the Wolof Diallo, most of the young Hausas who have moved to the United States have come not to replicate the kasua but to further journeys already begun in their premigration settings to be *akawo* (administrative managers). Consequently, their marked entrepreneurial presence in American cities signifies an unintended consequence and a detour from their original occupational plans. Pushed from their primary chosen fields because their premigration educational qualifications were unacceptable or by language barriers, a lack of the required immigration papers, or discrimination based on race or religion, many found in business a livelihood that bypassed many of these impediments. Strictly speaking, some of the new entrepreneurs were not actually driven from their previous jobs. They moved from work in the wage economy to start and manage their own ventures in order to capture opportunities that distinctly favored their West African backgrounds and American experiences.

The entry of West Africans into business arenas in America is a classic story of supply and demand. Their growing immigrant enclaves have created idiosyncratic requirements that only a similar enclave economy can fulfill. In a symbiotic dynamic, these ethnic communities are indispensable support zones for the entrepreneurs through the cultural resources they guarantee, like rotating credit pools (*osusu*), a rich communal associational life, and often the backing of local premigration-based ethnic and religious communities. In some specific contexts, even when the demand came from a larger American consumer base, the enclave economy still benefited from its ability to provide unique services, especially in areas where immigrant labor pools are crucial. Although the businesses are numerous and diverse, categorizing them reveals niches that have prompted and sustained the detour. The new entrepreneurs have capitalized on American need for immigrant labor and services in health care; growing American, especially African American, embrace of African hair and other beauty and fashion trends; and increasing knowledge about and appetite for African cuisine. While American patronage is an essential ingredient, the immigrant community continues to be the hinge for this variety of ethnic entrepreneurship. The economic culture within which the entrepreneurs function is crucial for the specific detour opportunity areas in which they have established their businesses, notably health care staffing and pharmacy, grocery stores or African supermarkets, restaurants and clubs, hair braiding, and fashion production and merchandising.

Health Care

West African–owned and –managed enterprises in American health care emerged and grew because the immigrants realized and capitalized on their worth in the labor force of that industry. Since the 1980s, across the country, hospitals, nursing homes, and American-owned agencies have consistently relied on West African women who not only worked for them but also, through their contacts in their communities, helped ensure steady recruitment. Nigerian, Liberian, and Sierra Leonean women, like their Afro-Caribbean counterparts, became adept at preparing new arrivals to work as nursing assistants. They lived in communities where the labor pool was located; they knew how to orient new arrivals and established immigrants who wanted to change careers; and through their own experiences working for health establishments and agencies, they had made valuable contacts with health care employers. So why not own and manage independent staffing businesses? By the 1990s, some of these women had answered this question by establishing their own nursing assistant schools and health care employment agencies, businesses spawned to manage, train, and place potential, mostly West African (but also a few Afro-Caribbean), nursing assistants, home health care aides, and nurses. These new health care entrepreneurs tapped into familiar cultural learning patterns, including instruction in Pidgin English, to ensure American certification.

Within a decade, females from West Africa had registered success, visible beyond their enclaves, as owners of health care establishments. Anna Kwakyewaah Pollard is among such women. Pollard, who was born in Ghana and raised in Liberia, is the sole proprietor of a medical supply company in San Diego with twenty full-time employees. Like many of her compatriots, she had been trained as a nurse and got the idea to open her own business while herself working in a hospital. Pollard faced many practical challenges related to obtaining start-up capital, proper certifications, and a satisfactory location for the venture, but she also had to grapple with those who questioned her very judgment at the idea of attempting such an initiative: "I remember people asked me why I was opening a business. They said I already had a good job as a nurse. I told them I was doing this so that someday we could do better for ourselves."[5]

While, like Pollard, many of these health care enterprises are owned by women, for the men in the diaspora who have wanted to become involved in the health-related professions, one avenue has been joint proprietorship, usually as part of a husband-and-wife team. Although a handful of the men are themselves qualified nurses, examples abound of how men from diverse academic and occupational backgrounds, whose wives are trained nurses, collaborate with the women to take new paths into nursing as business. Of course, the academic and professional credentials of the women are the anchors of these enterprises, even though in many instances the men are listed as CEO or managing director. In addition to providing temporary and long-term staffing to hospitals, nursing homes, hospices, and private homes, these agencies also serve as training schools for nursing assistants and preparation for college and university admissions as well as for licensing board exams. Needless to say, the staff and students of these agencies are overwhelmingly women. The New York–based agency of Nigerians Patience and Patrick Emenike, appropriately called Pioneer Home Care, is one of the first and most successful of the burgeoning West African health care businesses in major American cities. Similar husband-and-wife agencies can be found in Atlanta, Houston, and Dallas. Moreover, other immigrant health care professionals, while not setting up businesses in the United States, may well initiate related entrepreneurial pursuits in their homelands. They count on their relatives to run clinics, both for-profit and nonprofit, to operate pharmacies, or to provide mobile medical services.[6] Like other types of entrepreneurs in the West African community, proprietors of health-care-related enterprises utilize the economic and social networks of the coethnic community to help advertise these initiatives, bringing their business cards and flyers to immigrant social functions as well as publicizing their ventures throughout the West African business sector.

Another burgeoning West African occupational niche related to health care providers concerns the number of particularly Nigerian immigrants who are now making a living as pharmacists, estimated in 2010 at close to seven thousand by the Nigerian Association of Pharmacists and Pharmaceutical Scientists of America.[7] In the early 1990s, Nigerians, South Koreans, and Southeast Asians filled the void in a looming shortage of pharmacists in the United States. Trained pharmacists who were disillusioned with the corruption and economic hardship in their country needed no convincing to leave Nigeria in droves. More remarkable, some Nigerians already living in America changed their educational and occupational concentrations to pursue pharmacy studies in order to fill the opening. In the 1990s there was a surge of Nigerians earning pharmacy degrees in America. Many of these found work at major chains like CVS, Rite Aid, Eckerd, and Walmart as well as in hospitals and clinics.

Nigerian pharmacists increasingly became a visible representation of West African entrepreneurship in America when they began to own and operate their own drugstores by the end of the 1990s. In typical niche economy fashion, they moved into a void created mostly by the departure of big chains from inner-city, crime-ridden neighborhoods. Like the cabbies, they have ventured into perilous territory in search of prosperity, in this case, filling prescriptions and selling medicine and other health items behind a Plexiglas shield. Emmanuel Ezirim, who opened a pharmacy on the west side of Columbus, Ohio, in 2009, remarked, "You have to go where the need is, you can't be afraid."[8] But threatened by the high rate of deadly crimes in the neighborhoods where they work, many have had real cause to be afraid. Still, as impoverished and dangerous as these metropolitan areas have been, they present a unique incentive in the certainty of Medicaid payments that support the health care of most of their inhabitants. Such advantages are clearly encouraging the growth of Nigerian drug stores. In September 2010 at the fourth annual convention of the Nigerian Pharmacists Association held in Dallas, pharmacy business operation was incorporated into the agenda. There were workshops on how to buy existing drug stores and how to build them from scratch, how to adapt to seemingly undesirable neighborhoods with potential for the business, and how to benefit from Medicaid in honest and legal ways.[9] Taking notice of their adeptness at capturing a market abandoned by the mainstream, *Wall Street Journal* reporter Joel Millman compared them to audacious immigrants who had earlier displayed similar patterns: "Nigerian pharmacies are carving out an ethnic niche—particularly in African-American and Latino neighborhoods—not unlike those built by previous generations of immigrants, from the Chinese dominance of laundry business beginning in the 1850s to Gujarati immigrants—ethnic Indians largely from East Africa—who gained prominence in the lodging industry in the 1970s."[10]

Food Purveyors

Arguably, the most prominent index of West African entrepreneurship in America is the tropical food store, which is now visible on the landscape of many cities across the United States. Demand for African foods and other distinctive grocery items is a marker that separates the old and new diaspora. The pre-1970s cohorts lived mostly in student housing and spent time with American host families who attempted to immerse them in American culture, including food. With the substantial increase in the population of newcomers and more frequent connections to homeland sources of foodstuffs, familiar premigration staples have become available in residential areas with a consumer base of nostalgic West African immigrants. Individuals and families acquire the familiar foods for daily home meals, but also frequently families and cultural groups or organizations purchase large quantities to entertain as many as hundreds of guests at weddings, christenings, graduations, and birthday and other anniversary parties. The immigrants are willing to spend amply on homeland fare, which, as is typical of imported products, is relatively expensive. The tenacity of the customers was underscored in 2007 when news spread widely in West African communities across the country that, due to currency devaluation and other economic crises in Nigeria and Ghana, where the main sources of supplies are located, prices of African foodstuffs in the diaspora would rise drastically. Entrepreneurs and consumers did not panic. Both were assured that no matter the cost, African immigrant households in America would continue to crave homeland foods. As one confident store owner put it, "They are addicted to the tastes of home."[11]

Such dedication to maintaining customary foodways has created one of the biggest niches for West African ethnic business. Seeing the need for imported West African traditional products, some people have made drastic changes in their occupational paths to capture what has now proven to be an unending demand. From the late 1980s, men and women from a range of occupations, many requiring high levels of education and training to procure—computer specialists, accountants, insurance agents, teachers, bank tellers, and engineers—quit their jobs and opened tropical food stores in strategically selected areas. For example, in 1990, Ghanaian Kofi Roberts, a pharmacist, and his wife, Baba, a lawyer, opened It's Tropical, one of the first West African businesses in suburban Decatur, Georgia, just when West African immigration to metro Atlanta began to increase. Similarly, Gambian Stephane Kaffi left a computer job to open Ma Jolie African Market on 169th Street in New York to make money from the high demand for African foods.[12]

The basis for this economic niche—West Africa in America—is never lost on the entrepreneurs. Consequently, the African supermarkets have been symbolic and practical replications of home, from their very names to the products they carry, right down to distinctive name brands. Across American cities, West African grocery stores bear names that invoke well-known homeland markets—a fact appreciated by the immigrants but often unrecognized by the casual American observer. Examples of such transplanted names are Kumasi and Makola (Ghana), Dovecot and King Jimmy (Sierra Leone), Serakunda (Gambia), Sengada (Senegal), and Gbaja and Onitsha (Nigeria). If the outside façade is a symbolic representation, every aisle inside is a tangible reminder of home. Stacked on the shelves are foods common to the West African region as well as national and ethnicity-specific items: *garri*, various types of *fufu*, *egusi*, diverse fresh and frozen vegetables (cassava leaves, potato leaves, bitter leaves, and sour sour), dried and stock fish, *ogiri* and *kaanda*, palm oil, and snacks like groundnut cake, *chin chin*, and *puff puff*. These markets also carry canned, bottled, and boxed items with a long history in West Africa, for many as far back as the colonial period, when such manufactured products were valued as imported goods that came from the European imperial countries. Such favored "homeland" brands include St. Louis cubed sugar, Jacobs cream crackers, Peak milk, Nido and KLIM powdered milk, Exeter corned beef, Titus sardines, Milo and Bournvita hot chocolate powder, Sanatogen supplement powder, Lucozade energy drink, and Woodwards gripe water for infants.

The commitment to replicate West Africa through retail is continuously affirmed and reaffirmed by the vendors. For example, Global Grocery of College Park, an Atlanta suburb, advertises as follows: "Bringing Africa Home to You. Hundreds of African products and services available, including custom meat cutting." And Sierra Leonean American Leticia Jones, co-owner with her husband, former banker Eustace Jones, of Dovecot International Market in Cheverly, Maryland, described their services in this way: "We bring everything from home here . . . except for the relatives; we have everything here from home that they would want."[13]

Bringing home to the immigrants goes beyond edible products. The African tropical "food" stores also carry newspapers and magazines from the homeland and diasporic communities in North America and Europe. Furthermore, many of these local markets have begun to serve as video outlets where customers can rent and buy movies produced in Nigerian Nollywood and Ghanaian film industries. The sale of special phone cards and DVDs of West African and other African and Caribbean musicians is also an important function of the stores. Similarly, they serve as places to remit money and to get up-to-date information about upcoming events in the community, from soccer matches to performances of visiting celebrity artists from home. Professionals like plumbers, electricians, accountants, immigration lawyers, and real estate agents find these venues to be useful conduits for reaching

Food purveyors—West Africa in America. Photo by Marilyn Halter.

potential coethnic clients who can pick up their business cards usually strategically displayed at the front of the shop.

Restaurants and nightclubs, which also cater to a longing for home in the diaspora, have created viable outlets for occupational change. Like the tropical food stores, restaurants and clubs carry names that invoke premigration connections, like Calabar (Nigerian town) Kitchen, Nollywood I and Nollywood II, Calabash (traditional gourd or water container) Lounge, and Abuja (capital of Nigeria) International Kitchen. Beyond the names, advertising and other publicity materials elaborate on the commitment to bring the homeland to life in America. In tantalizing, graphically illustrative menus, they list regional and ethnic dishes like jollof rice, groundnut stew, various types of egusi soup, fufu, amala, banku, various vegetable soups, suya, and so forth. They also list regional favorite drinks like palm wine, Star beer, Fanta, Apple Sidra, and Vimto. Maruché Restaurant and Bar in New York promises that "African meals served at Maruché rival those of Lagos and Abuja."[14] And the proprietor of Buka launched the restaurant with the following announcement: "For love of my country and the pride of my people, with great honor I present Buka, New York, a place where Nigerians can bring their friends and meet each other possibly for dating, socializing, having fun and hanging-out Nigerian and American-style."[15]

The entrepreneurs who capitalize on the niche created by the demand for African foods have distinct backgrounds and experiences but demonstrate strikingly similar trajectories in their detour in that direction. Like new entrepreneurs in other fields, most of them point to great familiarity with business in premigration, their desire to acquire university education in America and excel in the professions and respectable salaried jobs, and their eventual decision to tap into home-land experiences to capture an American niche. Marie-Claude Mendy, owner of Teranga (Wolof for hospitality and mutual aid), the first Sen-egalese restaurant in Boston, opened in 2009, was born into a family of entrepreneurs in Dakar. In an interview she explained, "The spread of entrepreneurship is so in me that I always knew that I would branch out on my own."[16] Yet before embarking on the restaurant venture, she studied international law in London, then moved to Washington, D.C., where she earned a second degree before relocating to Boston in 2001.

Homeland tastes. Photo by Marilyn Halter.

Liberian restaurateur Nadia Assaf Cole relates a similar path. Forced from her country in the mid-1980s by the civil war, Nadia first thought she should capture the ironic opportunity to further her education and professional advancement in this forced migration. Consequently, she worked toward that end with her husband who was a university administrator, first in New York, then in Winston-Salem, North Carolina. They moved to Atlanta to be part of a more vibrant city and larger Liberian and African communities. When her husband fell ill and subsequently died, she found herself working three jobs. Recalling that "America is a land of opportunity, where you succeed if you work hard," she decided to look for a less stressful and more lucrative way to make a living.[17] She could clearly see the cultural potential in a demographic development: West Africans were increasing in numbers, and they would need a place to eat homeland foods, which they could introduce to their American friends. She was a good cook and had picked up unique talents from her enterprising mother and other female relatives in Liberia. She knew she was in a good position to give up at least two of the three jobs and open her own eatery, first called Diverse Zone, and then after a brief break Nadia's Restaurant.[18]

While many West African restaurant owners first started in other fields, some have taken a less drastic side trip, having worked in American food establishments from the onset. Starting from baseline positions like dish washers and bathroom cleaners to servers and cooks, some West Africans have used work in African and American-owned restaurants as stepping stones to opening their own place. This was the pathway for Senegalese Khadija Sow who came to own her own small six-table restaurant in the Bedford-Stuyvesant section of Brooklyn. When she first arrived in New York, she quickly got a job as a cook and in only three years time was able to save enough to operate her own establishment.[19]

Like Khadija Sow, Nadia Cole, and Marie-Claude Mendy, the overwhelming majority of West African restaurateurs are female. But it is not only women who are finding new careers in the culinary world. West African men in the diaspora are also working in the food business and sometimes in the process taking a very sharp detour from their original route in terms of gender expectations. Lamine Sawadogo, who migrated from Bamako, Mali, in the 1970s and who eventually became a successful international businessman and consultant, started his working life in the United States as a dishwasher and worried about how he would be perceived but rationalized the job this way: "And here I was from a middle class family in Mali having never washed a dish in my life, sort of culturally looking down on that type of work; because it's work either done by women or done by what we call a boy. I never pictured that I would be doing a job like that. But here I was. I have to pay my rent, I have to work to achieve my dream so, this I looked at as a phase in my life."[20] In another instance, the possibilities in the diaspora for ranging beyond expected occupational roles enabled a more recent immigrant, a Muslim man from Guinea, to eventually open a restaurant in Harlem where he also served as the head chef. He stressed that this was an endeavor that he never could have embarked upon back at home because of the strong cultural taboo against men, whether preparing hot or cold dishes, to be working as cooks at all.[21]

Nonetheless, although some men own restaurants or are co-owners with their wives or female relatives, the integral facet of cooking invariably is supported by women—owners and female workers alike. Even the women agree that this is the case because they have been able to transfer work and experiences from the premigration gendered domestic domain into a viable entrepreneurial arena. While there is no denying the women's long association with food and cooking, the restaurant business in America is still an area of occupational detour. The majority of the food entrepreneurs did not engage in that business before emigrating and, in most cases, did not set out to pursue it upon arrival.

Hair Braiding

Hair braiding represents another occupational arena of feminine domesticity, and the numerous salons that offer this service stand out as a signature of West African commerce in urban America. In the early 1980s, the seemingly sudden presence of African women braiders, especially in New York, began to generate attention. As mostly non-English-speakers, the women were even more conspicuous. They were Francophone West Africans, overwhelmingly from Senegal, and they came with the skills of their trade. Moreover, looking back at their homeland social environment, nothing could seem more natural. Throughout

West Africa since precolonial times, braiding as a beautifying trait and a craft has been central to the cultural and gendered dynamics of all communal life. This commonality notwithstanding, the various societies and localities developed distinctive braiding styles and work characteristics, some of them so minute as to signify specificities of ethnicity, residence, and political and social hierarchies.[22] Consequently, on the surface, plying such an entrenched trade appeared like a simple story of an extension of premigration skill sets. On the contrary, however, hair braiding is an exemplar of the convoluted trajectories that have reshaped the work experiences of the postcolonial West African diaspora in the United States.

First, it was a principal detour for the French-speaking women for whom language presented a formidable barrier to entering the largely Anglophone American labor market. Fortuitously, they arrived at a time that an Afro-centric hair revolution of the 1960s and 1970s had increased an appreciation and yearning for "authentic" African hair styles. At the same time, the braiding, weaving, and plaiting skills transplanted from Senegal infused the popularity of this trend as the latest hairdos and techniques were incorporated into the repertoire of diaspora stylists. Requiring very little capital, hair braiding as self- employment was one of the easier detour paths. Many of the women who started off working in American-owned salons were quickly able to set up their own hair-braiding establishments.

The rapid transformation belied the very important detail that most of the women did not come to America to braid hair. Typically, like taxi drivers, the women who braided hair for a living in Africa were not those who immigrated to the United States. In particular, Senegal, which continues to be the top sending nation for hair braiders, sustained a rigid caste system that historically demeaned hair braiding as a craft. Among the Wolof, hair-braiding specialists are members of the *ñeeño* class of artisans confined to the lower ranks. For a long time, it was mostly the *géer*, the nonartisan elite, who were given more opportunities for higher education in Dakar and France. Not surprisingly, it was primarily such women who also had the means to come to the United States. While a lot of them knew how to braid hair, picking it up as a business venture was definitely a social reorientation. Cheikh Anta Babou's 2008 study of female Senegalese hair braiders in Atlanta, New

York, Philadelphia, and Anderson, South Carolina, demonstrated that braiding in America involved some occupational shifts, and not just for the géer women.[23] Even the ñeeño artisan women who have immigrated to the United States do so to pursue nonartisan prospects that would elevate them from their premigration subordination. Naturally, they did not want to engage in braiding, but when they did as proprietors of their own salons, they were actually taking a detour. Thus, the Senegalese stylists in the diaspora tend to conceive of their jobs as professional—not service—work and as a profession that can be practiced no matter one's social class in Senegal.[24] And it can be a lucrative occupation, with profits that lead many on a path to upward mobility, which goes a long way to explaining why Babou estimated that 70 percent of all female Senegalese immigrants in the United States (and more than 90 percent in the region of the South) work in the braiding business.[25]

Although the migrants parlayed traditional skills into becoming successfully self-employed in the United States, the context certainly has changed, and the shifts have often resulted in the unsettling of entrenched gender norms as well as social hierarchies. Although the trope of the strong and independent market woman permeates the cultural iconography of traditional West African society, when the practical imperatives of earning a decent living are transplanted in the diaspora and immigrant women become the lead breadwinners in the family economy, it can be disruptive to these long-standing gender expectations. With that shift, wives may take on the role of head of the household, in charge of the business, even employing their husbands who help out as managers or to run errands. In those instances, the men might never let on to compatriots back home that they are involved in such a feminine business; some go so far as a cover, to open another kind of shop in the same building where the salon is located.

Such alterations in expected roles and traditional power relations within the structure of the family have the potential to wreak havoc on diaspora marriages. Whether successfully self-employed as hair stylists and restaurateurs or earning a decent living in another occupation, achieving financial independence and the heightened self-esteem that usually goes along with it have enabled women to step outside of entrenched patriarchal family dynamics to make the kinds of decisions such as filing for divorce if a high level of marital discord persists or contacting authorities if they become the victims of domestic violence, which they never would have considered initiating back at home.[26] Even when family life is more harmonious and the women are not feeling mistreated, the newfound economic autonomy has led to shifts in expected gender roles. For example, the woman of the house may decide to purchase real estate back at home, a financial transaction that has always been in the male domain, and they are also more and more likely to travel away from home with or without accompanying family members. Indeed, the Malian proprietor of a travel agency in New York reported that females composed almost half of his clientele on bookings for both domestic and international flights.[27]

Yet the transition to making the braiding business a distinguishing feature of Senegalese enterprise has not been seamless. Indeed, the arrival of large numbers of mostly French-speaking West African stylists created a formidable challenge to African American women, long entrenched in the hairdressing industry.[28] When African hair braiders began to set up salons in unwanted commercial space on and around Harlem's 125th Street and as their numbers increased, the charges for their services tumbled. Before long these more affordable prices lured diverse black women to the African proprietors and triggered a "braiding war." The situation was fodder for mainstream media, especially the *New York Times*, which covered the occupational rivalry with headlines like "Bargain Braiders Battle for Heads; Hair Stylists from Africa Arrive, Driving Down Prices."[29] Meanwhile in Atlanta, an African American salon owner expressed her frustration, complaining that "my grandmother was a stylist, my mother is a stylist, and here I am continuing an African American tradition, yet some of my clients have left me for African braiders not only because they are cheaper, but because some of our own African American sisters consider them to be more authentic when it comes to how black people's hair should look."[30]

Long after the hair revolution, braiding continues to provide opportunities for West African women beyond New York and other major cities. Soce Diop, who was born in Mauritania and raised in Senegal, lived in Atlanta, dabbling in the culinary business, but she really wanted to get a professional degree that would enable her to land a well-paying salaried job. In 2000, her cousin, Ibe Taye, a manager at a Sonic restaurant in Ashville, North Carolina, invited her to relocate to Ashville and pick up braiding because there was a niche. Although reluctant at first, she admitted to herself, "I just want to work. I don't want my kids to go through what I did as a child in Africa."[31] She moved and her cousin bought her two chairs, a few bundles of hair extensions, and a space at the Eagle-Market Streets Development Corporation. And Soce's African Hair Braiding was born. In the suburbs of Salt Lake City, a Sierra Leonean woman who runs a part-time business in her home used the cultural tradition of hair braiding to win a legal victory when in 2012 she successfully sued the federal government over the issue of licensing, contending that state cosmology requirements were too disconnected from actual hair-braiding practices to be relevant to the profession. While other states like California and Arizona exempt hair-braiders from obtaining full cosmology licenses, Utah does not. Yet, the classes she would have had to take to acquire such credentials do not include hair-braiding techniques. On these grounds, the judge ruled that the state violated the hair-braider's constitutional right to earn a living.[32]

Whether for their reasonable prices or their African authenticity, the momentum for African braiders continues to hold. By 2010, fierce competition was not so much between African and African American stylists. It had become more internal. Anglophone West African women had begun to compete with the Senegalese and other Francophone women who in the 1980s and 1990s had a virtual monopoly on the business. Nigerian, Gambian, and Sierra Leonean women, especially, have been opening braiding shops in Atlanta, Dallas, Houston, and Minneapolis and other cities across the country. The European colonial languages aside, French-speaking and English-speaking women come from similar West African ethnicities and communities where braiding is integral to the lives of girls and women. Therefore, even though the Anglophone West Africans are not faced with identical language barriers as the Francophone women, the reasons for and support of the detour are the same.

Fashion

Fashion production and merchandising have created similar outlets for occupational transformations. As with the hair revolution, appreciation for African styles began to be exhibited by African Americans and others ever since the civil rights era and has only increased with the growing presence of the new Africans. While this overall American base has been a crucial facilitator, the explosion of West African fashion businesses in the United States by the beginning of the twenty-first century owes much of its stimulus to the growth of ethnic communities with idiosyncratic fashion needs that only a cultural economy can fulfill. Similar to the situation with food, as the enclaves have grown in numbers and ethnic distinctiveness, so has the yearning for homeland fashions. A cultural practice common in almost all of the homeland societies has had a big payoff in the diaspora. For centuries, during a variety of functions, from naming ceremonies to funerals, it has been common practice for extended family members to wear identical or strikingly similar clothes, shoes, headgear, and jewelry to distinguish family and clan affiliations. The Yoruba term for this custom, also used by many other West African groups, is *aso ebi* (literally, kin or relatives' clothes). In the 1980s, many of the immigrants who wanted traditional clothing for *aso ebi* relied on family and friends in West Africa to send them the outfits and accessories. By the early 1990s, this had begun to change as businesswomen especially began to sell *aso ebi* garments in major American cities with large concentrations of West Africans.

By now the story is familiar. Some people changed educational and occupational paths to capture this niche. As in other arenas, many also tapped into premigration backgrounds and experiences that they had not initially banked on. Dosina Blemahdoo, who had grown up watching her mother sell fabrics in Ghana, came to Pittsburgh with her graduate student husband in 1973 to "advance the educational and professional prestige of the family." But in 1991, she opened a fabric and apparel shop where she serves as both designer and seamstress because, as she explained, "all of a sudden, I saw a clear opening and the potential for making and selling our colorful traditional clothing very much like my mother used to do."[33] Another Ghanaian, Dora Okrah, relates a strikingly similar experience. Also arriving in the United States in 1973 with her husband, who came to study medicine, she pursued a university education in business administration and accounting. Even though she was raised by a grandmother who was a market woman and her family owned a restaurant in her native country, her plans for the American dream did not initially involve business. In the early 1990s, however, she noticed the growing appreciation for African fashion, so she opened the Village Boutique in Memphis in 1993. After her husband died, she moved the enterprise to Atlanta in 2009 to capture an even bigger market of African and African American consumers.[34] While women dominate this field, some men have taken a similar detour. Nigerian Larry Alebiosu is a good example. He moved to the United States from Lagos in 1982 to study information technology and in 1987 relocated to Detroit to work for a telephone company. But in the early 2000s, as he saw West African communities expand in Michigan, he decided to open a retail clothing store.[35]

Stories like Okrah's and Blemahdoo's, stories about university-trained women making significant strides in the business of ethnic fashion, abound. Increasingly, publicity materials clearly state the nonfashion academic qualifications of fashion entrepreneurs. Advertisements, business cards, and shop signs consciously identify owners as holders of advanced university degrees. As Mojibola Ogunlade explained, it is important for them to unequivocally demonstrate that they are not the same market women as their forebears: "Although I truly admire my

Liberian and Guinean Mandingo women in *aso ebi* (matching outfits) at a wedding celebration in Dallas, Texas. Photo by Lesley Rickford.

Mandingo woman at the same wedding party carrying her child on her back, as is customary in most West African societies. Photo by Lesley Rickford.

mother and grandmother, both of whom sold foodstuff at Gbaja market and used the profits to educate me, I exhibit all the differences they wanted me to have. I am a business woman with three degrees in chemistry."[36] In addition to flaunting their degrees, fashion entrepreneurs like Ogunlade have adopted American/Western designations to identify themselves as presidents, directors, and CEOs of their businesses.

Indeed, these proprietors are not replicating the small market stalls of their predecessors; they are playing big on a vibrant global stage. African merchandising in America is widely international. The businessmen and -women crisscross the globe to sites in Europe, Asia, Africa, and the Middle East to buy assorted fabrics—lace, organza, ankara, damask—and shoes and jewelry. Their clientele pay keen attention to the international quality and prestige of their goods as these ads illustrate: "Modu's Fashion Textiles. Specializing in European and African Fashion: Italian 18K Gold, Austria & Swiss Voile Lace"; "For all your *aso ebi* needs, Debest Fashion carries the latest fabric, shoes, and jewelry from Europe and Dubai"; "Looks, the African and Continental Boutique, has the latest French laces, Bangkok blouses, and the best African asoké [traditional woven cloth]."

Simultaneously, as the diaspora consumer base is scrutinizing the prestige of the fashion businesses, international manufacturers, seeing opportunities for markets in the diaspora, are courting the new entrepreneurs. In 2007, a three-day conference in Houston on global investment, branding, and image management, titled "Nigeria: Heart of Africa," culminated in a gala fashion show staged by Legendary Gold Limited, an event production company, founded in 1995, based in Nigeria that represents the biggest names in high couture designers and models. Although their events had been primarily held in West African cities or broadcast on Lagos TV, they recognized the draw of diaspora buying power and have begun to expand to the United States to woo this segment of the market by displaying the latest styles in high end Nigerian fashion design. But it's not only continental African fashionistas who are taking notice. Europeans and other non-African industry leaders have also started to tap the African immigrant segment in the United States, as exemplified by this account from *African Abroad* regarding the visit to New York of Austrian fabric makers:

Sellers of African fabrics in New York, New Jersey and Connecticut are being wooed by Austrian fabric makers. To this end, a consortium of Austrian fabric makers, who manufacture lace, organza, and other embroidery products preferred by Africans, is organizing an exhibition for them [African fashion merchants]. . . . The five members LQE group from Lustenau, Austria is inviting all to the 3-day event, held at the LaGuardia East Hotel in Flushing, NY.[37]

Navigating the Path to Self-Employment

Not all African businesses are carried out in full view to be noticed by Americans outside of the ethnic enclaves, let alone worldwide. The hidden economy is very much a part of West African ethnic communities and also speaks to aspects of occupational detour. Although the extent of this sphere is not accurately known, by many accounts there are many men and women who have moved from salaried jobs to conduct businesses in their homes and strictly for a trusted co-ethnic clientele. For example, some of the most prosperous tailors and dressmakers work from home. In Atlanta, the house of a Nigerian seamstress is fondly known as Aso Ebi Depot. According to her clients, almost every day at least one group of party planners is at her house to be fitted for their *aso ebi*. Yet even though this is an under-the-radar establishment, what is most pronounced about the visual iconography of the business is that the proprietor prominently displays her diplomas from institutions of higher learning on her sewing room walls. She also never fails to renew her membership in the Association of Black American Business Professionals.[38] Similarly, in the Sierra Leonean immigrant community of Maryland, a woman who earned her degrees in early childhood education and formerly ran a highly regarded kindergarten in Freetown is now well known for her dressmaking business conducted from her house. Many talk about the spectacular shrouds she makes. Remarkably, some of her orders for shrouds come from Sierra Leone, from people who want to make a statement that their loved ones are buried in garments that are imported from "the U.S. of A."

In spite of the many success stories in both the hidden and visible economies, West African entrepreneurship in America suffers from considerable pitfalls. The high rate of retail business closings is indicative of this fact. According to the U.S. Small Business Administration, however, West Africans are not unique, as 50 percent of all small businesses fail within the first five years.[39] Nevertheless, some of the adverse situations that plague this particular group are intrinsic. Many of the self-employed continue to hold on to salaried jobs that detract from their enterprises. For example, Marie-Claude Mendy stuck with her demanding job at an asset management company while she ran her business. This is a common pattern among the entrepreneurs, so common that Sierra Leoneans have used a homeland term to explain the practice and its necessity. "Mammy Coker" (slang for moonlighting), they maintain, is a prerequisite for acquiring health insurance and other benefits for business owners and their families.

The coethnic base is so vital to the niche economy that the slightest insufficient patronage from that source is a death knell for some businesses. Even with its fullest participation, the ethnic base is often not enough to ensure continued sustenance of service retail. Aware of this drawback, many business owners have made conscious efforts to publicize and extend their services beyond the enclave. For example, the Ghanaian proprietors of the Southwest Farmers Market, a supermarket-sized tropical food store located in a multiethnic part of metropolitan Houston, have classified the long aisles of groceries on their shelves with signs above that read "African Foods," "Caribbean Foods," and "Spanish Foods." In addition to these packaged items, the store stocked a wide variety of fresh fruits and vegetables and included a butcher shop with display cases of pigs' feet and fresh hens, a fish market with many varieties of warm water fish and seafood, and a deli where shoppers could buy prepared dishes to take home. Whether West African or not, customers purchased these foods that are shared by the cuisines of many different tropical locations. Aziz Fade, an Ivorian who has described himself as "an opportunity entrepreneur,"[40] is one of the increasing numbers of shopkeepers pushing for "an American expansion" of the enclave economy. Fade emphasized that from the onset he was determined that the most effective way to make his International Food Market in College Park, Georgia, viable was to make sure that it was truly international, "a place where African, Caribbean and American food will bring people together, along with their money to spend."[41] His resolve paid off. His store has been patronized by various groups who have responded to his aggressive inclusive advertising. Interestingly, he believes that a particular kind of drink is the charm. Africans, Afro-Caribbeans, Hispanics, whites, and African Americans frequent his store to buy Karafi Bitter, a beverage popular for its medicinal value.

Unfortunately, most of the businesses have not been this successful in luring non–West Africans. Anecdotal evidence demonstrates the frustration over the failure to win significant numbers of American customers for the most ethnic of products. While American consumption of African fashion and cuisine has increased and now is more widely reported in the mainstream media, this development has not yet really impacted the subcultures of the ethnic enclave. The owner of Café de C.E.D.E.A.O., named for the coalition of West African states, had hoped that his restaurant, located in a diverse neighborhood such as the Bronx, would be a hub where "Americans would try his wife's cassava leaves soup and realize it's not so foreign after all."[42] But this did not happen. Mohammed Barrie's clientele remained solidly West African.

The realization of this dependence has prompted many of the businesspeople to continue to openly appeal to ethnicity in their advertising, even as they claim that their aim is to develop inclusive American businesses. In 2012, the Gambian-Senegalese owner of a tropical grocery and eatery business in Stone Mountain, Georgia, made the decision to get out of his failing venture and go back to his work in computer engineering. Undaunted by the hurdles that he knew caused the enterprise to fail, another West African, a Sierra Leonean, resolved to buy the store. The new owner, a professor at a metro Atlanta school of medicine, was convinced that while the Senegalese-Gambian population had dwindled in that area of metro Atlanta, the Sierra Leonean community was burgeoning, an advantage for his new business. Consequently, he put in motion an ethnic succession in entrepreneurship. He went after Sierra Leonean patronage assertively. Renaming the grocery, Sierra Leonean-Owned African and International Market, he targeted the community, sending a colorful flyer announcing the opening to the major Sierra Leonean churches and alumni and ethnic associations.

Indeed, the proprietors cannot take their ethnic base for granted. Often, its members have to be courted and convinced of why it is important to buy from the "home country" stores. Very often businesses have to fight against stereotypes and accusations of overpricing,

incompetence, and unprofessionalism. "We do not respect or patronize our own people" is a common refrain in the various West African
immigrant communities. How to get recognition and respect for ethnic enterprises is a subject that is constantly addressed. Many advocates have called for the "elevation of business image and practices to
'American' levels."[43] It was with this orientation that in 2009, the Ghanaian Women's Association of Georgia (G-WAG) launched the first free
business directory for the Atlanta West African community. Mrs. Agnes
Hayfron Barnor, vice president of the association, explained the rationale for the G-WAG Business Pages in this way: "It has the potential to
help the Ghanaian community thrive. . . . It is about coming together
and taking pride in the services that our community offers. By expos-
ing the various businesses, the directory invites patronage from both
within the Ghanaian and West African communities and outside."[44]

A firm way for the enclave economy entrepreneurs to elevate their
respect and image is to undercut the intermediaries and control the
wholesale import and distribution of their merchandise. Following
such an approach, by 2000 a few African-owned wholesale warehouse
and distribution companies had emerged.[45] But in general, most of the
small retail businesses relied on non-African companies for the pack-
aging and distribution of African products. In addition, by 2005 giant
American chains like Walmart, Kroger, and Publix had begun to carry
West African ethnic food and beauty products more cheaply.[46] By 2010,
word had spread that there was now lurking a foreign threat far more
perilous than American chains. The Chinese had already become enormously influential in the economies of Africa and were now expanding to the diaspora. By the beginning of the twenty-first century, the
Chinese had begun to gain the dubious distinction of neocolonialists
of postcolonial Africa.[47] What many on the continent did not readily
see or talk about was the growing neocolonialism of the diaspora as
well. But in immigrant communities, entrepreneurs and their customers have begun to relay stories of the Chinese attempts to capture all
aspects of the "African" ethnic market, from the cultivation of crops in
Africa to the exportation and wholesale and retail distribution of the
products among diaspora communities in Europe and North America. Some "African" store owners are now being "outed" as front men
for Chinese ventures. No longer embodying the standard student

professional turned trader, they are, instead, groomed and supported by Chinese investors who sponsor their immigration and business start-ups in the diaspora.[48]

Besides the Chinese and American foreign threats, almost nonexistent American patronage, and shifting African immigrant communities, another reason for the weakening or demise of West African businesses is the entrepreneurs themselves. Many are still very much the nonbusiness, highly educated professionals they set out to be. With one foot in business and the other in another job, they do not give their enterprises the required attention. Some of them do not establish a strong physical presence in businesses that bear their names. Instead, sometimes exploited newcomers are the real operators of the enterprises. While this shortcoming of the "uncommitted entrepreneur" is often raised, especially by members of the immigrant communities, it does not detract from the reality that business is still a most visible sign of the West African presence in America, even if the overwhelming majority of the entrepreneurs did not initially come to replicate a laudable entrepreneurial history. Ghanaian Kwaku Adwini-Poku, an automotive engineer and secretary of the United African Community Organization of Detroit, succinctly pointed to the shift in plans as he described how African entrepreneurship in Michigan has grown correspondingly with the increase in African immigrants settling there: "Historically, most African immigrants have been students or professionals who have academic-oriented careers like in engineering and the medical fields. But the new trends are showing that for practical considerations a lot of such people are moving into business. We [African immigrants] need them and they need us."[49]

4

Transnational Ties/Translocal Connections

Traversing Nations, Cities, and Cultures

"It's a small world," people say when I tell them about my life in Ghana, here in the USA and many other places. But is it really a small world? My universe is not only my home-town of Korle Bu in Ghana, which may have been the case if I had not immigrated; it now includes Chicago, Atlanta, New York, Philadelphia, Toronto, London, Antwerp, and, of course, Korle Bu and Accra. So, my world is not small and simple. It is big, complicated yet fascinating.
—Afua Quartey Sarpong, 2004

Migration stories have always been about multiple locations. From the Puritans who carved out new communities influenced by their experiences in Europe to Italian men who went back and forth as "birds of passage" to more contemporary newcomers from the Dominican Republic who all but split their time in half between the two countries, American immigration history has realistically been the history of numerous societies. By the late 1980s, scholars had settled on the term "transnationalism" as a crucial analytical category to describe and explain the immigrant experience. It was no coincidence that such conceptualizations were formulated in this period as the huge wave of post-1965 newcomers were streaming into the United States in record numbers and with this flow came recognition that breathtaking advances in travel and communications technologies along with the speed of the global flow of capital and commerce had profoundly elevated levels of connectivity across oceans and continents. Sociologists and anthropologists like Linda Basch, Nina Glick Schiller, Nancy Foner, Alejandro Portes, and Peggy Levitt were at the forefront of the new transnationalism.[1] As the field evolved and particularly as historians entered into the conversation, scholars emphasized that while some of its manifestations were of recent origin, transnationalism as a vital component of everyday life was not a new phenomenon; immigrants arriving from the late nineteenth century throughout the twentieth century have also systematically maintained homeland ties and transoceanic connections.[2] Most of the transnationalism studies of the 1990s focused mainly on a "dual" existence, "processes by which immigrants forge and sustain multistranded social relations that link together their societies of origin and settlement."[3]

Even though West Africans, as subjects of American immigration studies, are relatively new and their communities are still emerging, like other immigrants they display the many patterns enumerated by transnationalism scholars and in ever more complex ways. Ira Berlin notes that a high percentage of Africans sustain solid bonds between the United States and their African homelands through visits for vacations, weddings, burials, and the temporary relocation of American-born children; consequently, according to Berlin, "many men and women become comfortable in their old homelands and their new homes, literally transnationals."[4] This chapter discusses how the newcomers strive for "comfortable homes" in the United States while sustaining and enhancing ties across nationalities, ethnicities, continents, and American states and cities. Because the West African immigrant experience in America is more than a clear-cut "dual" existence, this chapter illuminates the variegated virtual and actual boundary crossings that reflect connections that go beyond a singular link between homeland and host societies. In the experiences of the postcolonial, post–civil rights West Africans, a complicated interplay among American localities, diverse West African ethnicities and nationalities, and African, European, and North American nation-states unfolds. Indeed, one sociologist studying the Cape Verdean diaspora characterized the multiple spokes of the primary sites of transnationalism—Boston, Providence, Lisbon, and Rotterdam—as "islands in a migratory archipelago."[5] Practically, then, the crisscrossings at the center of the new West African immigrant communities go beyond "transnational" relations; rather, they are more diffuse and intricate formations in an increasingly multifaceted new African diaspora.

American Communities, West African (Re)Creations

Restaurants, grocery stores, tropical food shops, and street vendors have been the most striking indicators of West African immigrant communities in America. This was how "Little Senegal" in New York first gained recognition in the 1980s. Increasingly, other indices are confirming the growing presence of the immigrants and the emergence of viable communities. Mosques, churches, community centers, and parades and festivals have joined businesses in making the West African presence visible. While prima facie, West Africans tend to dissipate within larger African and African American enclaves, actual population clusters create anchors for the development of ethnic diasporic translocal and transnational communities. The aggregation of Haal Pulaar coethnics from Mali, Mauritania, and Guinea resulted in Fauta Town, a West African neighborhood in Brooklyn. Similarly, by 2005 a West African community, made up mostly of Nigerians, Sierra Leoneans, Liberians, Ghanaians, Guineans, and Ivorians, had emerged in the Clifton neighborhood of Staten Island. The massive Tracy Towers apartment complex in the Bronx came to be home to literally hundreds of Ghanaians and became the basis for the development of the most recognizable physical enclave of this West African group in New York. By 2010, the residents had come together as the Tracy Towers Ghanaian Community. In the late 1980s and 1990s, Sierra Leoneans in the Atlanta suburb of Doraville clustered in a townhome complex and developed an enclave they called Big Yard. Similar demographic developments have resulted in hidden but flourishing West African settlements in almost every city where these populations have relocated in significant numbers.

Yet it's not only where West Africans live that demonstrates such geographic clustering; new spatial patterns in diaspora communities are also evolving where the dead ultimately reside. While the majority of the immigrants still believe that their souls will return to Africa, where their umbilical cords were buried, America has become the permanent physical home for the majority. Dissuaded by the high costs of transferring remains to West Africa, the immigrants began to seriously factor American cemeteries into their grand migration plans. Closely following residential patterns, cemeteries, like neighborhoods, have begun to exhibit the growing permanent presence of West Africans in America.

As a community leader in Staten Island observed, "Most American cities where we are settled have cemeteries that have sections that will continue to keep us together—the dead who are buried there and the living who meet when they go there to memorialize loved ones."[6] Individuals and groups learn about affordable and suitable cemeteries from attending funerals and through word of mouth. For example, the metro Atlanta Sierra Leonean community has developed an "afterlife enclave" in Hillandale Gardens in which, since around 1995, a "Sierra Leonean section," began to grow. The cemetery is in Lithonia, where, along with neighboring towns like Stone Mountain, Decatur, Conyers, and Ellenwood, a lot of Sierra Leoneans live. However, increasingly, even families who do not reside in these areas but live in other parts of Georgia such as Fayetteville or Macon are choosing to bury their dead in Hillandale Gardens because effectively, albeit morbidly, it marks a Sierra Leonean space in America.

While the physical, demographic concentration is what makes the communities possible in the first place, it is the cultural production that sustains them as American communities of West African re-creation. As with other ethnic groups, the family serves as a crucial base. It is through this unit that most individuals are poised to participate in and contribute to collective institutions that define the communities. Syracuse University fashion design student Ama Kwakye described this crucial basis for a transnational orientation: "Growing up in Staten Island, they [her Ghanaian-born parents] created an island within an island and kept their traditions alive."[7] All across the United States, families like Kwakye's create similar islands, which, technically, are not insular units because they are conduits for vaster activities that transcend cities, states, and nations. Families form the foundation for the organization and commemoration of transplanted markers through a variety of rites of passage such as naming, outdooring, graduation, engagement, wedding, and funeral ceremonies.[8] Interactions between members of extended families, old schoolmates, former/homeland, and new neighbors help to make their new homes comfortable enough to be conducive to encounters across city, state, ethnic, and national boundaries.

While many outside observers see these communities only as "black" or "immigrant" neighborhoods, their members fully grasp their hybrid societies that are akin to transplanted homelands. Cape Verdean immigrant Inez Britto underscores this:

> I like to say that when I look at my life, it's like a circle: I was born in Fogo, then I went to San Vicente—another island—and then I went to Portugal to study. Finally, at forty-three, I came here and found my childhood friends because they ended up here, too. And not just my childhood friends, but my whole island! Sometimes I think that America is more Fogo than other parts of Cape Verde, like San Vicente and Santiago.[9]

While this kind of fortuitous reunification cannot be underestimated, organized maintenance of community—through associations, ethnic media, and economic institutions (retail, travel, shipping, real estate, and money transfer)—is the foremost shaper of contemporary West African diasporic communities in America.

Based on ethnic newspapers and radio shows, flyers, and other publicity materials, it is safe to estimate that by the end of the first decade of the twenty-first century, there were no fewer than eight hundred West African immigrant-connected associations in America. They represent an array of categories, including ethnic, national, benevolent, sports, religious, political, professional, and school, college, and university alumni associations. Inarguably, ethnicity was a prime conferrer of premigration identity. No wonder then that ethnic-based affiliation came to be a central component of organized management of cultural production and community sustenance.

By 2000, ethnic associations had mushroomed. Nigerian immigrants alone had established at least three hundred ethnic associations. Although umbrella associations representing the main groups of Hausa, Igbo, and Yoruba exist, the majority of the Nigerian ethnic associations represent subdivisions of the main groups. For example, the Hausas have numerous organizations representing specific Hausa subgroups, from Adamawa to Zamfara. Similarly, the Yorubas have Eko, Ijesha, Ijebu, Ekiti, and other Yoruba subgroups represented in their associational life. And the Igbos have developed organizations representing Imo, Anambra, and Enugu, among others. The majority of these associations are affiliate members of the huge Igbo congress, which encompasses Igbo associations across America and Canada. In addition to the main ethnic groups and their subdivisions, Nigerian minority groups like the Nupe, Tiv, and Ogoni have also formed their own ethnic associations in America. While, undoubtedly, Nigerians lead in sheer numbers of ethnic associations, multiple ethnically distinctive associations are a visible pattern of all the West African nationalities in America. For instance, Sierra Leoneans have the Fullah Progressive Union, Tegloma, whose membership is mostly Mende and Sherbro, and Krio Descendants Union. Ghanaians have Ga, Asante, Fante, and Ewe associations. And Liberians have organized around their distinct ethnic groups of Bassa, Kru, and Congo.

These centuries-old ethnic groups (with the exception of Krios) are the same ethnicities represented in the Atlantic slave trade and the old diaspora in America. While in the old diaspora the brutality of slavery dictated the obliteration of African ethnicities, in the new era the projection of African ethnicities has been a significant hallmark. America has become an additional arena for the performance of ethnicity.

Confluence of homeland and American leisure: Sierra Leonean men, at a graduation and Fourth of July barbecue in Mesquite, Texas, playing English draught, a favorite pastime for men in both rural and urban areas all over West Africa. Photo by Lesley Rickford.

As a notice inviting members of the Anambra Association of Atlanta to a meeting proclaimed, "More than ever, we must come together. Being outside Anambra land, our identity and loyalty should be stronger because that is how we will keep up with our roots and glorify our home."[10] The pronouncements and activities of numerous other ethnic associations accentuate this heightened ethnicity in America. The Krios of Sierra Leone provide a useful illustration. Known in their home country as the most Western of ethnic groups, many Krio immigrants have admitted to embracing vital homeland cultural traits in America far more than they ever did in premigration times. In activities of the various branches of the Krio Descendants' Union, the leaders and members stress adherence to the Krio culture of their ancestors in everything, from dress to food to language. Men and women, who did not study Krio formally because they were immersed in English and other European languages in their curriculum, find themselves using written and spoken Krio for formal proceedings at events in their American West African communities.

As West Africans have continued to settle in the United States, the number of ethnic associations has kept increasing. Typically these collectivities are organized by cities. By the twenty-first century most of the branches had developed sophisticated ways of communicating across states and metropolitan areas. Group emails, listservs, Facebook and other social media groups, as well as phone texts and conference calls keep the members of various chapters of an ethnic association in contact. Conventions have also emerged as an actual and elaborate means to supplement the virtual networks. Community newspapers, radio shows, and flyers are replete with unending announcements of conventions around the country. Venues are rotated for these annual, massive, two- or three-day gatherings that bring together hundreds of men, women, and children to socialize and deliberate on pressing issues facing their many communities in America and their homelands. For example, the Urhobo (Nigerian ethnic group) Congress met in Orchard Beach in the Bronx in 2006. The previous year, they had held their convention in Iowa, a midwestern state that only a decade earlier would not have exhibited such diversity. The ethnic conventions are unequivocally focused on the respective ethnic groups. For instance, the 2011 convention of the Egbe Omo Yoruba North America drew thousands of Yorubas around the world. The events showcased traditional leaders who flew in to New York from Yorubaland, from the Alake of Egbaland to the Awujale of Ijebuland. The theme of the convention was "How to Turn Yorubaland to a Developed Region within Nigeria."[11]

While, undeniably, the affirmation and performance of premigration ethnicities have intensified in the new American setting, amazingly, simultaneously, so have cross-ethnic and national interactions. At the same time that the ethnic associations are fund-raising to develop their home villages and towns and to assist the townspeople, they are also supporting activities that nurture dialogue and practical cooperation across lines of ethnicity and nationality. The organizations based on national origins are the mainstay of ethnic amalgamation. These groups, with names like the Association of Sierra Leoneans in Georgia, National Association of Nigerian Organizations, National Council of Ghanaian Associations, Cape Verdean Community UNIDO, Liberian Community Association of Rhode Island, Senegalese Community for Aid and Self Development, Nigerian American Muslim Integrated Community, Ghanaian Women's Association, and Nigerian Lawyers Association, are premised on the blurring of intragroup divisions. They consciously tailor their activities, although not without lingering ethnic-oriented tensions, to achieve unity, ironically, based on their European-derived nationalities. The appeal to forego ethnocentrism remains a constant in the work of the umbrella national organizations, as illustrated by this plea from the United Nigerian Foundation–USA Inc.: "We are all related—North, South, West and East Regions. So, leave all tribalism at the door of this club."[12]

In many instances pan-ethnicity is more spontaneous. As vulnerable immigrants from the same African region, members of various ethnic groups have transcended ethnic, national, and linguistic boundaries to present a collective force in the face of American challenges. The DC-Maryland-Virginia Tristate Baffour Soccer Charity Tournament, which by 2011 had become an annual event, is illustrative of this trend. The event grew out of the desire to help Baffour, a Ghanaian immigrant in Virginia who, on his way from work one day in 2006, was in an accident that left him paralyzed. Baffour lost his livelihood, and without medical insurance, his situation was critical. Originating from his co-Ghanaian nationals, appeals to help him spread around the diverse West African communities. Individuals and ethnic and national organizations heeded the plea. The West Africans came together using a recreational medium common to all their homeland societies—soccer (or football, the label used in West Africa). Most of the soccer clubs founded by immigrants are organized along ethnic and national lines, like the Freetown Stars (Sierra Leonean immigrants) and Ashanti Kotoko–USA (Ghanaian immigrants). Yet, the tournament stands as a benevolent project that continues to provide a conduit for the gathering of West African immigrants of diverse ethnicities and nationalities living in different cities and states of America. NGOZI, a Nigerian benevolent group and AKWAABA a Ghanaian community radio station, emerged to spearhead this Baffour-inspired interethnic, intercity, and interstate initiative. They continually hammered home the point that the desired outcomes went beyond Baffour to enable people from Africa living in the tristate area to socialize and network. They also envisaged that in the near future they would raise far more than is needed for Baffour, so that they would help other families and projects in immigrant communities.

The keen focus on the welfare of the immigrant community is a trait openly displayed by all the associations, ethnic and national alike. The mission statement of the Senegalese Community for Aid and Self Determination is typical. This five-hundred-member, multistate organization pledges "to assist people with immigration and legal matters, promote education, training and networking for Senegalese in America, promote Senegalese values and identity among children and transport the bodies of Senegalese abroad home to Senegal."[13] Such vision, mission, and goal statements have elicited criticism from several quarters, most notably African Americans, who see the associations as un-American. According to critics, the associations, which are the bases of adaptation, prevent meaningful integration into American society because of their excessive focus on their communities as separate enclaves. This is reminiscent of charges levied on another group of foreign blacks, Afro-Caribbean immigrants of the first half of the twentieth century. West Indians, as they were called, were accused of being too clannish, the outcome of the objectives and activities of their associations.[14]

But how un-American is the evolving associational life of West Africans in America? Careful scrutiny demonstrates that while, admittedly, the organizations appeal to and employ familiar homeland practices, the communities that have emerged are not static and are not replicas of societies left behind. The result of far more cross-ethnic, cross-cultural, and mixed-class interactions, the communities are, in essence, based on negotiating cultures and finding and occupying niches in a diverse America. The hybridity that underlines the communities starts with the many "homeland" functions. Naming ceremonies, weddings, and funerals have been modified to accommodate the realities of living in America. Although dual wedding ceremonies—traditional and Western—still occur, the length of wedding ceremonies has been drastically shortened in America among members of several ethnic groups, for whom engagement and wedding celebrations at home are lengthy occasions that span several days.

In another example of the adaptation of life cycle events to new norms, for many ethnic groups in Sierra Leone it is taboo to bury the dead on Saturday. On the contrary, in America, funerals in Sierra Leonean immigrant enclaves are always held on Saturday, when many members of the community are off work and can attend, sometimes traveling in chartered buses hundreds of miles across state lines to pay their respects. Moreover, by the end of the first decade of the twenty-first century, the immigrants had begun to use the African American terminology of "homegoing" to describe funeral rites.

The celebration of baby showers is even more illuminating. The homeland societies did not have the concept of a baby shower in their cultural repertoire. In fact, among a number of West African populations, it is bad luck to shop for the baby before birth. Nevertheless, by the 1990s, grand baby shower parties had become one of the markers of the duality of the immigrant communities as West African and American.

Moreover, American holidays are momentous in the West African diaspora. Families, friends, and even entire organizations celebrate Thanksgiving, complete with turkey and candied yams, which, in most cases, have to share the table with festive West African dishes like jollof rice. The fact that relatives and friends in West Africa and Europe have begun to call their kin in the United States to wish them "Happy Thanksgiving" says a lot about the reality of the growing visible American facets of the evolving communities. Memorial Day, Labor Day, and the Fourth of July have become picnic and convention days. Like

Americans around the country, the immigrants have cookouts, theirs mostly organized by their community organizations. For example, in 1999 the Prince of Wales Alumni Association organized a Fourth of July picnic in Stone Mountain Park in Georgia. The event continued to grow every year, and by 2012, with other alumni associations collaborating with the Prince of Wales, the celebration had evolved into a huge gathering that annually brings together a diverse group of Sierra Leoneans representing the different ethnicities, religions, and classes as well as their American-born children. Labor Day weekend has become the most suitable time for elaborate conventions of ethnic associations whose members from all over the world converge in selected American urban centers for a global fest.

West Africans congregating on American holidays to eat foods from their countries of origin, listen and dance to homeland music, and hold conventions that affirm their African ethnicities might at first glance seem to confirm the charge of un-American, foreign black communities. But this view misses much of what is actually happening both at gatherings that bring coethnics together on American holidays and, at other times, spearheaded by the desire to celebrate national origins such as GhanaFest, organized by Ghanaians in Chicago, Philadelphia, and New York in July and August. Even the symbolism that surrounds the events clearly indicates the sense of dualism and the evolving process of integration. The American flag is always hoisted alongside the flag of the nation of the celebrating immigrants, while the "Star-Spangled Banner" inevitably follows the national anthem of the West African country represented. And in some instances the American Pledge of Allegiance is recited alongside the West African nation's pledge.

To be sure, the most public displays of the political culture of recent West African immigrant groups are Independence Day festivities marking the overthrow of colonialism in their respective home countries. Thus, the most widely celebrated holiday among Cape Verdeans in the United States occurs on July 5, Cape Verdean Independence Day, commemorating the successful ousting of Portuguese colonial rule in 1975. Parades, picnics, pageants, and cultural performances are held in Cape Verdean American communities throughout the country. The occasion provides an opportunity to acknowledge the historic significance of the event but, increasingly, also to highlight and legitimize Cape Verdean culture to the broader community. For Cape Verdeans in New Bedford, Massachusetts, the historic hub of the first wave of immigrants from the island nation, that wider recognition has already been accomplished. Since the holiday falls on the day after the Fourth of July, the cultural merger has been so complete that for more than three decades, the city's annual parade has actually been designed to simultaneously commemorate both of these back-to-back Independence Day celebrations; in recent years, it has even been officially referred to as the Cape Verdean Recognition Parade. Cape Verdean community leaders, youth groups, and entertainers wave from floats or march alongside city officials, high school bands, and members of other civic associations who represent the whole spectrum of residents of this diverse municipality, while the parade route is mapped to culminate in the South End neighborhood that is the heart of the Cape Verdean enclave.

Nigerians, the largest of the West African immigrant populations, provide other useful illustrations of how these groups are evolving as hybrid West African American communities. In 1995, the Organization for the Advancement of Nigerians (OAN) organized the first annual parade in America to celebrate Nigeria's independence from Britain (October 1, 1960). Occurring only a few weeks after the West Indian Labor Day Carnival, this parade has grown into one of New York City's spectacular multicultural events. By 2010, Nigerians had begun to tout the parade as the "largest celebration by Nigerians outside of their homeland."[15] The occasion draws thousands of Nigerian visitors, students, legal and undocumented residents, and naturalized American citizens and their children from almost every state in the United States with the banners of the different associations vividly conveying the diversity of the Nigerian population. The visiting participants represent other Nigerian diasporic communities in Europe and Canada, as well as dignitaries from Nigeria itself, from traditional chiefs to state governors, senators, and Nollywood film stars. Simultaneous Internet-fed broadcasts allow Nigerians in Nigeria and elsewhere to view the parade live. The national colors of white and green pervade the parade route on flags, T-shirts, and other clothing and decorations adorning the floats.

Commenting on the success of the 2006 parade, one Nigerian American reporter proclaimed, "This October 1st like several before is an outing on behalf of Nigeria . . . and we must remember that it is all about Nigeria and nothing else matters! Nigerians ought to thank OAN for keeping the flag of Nigeria flying high in New York."[16] But before jumping to a hasty conclusion that all this confirms the overriding, or sole, purpose of affirming and projecting the foreignness of Nigerians in America, a look at several other characteristics of the event modifies such an assessment. Interspersed among the waving Nigerian flags are the stars and stripes of the American flag. Rap and hip-hop music can be heard blasting from some of the floats, especially those with young people riding on them. And joining the Nigerian dignitaries are American notables, including politicians like Mayor Michael Bloomberg and New York Congressman Charles Rangel. The OAN leadership articulated the dualism they hoped the parade would demonstrate. According to the president, Michael Adeniyi, "[the parade] was designed to

Even when pride in their native country was at its height as Ghana faced the United States in a 2006 World Cup soccer match, the boisterous crowd gathered at a Ghanaian restaurant in Chicago was glued to a television placed directly underneath a picture with renderings of iconic American symbols, from the flag to the Capitol building to the Liberty Bell. Photo by Marilyn Halter.

The 2 to 1 lead of the Ghana Black Stars held, and there was no doubt which team was being celebrated afterward. Photo by Marilyn Halter.

show the growing influence of Nigerians in America back home where their estimated annual wire transfer to relatives has hit the $billion mark, as well as to emphasize their presence in the USA, where they have contributed their expertise in government, the law profession, the medical field, African supermarkets, fashion and beauty."[17] The organizers also declared in 2006 that the time had come to request that green and white lights be illuminated from the Empire State Building, one of New York's most important landmarks, in recognition of the Nigerian American celebration. The same reporter who excitedly claimed that "only Nigeria mattered," unknowingly, it seems, in the same piece pointed to how American to the core the Nigerian parade really is. He said, "In New York, there is always some parade or some flag waving ceremonies. . . . It feels wonderful that Nigeria has finally joined the fun in large numbers."[18] Indeed, Columbus Day for Italians and Saint Patrick's Day for Irish are widely acknowledged not as distinct markers of foreign exclusivity but as expressions of American ethnicity. Nigerian

Americans, newcomers to this trend, are well on their way to defining through a commemorative culture their position in America's multicultural tapestry.

The acknowledgment of the permanence of West African communities and what seems like their advancement to recognizable American ethnicities has helped to shape the activities of the ethnic and national associations. The development of the enclaves into well-informed, integrated, successful American communities is an important item on the agendas of the various organizations. From lectures and fairs on managing health to assistance with preparation of tax returns, the associations undertake practical efforts at development. By the beginning of the twenty-first century, community leaders and their organizations had embraced the view that productive participation in the American electoral process at the local, state, and federal levels was fundamental to the successful growth of West African American communities.

Because the prerequisite for this approach is the attainment of citizenship, ultimately it is not so paradoxical that the naturalization rates of West African immigrant groups increased significantly at a time when the projection of African ethnicities intensified.[19] The same influential members of associations who regulated the "ethnic project" were also the agents of the American politicization project. They incorporated into the activities of the organizations citizenship education for naturalization, voter registration drives, and lectures, workshops, and seminars on ballot issues. Often they went beyond the enclave to include Americans, especially African American activists and politicians in these activities. For example, throughout the late 1990s Congresswoman Cynthia McKinney was a fixture at numerous events of the diverse groups of West Africans in metro Atlanta. Interacting with such high profile U.S. representatives and participating in events designed to explain American politics, many immigrants gained insight into issues related to American foreign policy toward Africa as well as U.S. immigration policy, especially those laws related to refugee resettlement like the temporary protected status, which directly affected West Africans, especially Liberians and Sierra Leoneans. From participating in association-sponsored events, many of the naturalized citizens acquired an understanding of why they must vote. By the time of the historic 2008 presidential elections, immigrants from this region were no longer a negligible voting bloc. One of their newspapers articulated this in a bold headline that read, "America Is Home: African Immigrants Emerge to Make Impact in U.S. Election."[20]

As brokers between their communities and the larger American society, some of the leaders have used their own careers and involvement to convey the significance of political incorporation. A telling example is Nigerian American Okenfe Aigbe Lebarty. He worked tirelessly for the Obama campaign in 2007 and 2008, securing enough votes to attend the Democratic Convention in Denver in August 2008 as a delegate from New York. In 2010 he decided to run for the State Assembly to represent the district encompassing Far Rockaway, South Ozone Park, Rosedale, Laurelton, and Springfield Gardens. He moved easily within immigrant and nonimmigrant settings, explaining his platform. Addressing a group of West Africans, mostly Nigerians, he used American political lingo, describing how "Albany is broken," and he encouraged all eligible voters to exercise their right, thus making their own contributions to an "exceptional democracy." Lebarty said all this while proclaiming proudly in the same speech that he was from "Edo State in the great, historic Benin Kingdom."[21] Indeed, Lebarty represents the contemporary West African diaspora well in the ways that he legitimizes American communities with strong ties to the homeland, ties that he consciously and ostentatiously affirms and projects.

Transnational Networks

No meaningful investigation of West Africans in the United States can ignore the centrality of transnationalism. In fact, Ousmane Oumar Kane anchored his study *The Homeland Is the Arena* on the premise that "transnationalism is the dominant mode of adaptation of the Senegalese in late twentieth-century America."[22] The experiences of other West Africans certainly mirror those of Kane's Senegalese. By the late twentieth and early twenty-first centuries, Nigerians, Cape Verdeans, Gambians, Ghanaians, Sierra Leoneans, Togolese, Ivorians, and Liberians, like the Senegalese, had developed efficient networks that enabled their homes of origin as well as other locations of the diaspora to play pivotal roles in shaping their American experiences. Maintaining a strong dual identity or even multiple national identities has become much more feasible for members of the West African diaspora in recent years. The vast improvements in transportation and global telecommunications technology of the past two decades have facilitated the transnational quality of day-to-day lives in the diaspora, dynamics that also help to sustain strong cultural identifications.

But especially for Cape Verdean immigrants, this level of transnationalism is hardly new. By the end of the nineteenth century, as both the whaling and sealing industries in the United States sank into steep decline and as steamship travel came to replace sailing, not only was it difficult to recruit crew members to work in these occupations, but the old vessels themselves fell into disrepair. The whaling industry had been the strongest pull factor in bringing the initial Cape Verdean settlers to America's shores, and it continued its critical importance to the evolution of the Cape Verdean American community, albeit indirectly, as some of the most enterprising of this early wave took advantage of the opportunity to buy up the rickety Essex-built *Gloucester Fishermen*. They pooled their resources and converted them into cargo and passenger ships, used as packet boats that regularly plied between the Cape Verde Islands and the ports of New Bedford, Massachusetts, and Providence, Rhode Island. In 1892, with the purchase of a sixty-four-ton fishing schooner, the *Nellie May*, Antonio Coelho became the first Cape Verdean American packet owner. But he wasn't the last. Hiring former whalers as captains and crew members, Cape Verdean Americans became the owners of a fleet of these former whalers and schooners that carried goods (and some passengers to the islands for retirement) and returned full of hopeful new immigrants. Thus, in an extraordinary situation unlike that of most immigrant groups, black or white, the Cape Verdeans came to have control over their own means of passage to the United States.

Once the packet trade got under way, the transatlantic system of support greatly facilitated the newcomers' transition to the United States. While there certainly were instances of hazardous voyaging, that they were owned and operated by the Cape Verdeans themselves served to further strengthen the chain between the islands and the American settlement. To compensate for the risks of travel on these aged vessels, which have been described both as "floating shipwrecks" and "a cross between a caravel of Columbus and Huck Finn's raft," the Cape Verdeans were surrounded by their own compatriots.[23] On the crossing, they could hear the familiar sounds of their native language as well as enjoy the music of the *mornas* and *caledeiras* played by the passengers who brought instruments; they could also continue eating traditional *Kriolu* foods. Once landed at the pier in New Bedford, unlike the often bewildering scene at Ellis Island, where at its height as many as five thousand immigrants were processed daily, the arrival of a packet boat was always cause for celebration, as friends and relatives flocked down to the wharf to welcome the new arrivals, eager for news from the islands and the assurance that the voyage had been completed safely. Some would climb aboard to join in on the festivities, with much embracing, dancing, and drinking of *grog* (whiskey).

Because of the packet trade, transatlantic passage was readily available for both new migrants and return visitors, facilitating a significant flow of remittances, communication, and cultural exchanges. It was not unusual for the cargo of a packet boat arriving in Cape Verde to include American furnishings, from frying pans to bedding sent over to the wives and female relatives of the primarily male emigrants. The phenomenon of what came to be called the *casa mercana* (American house) was further evidence of the cohesiveness of the Cape Verdean American bond. The packet trade also made possible a constant line of communication between those who had departed and those who remained on the islands. With each trip, there were not only passengers to transport but also letters and packages to be delivered to friends and kin on both sides. A central part of this transnational connection was the custom of sending *mantenhas* (from the Portuguese, "to keep up" or "maintain"), verbal greetings that were essential to nurturing the ties among those who have been geographically separated. A trusted friend or family member would be selected to pass on a specific message overseas. Since Kriolu has traditionally been a spoken language, any letters that were written were likely penned in Portuguese, a language unfamiliar to most. Hence, the mantenhas took primacy over written correspondence as the conduit for news, gossip, and general good tidings. Delivery of these oral greetings was not a casual request or a message to be taken lightly, but a serious responsibility assumed by the traveler.

Furthermore, since many of those in the first wave of immigrants were primarily engaged in seasonal labor, especially cranberry and maritime work, a good deal of shuttling back and forth between the archipelago and New England occurred. The packet trade enabled seasonal cranberry pickers who would finish the harvest in late fall to return on the last boats out of New Bedford in November so that they could spend the winters in Cape Verde. Between 1900 and 1920, one out of three arrivals had traveled to the United States more than once.[24] The connection between the Cape Verdean American community and the Cape Verde Islands was so strong and transportation back and forth so accessible that the typical migrant, upon leaving for the United States, was not required to make a final commitment to resettlement, easing the anguish of separation.

Perhaps the most striking example of the bond between the Cape Verde Islands and the Cape Verdean American diaspora revolves around the return of the schooner *Ernestina* in 1982. After more than six years of transatlantic organizing efforts, the Republic of Cape Verde presented the United States with the gift of the historic vessel, the last Cape Verdean packet boat in existence. At the dedication ceremonies in the port of New Bedford, the Cape Verdean ambassador to the United States spoke eloquently of the ship as a symbol of the long-standing and ongoing interdependence that unites and binds together the Cape Verde Islands and the American diaspora community. In 1986, at the tall ships celebration of the Statue of Liberty centennial, the vessel took its place at the front of the flotilla, in recognition of its unique history as the only surviving ship in the parade that had actually carried immigrants to the United States.

At the center of today's transnational networks are two crucial pivots—remittances and phone communications. As Kane, concurring with transnationalism scholar Steven Vertovec, puts it, "Remittances and phone calls are two social glues of West African immigrant transnationalism."[25] While money has always been the defining element of transfer from migration destination to sending society, it is not the only staple. More than ever, by the end of the twentieth century other forms of transfer had become very important. Therefore, even though money still remained paramount, by 2000 nonmonetary commodities, including motor vehicles, generators, computer equipment, phones, medical and educational supplies, clothing, and food, had become instrumental in shaping the dynamics and broadening the definition of remittances.

"We are talking billions of dollars a year!"[26] This enthusiastic declaration by an ethnic association president underscores the enormity of the financial links with homeland societies. Indeed, since the 1990s, West Africans living in the United States have been transferring billions of dollars a year. In 2011 out of the $10.45 billion remitted to Nigeria, 40 percent came from Nigerians in North America, while for many years Cape Verde has been one of the top countries for remittances in all of sub-Saharan Africa, with amounts increasing an average of 10 percent annually from 1991 to 2011.[27] Similar patterns can be found for the other West African nations as well. Money transfer occurs on two levels—individuals/family units and collective units representing village, town, ethnic, and other organizations.

Although a quip, the following comment is dead serious in how aptly it conveys the reality of remittances in the life of the vast majority of those in the West African diaspora: "My paychecks disappear like a trick in a Houdini act because I have to give something to Uncle Sam in America [American taxes] and Uncle Bill, Uncle Sapé, Auntie Topee, Cousin Martha, and a host of others in Monrovia [capital of Liberia]."[28] The sense of obligation evident in this statement is what undergirds remittance as a formidable link of transnationalism. The migration venture is never an individual project. Through myriad ways, some going back to the time of birth, relatives, friends, and townspeople contribute to making the emigration of an individual possible. Tapping from their earnings abroad, the grateful migrants are expected to show appreciation in tangible ways made possible through remittances. Simply put, the social functions and value of remittances go beyond the mere financial transactions involved in the process. Remittances are embedded in the very fabric of the familial structure and are crucial to sustaining extended family membership. Remittances effectively fill the void of departure because they ensure a palpable presence of the family member living abroad.

Money and other commodities have vast implications. They serve as the ceaseless virtual return of the member physically resident in a foreign land. A Yoruba prayer beautifully depicts this phenomenon:

Olodumare je ki a ko ere oko dele
Ki a rajo kabo, ki a ma r'ajo gbe s'ajo
Ka ma pada l'orwo ofo

May the Almighty God grant the grace to come back home
With the proceeds from the land of sojourn
May we return from our sojourn, may we not perish in the land of
    sojourn
May we not return empty handed[29]

Numerous families are able to testify that the Almighty answers prayers, because remittances prove that the sojourner, though physically residing in America, constantly, albeit symbolically, returns home and not empty handed. Sojourners perform more effectively most of the responsibilities they would have undertaken if physically still at home.

West African immigrants often designate the money they send home for specific expenditure: school and college/university education (fees,

Cape Verdean schooner *Ernestina* in the Tall Ships Parade, New York, 1986. Photo by Michael K. H. Platzer.

uniforms, books, and other supplies), rent or contribution toward the building or renovation of family homes, and payment of utility and medical bills. The sustenance and advancement of the family in the place of origin not only confers a physical presence on the immigrant member, but also ascribes status to both the family in West Africa and the immigrant in America. It is partly for this reason that currency is augmented with strategically chosen nonmonetary goods. The kind of motor vehicles driven or parked in front of a house adds to the notion of success of family members abroad. Bumper stickers and decals, deliberately left to survive the transportation and arrival of the vehicles, amplify the transnational universe of a family. What is more American than decals of American institutions of higher learning and presidential election bumper stickers, from "Kerry-Edwards" to "McCain-Palin" to "Obama-Biden" and "Obama 2008—Yes We Can!"? Other symbols of success and perceived affluence continue to flow as remittances. These include flat screen TVs, DVD players, computer tablets, and "American-style" refrigerators. Even generators, turned on during the ubiquitous and infuriating power outages, are being embraced as symbols of status ascription. Ironically, the annoying noise and dangerous fumes from the generators help to identify families with relatives abroad who have shipped the menacing electricity providers or sent the money used to purchase them from local stores that carry coveted but prohibitive foreign goods.

Whenever the sojourners make actual returns home they are able to assess firsthand how their presence through remittance is being conveyed and consequently revisit how they demonstrate their connections with their homelands. On vacation in 2005 to see family in Serakunde, Gambia, David Njie noticed that the Acura that he had sent for the family several years before devalued his standing in the society. Looking around he saw the SUVs and other vehicles that people he knew in America who were less prosperous than he was had sent for their relatives. Therefore, as soon as he returned to the United States, he made arrangements to ship his Mercedes-Benz to replace the Acura, while he got for himself a "lightly-used pre-owned Jaguar."[30] Similar stories of the ostentation of immigrant prosperity abound.

While long-lasting commodities like motor vehicles and generators are prominent indicators of the consequences of remittances, more ephemeral displays in spectacular commemoration of birth, marriage, and death are increasing in significance as remittance-enabled illustrations of transnational prosperity. Homeland birthday parties and engagement, wedding, and christening ceremonies are planned in consultation with relatives abroad so that, as much as possible, visits to the homeland are made to coincide with the festivities. Having in attendance prosperous-looking "sojourners" and their American children, conspicuous from their accents and mannerisms, brings much-appreciated pomp to the celebrations. While the presence of the foreign-resident relatives is valued, the cash and nonmonetary imports are more important in ensuring the desired high-society quality of the celebrations. The foreign contributions run the gamut: from money to rent fancy event facilities and top-of-the-line limousines to imported outfits for the bride, groom, and entire party, including the parents and other relatives. Even *aso ebi*, identical traditional outfits for close relatives and friends, have undergone some transnational transformations. By the dawn of the twenty-first century, imported *aso ebi* shoes, head gear, jewelry, and fabric from Europe, America, and the Middle East had become reliable gauges of the extent of the transnational connections of the celebrants. Even basic items like plates, napkins, and party favors are shipped to West Africa by relatives eager to earn the highest scores in the transnational connection competition.

In most West African societies the rites of passage continue after death. Landmarks in the journey from the time of death to reuniting with the ancestors are commemorated in rituals like the Seventh Day and Fortieth Day *Awujor* (feast), and such wake-keeping, memorial, funeral, and internment ceremonies as well as annual anniversaries of the deceased—have become some of the most grandiose displays of the outcomes of monetary and nonmonetary remittances. By the late 1990s, in numerous West African urban areas, overseas-supported death commemorations had become identifiable by the opulence of the casket, the American or European-made suit or shroud worn by the corpse, the outfits of the mourners, and the American or European-printed programs. Added to these markers, food and drink, just by their sheer quantity, but also because of their brands, spell out the extent to which a funeral or other ritual remembrance of the deceased is foreign-aided. Family members in America and other parts of the diaspora to as far away as Australia increasingly are involved in the active organization of funerals, with the result that the length of pre-serving corpses before burial has increased tremendously in order to accommodate planning within multiple sites across continents and oceans. Funerals, as morbid as they are, do serve as occasions for kin and friends dispersed in various locations of the diaspora to reaffirm continuing ties and a sense of belonging to a homeland community. In a pioneering study, geographers and economists Valentina Mazzu-cato, Mirjam Kabki, and Lothar Smith, looking at funerals in a village in the Ashanti region of Ghana, showed why funerals, as multisited events that influence multiple economies, should be seen partly as economic events and thus should be included in economic analyses of remittances and migration.[31]

Although Mazzucato, Kabki, and Smith found that funeral spend-ing supported various economic sectors in Ghana and across the globe, transnational funerals have been criticized as one of the symptoms of the excesses of remittance designed more to show off the prestige of the giver than for the benefit of the recipient. As remittances grow even more in significance as links in transnational networks, so have the debates around what they actually contribute to lasting structural devel-opment beyond conferring high lifestyle status on individuals and small groups of beneficiaries. While there is no denying that remittances have helped to alleviate poverty and stimulated certain sectors of the econo-mies of developing countries, questions about the extent of their over-all impact are valid. As many scholars of migration and development point out, remittances often lead to the further widening of economic disparities in some societies, as those who do not have families abroad may not benefit in sustainable ways.[32] This outcome is conveyed by a Sierra Leonean single mother who found that by 2008 it had become almost impossible for her to afford to rent what used to be standard "modern" housing because it had become common practice for prop-erty owners of such flats to demand in advance a whole year's rent paid in dollars. She laments, "The people who sign such rental agreements without blinking have families abroad who pay the rent. When will they realize that not all of us live in the dollar zone? Those of us who have no one in America or England have been banished to the Leone [Sierra Leonean currency] zone."[33]

Inequities like this one and their potential adverse consequences for national development are often cited as reasons to revisit how remittances are planned and managed. Internationally renowned mathematician, computer specialist, and eminent Nigerian American Dr. Philip Emegwali once cautioned that African immigrants must do more than send money home to relatives: "Money alone cannot eliminate poverty in Africa, because one million dollars is a number without intrinsic value."[34] To turn numbers to intrinsic value, West Africans in America have also approached remittances and other transnational networks from macro levels through the agendas and activities of a variety of collective entities. Collective remittances transferred by organizations for homeland causes seek to go beyond the micro level of family welfare to much more transformative aid that can contribute in substantive and tangible ways to sustainable development of whole communities and, desirably, a whole nation. By the beginning of the twenty-first century, most members of West African American communities had been introduced to the term "501(c)," a crucial American tax-related component of philanthropy. At the same time that they are sending money to individual relatives, many of the immigrants are actively involved in the work of their 501(c) philanthropy-designated organizations, most of which are the same as their ethnic, national, and alumni associations. Collective efforts have been geared to achieve structural fortification that would ensure substantive, deeply entrenched transformations. To categorize the legion of the mushrooming 501(c) West African causes, they roughly fall under the following: infrastructural development, health, and education.

The precarious collapse of basic infrastructure—roads, bridges, water and sewage systems—is an often raised topic for venting at the average West African American gathering. Little wonder, then, that the many ethnic associations especially have tailored collective remittances to address the infrastructure of the villages and towns in which they grew up and still have relatives. Among a host of examples, the United Bassa Organizations of the Americas illustrates this trend. In 2011, the group launched a two-year mini-project to build wells and pipes for safe drinking water and to construct sturdy roads to connect a refurbished market to sources of supplies and outlets for business. The project was designed as part of the effort to reconstruct the Grand Bassa County of the war-torn Republic of Liberia.

From malaria to cholera and from prenatal complications to high rates of infant and adult mortality, the perennial health crisis in West Africa and the whole continent is one of the dire global concerns of the twentieth and twenty-first centuries. Post–civil rights West Africans in America lived in and some even suffered severely from these systems. Hence they do not need official reports of the World Health Organization or similar institutions to convey the urgency for aid to improve health care in their former homes; their lived experiences and continuing ties with the homeland are enough motivation for individuals to join in collective efforts to alleviate the crisis. All the sources—newspapers, radio shows, association events and records—point to the vibrancy in collective health care projects among West African associations since the 1990s. Ironically, simultaneously as the homeland societies are feeling the void caused by the departure of nurses and doctors, they are receiving assistance from the diaspora, including from America, in the form of hospital equipment and supplies, medicine, and monetary and other contributions toward the building, repair, and expansion of clinics and hospitals. Associations formed by health care practitioners are at the forefront of this. For example, the National Association of Nigerian Nurses and the Ghanaian Nurses Association routinely send a variety of aid to clinics, hospitals, and community centers in both the rural and urban areas of Nigeria and Ghana. Nevertheless, the ethnic associations have also developed frameworks to assertively address the health care of their kin beyond small family units.

Concentrating especially in the often neglected rural areas encompassing the villages, ethnic associations, from the Yorubas to the Igbos, Hausas, Bassas, Krus, Krios, Fulas, and Ewes, just to mention a few, have contributed to the improvement of health care in their hometowns, in some cases joining forces with coethnic organizations in other parts of the diaspora, especially in Canada and Europe. The Asante Mampong Kontonkyi Association of New York/New Jersey/Connecticut offers a useful example of this trend. Teaming up with branches in Chicago, Toronto, and London, it launched a multiyear project to provide easy, cheap, and effective access to health care in the Mampong district in their Ghana homeland. Their efforts included huge shipments of medical equipment and medicine and transfers of money and building supplies for the construction of a children's ward at the Mampong District

Hospital. Kofi Adu, chairman of the association, echoes the emphasis of this analysis. Cataloging the association's efforts to develop the homeland, he notes, "This is a classic example of collective action in the age of globalization and transnationalism, where distance and physical borders are less significant and networks are becoming as important as tools for community economic and other development."[35]

Education has always been at the center of the migration story of West Africans. In the first half of the twentieth century, West African students who studied in Europe and America eagerly returned home to contribute to the shaping of evolving postcolonial curricula. Since the last quarter of the twentieth century the proportion of students returning home has dwindled drastically, but the resolve to parlay benefits of migration to educational development, if anything, has increased. While the various organizations have one form or another of educational agenda in their repertoire, by the 1990s a growth spurt of school alumni associations resulted in a grand educational advancement campaign that put transnational educational projects principally in the purview of the alumni associations. By 2012, although there had been no comprehensive study and accurate figures, by most accounts there were probably more than two hundred of these West African associations around the country.[36] The primary motivation and rationale for their formation were simple, as stated in the announcement of the launching of the Isesa Grammer School (Nigerian high school) Alumni Association in 2007: "As we continue to count our blessings and successes in our respective endeavors, nothing is more honorable or gratifying than a commitment to giving back to the alma mater that nurtured and gave us the foundation for these successes."[37]

By the end of the twentieth century and the beginning of the twenty-first century, due to the legion of African postcolonial problems, including wars, the vast majority of these alma maters, which had shaped the migrants, were in dire straits, making the necessity to provide aid from the diaspora more urgent than ever. The associations are involved in similar projects: shipments of school furniture, books, pens, and other supplies. They have set up numerous scholarships, equipped libraries and laboratories, and established ongoing funds to maintain buildings and other school infrastructure. By the end of the first decade of the twenty-first century, many of the alumni associations had begun to insist on establishing projects geared toward substantial structural change instead of concentrating on small, cosmetic changes. To this end, increasingly alumni association branches in the United States are teaming up with branches around U.S. cities and states, in Canada, and in European cities, which have also witnessed a contemporaneous surge of activities on behalf of homeland schools.

This kind of intercity, interstate, and transatlantic amalgamation guaranteed robust coffers to support gutsy, long-lasting projects. In 2010, the Lagos African Church Grammar School Alumni Association kicked off a campaign to build a multimillion niara (Nigerian currency) building to house a fully equipped state-of-the art science laboratory. The St. Christopher Catholic School Alumni Association developed a five-year plan in 2006 to undertake massive renovations of some of the main school buildings. The project demonstrated foresight for structural impact by its inclusion of a blueprint for contributing to the reconstruction of feeder roads that students and teachers must use to get to the school as well as replacing pipes in the decaying water system surrounding the school. The members of the association in America, Canada, and Europe agreed that they were eager to see their school and Kakata, Liberia, where it is located, soar beyond the glory days when they were students before emigrating. The Prince of Wales Alumni Association decided to augment their computer lab project with a substantive solar power installation, which was seen as a realistic strategy for ensuring power for the school computers in a country where months-long power outages had become routine. These are a few examples of the long-term solutions-orientated projects that most of the associations are beginning to adopt. It must be noted that by 2012 many of these big projects were still evolving and some alumni associations had scaled back as soon as some of the projects proved to be too ambitious and incongruous to their projected revenues in the face of uncertain memberships and the occasional breakdown of alliances between branches.

Not only had the alumni and other associations begun to insist on structural change, they also demanded concrete interactions with and accountability from the beneficiaries of their aid. Gone are the days when the small number of mostly transient students and scholars were content with representation by their embassies and consulates. In the pre-1980s, such temporary West African communities relied on the occasional briefings from the embassies and the annual embassy invitations for the official celebrations of independence and other national homeland holidays. On the contrary, by the close of the twentieth century, the members of the now permanent West African American communities wanted more tangible connections with the homeland to which, unlike the earlier cohorts, they were most likely not going to physically remigrate, but in which they were still heavily invested. Consequently, visits of school principals, teachers, heads of departments, and incumbent and aspiring elected officials and government appointees had become regular notations in the associational calendars of the various communities.

In the 1990s, a new pattern began to develop whereby those seeking political offices in the homeland traveled to America to meet with diaspora communities to fund-raise, but also, importantly, to describe, explain, and be grilled about their manifestos and visions for the nation. Outposts or satellite branches of homeland political parties and organizations sprang up and began to lead the way in arranging what amounted to extensions of political rallies but held in the United States. For instance, in recent years, Cape Verdean presidential candidates routinely have included southern New England on their campaign trails. In addition to in-person appearances at planned town hall meetings, the politicians and their representatives give radio interviews, chat online, and submit to ethnic newspapers campaign advertisements and op-ed pieces about their plans and qualifications. The political visitors run the gamut—from city council to presidential elections candidates and elected presidents. Olusegun Obasanjo (Nigeria), Ellen Johnson Sirleaf (Liberia), Jorge Carlos de Almeida Fonseca (Cape Verde), Atta Mills (Ghana), and Ernest Koroma (Sierra Leone) are among the presidents who visited several communities of their nationals across the United States just in the first decade of the twenty-first century. Events around their visits were well publicized, well attended, and reported profusely in the West African subculture ethnic media.

Visits and other interactions with homeland custodians of development do not always proceed without controversies, tensions, and misgivings. Divisions and explosive confrontations develop around accusations of corruption, incompetence, and ethnic or tribal partiality.

Altercations that erupt at meetings and celebrations are reported in the ethnic press and discussed in small gatherings at homes of individuals and restaurants and other businesses. Some of the visiting politicians confront the diaspora belligerence head on. Take the example of the fiasco surrounding the planned visit of Chris N. Ngige, governor of Anambra State of Nigeria. According to the amalgamated group of Anambra State associations in North America, the governor had agreed to be prominently featured in the program of the November 2003 National Convention of the Anambra State Associations–USA. It was possible for the governor to do this as he had planned to stop to see relatives in the United States on his way back to Nigeria after a medical checkup and visiting with relatives in the United Kingdom. Eventually, however, very close to the time of the convention, the governor backed out. Freedom and Justice International, which was the intermediary that made the supposed agreement between the governor and the convention planners, threatened to sue the governor for breach of contract. The group took out a half-page newspaper advertisement that read, "Governor Chris N. Ngige, Saint, Conman or Crook?"[38] Firing back, the governor's office across the Atlantic explained that the governor did not have an agreement with the group and that he changed his mind when he suspected that the group acting on behalf of the Anambra Associations was controversial and had no stake in his state. All this was explained in a feature article in one of the Nigerian newspapers with the headline, "Go to Court!, Ngige Tells US Group."[39] This is one of many examples of the exchange of accusations and criticisms that periodically stemmed from requests and demands that developers of the homeland participate concretely in specified initiatives of the American immigrant communities.

Scathing skepticism about the efficacy of the physical presence of homeland leaders sometimes comes from within the immigrant communities. For example, in early 2012 several Ghanaian associations in Worcester, Massachusetts, were urging members to be involved in both presidential elections—Ghana's and America's. To that end, the Worcester branch of the Ghana Independent People's Party invited the party's candidate, Kofi Akpaloo, to speak at a town hall meeting on the party's platform: "Putting People's Lives First Through Technology." While many applauded and even contributed financially to the campaign, some took Akpaloo to task during the Q&A and continued the interrogation through social media. The following comment of a blogger is typical of the kind of misgivings expressed about political transnationalism: "Presidential candidates don't talk to the people who really need help . . . the village people between Kumasi and Accra where the roads are terrible. But rather they talk to Ghanaians abroad who are busy working their doubles [as in double shifts] and the elections don't affect them. If I lived in a village in Ghana with no electricity or pure water and sanitation I will be pissed off by these crooked politicians forcing to connect their home politics to our hard earned dollars in America."[40] As irritated as this blogger and others may have been, the reality is that West African elections do affect those who live abroad mainly by how they affect the relatives, friends, and institutions to which they are firmly tied.

The strong ties between homeland and diaspora are secured by the facilitators—phone communication and shipping and money transfer companies. The cell phone, which performs many more tasks than transmission of voice conversations—text, email, Internet, and still photography and video—is crucial for the many transactions that connect families across cities, states, and nations. From conveying routine "checking-up" conversations to arranging emigration, funerals, weddings, shipments, and money transfers, the smart phone is indeed glue in transnational networks. In almost every business in the communities, the glaring display of a wide array of telephone cards and discounted phone carrier advertisements affirms the centrality of the smart phone in the viability of the communities as transnational societies.

The proliferation of shipping companies owned and operated by West Africans is one of the indications of the intensification of transnational ties. As the twentieth century came to a close, West Africans in America were sending volumes of goods to families and institutions at home. Businesspeople and others captured the opportunities by either forming their own shipping companies or serving as middlemen for large American shipping enterprises. Small to medium-size bulk goods like phones, laptops, and small printers, clothing, and food are packed in barrels, which are then loaded into massive shipping containers along with large items like motor vehicles, building materials, and generators. The growing importance of shipping companies as facilitators of transnationalism is manifested in the increasing advertisements for shipping services in the ethnic media, at local businesses, and as part of community activities. Even the barrels in the garages and on the porches of the immigrants in the United States, as well as those (now used to store water and other necessities) on the verandas and compounds of families at home depict the new face of transnational maritime connections.

No consideration of facilitators of transnational connections would be complete without some attention to money transfer companies. While it is important to note that many immigrants still use informal networks like asking family and friends traveling to the homeland to physically carry cash home to relatives, the money transfer business has prospered rapidly since the 1990s because of immigrant remittances, including those to West Africa. One of the first indicators of the place of money transfer companies is their marked presence in the public activities of the immigrant communities. From Independence Day celebrations to fund-raising events of numerous associations, Western Union and MoneyGram are prominently acknowledged as sponsors. But at the same time, to many such events these companies send representatives to advertise the businesses, even as they distribute a variety of souvenirs that carry their logo, contact numbers, websites, and tips for sending money home.

By 2000, the money transfer business was massive and the competition fierce.[41] The major companies openly courted West Africans, like they did other immigrants. They reduced transfer fees and extended other incentives like prizes and scholarships. But for all their "generosity" Western Union and MoneyGram could not forestall the competition that they began to face from West African–owned companies. Matlababoul Fawzayan, a Senegalese American company based in Harlem, is one of the businesses that has devised ways to bypass the big money transfer companies. In the 1990s it came up with a system whereby immigrants in New York and elsewhere in the United States could pay at their stores for appliances like refrigerators, television sets, and DVD players to be picked up from their warehouses in Dakar, often on the same day. West African–based banks also tried to get their bite of the money transfer pie. The Banque de l'Habitat du Sénégal opened branches in New York and handled direct transfers and other forms of remittance, thus undercutting the business of the established money transfer companies. In 2006, the United Bank of Africa, based in Nigeria, agreed to a partnership with MoneyGram to ensure "improved money transfer services to Nigeria."[42]

Establishment of West African–owned money transfer companies directly challenged Western Union and MoneyGram. In July 2003, a group of Ghanaian businessmen and -women in Ghana and the United States formed Money Systems Cash Transfer. It wooed the Ghanaian and other immigrant communities using tactics similar to those of the established giants. As the customer relations manager for Georgia, Emmanuel Gyapong, boasted, this new company pledged to invest in associational life as much as MoneyGram and Western Union. And, indeed, in September 2007 it joined those two megacorporations as one of the main sponsors of the Atlanta Okuapemman Odwira Ohum Festival commemorated by the Atlanta-Canada Okuapemman Association. Money Systems went directly after the mammoth transfer companies, pointing out that the company was native to the core. It was owned by Ghanaians who speak the languages and understand the cultures. Gyapong unabashedly appealed to coethnic patronage, emphasizing, "We know Ghana. . . . We Ghanaians have to understand and cultivate the habit of spending with each other. If Money Systems makes money, it remains in Africa. If Money System works, it works for all of us as Africans."[43]

Literally on the same page as the report on the indigenous qualities of the newly established Money Systems is an article with the bold headline, "WESTERN UNION ANNOUNCES LAUNCH OF AFRICA CASH GIVEAWAY."[44] From July 30 through October 31, 2007, Western Union gave away $500 every day to one lucky winner. Every money transfer to Africa, excluding Egypt and Sudan, included an entry in the sweepstakes. The Africa Cash Giveaway ended with a $25,000 grand prize. Around the same time, MoneyGram was running its own sweepstakes, headlined in their advertisements with the caption, "Win $75,000 to Buy a House for Mom."[45] With such incentives and massive established networks in American and West African cities, Western Union and MoneyGram continue to be at the forefront of the business of remitting money. Yet the appearance of West African–owned companies as noteworthy competition speaks to the rapidly increasing significance of money transfer companies as key parts of transnational networks.

The (New) Diaspora in West Africa: Embrace and Resentment

In 2007, a number of people from specific ethnic groups and rural and urban communities around Sierra Leone met in a conference facility in Freetown to discuss trajectories for postwar development. They went around the room introducing themselves and identifying what local community or ethnic group they were representing. When it was his turn, one man in attendance said his name and then declared, "I am from The Diaspora." The whole room reacted, some people rolling their eyes, some struggling to stifle their laughter, and others clearly astounded by the bold affirmation of what sounded like a new ethnicity.[46] Indeed, by that time West Africans in the diaspora had become so physically and virtually connected to the homeland that they had begun to generate and demand recognition as an entity that was distinct but not foreign. From their conspicuous presence during vacations and long-term relocation to their contributions to development projects, West Africans of the new diaspora have become an imperative that even governments have begun to put on their legislative agendas.

"Our nationals abroad" is a conspicuous group in all the major urban areas, from Accra to Dakar to Monrovia, Praia, Conakry, and Banjul. Even beyond the urban areas, the visitors from abroad are now more recognized in the villages and other rural areas. They stand out. They exude Western lifestyles and prosperity. The locals of almost every major West African city have a label for these returnees who are now of the foreign land. In Freetown they are known as JCs (*Jus cam*, Krio for newly arrived). JCs are easily spotted by the towel around their necks to wipe the sweat from the African heat; the bottled water they drink exclusively; their children tagging along, speaking in American or European accents; and the dropping of American and European city names in conversations. In Ghana they are known as Joe Yankee or more commonly as American Burger. Burger is a term first used by Ghanaians to describe compatriots visiting from Germany, mostly from Hamburg, in the 1970s and 1980s. By the 1990s, the use of the term had broadened to include Ghanaians in the United States. By 2000, the

American Burgers had emerged as the most affluent nationals abroad. As a Ghanaian gossip newspaper reported, "Gone are the days when the European Burgers carried the day. Despite the monetary value of the Euro and the pound over the dollar, European Burgers are just too poor to compete with American Burgers."[47] And in Gbongan, Nigeria, the three hundred members who traveled from New York and New Jersey to attend their pastor's "intercontinental" funeral in his hometown noted with glee the preferential treatment given to the American Nigerians: "The USA group was assigned the nicest tents of the huge tents for the over 5,000 mourners."[48]

Increasingly, the presence of American West Africans in the homeland is becoming more visibly permanent. One major reason for this is the rash of real estate investments since the late 1990s. West African immigrants from a large spectrum send money home to relatives and contractors to build houses that attest to their American prosperity. Even though they talk about permanently relocating to live in these homes, more often they rent them out. By 2010, real estate and investment companies from West Africa had begun to venture into West African immigrant communities in the heart of American cities to promote this form of transnationalism. For example, on May 12, 2007, Nigerians living in New York, New Jersey, Connecticut, Rhode Island, Massachusetts, Pennsylvania, Washington, D.C., Maryland, and Virginia gathered at the Helmsley Hotel in New York to listen to representatives of a preeminent Nigerian financial institution talk about "Economic Pie-ticipation," an initiative launched to give Nigerians in the United States the opportunity to hold assets at home.[49]

Traveling to Africa to work on the development of the continent is not a new phenomenon for the diaspora. In the old diaspora, from Booker T. Washington to Marcus Garvey, diasporic blacks proposed and campaigned for the transfer of diasporic expertise. Immediately after independence, several American blacks, most notably W. E. B. Du Bois, actually relocated to West Africa to contribute to the postcolonial building project. But as Maya Angelou correctly analyzes, they were expatriates.[50] By the twenty-first century, members of the new diaspora were exhibiting the same sense of obligation to African development and a desire to work on site. West African governments encouraged their nationals abroad with specific, much-needed expertise to return home. Confident of the huge dividends from their training and exposure in the United States, some immigrants have willingly accepted government jobs in the homeland. For example, Mrs. Otiti-Alugbon, who accepted a position at the Health Management Board of Oyo State (in Nigeria), "vowed to use her New York connections to help the state."[51] Governments are not the major employers of the returnee new diaspora workers. Some returnees are self-employed, having launched their own businesses. But the majority are employed by private, mostly transnational companies and nongovernmental organizations (NGOs). Interestingly, the contract letters of many of the NGOs and transnational enterprises refer to the new hires as expatriates. Indeed, most of them are naturalized Americans, so technically they are expats. But as most would readily admit, they are living and working around family and friends and in some cases in the same towns where they grew up. No doubt they are a new breed of diaspora expatriates—they are homegrown.

Are homegrown expatriates superior to the loyal, hardworking local nationals who maintained an unbroken permanent presence? This question is being raised and debated in many West African countries, as the implications of the presence of the homegrown expatriate are becoming clearer. Some locals have begun to complain that the nationals abroad, who tend to get the jobs more easily, are in reality not better qualified. Moreover, their physical presence is guaranteed only during stable times. In Sierra Leone and Liberia, especially, where years of civil wars wrought tremendous hardships on their citizens, the returnees have been seen as opportunists desiring to get their hands on the provisions for post-civil-war reconstruction. In Sierra Leone, they are labeled disparagingly as *sugar yoni* (Krio for sugar ants).

Whether they are seen as opportunists or as better qualified, even if homegrown expatriates, the roles and place of these and other nationals abroad have become salient issues in postindependence West Africa. Family remittances, institutional philanthropy, real estate and other investments, the stimulation of economies through vacations and other short-term visits, and the transfer of professional expertise ensure that the vitality of such diasporic input has become integral to homeland development. As a result, governments of many West African nations have begun to pointedly address ways to cultivate official relations with their nationals abroad, especially in Europe and North America. Ghana, Nigeria, and Sierra Leone extended their government divisions to include a division for diaspora concerns and the Republic of Cape Verde has a recent initiative, Dias De Cabo Verde—Diaspora for Development of Cape Verde.

For their part, many groups in the diaspora have capitalized on such government recognition to make specific requests about the formalization of their transnational ties. Radio shows and ethnic newspapers report on numerous delegations to the West African countries to meet with government officials, sometimes in the stature of the president and vice president. Dual citizenship and voting by proxy from the United States emerged as two major considerations. For example, the government of Cape Verde now defines a Cape Verdean as someone born in the islands or having a parent or grandparent born there, while members of the diaspora community can vote in Cape Verdean national elections and have had representation in the National Assembly.

Local and diaspora newspapers are replete with the deliberations in the houses of representatives in various West African countries over these issues. After many heated debates, the Ghana House of Parliament passed the Citizenship Act of 2002 approving dual citizenship. At the end of that same year, diaspora citizens, mostly from the United States, Canada, and the United Kingdom, gathered in Freetown, Sierra Leone, for the Diaspora Homecoming Conference. Dual citizenship was the top topic of debate. One of the staunchest supporters participating in the conference was the Ghanaian high commissioner to Sierra Leone, Cabral Blay Amhire. He shared Ghana's experience and touted the positive results: "Dual citizenship encourages citizens to return home while enabling them to use their unique influence as citizens of Western nations to bring much needed development to their native countries."[52] The high commissioner and other impassioned proponents did not convince Sierra Leone lawmakers in 2000. After a series of more heated debates, the Sierra Leone Parliament passed the Dual Citizenship Act in September 2006. In 2009 the Nigerian House of Representatives appointed a Committee on Diaspora Affairs, developed a Diaspora Data Base, approved dual citizenship, and began to plan for voting abroad.

By the beginning of the second decade of the twenty-first century, all the West African countries either had adopted dual citizenship laws or were seriously debating them. And this time dual citizenship was not the symbolic variant that had been negotiated for native-born African Americans whose journeys to the motherland were charged with sentimentality. Rather, this new wave of conversations and actions has been about formalizing the links between home and America for the West African–born diasporic citizen, whose real ties to family, school and other institutions, ethnicity, and hometown beg for such official dual citizenship more than ever before. As the delegate to the 2007 conference in Freetown may well have been trying to convey, "The Diaspora" in many senses has become a new West African ethnicity.

5

More Than Black

Resistance and Rapprochement

Being black made the transition from Africa to America
extremely difficult because it introduced another complex
series of boundaries. In a racially divided country, it isn't
enough for an immigrant to know how to float in the mainstream. You have to know how to retreat to your margin,
where to place your hyphen.
—Ghanaian American Meri Nana-Ama Danquah, "Life as
an Alien"

West Africans, like other black immigrants, have adapted and assimi-
lated in three main domains—within the reconfigured African ethnicities, within the milieu of African Americans, and within mainstream
America. Unlike their predecessors of the period of the initial making
of the Atlantic World, the experiences of the newcomers have not been
regulated by the blatant oppression of the slave trade and slavery. Indeed,
in contrast, they are the beneficiaries of the dividends of the civil rights
movement since the post-1965 wave came to a country that was in the
process of remarkable change, largely due to the modern struggle for
racial equality. The complicated face of race in the United States nonetheless has been lost on many of the new African diaspora, who instead
see only a postracial America. Of the many immigrant success stories
that this study has tracked, whether residents of Boston, Chicago, D.C.,
Houston, or even Atlanta—home to Martin Luther King, Jr. and a city
with such a strong civil rights consciousness—when asked what they
see as the keys to their success, those interviewed rarely acknowledged
the role of African Americans in the civil rights movement as paving
the way. As Patrick Grant has observed, when it comes to race and

racism, black immigrants have arrived in the United States "with their eyes wide shut."[1] And, indeed, the eyes of African immigrants are even more tightly closed than those of their West Indian counterparts, who while still somewhat resistant are much more likely to give recognition to pathbreaking civil rights initiatives, largely because of their own legacy of Caribbean leaders, such as Marcus Garvey, Claude McKay, and Stokely Carmichael, in this cause. Many West African newcomers simply have no idea of the intricacies of American race relations and are blind to the pivotal role of the history of civil rights protests in facilitating their own adaptation. Moreover, if most in the new African diaspora do not acknowledge the direct foundational role of the historic push for racial equality in easing their incorporation into American society, they are even less aware of the ways that the post–World War II fight to eradicate institutional racism also fueled the momentum that resulted in a more liberal and nondiscriminatory immigration policy. Amid the mid-1960s era of monumental civil rights legislation, Congress passed the 1965 Immigration Reform Bill, a shift in policy that addressed the racism and ethnocentrism of national quotas and led to wide-scale voluntary immigration from the African continent in the first place.

Long before there was a significant settlement of new West Africans in the United States, a Pan-African perspective that emphasized the strong ties between continental Africans and the diaspora began to be expressed. In the late nineteenth century, when ruthless geopolitical agreements were made at the Berlin Conference to carve up the continent of Africa into partitioned areas under the control of the various European powers, notable leaders of the African diaspora began to put forth an internationalist black politics based on notions of a shared sociocultural lineage and a long history of suffering the exploitations of systematic racial inequality. Spearheaded by W. E. B. Du Bois, who articulated a vision of self-determination for black Africa writ large, this was a discourse of mutual identification that encompassed an incisive grasp of their predicament: whether colonial subjects or disenfranchised Americans, the pain of mutilation was a collective, transatlantic phenomenon. Booker T. Washington also recognized the deep-seated global interconnections. In 1909 when he was advocating for improved diplomatic relations and increased assistance to the struggling nation of Liberia, he made the following call for unity:

There is . . . a tie which few white men can understand, which binds the American Negro to the African Negro; which unites the black man of Brazil and the black man of Liberia; which is constantly drawing into closer relations all the scattered African peoples whether they are in the old world or the new.

There is not only the tie of race, which is strong in any case, but there is the bond of colour, which is specially important in the case of the black man. It is this common badge of colour, for instance, which is responsible for the fact that whatever contributes, in any degree to the progress of the American Negro, contributes to the progress of the African Negro, and to the Negro in South America and the West Indies. When the African Negro succeeds, it helps the American Negro. When the African Negro fails, it hurts the reputation and the standing of the Negro in every part of the world.[2]

By the mid-twentieth century the transatlantic connection became even more definitive as anticolonialist movements on the continent inspired the civil rights movement and especially by the late 1960s, the militancy of the turn to black power in the United States. Conversely those fighting for independence in Africa were influenced by the struggle for freedom and racial equality taking place on American soil. To Kwame Nkrumah, who had been educated in the United States and who led Ghana to independence from Britain in 1957, becoming the first sub-Saharan African country to overthrow colonial rule, the links between the civil rights uprisings in America and the sovereignty movements in Africa were inextricable. But Nkrumah's vision of Pan-African unity in the freedom struggle was short-lived as a 1966 coup swept him out of power and a more nationalistic Cold War politics took its place. Nonetheless, in some other sectors, Pan-African momentum lived on through the activities of revolutionary figures like Sekou Touré of Guinea, with whom Nkrumah collaborated in exile, and Amilcar Cabral of Guinea-Bissau and the Cape Verde Islands, who led the movement for liberation from Portuguese colonialism and who before Nkrumah was ousted had gotten permission from him to set up training camps in neighboring Ghana.

Despite the commonalities and an empathetic thread laced through their shared legacy, the history of the relationship between native and foreign-born blacks in the United States has often been an uneasy one, filled with ambivalence on both sides.[3] Fueled by misconceptions and pernicious stereotypes and layered with distrust, cultural differences have often superseded alliances based on color. Immigrants typically attempt to assert their cultural distinctiveness, foster ethnic solidarity, and resist identification with what has been the most subordinated sector of American society, while African Americans may exhibit bitterness at the perceived preferential treatment accorded the foreigners, regarding them as a competitive threat in an economy where resources available to racial minorities are scarce.[4] As Meri Nana-Ama Danquah recalled,

> At the time of my emigration, the early 1970s, Washington, D. C., a predominantly black city, was awash in a wave of Afrocentricity. Dashikis draped brown shoulders and the black-fisted handle of an Afro pick proudly stuck out in many a back pants pocket. However, despite all the romanticizing and rhetoric about unity and brotherhood, there was a curtain of sheer hostility hanging between black Americans and black Africans.[5]

The acrimony has been magnified by the juxtaposition of immigrant-origin blacks—first those from the Caribbean and more recently arrivals from Africa—as model minorities, emphasizing particularly their educational achievements but, in the process, making sure to call attention by contrast to the vulnerabilities of the native-born population. Heightened by pockets of persistent poverty and bleak urban conditions in the black community, distinctions of social class have factored into the tensions between the foreign and native-born. Yet it is useful to remember that such intraethnic dynamics have been fairly common to the process of immigration and adaptation, past and present. For example, when Jews from Eastern Europe began streaming into the United States in large numbers at the end of the nineteenth century, the more established German Jewish population who preceded them as settlers in an earlier wave were often less than welcoming to the newer arrivals, protective of the gains they had already achieved in the United States and embarrassed by what they saw as the old-country ways of the newcomers. Thus, to presume that long-standing African Americans, whose ancestry may well date back to seventeenth-century America, should automatically embrace, for example, Ghanaian arrivals of the twenty-first century just because both originally hailed from the African continent is rather illogical. Nonetheless, adding to the divide has been a simmering resentment whereby some African Americans hold contemporary Africans accountable for their forebears' role in selling their compatriots into slavery. As one of the Senegalese immigrants interviewed by Linda Beck in her study of West Africans Muslims in New York put it, African Americans are "foreign averse."[6] Usually, these dynamics get even more complex as the second generation of black immigrants begins to assimilate and to reshape their identities within the larger American and black American context.

Thus, West African newcomers, like their Caribbean counterparts, tend to initially feel detached from the black community, and very few forge close relationships with African Americans. James Burkes, who was the founding director of African Marketplace, Inc., an international cultural organization for people of African descent in Los Angeles, characterized the separation in this way:

> Black Americans who visit Africa are trying to get back home and connect with something. It is the land, it is the spirit, it is the ancestors, it is family, and the idea of being able to identify with Africa. By contrast, for African immigrants, the majority that I've engaged are here to strengthen their own outlook for economic purposes. I don't think I have ever met an African who has told me that they are here to connect with African Americans.[7]

In addition, some West Africans resist the label of "black" because, among other things, they see it as eclipsing their unique cultural identities and, furthermore, they arrived with preconceived pejorative ideas about this population that can manifest itself as disdain or arrogance toward them. Indeed, some West Africans, especially among the second generation, have started to call themselves "American African" in lieu of the term "African American."[8] And in a rather awkwardly phrased variation of the label, in his unsuccessful run for Congress several years ago, Peter Idusogie, a Nigerian American living in Minnesota, utilized the term "Africans of American citizenship."[9] At the same time, underlining the rift, some of the American-born descendants of slavery who come from a strident legacy of black pride, sometimes known as the "civil rights generation," have refused to include the African new-comers under the rubric of "black" in any case. For them being black is a badge of honor that they are not ready to bestow on the newest Afri-can Americans whom they believe to be undeserving of the label since their ancestors did not suffer directly through the atrocities of slavery and Jim Crow segregation.[10]

One local journalist covering Washington State's Puget Sound region where increasing numbers of African immigrants have settled graphi-cally summed up the disconnect between the foreign-born newcom-ers and the African American population by titling his feature on the subject "Black and African: As Different as Black and White." More-over, the sense of alienation was mutual, with one of the African immi-grants interviewed declaring, "We have the same skin color with Afri-can Americans, but nothing else together," while on the other side an African American respondent contended that "our relationship is built on misconceptions. . . . They don't want to deal with us, and we don't want to deal with them."[11] Similarly, across the country, a report on the interactions of African Americans and Africans in the Bronx referred to the dynamics as a "chilly coexistence," while a study exploring the relationships between African immigrants from Ghana and Nigeria and African Americans (that also included participants from the Carib-bean) conducted at several university sites in the D.C.-Maryland met-ropolitan area, demonstrated that even when there was positive con-tact, it was a shallow cordiality at best.[12] Almost all the respondents to a 2009 national market survey of African consumers agreed with the statement "Africans and African Americans differ greatly," with half asserting that they thought the two groups were completely different. The New Yorkers who answered the questionnaire perceived the schism as the most pronounced. Among the influences those surveyed overall gave to explain the divergence were their connections to their countries of origin, the absence of a history of slavery and discrimination, the emphasis they placed on education, and the fact that they came to the United States by choice.[13]

In *Disintegration: The Splintering of Black America*, Eugene Robinson parses the breach in this way:

These are generalizations, but they are true: Native-born African Americans often envy the immigrants their deep historical knowledge and heritage, and immigrants often look down on the native-born for their rootlessness. These deep and seldom-expressed differences over identity, I believe, may underlie the shallower complaints that the two groups voice about each other. The native-born say that the immigrants are arrogant and the immigrants say that the native-born have no pride in themselves.[14]

For example, several years ago, a mid-January issue of *Africans Abroad*, one of the leading publications of the new African diaspora, included an article titled "Remembering Martin Luther King, Jr." that appeared to finally demonstrate some recognition of the positive role of the civil rights movement in the lives of African immigrants. Not so. Rather the reader is immediately confronted by a subhead that only furthers many of the damaging stereotypes held about the native-born: "Remember Perpetual Welfare, Culture of Dependency, Laziness and Black on Black Crimes Are Not Part of Martin Luther King's Dream!"[15]

Constructing, maintaining, reconstructing, and making sense of identities have always been important processes in the black American experience. Throughout American history black leaders and organizations have had to tackle the questions of who they are and what to do about self-identification and imposed labels. When in the late 1980s Jesse Jackson called for blacks to embrace the "more dignified" term of African American, many of those who answered his call concurred with him that there was power in the label, which signified protest, a reminder that their ancestors suffered and survived slavery. But with the influx of Africans of the new diaspora, some of the supporters of Jackson's African American terminology began to urge a reconsideration of the label in order to grasp its new implications. John McWhorter, in a *Los Angeles Times* article titled "Why I'm Black, Not African American," emphasized that modern America was now home to "millions" of immigrants who were born in Africa, so "it's time we descendants of slaves brought to the United States let go of the term 'African American' and go back to calling themselves Black—with a capital B."[16]

Yet one advocate for African immigrants who has lived in the United States for over twenty years has protested, "But I am African and I am an American citizen; am I not African-American? . . . The census is claiming me as an African-American, if I walk down the streets, white people see me as an African-American. Yet African-Americans are saying, 'You are not one of us.' So I ask myself, in this country, how do I define myself?"[17]

In trying to solve the riddle of identity after twenty years in the United States, Kenyan writer Mukoma Wa Ngugi reflected on the question of whether this was the story of being African in America or African American. He spoke of "African foreigner privilege," positing the theory that those in the new African diaspora have experienced race differently from their black predecessors. Racism toward African immigrants has been largely expressed as condescension and, as such, has been more benign than the threatening, often virulent forms that their native-born counterparts have had to endure over many generations. Ngugi suggested that "racism wears a smile when meeting an African; it glares with hostility when meeting an African American."[18] Different, too, have been the ways that most Africans position themselves with regard to their racial identities. Even those who have aligned themselves with African Americans most often still privilege their ethnicity or nationality as their primary group attachment. Moreover, for many West Africans there really is no contradiction in simultaneously identifying in terms of both race and ethnicity.

Bridging the Divide

In the religious arena, West African Muslims sometimes find it difficult to interact with African Americans of the same faith. The former consider the brand of Islam of the latter watered down and excessively tailored to their long experience of inequality in America, while African Americans may find the language barrier of the primarily Francophone Muslim worshippers and their emphasis on communal ties prohibitive. An exception to the disassociation of the civil rights movement with the concerns of recent West African immigrants, however, as well as an example of unity between the foreign and native-born black populations is the dynamics surrounding New York's annual Cheikh Amadou Bamba Day parade. Since 1988 when David Dinkins, then president of the Borough of Manhattan, who was to become the first (and to date) only African American mayor of New York, designated July 28 as the day to honor Muslim spiritual leader and anticolonial activist Cheikh Amadou Bamba Mbacké, the Senegalese founder of the Murid Sufi Brotherhood, the gathering has drawn hundreds of celebrants and culminates more than two weeks of commemorative events. Indeed, Ousmane Oumar Kane, a scholar of the religious practices of the Senegalese diaspora in New York, has labeled the period between mid-July and mid-August in the city "Murid Month" because of the great flurry of cultural activities, visiting spiritual leaders, and resources mobilized at this time of year.[19] While most of the participants are West African Muslim immigrants, African Americans also take part. Indeed, one of the central aims of the parade itself has been to underscore a shared African identity as the Senegalese and African American pilgrims march together through the streets of Harlem in this very public display of unanimity. Oral interviews with participants confirm that the inclusiveness of both foreign and native-born Muslims that Bamba Day activities represent stands as a highlight of the occasion.[20]

Furthermore, as Kane has pointed out and as Zain Abdullah's ethnographic study of the festivities has demonstrated, a concerted effort has been made to connect the teachings of Cheikh Bamba to the nonviolent resistance strategy that has been the hallmark of civil rights protest, thereby unifying the new West African and long-standing African American populations in their understanding of racial oppression as well. Abdullah draws attention to a banner that marchers held at a recent parade, exemplifying the Murid perspective on race. Quoting Cheikh Bamba but echoing civil rights rhetoric, it read "OUR BLACK-NESS SHOULD NOT BE AN OBSTACLE TO OUR KNOWLEDGE AND OUR PERFECTION. ALL MEN WERE CREATED EQUAL."[21] Abdullah noted that some Murids believe that while in London Gandhi had been exposed to the writings of Cheikh Bamba and since Martin Luther King, Jr. was, in turn, so influenced by Gandhi, an indirect link can then be made crediting the earlier African visionary with shaping modern civil rights leadership:

> The suggestion that a Black African Muslim saint, rather than the Indian sage Gandhi, is responsible for key civil rights ideas modifies this crucial aspect of Black history. Such a proposition turns the foundation of

a Black Christian-based movement on its head, asserting instead that its
origin is African and Muslim.[22]

Similarly, Kane points to another parade banner displaying an excerpt
from a Cheikh Bamba text that further affirms a position of black racial
identity: "Let not my being of the blacks keep you from reading my
books, because the black skin does not cause foolishness and misunder-
standing."[23] Kane goes on to suggest another way that many see Cheikh
Bamba as in accordance with the principles of nonviolence since when
the Cheikh was finally released after suffering thirty-three long years in
exile, he emerged choosing forgiveness rather than retaliation against
those who had imprisoned him.[24] As further evidence of a connection
between the two spiritual traditions, Abdullah also observed that nearly
all of the neighborhood restaurants owned by African Muslims have a
photo of the Christian Martin Luther King, Jr. hanging prominently on
the wall, indicating that the inspiration symbolized by King's message
of racial equality and the dream of opportunity trumps identification
with him as guiding religious spirit.[25]

When the Senegalese Muslims first began to settle in Harlem in the
early 1980s, they were welcomed by Imam Tariq, the leader of the large
African American Malcolm Shabazz Mosque originally founded by
Malcolm X and located in the heart of what would become Little Senegal. He would also regularly invite visiting Senegalese spiritual leaders
to lead the congregation in prayer. And even though the relationship of
the mosque to the immigrant worshippers has at times been rocky—
after Imam Tariq's death in the early 1990s, relations cooled when his
successor proved to be less hospitable to the foreign-born members—
the majority of religious events and festivals organized by Senegalese
Sufi groups in New York are still held in the main prayer room of the
Malcolm Shabazz. Thus, the early legacy of embrace of the West African newcomers has prevailed.

Of the various expressions of the Islamic faith, the Murid Brother-
hoods have fostered one of the strongest bonds between African and
African American Muslims in the United States. African Americans
have frequented the first Murid house in Brooklyn since it was established in the 1980s and continue to be active followers of Muridism
today. Beck's research confirms an evolving link between the foreign

and native-born black populations, although far from seamless. The West African immigrants would rather interact with African American Muslims than with the members of the other immigrant Muslim communities residing in the city who are primarily of Arabic and South Asian origins, even though the numbers are greater and they share the same set of religious beliefs. Not only do West Africans have more daily contact with African Americans than they do with the immigrant-origin groups because they are more likely to live in the same neighborhoods as native-born blacks, they also consciously distance themselves, especially from Arab Muslims in a post-9/11 context, because of the stereotyped associations of terrorism with this sector as well as the West Africans' own anti-Arab biases.[26] To give stronger voice to this constituency, initiatives have been launched to both organize all of the approximately forty African mosques in the city as well as to form a coalition of African and African American mosques in Harlem, spearheaded by Senegalese Imam Konate of Masjid Aqsa and African American Imam Talib of the Mosque of the Muslim Brotherhood.[27] The affiliations with other black populations based on religion have spilled over to a nascent Pan-African politics as West Africans have begun to gravitate toward active support of the local campaigns and causes of politicians who are African American or Afro-Caribbean.

Through the dedication of its late leader, Shaykh Hassan Cissé, another Senegalese-based Sufi order, the Tijaniyya, has created notable ties to African Americans in the United States as well. Beginning in the mid-1970s, Cissé, who studied for his doctoral degree at Northwestern University, set out to bring African American Muslims into the Tijani fold. Today his disciples in the United States have an active presence in both New York and Atlanta. To further broaden the international scope of his work, however, in 1988 Cissé founded the African American Islamic Institute, an NGO organized not only to promote humanitarian initiatives for the improvement of education, health care, and the status of women but also to strengthen the relationship between West Africa and the United States. Despite such efforts to draw together West African and African American Islam and even with increasing incidences of intermarriage between native and foreign-born Muslims, the two religious entities still tend to operate in parallel rather than unified religious worlds.

Forty-One Shots through the American Dream:
The Killing of Amadou Diallo Revisited

While the rituals of a gathering such as Cheikh Bamba Day are meant to showcase an affirmative, unified blackness springing from within the ethnic community, more commonly the realities of institutionalized racism and outside discrimination have drawn these populations together, triggering, instead, a reactive solidarity. Indeed, the turning point in the public's awareness of a growing West African presence was the Amadou Diallo incident. The response to his death led to the consolidation of a West African community in New York that had previously been split by political and ethnic rivalries. In her book about his life, Amadou's mother, Kadiatou, explained,

> When a young person leaves home from Guinea, he becomes the *setté*. He is the explorer and the envoy, carrying the family name to unseen places. In the villages, towns, and cities, too, they will talk about him, imagining his triumphs and new riches. On his return, they will gauge his manner of speaking or of entering a room, the ease of his walk, perhaps a satisfaction that shows in his eyes, to determine if his travels have given him the bearing of a successful man. Beyond his conquests, they wait for the tales he will carry back. Even the man who has not filled his pockets with gold can still be a witness. For years he can tell people what happened when he finally stepped onto strange land, what surprised or scared him, lifted or saddened him, what he has discovered for them. Amadou was a *setté* for his brothers, sisters, cousins, friends, and for me, who anticipated a magnificent return.
>
> He returned a silent body with a tale untold. If there is anything as cruel as the taking of a man's life, it is the taking away of his story, the particulars that make him holy.[28]

Certainly, the special unit of the New York Police Department (NYPD) who gunned down Amadou prevented him from fulfilling this essential responsibility of the immigrant. On February 4, 1999, four officers of the Street Crime Unit fired forty-one shots at the twenty-three-year-old, a black immigrant from Guinea who had been in the United States for almost three years. Nineteen of these hit Diallo, who was killed instantly in the vestibule of his own apartment building in the Bronx. The officers, who were not in uniform, alleged that they had been looking for a serial rapist who, they said, resembled Mr. Diallo. They also claimed that they thought the young man was acting "suspiciously" and had reached for a gun. But it turned out that Amadou had no such weapon and what he had reached for was his wallet, perhaps fearing that the four men who were actually armed might be robbers. The police may have killed Amadou, but they did not put an end to his story; in fact, they made it poignantly bigger. Coming on the heels of the beating and sodomizing of Abner Louima, a Haitian immigrant, in 1997, this incident provoked public outrage and provided yet another example of the racist brutality of Mayor Giuliani's police force. Within a short time, the media, in all their forms, were saturated with various perspectives about the incident, coverage that continued from the time of the killing right through the trial and acquittal of the officers to the civil settlement in 2004 between the city and the victim's family. The mainstream media brought full coverage of the tragedy to the nation, and thus they became the tale bearers of Amadou's life.

Almost every headline identified the victim as a foreigner—"an unarmed West African," "an immigrant," "a Guinean street peddler." What they did not report was that he was born into a prosperous middle-class family whose business ventures had resulted in his birth in Liberia and his sojourn in several other countries in West Africa and Asia, where he attended some of the finest schools. Neither did they recount his determination to come to the United States to realize his dream of becoming a computer specialist nor his fervent belief in America as the land of unparalleled opportunity. Amadou's hopes for life in the United States were typical of those of the many other African immigrants who began to arrive in large numbers beginning in the 1980s.

As sizeable as the late twentieth-century wave of African immigrants and refugees was, however, they still represented a small proportion of American blacks. In New York, for example, in the 1990s, they constituted less than 3 percent of the total black population.[29] Africans did not create clearly visible enclaves, but they found niches in specific neighborhoods where they began to leave definitive imprints. Although they sought to distance themselves from American blacks, they tended to live in close proximity to them as well as Caribbeans and other immigrants. In the 1990s, their presence was most visible, however, not in their residential neighborhoods but on the streets of Manhattan, where Francophone West African vendors were hawking their wares. Arriving in the United States in September 1996, Amadou belonged to that group of ubiquitous African peddlers. He sold a variety of items on Fourteenth Street—socks, batteries, juice, soda, chewing gum, Life Savers, and, as the police relentlessly pointed out, bootlegged videos.

The Diallo killing was racially charged from the onset as it spoke to a chronic domestic problem—an innocent *black* man killed by four *white* men. The episode further shattered the prevalent misconception among the immigrants of immunity to American racism, jolting many into the realities of racial profiling. This recognition spurred the Africans and African Americans to join together in their efforts to demand justice. For their part, the African American leadership recognized that the action was not just an attack on an immigrant, but a continuation of a pattern of historical racist assaults on black Americans. Already steeped in the tradition of their struggle, they were poised to lead protest activities. For many this was clear evidence of continuing racial injustice. Almost everyone interviewed by the journalists in the aftermath said they believed that Diallo was condemned as a criminal because of the color of his skin. Some pointed more specifically to the perennial assault on the black American male. The Reverend Jesse Jackson described the tragedy as "open season on blacks." Prominent African American attorney Johnnie Cochran unequivocally indicted what he saw as America's racist system:

> This isn't only a case of driving while black. It's walking while black, it's living while black, it's breathing while black . . . there was absolutely no question in my mind that this would not have happened if Amadou Diallo had been white. If he were white, he would still be alive. If Diallo had been white these cops wouldn't have kept shooting. But they lived in a culture where it is assumed that a young black man must be doing something wrong.[30]

Even as the press stressed the foreignness of the victim, African Americans took the incident as one more affront against "black America." The actions of these well-known African American leaders underscored this stand. Diallo's autopsy was hardly completed when the Reverend Al Sharpton, a significant face of contemporary black resistance, began to chart a public protest with a black immigrant presence. Sharpton and several other African American sympathizers joined the Diallo family and members of the Guinean and West African immigrant communities at the *Salat-al-Jumah* (Friday afternoon prayer) at the Islamic Cultural Center. Diallo's remains were brought there for the prayers for the dead. A much bigger show of solidarity followed at the homegoing memorial service. By most accounts, this event, attended by two thousand people, was a protest rally. Activists were visibly represented, some taking the podium to affirm their resolve and rally others to the cause of seeking justice. And Kadiatou Diallo made her debut as a face in the black struggle in America. Holding Amadou's Koran, his book on Martin Luther King, Jr., and another on dialogue between Christians and Muslims, Mrs. Diallo declared, "We have to work together to save all our children."[31]

This show of African–African American solidarity crossed the Atlantic with Sharpton and the entourage that accompanied the Diallos to Guinea for Amadou's funeral and a transatlantic, transnational statement of protest against racial profiling and police brutality in the United States. The motorcades and the presence of American journalists and activists helped hammer home publicly in Africa the continuing race struggle in post–civil rights America. But the site of contestation remained the United States. Demonstrations, which had begun as soon as news of the shooting got out, were stepped up after the funeral and the return of Sharpton and others. There were daily protests outside Amadou's Bronx residence, NYPD headquarters in Manhattan, the State Supreme Court in the Bronx, and the Justice Department in Washington, D.C. On April 15, 1999, thousands marched across the Brooklyn Bridge to draw attention to police brutality nationwide and to promote a ten-point plan for police reform. Besides the numbers, the names of some of the protesters spoke to the momentum of the campaign. The list read like a who's who in celebrity activism—Harry Belafonte, Ossie Davis, Dick Gregory, former New York mayor David Dinkins, actress Susan Sarandon, to name a few. A year after the shooting, the demonstrations received new life when the four officers were acquitted on February 25, 2000.

The results went beyond mere arrests. The protesters got the attention of the city, state, and federal governments. Their actions led to the investigation of police relations with minority communities and the eventual disbanding of the notorious Street Crime special unit; they forced the Justice Department to look into the Diallo case, even though it concluded that it did not find beyond a reasonable doubt that Mr. Diallo's civil rights were violated. Furthermore and perhaps most significant was the level of coalition building that the campaign sparked, giving new life to liberal Democratic politics in New York. Remarkably, one hundred chanting rabbis and rabbinical students were among those whose arrests Sharpton had orchestrated at police headquarters.[32] Similarly, the campaign appealed to organized labor activists as well as advocates of gay and lesbian rights. The campaign brought people and groups together, and as a *New York Times* reporter rightly pointed out in a front-page article in March of 1999, daily protesters in handcuffs kept the focus on the Diallo shooting.[33] Rage over the killing of a black man had galvanized a diverse group of people who helped broaden racialized politics and protest into a case not just for justice for blacks but one for American justice. Four months after the acquittal verdict, the legendary Bruce Springsteen immortalized this episode of racial violence when he debuted his protest song "American Skin" with its throbbing "41 shots" refrain and including the lyrics:

> Is it a gun?
> Is it a knife?
> Is it a wallet?
> This is your life
> It ain't no secret (it ain't no secret)
> Ain't no secret my friend
> You can get killed just for living in your American skin

Yet while commentators pointed to the various coalitions among groups of liberal democrats, organized labor, religious and ethnic minorities, African American activists, gay and lesbian leaders, and other sympathizers, very little was said about African immigrants themselves.

While Americans were dissecting this incident involving a black African, what were the Africans in America saying and doing? Although

Amadou's parents, Saikou and Kadiatou, were paraded prominently in rallies and the media, it was clear that American-born blacks were in charge of the public protest. Guinean leaders worked with the Diallos and tried to rally their compatriots and other West Africans of the city. The Bronx African Islamic Center offered special prayers for a fellow Muslim. Although the protesters in front of Diallo's home were over-whelmingly African American, African demonstrators were still con-spicuous. The *New York Times* reported that there were several dozen African Muslims offering prayers to Allah and a group of Guineans dancing around a drummer (a dance of mourning, no doubt).[34] This specific mention notwithstanding, the activities of Africans in reaction to the tragedy remained in the shadows, to the extent that in one of its editorials published two years later, a West African publication lam-basted what the writer saw as a disgraceful lack of concern and raised the question of "Where were the continental Africans"?[35] The president of the Guinean Association of America admitted that his organization did not do much beyond raising funds at "informal sporadic gather-ings" to help repatriate the bodies of those who have died in the "strange land of America."[36] Although African immigrants were incensed by what happened to a fellow immigrant, the majority did not publicly demonstrate this outrage. Instead, they explained the events as random, unfortunate, typical American violence. Some were convinced that if they only stuck to the business of "making it" in America, they could avoid, to quote a Nigerian immigrant, "all the dizzying complications of race, race relations and subtle and not so subtle racism."[37] They were there and they had opinions, but did not voice them publicly. In infor-mal conversations, electronic chat rooms, and oral history accounts, the immigrants seemed to dwell on what the tragedy did to Diallo's pursuit of the American dream and the wider implications for the attainment of that dream by others like him.

By the 1980s glowing reports about America were finding their way to various parts of Africa. Some immigrants who had settled in the coun-try by that time, through letters and gifts they sent home, relayed a very positive African immigrant experience. An equally influential source of information was exported American popular culture. Those living in urban areas with access to television—theirs or their neighbors'—were able to consume American popular culture, and from programs like

The Cosby Show, Dynasty, and *Dallas"* they developed their impressions about the United States. By the 1990s, the success of African-born athletes like basketball players Hakeem Olajuwon and Dikembe Mutombo was symbolic of the opportunities in America. Diallo's fate offered a vivid lesson in the complexity of a phenomenon often invoked as an uncomplicated American trait. As many African immigrants already knew, not everything is possible in the United States and the American dream is not so easily realized. When Mrs. Diallo visited her son's surprisingly tiny and sparsely furnished room, she was amazed to discover that "the alien West African street peddler" had managed to save three thousand dollars.[38] But all this resilience, endurance, and perseverance were no match for the bullets that put an end to any hopes of continuing in the rough path to the dream.

How much did African immigrants really know about the obstacles that emanate from their new identity as blacks in America? What did they take out of the Diallo tragedy? That this exemplary African met with such a violent fate sent some terrifying messages to other African immigrants about race and opportunity in their adopted country. Although the voices of the African American leaders dominated the "black reaction" to the incident, Africans also dissected the tragedy and contemplated its ramifications. They did so not in "American" public spaces with American-born blacks, but within their own ethnic enclaves. They engaged in long, passionate conversations in what had become familiar sites of interaction in their diasporic world—restaurants, tropical food stores, and leisure-time gatherings like soccer matches, weddings, naming ceremonies, and independence anniversary celebrations. Farafina's Coffee Shop on West 116th Street in Manhattan was one such venue. This restaurant, owned by Maimouna Ndiaye, an immigrant from Mali, was, by 1990, perhaps the most popular stop for the many African cab drivers and delivery men. They came to patronize the business, mainly because of the authentic African dishes like fufu, groundnut, and goat stew that it offered. As they ate and socialized, they talked about a variety of subjects about life in their respective homelands and the continent in general. But for weeks after the Diallo killing, they focused almost exclusively on that incident and what it meant for their immigrant experience. Silla Sidique from Guinea expressed the terror the incident sent through the African immigrant enclaves:

"We are afraid, we are afraid. I want to go back home before somebody kills me."[39]

Indeed, the extent of violence in the United States, represented by the tragedy, was a major topic of conversation in other parts of the country. At Its Tropical, a food store in Decatur in metro Atlanta, the mostly West African shoppers talked about violence in America and took the opportunity to assess the scale of violence in their own rapidly expanding metropolis. A few months after the incident, Ethiopians in Washington, D.C., who gathered to play soccer one Saturday morning discussed the violent nature of Diallo's death and how representative this was of the situation in the United States.[40] Ida Njie from Gambia was convinced that the incident, though conspicuous, was just one more typically violent assault in America: "All of us at the naming ceremony that day agreed that any of us could easily be an Amadou Diallo. We could be attacked and killed by a drug-addicted thief on our way home." At the same event, according to Njie, another Gambian immigrant pointed out that it made sense that many of them there had earned and saved enough money to live in the safe Houston suburbs where they had bought houses. Some of them believed that living in a "rough Bronx neighborhood" may have cost Diallo his life.[41] As discussed in chapter 3, perhaps no other African group knew more about violence in America than the taxi drivers. From 1985 to the time of the Diallo killing—a little over a decade—by some estimates, more than fifty African (mostly West African) cab drivers had been murdered in New York.[42] As Mohamed Mouktar Diallo, a cousin of Amadou Diallo, noted, "We know that many Guineans before Amadou were killed in New York. But they are usually doing something dangerous, like driving a cab in Harlem."[43]

Like their African American counterparts, many Africans did point to the racialized implications of the incident but were hesitant to assert that Diallo's killing was definitively the result of racism, maintaining instead that he *may* have been the victim of racism. Nevertheless, the incident prompted many to begin to examine and talk about race and racism in America. *New York Times* reporter Amy Waldman noted that interviews with more than one hundred Africans in the city revealed that "they cherish America's economic prosperity, its political freedom and its education system, but they dislike its racism and its violence, and they disdain its values."[44] In their "ethnic spaces," like Farafina's Coffee Shop and tropical African food stores, many of them related their own experiences that provided insights into issues of race and racism that might have been factors in the Diallo killing. Mamoudou Jawara, a Guinean, talked about being repeatedly stopped by police near his Staten Island home and asked for his license and occasionally told by officers to "go back to Africa." Tingah Mohammed, a forty-nine-year-old Ghanaian, who by the time of the tragedy had been living in the United States for fifteen years, recalled one night walking down a TriBeCa street and seeing a white woman running. She ran and hid behind a rubbish heap. She was afraid of him, a realization that almost brought him to tears.[45]

Perhaps most perplexing for many of these foreign blacks was the emphasis by African American leaders, as well as African-born intellectuals and community leaders, that their "foreignness" cannot secure for them an immunity from the insidiousness of American racism. Fordham University professor Mojubaolu Olufunke Okome, originally from Nigeria, pointed to the inevitable racial implications of the killing of Diallo and their larger significance:

> Both Amadou and I are black. As black people in the United States, we have walked into a situation where historically, whether you like it or not, the color of your skin determines your identity. Many recent African immigrants to this country eventually come to realize that the first thing that the external observer sees about you is the color of your skin. Like it or not, that color marks you and makes you subject to the treatment that other people may never experience. We . . . by coming to America, have come into the stream of American history that continues to perpetuate inequities against African Americans, simply by virtue of their color. While Amadou died, I am here now. As an African who may have faced police harassment, but who was not shot at, I have a responsibility to consider what is happening carefully, analytically. If I do not look into this tragic matter, I will be doing myself and others an injustice.[46]

NYU professor Manthia Diawara, who moved to the United States from Mali, expressed similar sentiments.

Part of my profound disappointment with the world stemmed from a realization that Amadou Diallo was shot in New York because he was a black man. Amadou Diallo's death left a sour taste in my mouth. Just as my success story in America could have been his, the tragedy that had befallen him could have been mine. . . . They cut Amadou Diallo down like a black American, even though he belonged to the Fulani tribe in his native Guinea. There is a lesson here for all of us to learn.[47]

What are the lessons, then? And did African immigrants really learn these lessons from the Diallo tragedy? Did even the gunning down of one of them as a black man fail to convey to many of the African immigrants the reality of their position as inheritors of the legacies of America's complex racial history? Although many black Africans who immigrated to America were ignorant of the gravity of the repercussions of the history of race and racism in America, some of them had been exposed to some valuable insights into the problems in their pre-migration settings. The protagonist of the tragedy was one such African. Diallo's privileged schooling at an international school in Bangkok exposed him to American history where he read about Martin Luther King, Jr. and Malcolm X. And his mother once heard him declare passionately, "The changes [brought about by the civil rights movement] happened because of the actions of black people."[48] Like Diallo, many Africans who had been exposed to similar educational opportunities or lived and worked in urban areas where they gained access to American news and popular culture came to America with varying degrees of awareness of the salience of race. Still many continued to detach themselves from the history; the narrative, they believed, was not about them, they were, after all, "the other blacks." Thus, although some African immigrants did address issues of race and racism, their voices did not translate into recognizable, viable African immigrant activism in response to the police killing of a fellow immigrant. In fact, although cab drivers, hair braiders, street peddlers, security guards, as well as nurses, nursing assistants, engineers, doctors, teachers, and professors talked about the racial implications, in general, the majority of these black foreigners were more focused on "making it" in America and attaining the American dream.

It is this apparent disconnect from the African American agenda that helped shape the African immigrants' responses to the Diallo tragedy. Many of them failed to see the probable links between the Diallo tragedy and other incidents like the police beating of Rodney King in Los Angeles and the police brutalization of Abner Louima in New York City. Did the immigrants even consider reports that the police who shot Diallo that night were looking for a black male rapist, and, if so, how much importance would they have placed on this information? Indeed, what do they know about the role of the image of the black male rapist in the history of race, racism, and race relations in America? As Elizabeth Alexander emphasizes, "Black bodies in pain for public consumption have been an American national spectacle for centuries."[49] What do the African foreign-born know about, and how do they interpret the lynching of blacks in American history or the horrific murder of Emmett Till?[50] When they see pictures or read about that "strange fruit" hanging from trees, can they feel the pain not only as any decent human beings committed to human rights, but also as an integral part of the agony on display? Even those among the continental African population who did register their points of view on the incident did not necessarily speak to a collective black traumatized past.

Perhaps the clearest illustration of the divergence in agendas in this story can be found in the breakdown in relations between the Diallos and African American leaders—specifically, Al Sharpton, Johnnie Cochran, and Jesse Jackson. The national tour that was supposed to have been an opportunity to showcase African and African American solidarity ended suddenly only after appearances in two cities. Furthermore, Mrs. Diallo terminated the services of Cochran. Both sides made every attempt to be civil about the breakup—Cochran lamented that probably due to cultural differences, Mrs. Diallo could not understand or cope with his busy schedule.[51] Mrs. Diallo, for the most part, remained silent about why she parted company with her African American advisers. Still, observers read between the lines, and what they found was mostly a discrepancy in ideologies concerning American racism and black protest.

In Chicago, during the short-lived national tour, Jackson and Sharpton lambasted America's historical and contemporary treatment of minorities, especially blacks. Sharpton went further to raise the point about the naïveté and delusion of black immigrants who believed that, as a different kind of blacks, they were somehow immune to the consequences of America's racist past and present. Although Mrs. Diallo did not publicly admit it, according to some observers she did not agree with Sharpton's acidic assault of a country she maintained her son truly loved.[52] Roving writer Ted Conover eloquently describes the divergence:

> When discussion moved from the particulars of her son's case to a broader critique of American society, Sharpton's political narrative ceased to be her own. . . . The rift between Sharpton and Kadi seemed to be about a built-in fork in the road, the place where an immigrant narrative of opportunity and fair treatment diverged from an African American narrative about civil rights and historical injustice.[53]

Sharpton and other American-born blacks insisted, as Jesse Jackson put it, "there is power in innocent blood." For them, Diallo's blood should go a long way to helping blacks attain long-term goals of a complete overhaul of the status quo and the reclamation of the gains of the civil rights movement. Mrs. Diallo, on the other hand, appealed to an end to demonstrations and a resolve to work toward healing by making peace with Giuliani and his administration. She also hoped that a major step toward reconciliation would be through the work of the Amadou Diallo Foundation, especially with regard to its provision for young black Africans to attain the American dream made possible by scholarships awarded by the organization.[54] Were the Africans so out of tune with the history and nature of black, racialized protest in America?

Mrs. Diallo's conciliatory tone and the faint voices of her fellow African immigrants connoted a detachment from the black American struggle and were misconstrued by many as absolute nonchalance. True, the failure of Africans, and indeed other black immigrants, to fully grasp the traumatic past and problematic present of American blacks cannot be denied. This, however, does not mean that the perceptions that African immigrants have of American pluralism, especially as it relates to issues of race, are static. As the newcomers have adapted, their responses have also evolved. Particularly for the undocumented, however, outspoken protest of such practices as racial profiling and police brutality must be tempered by the reality of immigration law enforcement. Nonetheless, an episode that should have provided the perfect scenario for foreign- and native-born blacks to come together in protest of American racism ultimately failed to create and sustain a united front. Furthermore, alongside the outcries of the African American activists as well as the commentaries of the many and diverse journalists, the voices of Africans in the interpretation of the killing of young Diallo, however muffled, are essential to fully understand what was ultimately an American tragedy but one that is at the center of the black immigrant experience.

Shades of Black

A reversal of sorts has occurred over the past several decades regarding racial politics and alliances between black immigrants and African Americans. Afro-Caribbean activists of the early twentieth century were criticized for their "pushiness" and arrogant meddling in the American black struggle, while the post–civil rights era African diaspora is faulted, instead, for its reticence to join the continuing fight.[55] Deep involvement in homeland politics and other "non-American" issues may well be a justifiable characterization of the contemporary West African community who can be seen as paying so much attention to pan-ethnic issues and transnational prerogatives that their response to American problems with uniquely racial ramifications is inadequate. This is precisely what Jill Humphries found in her research on the ways foreign-born African constituencies have engaged in multiracial political action coalitions in the United States. Utilizing a case study of Southern California participants in the National Summit on Africa, an initiative launched in 1997 to guide America's policy on African affairs, she summarized her findings with the phrase "Resisting 'Race,'" as she concluded that while the immigrant cohort acknowledged the salience of race in the African American context, they did not privilege its significance, nor did they see confronting the racial order as a unifying platform to mobilize and bring together native and foreign-born subgroups. Preferring to maintain a separate agenda, the African-born turned away from a political strategy that would readily encompass the concerns of their African American counterparts.[56]

Certainly the black foreigners have capitalized on the vastly more tolerant climate in the United States, when compared to the African continent, to voice their opinions about conditions at home and to chart actions. A close examination of the mission statements of African organizations in New York City revealed that as many as half are dedicated to the sociopolitical concerns of their respective homelands,[57] while the increasing numbers of those in the diaspora who hold dual citizenship further facilitate the possibility of direct involvement with political campaigns and government policy making in their countries of origin. Some in the diaspora may even hold political office in their homelands or, short of that, have substantially funded the bids of other candidates. Thus, Nigerians abroad immersed in ensuring the hegemony of their respective ethnicities in the complex Nigerian federation or Sierra Leonean immigrants too focused on rebuilding their former schools—indeed, a whole country—after a protracted war and a temporary collapse of the state could potentially lessen their ability to be proactive about pressing issues in the United States. At association meetings, in specialty stores, nightclubs, and house and hall parties, the West African foreigners, especially the men, spend an enormous amount of time dissecting homeland problems, hotly debating current African affairs and assessing the actions of past and present leaders, from Nkrumah to Senghor to Tejan Kabba and Olusegun Obasanjo. As diasporic citizens, this should be expected. The question is to what extent these emerging and new Americans can juggle their transnational existence to also apply this determination—to question and agitate—to their experiences in their new home, especially as they relate to their being black in America. In his efforts to persuade his fellow African taxi drivers to get more politically active, one Seattle immigrant expressed the extent to which he has made the adjustment with his recognition of the advantages he has gained by becoming an American citizen: "What excites me every day is that I could go protest without fear of deportation or being sent to prison. . . . I could lobby, jump up and down, start my own business, and nobody could question me. The country I was not even born in is allowing me to dream."[58]

In time and to varying degrees, contemporary African immigrant communities have become more cognizant of the metaphoric "pain of the black body." Since the 1990s, intellectuals, professionals, and leaders of various diasporic associations have been encouraging members of their communities to consider "American" issues not just in general terms but through the prism of race as well. Diawara articulates the rationale for this stand:

> Little do the Amadou Diallos of the world know that the black man in America bears the curse of Cain, and that in America they, too, are considered black men, not Fulanis, Mandingos or Wolofs. . . . They cut Amadou Diallo down like a black American even though he belonged to the Fulani tribe of his native Guinea. The tragedies of Abner Louima and Amadou Diallo—two immigrants submitted to the ritualistic white violence generally reserved for African Americans—should finally suffice as a political awakening for Africans and Caribbeans to the issues of race in America.[59]

Although typically those who compose the new African diaspora have not been conversant with the history of civil rights, with the election of Barack Obama in 2008 African immigrants who had rarely been involved with the discourse on race began to shift the usual focus on homeland politics as the primary topic of what were often heated discussions to conversations, instead, that have revolved around some of the domestic debates that have been raised by the Obama presidency. The ongoing allegations that questioned the veracity of his American citizenship promulgated by the birther movement, especially that he was born in Kenya, conspiracy theories that were not quelled until well into the president's third year in office (and even then they persisted among some sectors), served as a lightening rod particularly for the highly educated and professional cohort of West Africans who saw this confrontation as a direct assault on their own legitimacy. The racial politics implied by such attacks have galvanized the continental African community to align themselves with African Americans in a shared blackness, seeing their long-standing struggles with new eyes and understanding, in some cases for the first time, the rationale behind a more activist position when it comes to countering racial bias and discrimination. Such priorities have led to the formation of new organizations such as the African Advocacy Network in the San Francisco

Bay Area. Its founder, Adoubou Traore, who is from Côte d'Ivoire, explained the interchange:

> We are different from each other: many African-Americans no longer know much about Africa. Many African immigrants only know of the mass media's narrative when it comes to African-Americans. . . . African-Americans can serve as powerful source of support for newly arrived African immigrants. And we can help them to recover their historic roots.[60]

In *The Making of African America*, as part of his argument for the legacy of diversity among peoples of African descent, past and present, Ira Berlin cleverly characterizes this juxtaposing history of the long-settled and migratory cohorts as "roots and routes."[61]

In the spring of 2013 as consensus was building to overhaul U.S. immigration policy, a coalition spearheaded by leaders of African diaspora communities from across the country organized a series of rallies in Washington, D.C., on Capitol Hill to advocate for comprehensive immigration reform, an initiative that had the full support of civil rights and faith-based groups as well as representatives from various Caribbean American constituencies. The gatherings drew the attention of the Congressional Black Caucus, with Representative Charles Rangel from New York declaring at the first Day of Action event, "We're all immigrants and it's time for change, reform and justice," signifying a shared black American vision that superseded national origins.[62]

Beyond political advocacy, other creative initiatives have generated platforms for the exploration of the dynamics among native-origin and immigrant-origin blacks. When Ghanaian-born filmmaker Kobina Aidoo, director of the 2009 documentary *The Neo-African-Americans* on black immigrant identities, told his friends and family at home that he was coming to America to study film, they gave him their well wishes to become the next Steven Spielberg. Once he arrived in the United States, however, when he told people of his plans, although they also wished him the best of luck, it was, instead, to become the next Spike Lee:

Great filmmakers, both . . . but the significance of the difference in their respective blessings was not lost to me. Through this and other experiences, I was forced to start thinking of myself as black. Not that there's anything wrong with that or I didn't know that already, but I mean exactly that: think. Having come from an overwhelmingly majority black country, I had only thought of my being black in philosophical terms. Living it as a minority was new to me, and I felt myself getting squeezed in boxes with which I was unfamiliar. For instance, I didn't know why people in the gym wanted me on their basketball team. Of course, I knew why, but I didn't know why, given that I would only go on to embarrass myself—and all black people.[63]

From his personal experience, Aidoo began talking to other black immigrants, immersing himself in the literature on the history of race in America and subsequently launching the *Neo-African-Americans* documentary project and accompanying website. Between the screenings nationwide, primarily on college campuses, where there is always time for discussion and the enormously popular online interactive forum on the subject, the conversations have touched on the myriad facets of the meaning of race for black immigrants in America.

Indeed, when Barack Obama, son of a black African father and white American mother, first declared his candidacy in the Illinois senatorial race in 2004 and became a rising star in the Democratic Party, Alan Keyes, the black Republican nominee who opposed him, sparked a heated debate in the African American community by questioning Obama's credentials as a black man, an issue that continued to nag at the Democrat in his later successful run for the presidency. Such narrowly construed notions of black authenticity are being revised by the rapidly changing demographics of race in contemporary America. As one African American commentator put it, "At bottom, the hue and cry over Barack Obama's identity stems from a failure by black traditionalists to recognize multiracial versions of themselves. Soon enough, the Obama story, which seems so exotic to so many people now, will have found its place among all the other stories of the sprawling black diaspora."[64]

In general, the longer the new West African settlers live in the United States, the more they realize and accept that in America, they are identified more by the color of their skin than by their nationality. Such a shift in self-perceptions accompanied by a better understanding of the meaning of race and how to navigate those hierarchies in their new country can lead to an easing of intraracial tensions. Five years after immigrating to the United States from Lagos, Nigeria, in 1982, clothing retailer Larry Alebiosu opened a store in metropolitan Detroit largely because of the racial makeup of residents in that part of the city: "I blend in very well with the African-American community because we are black people. It's easy to get along with people that are the same as you are. And you have a lot of African-Americans here who are interested in Africa."[65]

In the arena of social life, capitalizing on the notion of Afropolitanism, the Boston-based Afrique event planners have organized an annual "Afropolitan Cruise," a midnight soiree aboard the *Spirit of Boston* luxury ship billed as "all black" (upscale black attire recommended), where the music combined African and West Indian beats.

At times, the immigrants have realized that alliances with the wider black community can be politically advantageous, and they

Afrique Events Second Annual Afropolitan Cruise publicity flyer, Boston, September 2012.

purposefully seek common ground. These overtures may well be readily reciprocated. For example, despite all the reported friction between African origin and native-born blacks in the Pacific Northwest, the NAACP branch in Portland, Oregon, recently elected a young Liberian immigrant as its president. For others, barriers to an inclusive black identity were never an issue. Once Marcus Samuelsson got the idea to open a high-end African restaurant in New York, he found that he was unable to persuade anyone to invest in such a concept. After two years of knocking on closed doors, Samuelsson reported that he wasn't at all surprised that it was an African American businessman who finally understood the potential of his venture and agreed to back him. Unfortunately, a mere two days after shaking hands on the deal, the man died of a heart attack. Undaunted, Samuelsson eventually got the financing he needed from a Haitian American club promoter, and consequently his quest was realized in a collaboration truly representative of the wider African diaspora.[66]

Through the increasing interactions of the new immigrants with the native-born, the meanings of African American race and culture are continuously being redefined. As individuals, a common pattern has been to initially self-identify most broadly as African upon arrival in the United States or to define oneself in terms of a distinctive ethnic or nationality group and later, after making a more permanent adjustment to the urban neighborhoods in which they live, to gradually affiliate themselves with the larger black community; some may even identify as African American. Over the course of two decades, Kenneth Udoibok, who left Nigeria for the United States in 1981, slowly came to consider himself an African American: "Ten years ago I told people I was an African. Fifteen to 20 years ago I told people I was a Nigerian." And while Udoibok calls himself African American today, he still finds it difficult "to wrap his African mind around American racism."[67] In another instance, an American-born Ghanaian married to a first-generation African confided that she and her husband viewed the concept of race differently. Her spouse did not recognize race as a meaningful social category, but she readily acknowledged that blackness can, indeed, constitute a cultural identity: "My husband doesn't understand this issue. But I can see the African American side of things and the

African immigrant sides of things. I know what they [African Americans] mean when they talk about 'being black.' It's not just skin color."[68]

Most significant, though still not as free as white ethnics are to choose when and with whom they want to identify, increasingly the nonwhite immigrant population, including members of the new West African diaspora, have the leeway to exercise ethnic optionality, emphasizing individual nationalities and cultural identities in certain contexts while joining with the native-born black population in other situations. In an autobiographical essay, the Anglo-Nigerian writer Sarah Manyika, who is based in San Francisco, ruminated on the process of seeking equilibrium in relation to the racial barriers she has faced: "As I now trace the life experiences that engendered my racial consciousness, I strive to find balance between the value of being mindful of race and the danger of being consumed by it."[69] Rather than a cohesive and fixed notion of racial or ethnic identity, new West Africans, like many others among the foreign-born, exhibit variegated identities that are continuously in flux. As Fallou Guèye, a former president of the Association of Senegalese in America who lives in New York with his wife and young child, explained it, "I like to think that I am multidimensional. Look, even in Senegal there are bad influences and kids are affected there by the media and rap music. But if my kid can be African and American together, it's good. People can pursue this idea of being pure, being one thing. But it's not doable."[70] The rate of intermarriage between second-generation West Africans and African Americans is increasing as well and is another factor that minimizes the wedge. In the course of adaptation, many new immigrants eventually do successfully juggle becoming ethnics with acceptance of being black in the United States, often representing integral threads in the fabric of African America.

6

Young, Gifted, and West African

Transnational Migrants Growing Up in America

> The myth of return will always remain a myth. . . . If you
> want to know if you are going home, just listen to the accents
> of your kids and you know you're not going anywhere. This
> is their country.
> —Sulayman Nyang, *Dollars and Dreams*

Ghanaian American Kofi Apraku, who came to the United States in his teens, recalled his first impressions:

I had been told that the United States is the ultimate land of opportunity, that the limit to one's achievement is set only by one's own imagination, and that a determined person can literally reach for the stars. . . . Didn't America literally reach for the stars when it landed a man on the moon? Sure, everything is possible in this country.

For the next ten years, I was determined to take America at its word—it was the land of opportunity where if you played fair you would be rewarded.[1]

Miriam Jalloh, who arrived as a young refugee from Sierra Leone in the late 1990s, expressed similar resolve: "There is nothing impossible here. If you want to do it, and you are strong enough, you will do it. I think I will do it."[2] Nigerian American Sabella Abidde concluded,

America has been very good to a select group of Africans. For this august group of men and women, America is the ultimate destination. . . . These are men and women who toiled night and day and all hour's in-between to get to where they are in life. These are an honest bunch of people who

pulled themselves by the bootstraps and made it to the top of the mountain. They live the good life. They live the American dream.[3]

These quotes represent two key patterns of thought that have played
significant roles in the adaptation of West Africans to life in the United
States and are crucial for understanding and evaluating the success of
young West African immigrants and refugees as well as the 1.5 and second generations.[4] The convictions expressed—strong belief in the avail-
ability of almost unlimited opportunities in the United States and the
outstanding performance of immigrants—admittedly are not unique to
West Africans. However, discrete premigration histories and traditions,
the specific trajectories of immigration from that region, and the racial-
ization of the identities of the newcomers in the United States bring
some distinctiveness to the West African story. The amalgamation of
homeland traditions, collective memory, and social capital has translated into a powerful immigrant narrative with a definitive emphasis on
the drive to succeed.

When Olufunke A. came from Nigeria to join her aunt and uncle in
Atlanta, one of the first statements they made to her, "only minutes after
her arrival from the airport," was "in America, every Naija is successful! That has been the story since people from that part began to come
here even before independence."[5] According to Olufunke, "I will not be
the one to change that history. I put it in my mind, there and then, that
success is mine for the taking."[6] Indeed, like the relatives of this young
immigrant, many West Africans in the United States are recounting a
past of remarkable group progress. The trend is significant as it begins
to show how this population has been constructing a collective mythos
of success designed to bolster their resolve for further achievement in
the next generation. This shared oral history, circulated in the immigrant community, is substantiated by the documented history.

Accomplishments of West Africans as voluntary immigrants to the
United States started with the first group from that region, young Cape
Verdeans who seized the chance to leave home in search of a better life
as crew aboard the New England whaling ships that were beginning
to arrive at the archipelago's protected harbors. They worked hard in
maritime-related jobs, in the textile mills, and on the cranberry bogs

and were industrious enough to establish a permanent settlement in the United States.[7] While this initial influx made an impact, the evolving narrative of West African success is heavily weighted with accounts not of the Portuguese-speaking laborers but of the English-speaking student pioneers who came some years later. The protagonists are men like Nnamdi Azikiwe and Kwame Nkrumah who not only pursued their undergraduate education in the United States (Lincoln University, an HBCU) but went on to receive their master's degrees (both also at the University of Pennsylvania). Their accounts of their experiences in the 1920s and 1930s give useful glimpses into the small, little-known African émigré communities of the pre–civil rights era. Yet they were sojourners, eager to go back to their homelands to participate in the tasks of independence and nation building.[8] It was not until several decades later, however, beginning in the 1980s, that, disillusioned by the political and economic woes in their countries, West African students in the United States, whose numbers had increased considerably, became reluctant to return. They adjusted their status to become permanent residents, acquiring desirable professional positions such as teachers, engineers, and accountants.

The "student-immigrant" tradition, then, has become a key element in the narrative of success. Adama K., a second-generation Sierra Leonean, recalled how her father would stress that "West Africans in this country are among the few groups of immigrants whose communities were laid not by 'uneducated workers seeking work' but by bright people who came to further their education."[9] Scholarly investigation helps reinforce this claim emphasizing findings from the 2000 census that showed that Africans composed the most highly educated group in the country, surpassing white Americans, Asians, and Latinos.[10] The results of two different studies of the educational performance of black immigrant youth, one based on the National Education Longitudinal Study of 1988 that followed a national sample of students who were in eighth grade that year and the other based on the National Longitudinal Study of Freshman (NLSF) that surveyed freshmen entering twenty-eight selective colleges and universities in the fall of 1999, also confirmed a significant overrepresentation of high achievers among their subjects. Again, it was not just that the immigrant-origin black students outperformed their native-born black peers; they also did better than the white students.[11] Furthermore, investigators on the NLSF project disaggregated their data to show that among the African-origin students, Nigerians and Ghanaians were the most likely to attend top universities.[12]

Education as the most effective avenue for success is a conviction embraced by the adult immigrant generation and transmitted to young immigrants, the 1.5 and second generations. As the evolving West African immigrant story line emphasizes, this creed is rooted in their pre-migration settings. Emphasizing the extent to which education has been a priority over other aspects of life, Nigerian scholar Ehiedu Iweriebor has put it very simply: "In Nigeria education is actually a secular religion. People believe so strongly in it."[13] Schooling, which in the African nations is specified as Western education, has been valued and has proved to be a formidable criterion for upward mobility since the days of European missionaries. As many are quick to point out, although Western education is a European import, hard work is at the core of African traditional life. Thus, it is this blending of a European product with an African cultural resource that shaped the premigration backgrounds of the majority of the adult immigrants and is influencing the lives of their children in America. Robert Owolabi, who came to the United States for undergraduate studies, vividly recalls,

> A popular poem in western Nigeria titled, "Work is the Medicine for Poverty," truly epitomizes the work ethic in the United States. The poem was very popular when I was growing up. . . . Basically, the poem, written in Yoruba—the predominant language in western Nigeria—talks about the importance and dignity of labor in a person's life. It infers that with hard work, one can be successful. . . . So, in short, this popular Yoruba poem capsulizes [sic] an ideal work ethic for anybody anywhere.[14]

This statement is an example of the sense of preparedness felt by West African immigrants, especially those from Anglophone nations. They were not introduced to the ideal of the American work ethic upon arrival in the United States; they came from societies with an identical work ethic and could thus readily step in as the new Puritans.

West African Advantage

Although no West African groups were included in the ambitious and wide-ranging research that resulted in the publication of *Inheriting the City: The Children of Immigrants Come of Age*, a recent study of the post-1965 second generation in New York City, the experiences of a good number of young West Africans clearly resonate with many of the findings of this volume.[15] The investigation by social scientists Philip Kasinitz, John Mollenkopf, Mary Waters, and Jennifer Holdaway tested the efficacy of the dominant theory of segmented assimilation that posits a stratified second generation decline, whereby the children of recent immigrants who are largely racialized as nonwhite often face downward mobility and limited opportunities for advancement and are likely to be absorbed into more long-standing African American and Latino communities that are mired in poverty. In such a scenario, the best strategy for achieving upward mobility is to resist integration for fear of falling into the abyss of the urban underclass by remaining closely tied to the coethnic enclave economy as a source of both material support and symbolic cultural differentiation from the native-born minority population.[16]

The authors of *Inheriting the City* found, instead, a more complex and fluid set of dynamics rather than a normative downward trajectory of assimilation in which this cohort held what they termed a "second generation advantage" based in part on their ability to capitalize on the dexterity of their "in-between" status. Rather than feeling caught between two worlds or being held back by their new surroundings, they benefited from being able to combine the influence of their homeland cultures in the socialization process with the development of the necessary cultural literacy as well as their familiarity with the expectations of mainstream American society to work in their favor. For example, as a practical matter, unlike their native-born counterparts who are eager to become independent and strike out on their own, many of the immigrant youth that they surveyed delayed leaving home, sometimes well into their twenties and early thirties, an arrangement that is supported by their families where living in multigenerational households is often customary. Staying in the parental home can be advantageous to young people, postponing the need to work full-time to support themselves and enabling them to concentrate on completing their education. For those young women who have children but want to continue their schooling, living at home brings the greater possibility of having family members available to help with child care, which also cuts down on expenses.[17] Among West African youth, a similar pattern can be found of remaining in extended multigenerational households until they finish college, find a decent job, and are able to manage living on their own. In addition, more often than not, the children are being raised in two-parent households, a factor that some researchers have found increases the odds that students will attend an elite college.[18] Overall, the New York study concluded that second-generation gains were modest but still represented definitive progress beyond the achievements of their parents' generation.

Among the West Africans, especially those from Anglophone West Africa, the higher educational attainment of the parents and their success in the professions have been transmitted as a form of social and financial capital that benefits their progeny, helping them to maintain middle-class status and steer clear of the downward slide in socioeconomic status expected of black immigrants in the United States by segmented assimilation theorists. Even when parents have had to take an occupational detour such as having to work as a security guard in the United States after practicing law in their native country, they have undergone the experience of finishing a degree and know firsthand the kind of discipline it takes to successfully complete professional training. As they communicate that process to their children, their reverence for education becomes palpable and they can be effective role models.

Nigerian American professional football player James Ihedigbo grew up in Amherst, Massachusetts, near the University of Massachusetts campus, where his parents had relocated in the 1980s to pursue their goals of obtaining a higher education after initially having left Nigeria for New York City in the 1970s. Parents of five children, Rose and Apollos Ihedigbo both eventually obtained doctoral degrees, but to make ends meet, among their many jobs along the way, Apollos worked part-time delivering pizzas while the whole family capitalized on living near a college campus to collect the inevitable plethora of empty bottles and cans on weekends that could be recycled for extra cash. Even though all the children played sports, their parents were adamant that their studies came first. James stressed that "[my father] always instilled the fundamentals of our faith and yet always excelling in education to be the best. I mean, it was education, education, education. I couldn't even go to basketball practice [he played basketball, football, and lacrosse in school] without homework and everything being done." Before they left Nigeria, Rose and Apollos had founded the Nigerian American Technological and Agricultural College, and as Rose explained,

> One of the goals of why we left Nigeria for the United States was to study and achieve and go back to Nigeria to establish a school that will support the children or families who could not do it on their own. So education became very important to us. We wanted all of our children to achieve some form of education. My commitment to them—including James— was I would support them, but you have to graduate.

With a successful career in football and watching his parents dedicate their lives to education, in 2008 James was inspired to establish his own educational initiative, the Hope Africa Foundation, dedicated to underprivileged children. The foundation has teamed up with the University of Massachusetts to provide scholarships to children from Africa who want to pursue higher education and return to their countries to make an impact.[19]

Ngozi A., whose parents are from Nigeria and Sweden and who moved to Atlanta in the early 1990s, remembered that her Nigerian father once remarked, "No young African person needs to be in the United States without pursuing an education. The business of being here is the business of education."[20] Her statement hits at the core of the young West African immigrant experience. School, after-school activities, and related extracurricular activities provide the crucial milieu within which the experiences of the young immigrants and second generation unfold.

Rather than foundering between the traditional and the new or the insular and the cosmopolitan, young West Africans utilize their multiple social networks and globalized cultural knowledge as plusses to improving their odds of successful incorporation. Preliminary findings of the doctoral research of Shelly Habecker supports this bridge-building aspect of the notion of second-generation advantage as she observed African youth in Washington, D.C., who straddled both the African American peer group and their African immigrant communities, drawing on manifestations of cultural hybridity to ameliorate the divide between the native and foreign-born as well as racial- and ethnic-based cleavages.[21] They are exemplars of situational ethnicity, accentuating their homeland ethnicities in settings that encapsulate family or church activity but able to "act black" to fit in with their African American peers when circumstances call for such expressions of identity. Many become quite adept at code-switching and can read the cultural terrain with fluency, skills that certainly are advantageous in navigating the increasingly multidimensional and complex ethnoracial landscape of twenty-first-century American society.

Growing up with African Americans as well as being more likely to have lived and gone to school within integrated neighborhoods suggests the likelihood of greater comfort and familiarity with a range of both black and nonblack cohorts and may well put second-generation Africans in the best position to take on the role of consensus builders, able to mediate differences, form coalitions, and get beyond more rigidly defined identity politics. Similarly, early results of research on identity choices among Nigerian young adults of the 1.5 and second generations in Britain demonstrate that while the first generation closed themselves off from the other major black population living in England—the more established Afro-Caribbean community—their children, while still heavily identifying as distinctly Nigerian, did not erect such rigid barriers between themselves and their Caribbean counterparts.[22]

Msia Kibona Clark also found that among those children of African immigrants whom she surveyed in her doctoral research, the cohort that was multiply-identified, especially those who had grown up primarily in the United States without vestiges of a foreign accent, readily gained familiarity with both the African American and African immigrant communities, and thus were comfortable in both settings. Educated in American schools where black history and especially the gains of the civil rights movement have by now become a standard part of the curriculum and with constant exposure to American popular culture, they still return home at the end of the day to meals with fufu or jollof rice on the table and conversation in their native languages of their parents.[23] As one young American-born college student whose parents emigrated from Nigeria and who considers himself both African American and Nigerian phrased it, "I definitely identify with all the struggles that we as African Americans have had to go through. But at the same time, I have this (other) history from my parents."[24] Not surprisingly, young people who are the product of unions between an African American and African immigrant parent, a phenomenon that is on the increase, especially relationships between African American women and African men, were particularly adept at bridging both worlds.

While it is difficult to measure the extent to which high aspirations for their children and the student-immigrant tradition influence the actual achievement levels of younger generation West Africans, the phenomenon does appear to vary by nationality and is likely tied to language ability as well as immigrant versus refugee status. Those from Anglophone countries, especially those from Nigeria, Ghana, and Sierra Leone, are better positioned to utilize their immigrant advantage and thus more likely to fulfill such high expectations of success than those English speakers who migrated as refugees, such as the recent Liberian influx. Because of the long civil war, young Liberians may have had their schooling interrupted, lived in refugee camps along the way, or simply arrived with far fewer economic and emotional resources. They may still be able to draw on a legacy of achievement but face greater challenges to realizing more immediate success.[25]

Little research has been conducted on the Francophone West African second generation, but while they did develop their own version of the "student-immigrant" tradition in France, unlike the Anglophones who much earlier extended their shared history of educational accomplishment beyond England to the United States, the transplantation via Europe for the French-speaking population has been less definitive. Most of the existing studies seem to suggest that the Francophones, especially the Senegalese who are the largest group, more often come to the United States in search of commercial prosperity rather than educational success. Nonetheless, anecdotal evidence indicates that the Francophone children have also contributed to the remarkable statistics of educational attainment among West Africans. Although they confront language problems and are more likely to be streamlined to ESOL (English for speakers of other languages) classes, their own enclaves do stress similar educational aspirations. For example, the Miss Senegal-USA pageant, introduced in 2009 for ECOWAS participants, emphasized scholarships and education for girls and young women, while the Senegalese Association of Houston cites education as a major part of its mission.[26]

Among the Cape Verdean population, the "student-immigrant" component of the narrative is even less pronounced. Cape Verdeans, past and present, have been pushed and pulled by similar factors. Economic necessity at home and economic opportunity abroad as well as family reunification drive the dynamics of diaspora. However, the desire to seek a better education plays more of a role today in motivating migration than it did a century ago when the first wave of immigrants began to settle in the United States. Moreover, recent Cape Verdean arrivals are more widely educated—most adults enter having completed a high school education in Cape Verde—than those who came in the first wave. At that time there were only two high schools on the entire archipelago, one in Mindelo, São Vicente, and one in Praia, São Tiago. Neither island was home to the great majority of Cape Verdeans who actually immigrated to the United States in those days. Thus, only the children of the wealthiest would have had the opportunity to be sent to another island or abroad for a high school education. As a result, on average most of the immigrants in the past arrived with minimal schooling, usually only a fifth grade education. Women were even less likely to be educated, whereas since the 1975 independence of Cape Verde, girls have been going to school right alongside the boys. With secondary schools in place on all of the islands today, unprecedented numbers of young people of both sexes attend high school. Still, by the year 2000, only 19 percent of the population had completed secondary schooling and only 1 percent held a university degree.[27] Current newcomers also are much more likely to be able to speak English since English language classes are a required part of the curriculum in Cape Verdean schools beginning in ninth grade.

Once in the United States, like their Cape Verdean American counterparts, many more are going on to college than in the past. Consequently, for the first time in the history of Cape Verdean settlement in the United States, a significant proportion of young adults are receiving higher education. The wide network of Cape Verdean student organizations on New England college campuses testifies to this trend. Despite these gains, however, according to 2000 census findings, Cape Verdeans in the eighteen to twenty-four age cohort were still the least likely of the minority groups in the city of Boston to be enrolled in college or graduate school.[28] For those students who are matriculating at area colleges, however, the well-organized Cape Verdean student networks provide both an academic support system and opportunities to celebrate their members' ancestry and promote greater awareness of Cape Verdean history though a full schedule of conferences, fund-raisers, social events, and lecture series. Usually at least one program on the school calendar pays tribute to the legacy of Amilcar Cabral as young Cape Verdeans of the early twenty-first century, whether new immigrants or American-born, are likely to be familiar with the monumental role that Cabral played in the history of Cape Verdean independence.

The Role of "Intellectual Subcultures"

The communities formed in the diaspora are the foremost conduits in transmitting and maintaining a mentality of success, continuing to reify the role of education while emphasizing the importance of solid grounding in homeland customs as essential to upward mobility. Kadiatou K., who fled Sierra Leone with her teenage daughters at the height of the civil war in 1998, provided some useful insights: "What we have created in the United States are 'intellectual subcultures.' Therefore, we cannot hand over our children to America. We must keep them in our subcultures where they can benefit from our traditions and values and be ready for America."[29]

The worry is that losing touch with their roots will make the young people more susceptible to American-made problems, anxieties that speak to an underlying fear that the immigrant children will fall into the oppositional culture that has developed among some disaffected American-born adolescents, especially among the black and Latino populations, whose attempts to move up the social ladder through educational pursuits have been so thwarted by the dire socioeconomic circumstances that they find themselves in that it has led them to reject academic aspirations and to scorn scholastic achievement among their peers.[30]

Such priorities led one Nigerian educator to self-publish a primer, *Readings for Amerigerian Igbo*, with the aim of providing "a legacy, road

Second-generation Sierra Leonean American children march into church holding the American and Sierra Leonean flags at the 2012 annual Thanksgiving service of the Krio Descendants Union (KDU)–Texas Branch. Behind them in the procession are two women wearing print (traditional Krio costume) *aso ebi*. Photo by Lesley Rickford.

map and information source for . . . educating and acclimatizing their American-born Nigerian children (Amerigerians) with the ethos of life in the Nigeria that these parents left behind as students."[31] More recently some community groups have initiated summer camps for youngsters where they can receive intensive cultural heritage training, a telling and ironic development since there is no such thing as summer camp in West Africa, yet that is the vehicle used in the United States to inculcate such traditional values. Thus, for example, when the Ote Ummune women's organization in Atlanta created an annual summer camp for the sole purpose of educating Igbo children in the city in the principles of their culture, they were combining these treasured transplanted customs with the time-honored American summer ritual of sending kids off to camp.

The majority of young West Africans, both immigrant and second-generation, are closely connected with their respective ethnic enclaves through the family and other institutions, including church, mosque, and a variety of secular associations. Such resources constitute a level of social capital that can often assist in successfully overcoming the challenges of resettlement. The family attempts to oversee the children's adaptation, from selecting their circle of friends and insisting on the retention or learning of African languages to stipulating appropriate social activities. Crystal S., a high school senior whose mother is from Sierra Leone, explained why her mother approves of her best friend: "She [the best friend] was born here [America] but her parents are from Nigeria, so my mom said she has 'training.'"[32] West African immigrants have attempted to replicate traditional family structures like the extended family in their new homes. The children are exposed to the influences of a host of uncles, aunts, grandmothers, and grandfathers. While some of these are biological kin, many of these "relatives" are friends and acquaintances of the parents. A number of the relationships are new ones forged in the United States. Such efforts to reconstruct a cohesive familial network, even when the original family unit might have been disrupted in the migration process, as can often be the case particularly for refugee populations, mirrors settlement patterns that have been well documented for other immigrant groups such as the Vietnamese.[33]

Other institutions, even if they do not blatantly dictate to the children, attempt to steer them toward the values of the homeland cultures. Sermons of church pastors and imams of West African Muslim congregations remind youngsters about life in the homeland and admonish them to tap into that background for success in America. The religious institutions have developed ministries that are specifically devoted to young people such as the Masjid Lwabahu, a small Gambian mosque that started in a small apartment in the Bronx and runs an after-school program for children to study the Koran in Arabic. Secular associations also address the advancement of the youth in their mission and goals. For example, the Nigerian Women's Association of Georgia offers scholarships to qualified high school seniors who are Nigerians or of Nigerian descent and organizes an annual summer enrichment program to acquaint the youth and children in the Nigerian community of Atlanta with Nigerian culture, values, and lifestyle. The young people themselves are beginning to address the realities of their "in-between world." The organization, Youth for Sierra Leone, offers a good example of this trend. Founded by mostly young immigrants and refugees with a few second-generation members, the association, with branches in Washington, D.C., Atlanta, and Freetown, Sierra Leone, was created primarily to "improve the conditions of young people" in that West African country. Initially, Sierra Leone was its exclusive focus. Recently, however, a discussion has begun about why and how to talk about issues affecting the members in the United States. Similarly the Cape Verdean Alumni Network regularly sponsors events in conjunction with the consortium of Cape Verdean Student Associations to foster the link between cultural literacy and educational attainment.

The immigrant press is another viable contributor to the grounding of the young ones. *African Abroad*, which has a wide circulation in West African communities in New York, Atlanta, Chicago, and Houston, devotes much attention to youth development. Its most notable contribution is its policy to cover the accomplishments of young West Africans, immigrant and American-born, from graduations and awards to service in the U.S. military. The editor, Alex Kabba, believes that not only the young people but entire West African immigrant communities are encouraged and emboldened by such reports.

The efforts of the enclaves in guiding their progeny are undoubtedly well meaning and useful. The children do acknowledge this and express their appreciation of the intellectual subcultures in ensuring continuity with the homeland and grounding them in their multifaceted American existence. When Ngozi M., who fled Sierra Leone with her parents and siblings, graduated with honors in journalism from the University of Tampa, she stressed in her graduation party speech that she owed that success to her parents and, importantly, the extended family in Atlanta, who raised her in "the African way." Such outcomes are consistent with studies of other recent immigrant groups that show that those who come from families who are able to remain intact or, if separated, can maintain tightly knit social networks that replicate the support of the close ties of an extended family have higher levels of educational achievement and better rates of psychological adjustment than those from more socially isolated families, whether immigrant or native-born.[34] Moreover, recent research has shown that children of immigrant parents who are stern disciplinarians also perform better in school and have more successful career outcomes. The tight hold the parents impose on their kids combined with an emphasis on traditional homeland values can serve to protect young people from becoming vulnerable to the dangers of street life.[35]

In his case study of Liberian students in an ESOL program at an urban high school in Philadelphia, Richard De Gourville found that the parents often complained that their children's American education lacked the rigor of their schooling in Liberia, even with the turmoil there caused by the civil war. Like Sierra Leonean refugees, Liberians do not see language as an educational barrier in this country, and thus their expectations of excellence in academic preparation are generally higher than those of their counterparts from other African countries such as Somalia and Ethiopia. The students in De Gourville's study also lamented the absence of the kind of close working relationships with their teachers that characterized the Liberian pedagogical approach. By contrast, their teachers in the U.S. seemed distant and aloof, even when they offered their pupils extra help with their schoolwork. The youngsters in the American classroom sorely missed the personal quality of the teacher-student relationship, the interest that teachers took in their academic and social progress, and the importance of mentorship in the educational system of Liberia.[36]

An exception to this pattern can be found in the Providence, Rhode Island, public school system where the principal of one of the middle schools is Liberian himself. Following the Liberian model of personal involvement with his students but in the American setting, he was the catalyst for the organization of the citywide Liberian youth association and in countless ways demonstrates his devotion to the education of his students inside the school and out—from personally driving pupils home when their after-school activities keep them late to meeting with their parents at their homes, if that is what is warranted. The principal is a strict and demanding administrator, a galvanizing role model, and a stellar mentor to his young Liberian charges, and under his tutelage students have found much success in the classroom and beyond.[37] As more and more West Africans who were refugees themselves obtain their teaching credentials, they have been able to work within the school system to provide a more responsive educational environment for immigrant youth.

Another feature of their premigration schooling that some of the students whom De Gourville interviewed still wished for was the required school uniforms. Whereas fitting in and the status achieved through dressing in the latest styles at their urban American high school was fraught with anxiety, challenging to negotiate, and expensive to attain, in Liberia it was the wearing of school uniforms that signified status as members of a privileged group whose families could afford to send them to these select schools. Students wore the uniforms, as symbols of school community, with pride and as markers of their social identity. In the United States the freedom of individual expression gained by being able to choose what they wore to school came at the price of risking ridicule or peer group exclusion and ultimately a loss of status if they somehow got it wrong, which was easy to do and, consequently, a frequent occurrence.[38]

While a proportion of the 1.5 generation still remembers wearing uniforms to school before emigrating, for those who have vague or no memories of this dress code and for the second generation, references to the value of uniforms have found their way into the unfolding West African immigrant narrative. Parents nostalgically recount the role of their "clean, well starched uniforms" in emphasizing and upholding decorum and discipline in their high-quality European-molded African schooling. Consequently, tapping into a premigration past, parents and other relatives and family friends define and often stipulate proper dress, which to their chagrin the culture of American schools does not encourage.

Simultaneously, the realities of school life, heavily influenced by popular culture, tug at the young West African Americans. As one young second generation high school sophomore expressed it,

> When you're young, you feel like you need to be around your parents a lot so that's when you start to connect with their culture, but then you grow up . . . you stop bringing Liberian food to school for lunch, you finally start connecting to the black kids, you start listening to black music instead of African stuff . . . you can sag your pants a little bit when they're not looking . . . and then when you get home you can pull them back up.[39]

Admittedly, unlike many East African students such as those from Somalia, the West African pupils who are Muslim typically do not conform to a strict Islamic dress code. Yet their clothing, supervised and approved by their parents, has been a source of ridicule and taunts from schoolmates. Moreover, many of the females are convinced that they endure far more strain and stress with regard to what they wear and other aspects of cultural identity and belonging than do their male counterparts. Intergenerational conflict may be especially tense around such issues as they relate to sexuality and dating norms, concerns that are often heightened in the level of control that immigrant parents attempt to assert over their daughters in particular.

Second-generation teenager Efua C. resented the leniency that her Ghanaian and Sierra Leonean parents showed toward her brother: "My mom and dad never say anything to him when he wears his pants way down. But the moment I try to go out with a decent low-rise, I get the third degree about what 'wayward girls look like back home!'" Efua and many like her have resorted to lying to their parents about clothes, makeup, trips to the mall, and dates.[40] Scholar and advocate for social justice Laurie Olsen describes similar experiences in her study *Made in America*, based on her examination of a public high school in California. Olsen found important gender differences among the Hispanic, Chinese, Vietnamese, and East Indian students of the school she investigated, similar to findings for West African youth.[41] These dynamics can lead to young women feeling torn between their desire for greater autonomy in their social lives and their wish to be dutiful to their parents. The clash of cultures regarding normative adolescent sexual and social behaviors is not always generational, however. One Liberian refugee described her shock and dismay on her first day of high school after arriving in the United States at seeing female classmates who were pregnant and unmarried. She had led a sheltered life in Liberia, attended a private Baptist school there, and was stunned by the visible signs of differences in moral values from that with which she was accustomed:

That was a big shocker for me, seeing girls who were pregnant and in school. In Liberia you never saw that. We believe, "no kids until marriage." Liberian fathers are strong on that. Plus, I was used to wearing uniforms. Here you had to dress up—but the way the girls are dressed! You saw that on TV but you didn't expect that they would actually dress

that way in school. I had a lot of problems with a few of the girls, the wild
girls.[42]

Nonetheless, of particular interest here are the findings that show that
strict parental monitoring of the lives of the second-generation daughters can produce positive results. Although the girls may resent the
greater limitations placed on them, Robert C. Smith's research on Mexi-
cans and Nancy Lopez's study of Caribbeans, both conducted in New
York, suggest a positive correlation between more restrictive and structured child-rearing practices with girls and the young women's ability
to outperform boys in school.[43]

Transatlantic Time-Outs

One alternative to the struggles of trying to reconcile African and
American pedagogical approaches in the U.S. classroom, however,
has been for some parents to opt out by sending their children to be
schooled in their homeland countries. While research on the actual
numbers who participate in this reverse temporary migration has not
yet been conducted, it has become quite a common practice, particularly among those who hail from Nigeria and Ghana, countries where
well-established systems of boarding schools are in place that are more
affordable than their private school counterparts in the United States.
For example, at one of the more well-regarded private schools in
Ghana, Akosombo International, a coed institution, 20 percent of the
student body is composed of Ghanaians living abroad.[44] Moreover, at
such schools, the curriculum, taught in English, is certain to be rigor-
ous and the schedule of the average school day much more demanding than is the case in the United States. The strict disciplinary procedures compared to the American classroom are a welcome alternative
to parents who worry not only that traditional cultural values are not
being instilled in their children the longer they are in the United States
but also that exposure to American socialization patterns will lead the
young ones to become increasingly disrespectful of their elders.

Typically, children are sent abroad in the middle school years and
return to complete high school and take the SAT exams, with hopes that
they will go on to matriculate at well-ranked colleges and universities in

the United States. Such a plan, of course, is not an option for those who have fled war-torn countries, such as Liberia, that may still be politically unstable or have not yet rebuilt their educational infrastructure. Sometimes the strategy backfires and the time away represents a setback. Indeed, in one unfortunate and extreme instance, the temporary time-out became permanent when the son of a church minister in Boston was sent home to Sierra Leone because he was skipping school and had joined a band of teenagers who routinely broke into neighborhood houses. Before the young man was scheduled to return to the United States, however, the war broke out and he was stuck there, eventually losing his green card status because he was out of the country for more than a year. Despite such cases, when this form of sojourner migration is successful, it exemplifies the best of what a transnational outlook can offer. Viewing the challenges of child rearing as a global endeavor where resources from both American and West African societies are mobilized, some parents have decided that, ironically enough, the best way to ensure long-term success in the United States is to ship their budding adolescent offspring away from their adopted homeland for an extended stay. They hope that such a cultural time-out will enable the second generation to absorb a good dose of African influences that will, in turn, fortify them for the next stage of development on their return to the United States and young adulthood.[45]

Even if parents do not go so far as to enroll their American-born youngsters in schools back home, they may arrange for them to at least spend their summers with extended family in their countries of origin as another route to sustaining the cultural connection in the second generation. Some kids may resist these trips, not wanting to leave their friends and their familiar social scene behind. Although by the time he reached young adulthood he came to appreciate the education his parents were trying to give him, one second-generation Nigerian who grew up in Houston, but routinely had to spend his summer vacations in Nigeria, found the whole experience trying and had only negative memories: "I'd be like 'Why are we going? They don't even have electricity. They don't have water. I just want to play Nintendo' . . . that was our summer vacation. No hamburgers, no hot dogs, it was terrible."[46] Similarly, when standout NFL defensive player Adewale Ogunleye, a second-generation Nigerian born and raised in the tough projects of

Staten Island, New York, and the grandson of the provincial king of the city of Emure in Nigeria, visited his ancestral homeland at age thirteen, he was singularly unimpressed. Despite his royal lineage, "I couldn't really appreciate it. I wanted to sit in air-conditioning, enjoy my cartoons and get back to my friends."[47] Ogunleye managed to survive the violent turf wars of his neighborhood largely through attendance at a more middle-class high school at the other end of Staten Island, where he took advantage of an initiative to make the student population more racially diverse.

But especially if the young people are getting into trouble or showing signs of more serious behavioral problems, parents will insist on these transatlantic time-outs as a strategy to manage unruly teens by removing them from the influences of their peer group. When Alex Kabba addressed these concerns in an issue of *African Abroad* with the headline-grabbing article, "Immigrants' Children Gone Wild! The Difficulty of Raising Black Children in the USA," he concluded with a column of "5 Ways to Prevent Children from Trouble." Last on the list is the "Africa Option": "If you are unable to afford a private school, there is no law against sending your child to Africa to school and learn the disciplined life which has made many parents—also known as African immigrants—to be such a success story in the USA."[48] African parents in the United States making arrangements to send their kids back home is what inspired director and screenwriter Emmanuel Ijeh to make the recent film, *Tobi*, a production that came out of what has been called the new Nollywood in the Diaspora cinema about a second-generation Nigerian high school dropout who is in constant conflict with his parents.[49] Himself an emigrant from Nigeria who arrived in the United States in 2000 at the age of seventeen, Ijeh was taken aback by the frequency of this strategy and wanted to explore the dynamics that were leading families to go to such lengths to try to resolve these intergenerational difficulties. Not only does the first generation hope that such experiences will interrupt delinquent behavioral patterns, they also anticipate that these excursions will give their sons and daughters a fresh perspective on what America has to offer them and that they may even come away with a new appreciation of their West African heritage.

Sometimes though such visits are not a matter of damage control but are the result of the resilience of transnational ties that include family trips that are embraced by the young people as a way of deepening their West African roots. Moreover, some young adults, especially recent college graduates who have been immersed in the new realm of global consciousness are combining their strong family bonds with a sense of international social responsibility and want to direct their energies to their homelands in order to make a positive difference. Yet the dynamics that ensue once the connection is made can, at times, be startling for the Americanized visitors, especially when they return displaying visible signs of wealth and success in the United States. Under these circumstances, rather than being welcomed as, for example, fellow Nigerians or Ghanaians, they are, instead, seen as Americans only and sometimes even called out as "white people" because of the socioeconomic status of their families and the perceptions of privilege associated with whiteness that their compatriots in West Africa may hold. Or they may be viewed, instead, as another kind of African as with the recently invented label of "Jus Cam" or "JC," used in Sierra Leone to differentiate a Sierra Leonean in the diaspora. In these instances, the journey "home" can be bittersweet at best and terribly disappointing at worst, especially if the travelers came with high expectations of finally alighting in a place where they can readily belong and are caught off guard by the realization that they do not automatically fit in and that there is a significant gulf between how they see themselves and how they are perceived by their hosts. Indeed, rather than automatically reinforcing their transnational identities as would typically be presumed, second-generation visitors may find, to the contrary, that such experiences actually make them feel more American than they did before they left. These dynamics, however, have been influenced by the power of social media as engagement in precontact dialogue on social networking sites such as Facebook and Twitter can serve to assuage the alienation often felt by diaspora returnees when they finally arrive.

Identity Matters

For the diverse West African immigrant groups, identities matter. They are crucial in shaping the trajectories of adaptation, assimilation, and socioeconomic mobility. For the majority of the first generation, fostering seemingly uncomplicated homeland African identities is imperative. They believe that the success of the community beyond the second generation depends on the sustenance of viable, diverse African identities. This phenomenon is not new or unique to West African immigrants. Similar patterns among other groups have been identified and examined by scholars such as Mary Waters in her study of West Indians in New York, *Black Identities*. Waters discusses the parents' hopes and convictions for continuity and their fierce cultural pride, while the realities of their children's lives, especially peer influences, often lead the young ones to assimilate instead into a broader ghetto youth subculture. Sociologist Milton Vickerman, looking mostly at the first generation in his work *Crosscurrents: West Indian Immigrants and Race*, analyzes some of these same dynamics.[50] Thus, initial trends suggest that West African adaptation patterns resemble those of other foreign-born blacks such as West Indians, whereby the immigrant generation attempts to emphasize distinctive cultural traditions and defies being grouped with African Americans while the second generation is much more likely than their parents to associate and identify with native-born minorities. Alternatively, research on Dominican youth in Providence, Rhode Island, has led one scholar to argue that post-1965 immigrants and especially the second generation are transforming entrenched notions of black/white racial categorization altogether. The young people in the study privileged their ethnolinguistic and cultural background as their racial designation whether as Dominican, Spanish, or Hispanic rather than identifying in terms of black or white.[51]

Ruben Hadzide, president of the Ghana National Council of Metropolitan Chicago, echoed the typical first-generation hope:

> May I ask you to pause for a moment with me and ponder over what will happen to the next generations of our children if we do not put in place structures that will bring them together when we are no more. . . . Our identity as a people will be lost and our community as we know it today will be wiped off if we do not lay that foundation! That is the stark reality.[52]

Holding such a perspective has led the immigrant generation to work very hard to erect this formidable foundation. Many communities have devised vehicles to formally transmit the immigrant cultures to the children. By the end of the 1990s, language and culture schools had sprung up in several West African communities in New York, Washington, D.C., Atlanta, and Houston. For example, families banded together to organize dance and cooking classes in their homes in D.C. and Maryland. They explained that they were prompted by the desire to "provide the younger generation with cultural roots that will hold them firmly, help them grow, and give them a sense of identity, which many believe has helped them cope with the difficult transition to life in America."[53] Dr. Akinyele, one of the Yoruba language instructors for the D.C.-based Isokan Yoruba Organization, explained, "We believe that by teaching our children our culture we will one day go back to our fatherland triumphantly."[54] For the overwhelming majority of the West African associations, most of which do not have formal, clearly defined culture schools, the "African socialization" of the younger generation is central to their mission. A founder of the Guinean Association of Philadelphia underscored this imperative: "One of my own motivations for creating the association was I wanted my own kids to be introduced into the Guinean community."[55]

What, then, is the "stark reality" for the young members of West African immigrant communities? Contrary to preconceived notions held by the immigrant generation, perceptions and negotiation of identities produce some of the most complex experiences in the youths' multiple worlds. One young woman, Meri Nana-Ama Danquah, who left Ghana when she was six years old to join her mother in Washington, D.C., explained, "Being black made the transition from Africa to America extremely difficult because it introduced another complex series of boundaries. In a racially divided country, it isn't enough for an immigrant to know how to float in the mainstream. You have to know how to retreat to your margin, where to place your hyphen."[56] The immigrant subcultures of the parents are not the only context that molds the identities of the 1.5 and second generations. They are shaped simultaneously to varying degrees by the other social spaces that constitute the children's realities—public and private schools, after-school programs, the workplace, restaurants, clubs, theaters, and other arenas of entertainment, and, very important in the twenty-first century, the variety of cyberspaces. These environments are just as potent, for they are where the young West Africans bump into American obstacles that require a more efficacious set of identities than what a narrowly focused foreign black subculture might provide, although sometimes these same venues can strengthen cultural identifications. Waters, discussing West Indians, offered a useful list of the challenges the young people encounter—the materialistic U.S. culture, an oppressive racial environment, and segregated city neighborhoods.[57] How the West African 1.5 and second generations experience and confront these barriers is important in defining and projecting their identities.

In the unfolding discussion of identities in black America, a bifurcation between descendants and immigrants has emerged. According to this division, those who trace their ancestry to the earlier, involuntary diaspora are the descendants; and those blacks not born in the United States, and even their American-born children and subsequent generations, all products of the new diaspora, are not truly part of the American black historical experience—therefore, they are not descendants. Thus, who or what, exactly, are the young West Africans in the context of black America? The complexity of identities among 1.5- and second-generation Nigerians, Ghanaians, Sierra Leoneans, Cape Verdeans, and so forth is forged by the debates and changing circumstances within their immigrant cultures as well as black and mainstream America.

The distinction being made between black descendants and immigrants has recently been most clearly articulated in the raging public debate over what sociologist Rodney Coates calls the "outsourcing of Affirmative Action."[58] The questions being asked are these: Who should be entitled to the benefits of the civil rights struggle, fought to rectify historical injustices created and sustained by a long-lived racist, oppressive system? And, as the system currently stands, who are the real beneficiaries? With Harvard professors Lani Guinier and Henry Louis Gates, Jr. at the forefront, some skeptics have called for revisiting the workings of affirmative action for America's blacks. They believe that the main recipients among young people, at least at Ivy League institutions, are black immigrants and the American-born children of black immigrants.[59] The conclusions in *Inheriting the City* support such claims, as the research showed that one of the key components of second-generation educational success has been that many of the young immigrants of color in their study have taken advantage of just such policies as affirmative action and the creation of other kinds of diversity programs. The authors point to the irony that initiatives coming directly out of civil-rights-era activism as a strategy to repair long-standing racial inequities often end up helping the foreign-born black population rather than the black descendants for whom they were intended.[60]

Outside the rigors of intellectual discourse, the young immigrants and those of the second generation experience the unfolding identity tussle firsthand. For example, some students at a predominantly white college, who are American-born of Nigerian and Ghanaian heritage, were criticized by African American "descendant" students for joining the African and West Indian Student Association, even though they had been born in the United States and had, according to their chastisers, shamelessly accepted financial aid as American minority students. Incidents like this reveal how far-reaching and complex issues of identity among the children of West African immigrants are. They are not isolated concerns completely unique to the group or played out exclusively within West African immigrant subcultures. Rather, the identity issues that young West Africans and their immigrant parents grapple with are similar to those of some other groups and are influenced by circumstances beyond their communities. Relatively speaking, the young West Africans are new and so their history in America, including the history of their identities, is only just unfolding, even if rapidly and vibrantly. The diasporic, transnational identities that are emerging from the experiences of these young immigrant black Americans are, like all evolving developments, sometimes difficult to grasp.

The nuances of racial labeling are also variable and contested. One second-generation Liberian teenager made a definitive distinction between her black and African American peers. She grouped the former based on their being slave-descended, explaining, "They say they're not from Africa because it's too far down the line, so they are just Black," while she used the term "African American" to refer to African immigrants and their American-born children. Yet, at the very same time, she resisted calling *herself* African American, self-identifying, instead, as Liberian or occasionally as African. This was a source of contention with her father, as she explained:

> My Dad tells me all the time that I'm not Liberian—you weren't born there. He says you're just African American. We always argue. I reason

that both my parents are Liberian. I tell him, if Mommy was Caucasian and you were black, I would say I'm mulatto because I'm 50 percent white, 50 percent black. But I say you are both Liberian so I'm 50 percent Liberian on both sides so that makes me 100 percent Liberian.[61]

This is a rare instance, however, as the more common scenario has the parents insisting on African/homeland identities for their children, while the young people defy them and try to be more practical by affirming their Americanness or African Americanness. And although most who do invoke their African heritage prefer to self-identify by national origin group, for one young woman hailing from Guinea, her nationality never entered into the discussion. Instead, she clearly and repeatedly identified and referenced Africa, proclaiming, "I'm African—100 percent African."[62] Yet another young man, a second-generation Liberian, who spent time with his family in Liberia when he was five years old, declared, "I know this is kinda weird, but here [in the United States] I'm a black kid but there [in Liberia] I'm just a kid." At age seventeen, he considered himself "a full black kid but with African roots and not afraid to show it."[63] But for another young Nigerian woman, it took several years in the United States for a black identity to even sink in: "I discovered my blackness at Syracuse, well into my fifth year in America. Suddenly, in something of a blind revelation, I saw myself as a black person for the very first time. Of course, I'd known I wasn't white, but I did not see myself as black either. It was as though I believed I belonged in a no-color zone."[64]

Among Cape Verdean youth, the long-standing position of being "in-between peoples" continues to manifest itself among the current wave. Unlike the history of other West African groups that have immigrated to America, Cape Verdeans have been settling in the United States in significant numbers for well over a century. Consequently, the multigenerational dynamics typically differ from those of their other West African counterparts, making issues of ethnoracial identity formation even more nuanced and complicated. Whether migrants from the earlier period or contemporary arrivals, identity concerns have been paramount in the life stories of members of the Cape Verdean diaspora. The legacy of both colonialism and creolization has continued to divide the population over conceptions of race, color, and ethnicity.

As was the case a century ago, many Cape Verdeans today still wrestle with these fundamental questions of identity, and those who migrate as young people are no exception.

What is most apparent about the contemporary Cape Verdean diaspora in the United States is that it is no longer possible to speak of a monolithic Cape Verdean community. Apart from the continuity of regional geographic concentration in southern New England, from the newly arrived to fourth-generation Cape Verdean Americans, this population represents a multiplicity of educational backgrounds, socioeconomic positions, ethnoracial affiliations, religious beliefs, political perspectives, and island and national origins. Individual biographies typically reflect these complex diasporic histories. As one immigrant who was born on the Cape Verdean island of Brava, migrated to Dakar, Senegal, when she was two years old, and then moved to the United States at age five and who is trilingual in Cape Verdean Creole, English, and French put it, "I'm a well-seasoned salad."[65] Another second-generation Cape Verdean who grew up in the Boston area distinguished herself from her immigrant parents by privileging the American side of her hyphenated identity, declaring that unlike those who were born in Cape Verde, she is "American Cape Verdean," not "Cape Verdean American."[66]

Among the long-standing American-born segment, there are those, especially of lighter skin color, who continue to refer to themselves as ethnically Portuguese, while others, particularly those who live in predominantly black communities, who themselves identify as black. As one immigrant, now in his early thirties but who arrived as a teenager in the 1990s, succinctly phrased the dilemma,

> We aren't accepted being black because I am Cape Verdean and my culture is different and I am lighter. We know we are from Africa, but we are from Cape Verde. We are not accepted in the white culture because we are dark and speak Portuguese. We are caught in the middle of blacks and whites.[67]

And despite Cape Verde's nearly forty years as an independent nation of Africa, some Cape Verdean immigrants and many more of the American-born still resist the label of African. There are notable exceptions, however, especially among those families who were active in the revolutionary struggle or who have lived in continental Africa en route to migrating to the United States, such as Adonis F., who was eight years old when he arrived in this country:

> The difference for us, we were more conscious of our Cape Verdeanness, number one, and secondly I remember when coming here [to the United States] being really proud of my Africanness. . . . We knew who we were because our parents lived through that. They lived in a predominantly African community in Guinea-Bissau . . . especially coming here when the image of Africans as a whole from the continent is already Tarzan and jungle and those types of things. And the other kids would ask, "how can you be proud of being African?" Because we heard those stories at home in terms of the revolution, in terms of Amilcar Cabral, so our roots were already there. . . . At no point did I ever negate any part of my Cape Verdeanness.[68]

At the intragroup level, contested identities reflect shifts in meaning based on changing historical circumstances that challenge the creation of a cohesive community. The deepest divisions are generational. Given that there was a fifty-year hiatus in migration flows, differences related to education, culture, and social levels separate those families who have been in the United States for generations and those who immigrated after independence. The results of ethnographic research conducted several years ago on identity structures among the Cape Verdean diaspora in Boston also underscore the division between immigrants and the American-born.[69] For starters, the immigrant community tends to continue to converse in Cape Verdean Creole while the American-born residents speak English. But the splintering is much more complex than that.

An equally important element of cultural fragmentation, then, is the extent to which diaspora Cape Verdeans identify as Portuguese versus as African Americans. The 1960s were watershed years for Cape Verdean Americans as the rise of black nationalism and its attendant emphasis on pride in one's African heritage had a transformative effect on many. Thus, the struggles for liberation from Portuguese colonialism on the continent of Africa coincided with turbulent social change on the domestic front. The process of rethinking racial identifications touched most Cape Verdean American families in this period, often creating intergenerational rifts between the parents and grandparents, who were staunchly Portuguese, and their children, who were beginning to ally themselves with the African American struggle not only in political thought but also in cultural expression.

More recently the intergenerational struggles have centered, instead, on what is viewed as an erosion of traditional family controls. The past decade has witnessed a significant upsurge in drug and gang-related violence among Cape Verdean youth, especially in the cities of Boston and Brockton, Massachusetts, that has been gravely undermining the quality of life. The crisis has been attributed to this generation's lack of respect for its elders and the community itself. Lamenting the difficulty of transplanting the time-honored approaches to child rearing that shaped the socialization of young people in their homelands, especially as parents compete with the influences of American television, new media, and popular culture, Nigerian American journalist Rudolf Ogoo Okonkwo declared, "In Africa, it takes a village to raise a child. In America, it takes a village to ruin a child."[70]

Problems related to drugs and petty crimes are certainly not solely the domain of Cape Verdean adolescents. Incidences of teens caught up in the criminal corrections system and reports of eruptions of violent crime have come out of the Sierra Leonean communities in Perth Amboy and New Brunswick, New Jersey, as well as from Nigerian youth living in New York City.[71] Parents are especially worried that their children will be lured into membership in gangs, a step they fear brings them only closer to permanent criminal records. These dilemmas have become so intrinsic to the West African experience that the central narrative of the Nollywood in the Diaspora movie *Tobi* revolves around the desperate attempts of the parents of the lead character to inculcate the traditional values upon which they were raised to protect their wayward son against negative peer-group influences; however, they simply cannot compete with the pull of American street life.

Yet although cases of gang violence have been reported involving East African youth in Seattle and Minneapolis in recent years, apart from adolescents in selected Cape Verdean communities, organized gang activity has not made much news among other West African populations.[72] That does not mean, however, that instances of individual delinquency have not occurred, especially concerning male refugees from the war-torn countries of Liberia and Sierra Leone, who when they find themselves the targets of verbal taunts or hostility from their peers, have reacted with what is familiar from the trauma of wartime experiences—fighting back with fists or weapons, thereby escalating the confrontation. "If you have been in a war as a kid, you don't know anything different. You have to fight, that's all you know," conceded one young man from Sierra Leone.[73]

Community activists have begun to address such problems with programs geared to African teenagers. In Providence, Rhode Island, where a large population of Liberians resides, the Liberian Association of Rhode Island has been actively engaging the younger members of the community, sponsoring an annual Youth Summit. In 2006, the focus was on "Youth Confronting Violence," and it drew on the resources of educators, government, and social service providers to create a forum for "Real Talk" on this urgent subject. Similarly, in order to help quell the simmering rivalry between African American and African students at the local high school, leaders of the Liberian community in southwestern Philadelphia organized a successful youth summit in 2009 to tackle problems with drugs and violence. In the Washington, D.C., area, in addition to tutoring and after-school clubs, the youth program of the African Refugees and Immigrant Foundation has devoted time to forums for violence prevention. And with regard to the troubles among Cape Verdean adolescents, a conference was convened in Boston in the summer of 2010, titled "Youth in Dangerous Times: The Capeverdean Challenge," to address head-on the escalating violence plaguing the local community. Former gang members and young people with criminal histories met with students successfully enrolled in area colleges who were able to demonstrate an alternative path of pursuing an education.

Related to the intergenerational strife is an increasingly pronounced conflict between the American-born diaspora and the newest immigrants. Barriers between newcomers and those born in the United States are especially high among the adolescent population. The consequences of the rash of crimes in the greater Boston area have reverberated across the Atlantic as recent policies have resulted in the deportation of a number of convicted youth back to the Cape Verde Islands, often to settle, if they migrated at a young age, in a place with which they are no longer familiar. The difficulties of reintegrating these return migrants into Cape Verdean society—young people who already feel like outcasts—and preventing further delinquent behavior have created new challenges in a country without a history of this type of gang activity. At the Boston symposium, as a sign of the transnational impact of the problem and the extent to which it has undermined the quality of life both in the United States and abroad, the prime minister of Cape Verde traveled to the city to deliver the keynote address. Yet it has not only been the Cape Verdean community in the greater Boston area that has been plagued by such neighborhood disruption. By 2012, there were enough young people of Nigerian descent residing in the city for local Nigerian American organizations to sponsor an educational forum on violence prevention titled "Empowering Our Youth!"

Expressive Culture

As is the case with all Americans negotiating their hyphenated identities, young West Africans find creative ways to blend the variegated cultural components of their fluid ethnic affiliations especially in the arenas of music, food, fashion, and festive culture. And they do so with pride in these distinctive cultural expressions. Such a cultural trajectory echoes the findings of the research on the West Indian sector of the groups studied in *Inheriting the City* where the crossover popularity of Jamaican music in particular served as a positive vehicle for bridging connections to other black and white groups in New York.[74] When Candida Rose, a second-generation Cape Verdean singer whose musical training was in R&B and jazz began to explore her ethnic heritage, it transformed her music and she invented a new genre to reflect that journey: "Every song has that kind of thing in mind, Cape Verdean-rooted music with my American influences which I call 'KapuJazz'... it's a combination of new and old."[75] Rather than using music to express her ethnic heritage, Obehi Janice, a young Nigerian American from Lowell, Massachusetts, has instead articulated her personal journey of cultural hybridity through theatrical performance, creating a one-woman show with the clever title of "Fufu and Oreos."[76]

The ethnic revival that began in the mid-1970s in the United States with its emphasis on cultural pluralism was just taking hold when West Africans began to arrive in significant numbers. Thus, the newcomers and their children have been settling in America in an age of multiculturalism where claiming a hyphenated identity has become normative, even fashionable. Unlike the children of earlier generations of immigrants who may have felt ashamed of their parents' language or traditional ways of living, no matter what their ancestry, young people today celebrate the unique features of their diverse ethnic origins, taking pride in their cultural distinctiveness, and are encouraged to do so by a wider society bent on increasing tolerance of difference.[77] Furthermore, the influx of large numbers of nonwhite immigrants from many parts of the globe in the past four decades combined with the increase in rates of mixed-race marriages and reproduction have transformed the United States from a largely black and white world to a kaleidoscopic ethnoracial landscape where the boundaries between groups are becoming less and less sharp.

The young people attending the celebration of the 2005 annual New York Nigerian Independence Day found creative ways of asserting their Nigerianness while blending both sides of the Nigerian American hyphen. They were dressed in the green and white colors of the Nigerian flag, and the slogans on their T-shirts typically pronounced sentiments like "Born Nigerian, Nigerian Always," "I am 100% Nigerian," "Nigerian born in the USA," and "Nigerian Girl Powered by Garri [a staple Nigerian food]." Yet cultural hybridity abounded as one young woman at the parade signified her Nigerianness by wearing green but in the form of a Boston Celtics basketball jersey, while another variation on the pastiche theme found a young man in the crowd sporting a green Yankees hat to mark the day's festivities—even the usual white-on-navy Yankees logo was set in green. At Nigerian Culture Night, an event organized for young people by the Organization for the Advancement of Nigerians and held at Brooklyn College as part of the annual Nigerian Independence Day Celebrations, the 2008 program featured a talent and fashion show as well as the Miss Nigeria Independence Day competition. Whether modeling in the show or not, those in attendance, especially the women, almost all combined traditional clothing with a contemporary twist. Nigerian cloth was cut into funky and hip designs; printed sashes made for wide belts draped across the waist. The traditional national costume combined with stylish Brooklyn attire making for a uniquely Nigerian American fashion statement. Similarly, among the garments that a twenty-one-year-old aspiring fashion designer from Ghana who now lives in the Bronx brought to the Soho preshow for New York's annual Africa Fashion Week in 2011 was an original creation made from West African kente cloth but cut like a short, puffy prom dress.

Indeed, a group of the mostly young 1.5- and second-generation designers and fashion bloggers who participated in African Fashion Week have adopted the notion of Afropolitan and extended it to define a new trend in style. As such, Afropolitan fashion displays "a consciousness that blends Africa's lively prints with vintage cuts and sensibilities . . . Nairobi meets New York." [78] One ambitious fashion promoter has created a website solely dedicated to increasing awareness and recognition of high-end Afropolitan brands and the designers who produce them, while one of the organizers of the week's events, a young Nigerian American, declared, "It's our moment, and it's just beginning. Young African designers are becoming real players now. People have been taking resources from Africa for generations. But our generation, raised in both worlds, is changing that."[79]

Afropolitanism has also been making its mark in the world of music. The band featured in a series of interviews for a 2011 piece in *Arise Magazine* titled "Generation Next: Meet the Afropolitans, Africa's Transcontinental Children," whose members come from all parts of the continent and combine ska-punk, township jazz, and hip-hop in their eclectic repertoire, have christened their group the "Afropolitan Society."[80] In general, the hip-hop genre with its mash-up of sounds and styles has become a ready and influential vehicle for expressing the multiple racial and ethnic identities of the new young Americans from West Africa. As Temistocles Ferreira, aka Tem Blessed, a New Bedford, Massachusetts, rapper who emigrated from Guinea-Bissau in 1977 when he was three years old, explained, "For me Cape Verdean and black were synonymous. . . . The hip-hop culture had a lot to do with that and hip-hop at that time was about being black and proud and being African and all of that . . . so cool, I'm going with this."[81]

Some have even found ways of overcoming what would seem to be the clashing values of the powerful mythos of successful upward mobility and the alternative expressions of hip-hop culture. One young Nigerian American artist, Madarocka, known as the "Original" African Queen of Hip Hop, has deftly positioned herself at just such a nexus. Simultaneously showcasing the status of her educational achievements and her coast-to-coast street credentials in one sweep, she promotes herself with this billing: "Born of a proud Igbo family the African Queen was raised in D. C., educated at the University of Delaware, Howard University, and in the streets of D. C., New York and LA." And, in the very next breath, true to her African upbringing, she honors her elders by explaining that over the past forty years, her father "assisted nearly a whole village in the migration from Imo State to the East of America. In recent years, this migration translated to success for many Nigerian families in America." In a final Weberian homage she underlines her entrepreneurial drive and business acumen when she tells us that she has a background as "a graduate of fine arts, has worked on Hollywood sets and been an innovator of Nubian hairstyles, who has been a wicked braider and natural hair care stylist for many entrepreneurs and professionals." But that's not all. Madarocka also has clearly announced herself as embracing the subgenre of conscious hip-hop when she writes that she has been inspired to motivate young Americans to "explore the sands of the Motherland." She also speaks and mentors to youth in urban communities. "Utilizing her God-given artistic abilities in a positive way," the promotional flyer explains, "Madarocka became an art coordinator for youth education programs."[82]

Conscious hip-hop aims to teach those who choose to listen in a format that is considered rooted in African traditions. The hip-hop movement, which began in the early 1970s, was created by the children of parents who lived through or participated in the civil rights movement. These artists used the modern technology of sound systems and turntables to establish a cultural form that specifically addressed the socioeconomic conditions of their surroundings. Inspired by African musical traditions, the genre was intended to teach and raise the consciousness of those who listened. This form of hip-hop thrived through the early 1990s, promoting a Pan-Africanist stance and delving into topics that affected urban communities of color such as racism, police brutality and incarceration, drugs (specifically the crack epidemic and the havoc it was wrecking in urban locations), AIDS, black-on-black violence, apartheid, and teenage pregnancy.

While maintaining street credibility has always been an important component of hip-hop culture, rap style took a major turn in the late 1990s when gangsta rap became the dominate force in the global hip-hop world. Mainstream hip-hop, which has become the nation's popular music, employs the rhetoric of the world of "ghetto fabulous." It's all about jewelry, cars, hot chicks, guns, money, power, sex, and drugs.[83] For many West African parents, it is the very promotion of "ghetto fabulousness" that they worry will seduce their youngsters, poisoning the traditional values they have tried to instill. In the concluding sections of his sweeping history of the great migrations of Africans to the United States, *The Making of African America*, Ira Berlin reiterates the difficulties African newcomers, dismayed by the lyrics and put off by the glitzy and violent lifestyle, have had identifying with hip-hop culture. Berlin emphasizes the irony that "the Afro-centrality embedded in hip-hop seemed to have little appeal to Africans, at least on the east side of the Atlantic. Rather than provide cohesion to black life the new culture seemed to be a divisive force."[84]

While this distaste certainly has been a common reaction, especially among the first generation, as hip hop has continued to evolve, young people persist in responding with new iterations of the genre. Bam Savage, a hip-hop producer living in Lawrence, Massachusetts, remembers that as a child growing up in Freetown, Sierra Leone, his parents liked listening to Marvin Gaye and Bob Marley. This was his introduction to the music of the Americas, songs that told a story, much like the popular music of his homeland. By the time he immigrated as a teenager with his family to Washington, D.C., gangsta rappers like N.W.A., whose lyrics spoke of killing police and dealing drugs, were peaking in popularity. Young Savage found the music strange but not outrageous; his parents, by contrast, had a much different reaction, as did many of the other West African adults. They were offended by the entire gangsta rap genre and tried to steer their kids away from what they viewed as a dangerous world. Savage, like so many of his peers, nonetheless was irresistibly drawn to this music, but when he heard the lyrics of Boogie-Down Productions' "Criminal Minded," sentiments that gave the possibility of being a rapper, but also an educator, a preacher, and a leader all at once, he found his inspiration. "It was overwhelming," he recalled. "I was like, 'Wow' . . . he was kicking so much knowledge to me at once." Savage has gone on to make his mission the fusion of rap and the West African music he grew up with, hoping to "subvert mainstream hip-hop and bring it back to its socially conscious and traditional roots."[85]

What Berlin did not take into account, then, was the extent to which the crossovers and connections between native and immigrant-origin blacks, particularly of the second generation, have assuaged the breach in the hip-hop world and the ways that African motifs and geopolitical realities have crept back into rap music. This trend is perhaps best exemplified by the African American artist Kanye West's Grammy-award-winning song "Diamonds from Sierra Leone," released in 2005. Riffing on the theme song from the classic 1971 James Bond film *Diamonds Are Forever*, West spotlights the exploitation of Sierra Leone's children and the role of mining conflict diamonds in the country's long and bloody civil war of the 1990s. Furthermore, a sprinkling of African musicians have crossed over and risen to prominence on the American *Billboard* charts such as Akon, a major rap/hip-hop singer and songwriter who has bridged the divide and been embraced by both African American and African immigrant youth. His biography embodies a transnational identity as he was born in St. Louis, Missouri, to parents who are from Senegal and was raised in both Dakar, Senegal, and Jersey City, New Jersey.

In the early years of the twenty-first century, other artists besides Kanye West and Bam Savage, such as Common, Talib Kweli, Mos Def, and Outkast, began presenting a different sound and message that focused on a return to roots and positivity. These performers aimed to speak to youth and provide an alternative example to the high-rolling, womanizer gangsta that most hip-hop portrayed. For the most part, with the rather recent exception of Outkast, these artists have been marginally successful in a music market that cannot seem to get enough of rap. However, they have remained true to an individual style that is conscious in its message and aware of the influence and power that the microphone affords them. Inspired by this movement, some young West African rappers are creating music that they hope will address some of the problems that their peers face in the United

States as well as their native countries. Madarocka says that she wants to be "a part of the solution for Nigeria, for D.C. and for the Third World and the slums that resemble them." Similarly, Tem Blessed explained on a recent CD, *Y'll Aint Ready*, "There's a track speaking to the youth. We shouldn't be out here killing each other, in New Bedford, Lebanon or Israel." Emphasizing the continuing violence taking place locally and around the world, he declares, "I wanted to bring that consciousness because sometimes we forget and that is part of the problem."[86]

This is not to say that many other young people growing up in West Africa were not already exposed to gangsta rap in their homelands prior to migrating, however, since the dynamics of globalized popular culture made it possible for the music to permeate even the most remote areas. Indeed for Ishmael Beah, best-selling author of the autobiography *Long Way Gone: Memoirs of a Boy Soldier*, the Western cultural forms that reached his *upline* (backcountry) village as he was growing up in Sierra Leone were the music of rap and the works of Shakespeare, each in turn paradigmatically representative of popular and canonical culture. Beah imbibed both art forms. Improbably, months into the horror of being abducted into warfare as a preteen, the reader finds him at an encampment between killing sprees, reciting Shakespeare with his commander, Lieutenant Jabati, an AK-47 strapped to his youthful body, and cassettes of American rappers LL Cool J and Naughty by Nature stuffed into his pants pocket. It was the music that shaped Beah's premigration notions of America as he recalled his first impressions upon arrival, "My conception of New York City came from rap music. I envisioned it as a place where people shot each other on the street and got away with it; no one walked on the streets, rather people drove their sports cars looking for night clubs and for violence."[87]

By contrast, drawing from a history of using rap and hip-hop to raise awareness of the issues and problems of the urban world, the new generation of West African artists and their American counterparts through conscious hip-hop has come full circle. Reviving the objectives of the 1970s originators of the hip-hop movement, they have sought to utilize their African heritage to address the troubles vexing their communities at home and abroad with a positive message and as a vehicle for cross-cultural understanding and social change.

Interethnic Relations

Although West African young people are likely to forge their strongest friendships with compatriots, that tendency coexists with another common pattern of developing social relationships beyond the boundaries of their own nationality groups, not only with other West Africans, but with members of other minority populations such as those from the Caribbean and Latin America with whom they often share similar cultural affinities and social experiences. Looking back at the early years of her adjustment to a new life in the United States, Meri Nana-Ama Danquah recalled,

> The one place where I found acceptance was in the company of other immigrants. Together, we concentrated on our similarities, not our differences, because our differences were our similarities. . . . Of all the other immigrants, I got along best with my Spanish-speaking friends. For me, they were the middle ground between America and Africa.[88]

She even discovered that *pan*, the Spanish word for bread, also means bread in her native language of Twi.[89] Evidence of meaningful interethnic relationships is particularly manifested in activities related to sports and to music. Liberian refugee Winston S. and his best friend, who was an immigrant from Cape Verde, were both standout players on their high school soccer team. Indeed, there were so many different countries represented on their Hope High School team in the city of Providence, Rhode Island, including the coach, an immigrant from Italy, and the assistant coach who himself hailed from the Cape Verde Islands, that they called themselves the Hope United Nations. When they had a match against nearby Central Falls High School, another team with players from all over the world, the kids dubbed it "The Battle of the Green Cards."[90]

Yet interethnic friendships do not always require participation in athletics or other organized activities. A ninth grader from Liberia whose social circle includes many other Liberian youngsters at school and through her church group declared that her best friend was Spanish, from the Dominican Republic, while a Cape Verdean teenager who migrated to the United States in 1998 at the age of fifteen simply proclaimed, "I got Haitian friends. Jamaican. African American. Spanish. All over."[91] Even the American-born Liberian high school senior whose five closest friends are all not only Liberian but also second generation like herself prefers to date and ultimately marry someone outside her ethnic group:

> If I was to get married, it would not be to a Liberian man . . . when I was younger I always liked Spanish boys now I like regular, as they say, Black boys. I'm just not the girl in the house who is just the wife—does all the cooking and cleaning. I want fifty-fifty. If I met a Liberian man, he couldn't have those customs—because we're not in Africa, we're in America.[92]

For some young people, the social pressures of teenage cliques result in a lessening of cross-ethnic interaction as the children reach adolescence. As one high schooler explained, "When I was little, I had friends from different nationalities, but as you grow up, you tend to cling to your own kind."[93] Malik A., who migrated from Senegal when he was sixteen and who lives with his two brothers in Newark, New Jersey, where he also works at a small shop owned by a compatriot and attends community college part-time, spoke about the large network of multinational French-speaking West Africans with whom he is acquainted in the city. Yet while he claims to enjoy their company, in the end he says, "I get along just fine with the other Africans, it's all one love, but I prefer to be around other Senegalese."[94]

Although young people can feel pride in their particular African heritage, it is also not uncommon for them to show discomfort or embarrassment about their ancestry. Chinedu Nwokeafor, the teenage son of Nigerian parents, once cut out a picture from the family photo album of his relatives in their village of Umubasi, Nigeria, standing next to their new Mercedes-Benz, which was parked in front of their spacious home, and took the snapshot to his suburban Maryland high school so that he could "prove to teasing classmates that Africans did not, 'live in trees, like monkeys.'"[95] Beyond the typical adolescent desire to fit in and not be seen as different from one's peers, the young people, both immigrant and American-born children of African parents, are often proactive in disaffiliating themselves from the continent, particularly from the rampant associations of jungle imagery and primitivism thrown at them. Such a stance only gets exacerbated by the steady deluge of negative media depictions of African countries rife with poverty, hunger, and disease, of which the teenagers simply want no part.

While there is no denying the usefulness of the West African subcultures for the development of their young members, the immigrant success narrative is far from flawless. As positively assertive as it is, it can be too lofty, with the tendency to blur realities and elicit resentment and alienation. Sierra Leonean American Joy Roberts, a high school teacher in Lithonia, Georgia, lamented that its proponents are so preoccupied with savoring the abilities and accomplishments of the young members that they often do not recognize the nature and extent of the challenges that young people face outside the safety of the immigrant enclaves. Roberts, from her vantage point as a member of an immigrant subculture and a teacher in an American public school, has observed the psychological strain felt by teenagers who, feeling that they do not fully belong, may try painfully hard to fit in or might, instead, recoil or become belligerent in defiance.[96] Native-born young Americans berate the African-born about a number of issues—their appearance and mannerisms, not being able to speak English or speaking with "funny" accents, and their perceived inferior backgrounds coming from a beleaguered part of the world. For example, Nassou Camara, a fifteen-year-old whose parents are from Gambia and Senegal, recalled what happened when she wore a necklace with a charm in the shape of the African continent around her neck. One of her classmates in her Harlem school said to her, "You are not going to bring no disease here, right?"[97]

When Chinedu Ezeamuzie, a young Nigerian who had spent most of his childhood in Kuwait, arrived in Athens, Georgia, at age fifteen and started high school, it took him awhile to adjust to the expected norms of black kids. Getting ready for his first day of school, he dressed in khaki pants, a pressed button-down dress shirt, and a good-looking pair of leather shoes. But when he walked into the cafeteria for lunch, the African American students came down on him: "They gave me the look," he recalled. "Why is this guy dressed like the white folks, like the preppy guys?" It took time for Ezeamuzie to grasp the unspoken code of lunchroom segregation and why his black classmates accused him of not liking black people because he sat with white students. Before long he changed his attire to baggy pants, T-shirts, and sneakers, relaxed his more formal British accent, and, standing at six feet five inches, tried out for and made the basketball team. While these changes did not win him full acceptance from his black student peers, he conceded, "They kind of accepted me. They saw me a little differently, but I was thinking this is a very narrow mindset."[98]

Similarly, the teenage daughter born in Houston, Texas, to parents from Ghana, both professionals, and who grew up in a suburban neighborhood got along fine socially with kids from many different backgrounds until she started high school. Typically at this age, of course, figuring out in which group one belongs or is accepted can be a challenge no matter what the teenager's ethnoracial heritage. In a community with few other African immigrants, in the case of this young woman, the group that was her skin color, the African American kids, was where she desperately wanted to be. Yet she was rejected by them. As she was a student in all honors classes, they said she dressed and acted too preppy; they also criticized how she talked. What was most difficult for her was the pressure she continually felt to explain to her peers how it was that she is black but doesn't sound like them. To African immigrant kids she sounded like an American, but to African Americans the slightest hint of the accent she absorbed by simply growing up in a household with Ghanaian parents marked her as different. Her solution to navigating the complicated racial landscape was to spend less time on homework and, like Ezeamuzie, to get involved instead in the extracurricular activities in which the African American students participated, especially drama and sports. She joined a dance group and performing successfully as part of a talent show, and the other black students finally pronounced her "cronk" (hip). As her mother commented, "The children have a unique problem. It's that they look black—they *are* black—they are Africans, but they don't fit in easily in the African American community. They don't sound the same; they don't dress the same. They feel ostracized."[99] Such dynamics were precisely her rationale for the necessity of a strong African associational life.

The friction, then, within and outside of school is not simply with American kids; it is more specifically with young African Americans. A study of the adjustment of African students enrolled in a public school in Philadelphia's inner city found that preconceived ideas about each group were rife with negative assumptions and an appalling lack of knowledge about each other with, again, the jungle stereotype looming large. When the investigator, Rosemary Luckens Traoré, posed the question of what the African newcomers would most want Americans to know about them, one young woman responded, "The first thing I want them to know is that Africa is not a jungle. Second, that people who live in Africa are not animals and third that Africa is a beautiful continent."[100] But the rabid misconceptions went in both directions; Traoré summarized the level of animosity in this way: "To the African Americans, the Africans were primitive and ignorant; to the Africans, the African Americans were lazy and rude."[101]

The tumultuous relationship between the two groups simply cannot be ignored. Almost every American city with an African immigrant presence has seen this conflict unfold, sometimes in the most vicious ways. African children have accused African Americans of physically assaulting them, sometimes in the process of robbing them, but very often just because they feel resentment toward their foreign, black counterparts. In November 2005, the situation in southwestern Philadelphia, a predominantly African American neighborhood, came to a head. Tension had been escalating for months before, as a result of the rapidly growing Liberian community, which had also made its home in that "black" area. A thirteen-year-old Liberian boy was severely beaten by African American youngsters. The extensive coverage of the incident by the media revealed the extent of the problem and prompted reactions. Members of the Liberian community were sure of the reasons for the assaults, including the much-publicized attack on the thirteen-year-old. Sekou Kamara explained, "Some African Americans perceive the growing American-born community as a threat." According to Orabella Richards, a Liberian businesswoman, "There is anger about African immigrants coming here and doing so well." And Varney Kanneh, who claimed that his children had been harassed and attacked in school, believed that "the immigrants make some of the American students look bad."[102]

These dynamics have also permeated the relationship between young West Africans in America and the HBCUs. In recent years, many parents have discouraged their children from considering these schools while others support the decision. The experiences of West African immigrants and the second generation at HBCUs have been mixed. Some relate a positive outcome that enhanced their identities as blacks, while others transferred to other institutions because of their dissatisfaction with what they felt was a "racialized" college environment. A young Sierra Leonean student who could not wait to enroll in an HBCU switched to a state school in Georgia after only one year there. "I was overwhelmed by blackness," she explained. "Not really thinking of myself as black before going to college, it was too much, too fast."[103] Another HBCU "dropout," a young Gambian who immigrated to Atlanta to join an aunt, resented that "everyone expected him to fight." He said he was always told "you are part of the struggle." Convinced that the "struggle" was getting in the way of a good education—his whole reason for being in the United States—he quit and went to another school. The level of skepticism about HBCUs displayed by contemporary West Africans is a departure from the era of Nkrumah and Azikiwe, who emphasized the role of their educational environment at HBCUs in nurturing their Pan-African black consciousness and preparing them for leadership roles in the nationalist and independence struggles at home.

Fortunately, not all interactions between young foreign and native-born blacks are conflict-ridden. For example, the Umoja Media Project, part of Harlem Children's Zone, a nonprofit agency, was launched in 2001, in part as a response to the tension between African Americans of Harlem and African immigrants, especially Muslims, generated by the 9/11 tragedy. Under this initiative, African American youngsters and the children of African and Caribbean immigrants were provided with the necessary equipment to produce a documentary about their communities and their perceptions of and relationships with others. The project gave the participants a chance to share their collective histories and discuss issues of identity and ethnoracial stereotyping. Yet apart from such programs aimed at improving these relationships, can members of the contemporary West African second generation afford to be simply achievers and remain immersed in the sanctuary of their parents' subcultures? No one is denying the potency of their social capital. Indeed, they are young, gifted, and West African, but so was Amadou Diallo, and his life came to a premature and violent end on the streets of America. Cases like his provide evidence that West African and other black immigrants need to give recognition to the African American collective narrative as well.

Moreover, the adaptation process is not solely about traversing the terrain between African immigrant and native African American identity structures. The second generation encounters a mélange of blended manifestations of contemporary youth culture and, depending upon where they live or attend school, a peer group that often defies the customary, oversimplified, and often outdated categories of black and white; even adding brown to the mix does not account for the permutations of populations of African, Asian, Latino, Caribbean, and European descent that are crisscrossing the traditional racial divide, particularly in the arenas of music, sports, and consumer culture. Because West African youth already have a transglobal perspective and, for the most part, have not been socialized with a racially polarized worldview, they often demonstrate a level of cultural versatility that reverberates well with current and evolving landscapes of cultural hybridity, and as such, many remain unfazed by the blurred boundaries of multiple identifications.

Conclusion

Further into the Twenty-First Century

Although we began life in the villages and towns of Nigeria, Ghana, Senegal, Liberia and Sierra Leone, we must work to fully understand our rights in America and the sacrifices made by civil rights activists; we must fully participate in the political process and seek our interests as African Americans, because that is what some of us have become and others will eventually be.

—Alpha Jalloh, 1994

We opened this book by posing the pivotal question of whether post–civil rights era immigrants from continental Africa are, indeed, becoming the newest African Americans. While Alpha Jalloh would likely agree that they are, others have been more skeptical. Consider linguistics and race relations scholar John McWhorter's thoughts on this conundrum:

> Modern America is home now to millions of immigrants who were born in Africa. Their cultures and identities are split between Africa and the United States. They have last names like Onwughalu and Senkofa. They speak languages like Wolof, Twi, Yoruba and Hausa, and speak English with an accent. They were raised on African cuisine, music, dance and dress styles, customs and family dynamics. Their children often speak or at least understand their parents' native language. . . . My roots trace back to working class Black people—Americans, not foreigners—and I'm proud of it. . . . They and their dearest are the heritage that I feel in my heart, and they knew the sidewalks of Philadelphia and Atlanta, not the sidewalks of Sierra Leone.[1]

Such divergent points of view reveal the extent to which the place of these newcomers is still contested and unfolding.

As such, our investigations have confirmed that the populations that compose the new West African diaspora in the United States are very much communities in the making. While Eugene Robinson sees contemporary black America, including its cohort of emergent African immigrants, seeped in the process of *dis*integration, as he titles his recent book, our assessment of the current dynamics is rather one of *re*integration. After all, these West African newcomers represent many of the same ancestral groups that formed the very foundation of African America when their forebears arrived in bondage generations ago. Once original settlers, the latest arrivals from the region of West Africa are now remaking what it means to be both African and American in the twenty-first century.

To understand the experience of the massive influx of immigrants from Southern and Eastern Europe to the United States at the turn of the last century, scholars in the field have offered various theories of assimilation and adaptation, including the notion of ethnicization to describe the ways that new immigrants reinvent their collective identities as they adjust to the shifting realities of the host society.[2] We have observed a similar process of ethnicization in recent decades, this time as it applies to African America, whereby the factors of both nationality *and* race figure significantly when members of the new West African diaspora proceed to negotiate and re-create their status in their adopted homeland. Thus, the question may not be whether this population stands as the newest African Americans but rather how they are simultaneously becoming *both* African and American. In a contemporary cultural climate more receptive to the nuances of ethnicity within broader frameworks of race than has been the case in earlier periods of American history, the valances of generation have also mattered. In general, 1.5- and second-generation West Africans have been able to navigate the layers of race and ethnicity within the putative black community more successfully than their first-generation counterparts.

Yet whether choosing to identify as African American, West African American, or one of the range of possible hyphenated nationalities such as Nigerian American or Cape Verdean American and whether or not the native-born African American population welcomes these foreign-born arrivals into the fold, this is a population that, nonetheless, is becoming more visible. At the dawn of the twenty-first century when John Arthur published one of the first studies of the new African diaspora in the United States, he titled it *Invisible Sojourners*.[3] While still obscured in much public and scholarly discourse on the American immigrant experience, over the past decade African newcomers have become more recognizable as part of the fabric of American political and cultural life. For example, in 2013 three West African–born men and the daughter of West African immigrants made headlines as front-runners for the Bronx District 16 seat in the City Council election. By this time, several Bronx neighborhoods had become home to large numbers of African residents, whose growing political presence was manifested in this feisty race that pitted them against a formidable African American candidate, Vanessa Gibson, looking to continue the native-born black hold of a political district dubbed "the Black Seat." Ironically, one of the foreign-born vying to have his profile stand out to represent this constituency, Ahmadou Diallo from Guinea, has the same name (though spelled differently) and national origins as the young Amadou Diallo who had been gunned down nearly fifteen years earlier in that very neighborhood and whose individuality had been so erased by persistent marginalizing media portrayals of him as simply an undocumented African.[4]

The Obama factor certainly has made a difference in raising awareness overall of Americans of African descent, but in an era of globalized consumer culture, advanced electronic technologies, and virtual melting pots, West African immigrants are making their mark on their local communities as well as through the influences of various West African cultural transplantations on mainstream American forms of expression. From Nollywood film to World Music artists to professional sports figures, from African restaurants and hair-braiding salons that dot the commercial landscape to the DNA tracings of prominent African Americans, the interpenetrations and heightened connectivity of African and American cultures continue to pulsate and evolve in new and expansive ways as we forge ahead further into the twenty-first century.

NOTES

NOTES TO THE INTRODUCTION

1. Kadiatou Diallo and Craig Wolff, *My Heart Will Cross This Ocean: My Story, My Son, Amadou* (New York: One World, 2003), 246.

2. Paul Gilroy, *The Black Atlantic: Modernity and Double Consciousness* (Cambridge, MA: Harvard University Press, 1993).

3. According to the pioneering research of Linda Heywood and John Thornton, leading scholars of African and African American history, most of today's African American population can trace their ancestry back to one of just forty-six ethnic groups. The three large regions of the continent, all on the Atlantic side, that were the major contributors to the slave trade are Upper Guinea, including the modern countries of Senegal, Mali, Gambia, Guinea, Sierra Leone, and Liberia; Lower Guinea, including the southern portions of eastern Ivory Coast, Ghana, Togo, Benin, and Nigeria; and West Central Africa, which encompassed mostly the western portions of the Democratic Republic of Congo and Angola. See Linda Heywood and John Thornton, "Pinpointing DNA Ancestry in Africa" and "African Ethnicities and Their Origins," *Root*, October 1, 2011, http://www.theroot.com/views/tracing-dna-not-just-africa-one-tribe?page=0,1 and http://www.theroot.com/buzz/african-ethnicities-and-their-origins (both accessed November 5, 2011).

4. Ira Berlin, *The Making of African America: The Four Great Migrations* (New York: Viking, 2010), 73.

5. Michael Okwu, "Family Tree Project Helps Trace Deep History," *Today*, November 18, 2005, http://today.msnbc.msn.com/id/10095659/ns/today/t/family-tree-project-helps-trace-deep-history/.

6. Percy Claude Hintzen and Jean Muteba Rahier, eds., *Problematizing Blackness: Self-Ethnographies by Black Immigrants to the United States* (New York: Routledge, 2003), 7–8.

7. At the project's centerpiece is an expansive website of 16,500 pages of essays, manuscripts, maps and illustrations, including a section in which the history of the Cape Verdean diaspora is showcased.

8. Ian Goldin, Geoffrey Cameron, and Meera Balarajan, *Exceptional People: How Migration Shaped Our World and Will Define Our Future* (Princeton, NJ: Princeton University Press, 2011), 241. See also Thomas Hatton and Jeffrey Williamson, "Demographic and Economic Pressure on Emigration out of Africa,"

Scandinavian Journal of Economics 105, no. 3 (2003): 467–468; Hendrik van Dalen, George Groenewold, and Jeannette Schoorl, "Out of Africa: What Drives the Pressure to Emigrate?," *Journal of Population Economics* 18, no. 4 (2005): 741–778.

9. Eugene Robinson, *Disintegration: The Splintering of Black America* (New York: Doubleday, 2010), 9, 165.

10. Susan Greenbaum, *More Than Black: Afro-Cubans in Tampa* (Gainesville: University Press of Florida, 2002), 9.

11. Olúfémi Táíwò, "This Prison Called My Skin: On Being Black in America," in Hintzen and Rahier, *Problematizing Blackness*, 41–42, 47–48, emphasis original.

12. Chimamanda Ngozi Adichie, "The Color of an Awkward Conversation," *Washington Post*, June 8, 2008, B07.

13. Chimamanda Ngozi Adichie, *Americanah* (New York: Knopf, 2013), 222.

14. Baffour Takyi, "Africans Abroad: Comparative Perspectives on America's Postcolonial West Africans," in *The New African Diaspora*, ed. Isidore Okpewho and Nkiru Nzegwu (Bloomington: Indiana University Press, 2009), 243. Cape Verdeans are the exception here as this study found that 77 percent of immigrants from Cape Verde identified as *nonblack*.

15. Gerald Lenoir and Nunu Kidane, "African Americans and Immigrants: Shall We Hang Together or Hang Separately?," *Black Scholar* 37, no. 1 (2007): 51.

16. Jacob Olupona, "Communities of Believers: Exploring African Immigrant Religion in the United States," in *African Immigrant Religions in America*, ed. Jacob Olupona and Regina Gemignani (New York: New York University Press, 2007), 28.

17. Yvette Alex-Assensoh, "African Immigrants and African-Americans: An Analysis of Voluntary African Immigration and the Evolution of Black Ethnic Politics in America," *African and Asian Studies* 8, nos. 1–2 (2009): 89–124.

18. Msia Kibona Clark, "Identity among First and Second Generation African Immigrants in the United States," *African Identities* 6, no. 2 (2008): 172.

19. See this comment referenced in the introductory chapter by Isidore Okpewho in Okpewho and Nzegwu, *New African Diaspora*, 13–14.

20. Zain Abdullah, "West Africans," in *Encyclopedia of American Immigration*, ed. James Ciment (Armonk, NY: M.E. Sharpe, 2001), 1072–1073. Toyin Falola and Niyi Afolabi also offer a framework of three waves of overall continental African migration but within a much narrower time frame. They suggest that the flow of the past two decades (from 1986 to 2006) can be broken down into a first wave of primarily professionals who were able to regularize permanent residency status due to the provisions of the 1986 Immigration and Control Act, a concurrent second influx of refugees seeking asylum in the United States, and finally the tide of African newcomers who benefited from the Diversity Visa Lottery beginning in the 1990s. See Falola and Afolabi, eds., *African Minorities in the New World* (New York: Routledge, 2007).

21. Elizabeth Grieco, "Race and Hispanic Origin of the Foreign-Born Population in the United States" (U.S. Census American Community Survey Report, January 2010).

22. Kristen McCabe, "African Immigrants in the United States" (Migration Policy Institute, July 21, 2011), http://www.migrationinformation.org/USfocus/display.cfm?id=847 (accessed August 17, 2011); John Logan, "Who Are the Other African Americans? Contemporary African and Caribbean Immigrants in the United States," in *The Other African Americans: Contemporary African and Caribbean Immigrants in the United States*, ed. Yoku Shaw-Taylor and Stephen Tuch (Lanham, MD: Rowman & Littlefield, 2007), 49–67; Jill Wilson, "Spatial and Demographic Trends in African Immigration to the U.S." (paper, Colloquium on New Americans from Africa and the Immigrant Experience in the United States, George Washington University, May 19, 2010).

23. Randy Capps, Kristen McCabe, and Michael Fix, "New Streams: Black African Migration to the United States" (Washington, DC: Migration Policy Institute, 2011), 1, 18, http://www.migrationpolicy.org/pubs/AfricanMigrationUS.pdf (accessed July 24, 2011). By contrast, according to research based on data from the Census Bureau's 2008 American Community Survey, Jill Wilson found that the significantly larger populations of the foreign-born from both Asia and Latin America grew at the much slower pace of 25 percent. See Wilson, "Spatial and Demographic Trends." It should also be noted that in the years since the attacks of September 11, 2001, the U.S. State Department has made entering the United States more difficult for some Africans.

24. Capps, McCabe, and Fix, "New Streams," 3.

25. 2003–2004 New Immigrant Survey (NIS), table A.10 in Shaw-Taylor and Tuch, *Other African Americans*, 284.

26. McCabe, "African Immigrants in the United States"; as is the case with population figures for many immigrant groups, official records regarding West Africans typically represent significant undercounts. However, relying on the estimates of ethnic community leaders also has its limitations since often, to compensate, those totals can be exaggerated in the other direction.

27. Nigerians also compose the largest immigrant population of all the countries of origin in Africa, not just compared to those from West Africa, and are followed in numbers by Ethiopians.

28. Takyi, "Africans Abroad," 241.

29. McCabe, "African Immigrants in the United States"; Aaron Terrazas, "African Immigrants in the United States" (Migration Policy Institute, February 10, 2009), http://www.migrationinformation.org (accessed February 19, 2009).

30. Takyi, "Africans Abroad," 243–244.

31. Mary Mederios Kent, "Immigration and America's Black Population," *Population Bulletin* 62, no. 4 (2007): 1–16.

32. John Donnelly, "Americans Adopting More African Children," *Boston Globe*, May 19, 2006.

33. McCabe, "African Immigrants in the United States"; see also U.S. Department of State, "Reports of the Visa Office 2000 and 2008, VII. Immigrant Number Use for Visa Issuances and Adjustments of Status in the Diversity Immigrant Category: Fiscal Years 1995–2000 and Fiscal Years 1999–2008."

34. In the most general sense, asylum or refugee status is a political classification that characterizes persons seeking refuge. For the Immigration and Naturalization Service, a refugee is "a person who has fled his or her country of origin because of past persecution or a well-founded fear of persecution based on race, religion, nationality, political opinion or membership in a particular social group." The difference between refugee and asylum status is based on where the application is filed: refugees file their applications prior to entering the United States and asylees file after their arrival (on temporary visas, illegally, etc.). Most often gaining refugee or asylee status means permanent resettlement outside of one's homeland.

35. Aaron Kase and F. H . Rubino, "Refugees Settling in Philadelphia," *Philadelphia Weekly,* March 2, 2010, http://www.philadelphiaweekly.com/ news-and-opinion/cover-story/Refugees-settling-in-Philadelphia. html?page=1&comments=1&showAll= (accessed September 19, 2011).

36. April Gordon, "The New Diaspora—African Immigration to the United States," *Journal of Third World Studies* 15, no. 1 (1998): 79–103; John A. Arthur, *Invisible Sojourners: African Immigrant Diaspora in the United States* (Westport, CT: Praeger, 2000); Kwado Konadu-Agyemang and Baffour K. Takyi, "An Overview of African Immigration to U.S. and Canada," in Kwado Konadu-Agyemang, Baffour Takyi and John Arthur, eds. *The New African Diaspora in North America: Trends, Community Building, and Adaptation* (Lanham, MD: Lexington Books, 2006); Kwado Konadu-Agyemang and Baffour Takyi, "African Immigrants in the USA: Some Reflection on the Their Pre- and Post-Migration Experiences," *Arab World Geographer/Le Géographe du monde arabe* 4, no. 1 (2001): 31–47; Kent, "Immigration and America's Black Population."

37. U.S. Congress, House of Representatives, *Congressional Record,* 89th Congress, 1st Session, August 25, 1965, 21, 758.

38. For more on the legislative links between advocates for civil rights and immigration reform, see Cassandra R. Veney, "The Effects of Immigration and Refugee Policies on Africans in the United States: From the Civil Rights Movement to the War on Terrorism," in Okpewho and Nzegwu, *New African Diaspora,* 196–214.

39. van Dalen, Groenewold, and Schoorl, "Out of Africa," 753.

40. Ibid., 753–754.

41. U.S. Department of State, Bureau of Population, Refugees, and Migration (PRM), Worldwide Refugee Admissions Processing System (WRAPS), "2008 Yearbook of Immigration Statistics."

42. Capps, McCabe, and Fix, "New Streams," 1.

43. See esp. John Arthur, *African Diaspora Identities: Negotiating Culture in Transnational Migration* (Lanham, MD: Lexington Books, 2010), 35–77.

44. Remittance totals typically represent significant undercounts since only half of sub-Saharan African countries regularly collect and report such data. Dilip Ratha, Sanket Mohapatra, Caglar Ozden, Sonia Plaza, William Shaw, and Abebe Shimeles, *Leveraging Migration for Africa: Remittances, Skills and Investments* (Washington, DC: World Bank, 2011), 4–5, 49, http://siteresources.worldbank. org/EXTDECPROSPECTS/Resources/476882-1157133580628/AfricaStudyEntireBook.pdf (accessed August 23, 2011); David Crary, "African Immigrants Find Opportunity," *Seattle Post-Intelligencer*, June 16, 2007; Howard Dodson and Sylviane A. Diouf, *In Motion: The African American Migration Experience* (New York: Schomburg Center for Research in Black Culture, 2004), 204–205.

45. "The African Consumer Segment" (Los Angeles: New American Dimensions, April 27, 2009), 30, http://www.newamericandimensions.com/.

46. In all, 25 percent held bachelor's degrees and 16.7 percent graduate or professional degrees.

47. McCabe, "African Immigrants in the United States"; U.S. Department of Homeland Security, Office of Immigration Statistics, "2007 Yearbook of Immigration Statistics"; Douglas Massey, Margarita Mooney, Kimberly Torres, and Camille Charles, "Black Immigrants and Black Natives Attending Selective Colleges and Universities in the United States," *American Journal of Education* 113 (February 2007): 243–271.

48. Paul Tiyambe Zeleza, "The African Academic Diaspora in the United States and Africa: The Challenges of Productive Engagement," *Comparative Studies of South Asia, Africa, and the Middle East* 24, no. 1 (2004): 268.

49. Kevin Thomas, "What Explains the Increasing Trend in African Emigration to the U.S.?," *International Migration Review* 45, no. 1 (2011): 22; Capps, McCabe, and Fix, "New Streams," 10.

50. Capps, McCabe, and Fix, "New Streams," 1.

51. Ratha et al., *Leveraging Migration for Africa*.

52. Arun Lobo, "US Diversity Visas Are Attracting Africa's Best and Brightest," *Population Today* 29, no. 5 (2001): 1.

53. Ibid.

54. According to McCabe's 2011 analysis of the 2009 American Community Survey and 2000 decennial census findings, those from Cape Verde were the most likely among African immigrants to have limited English proficiency, while those immigrants from Liberia, Nigeria, and Sierra Leone were among the top six African groups to have the highest English proficiency.

55. Massey et al., "Black Immigrants and Black Natives"; Arthur, *Invisible Sojourners*.

56. Michael Fix and Jeanne Batalova, *Uneven Progress: The Employment Pathways of Skilled Immigrants to the United States* (Washington, DC: Migration Policy Institute, 2008).

57. McCabe, "African Immigrants in the United States."

58. Wilson, "Spatial and Demographic Trends."

59. Ibid.

60. Capps, McCabe, and Fix, "New Streams," 19; McCabe, "African Immigrants in the United States."

61. Wilson, "Spatial and Demographic Trends."

62. Logan, "Who Are the Other African Americans?," 54–56; Alex-Assensoh, "African Immigrants and African-Americans," 102–103.

63. Takyi, "Africans Abroad," 249.

64. According the 2000 census, 95 percent of African immigrants living in the United States resided in metropolitan areas.

65. Takyi, "Africans Abroad," 243–244.

66. Logan, "Who Are the Other African Americans?," 51–54.

67. Rachael Horowitz, "Eat, Stay, Love," Imprint, January 30, 2010, http://imprint-mag.org/2010/01/30/west-africa-in-harlem/#more-7 (accessed August 23, 2012).

68. PRI's The World, September 15, 2010, http://www.pri.org/stories/2010-09-15/chef-marcus-samuelsson (accessed September 15, 2010); see also Nana Kanam, "Uptown, Africa Toujours," New York Times, July 22, 2007, http://www.nytimes.com/2007/07/22/nyregion/thecity/22harl.html?_r=1 (accessed January 25, 2010). Note that in his study of African Muslims in Harlem, Zain Abdullah refers to this neighborhood as "Little Africa." Black Mecca: The African Muslims of Harlem (New York: Oxford University Press, 2010), 13.

69. Tracie Rozhon, "TURF; Grit and Glory in South Harlem," New York Times, March 16, 2000.

70. In Linda Beck's research on West African Muslims in New York City, she suggests that the affinity of African immigrants for living in African American neighborhoods stems from a desire to be less visible; especially for those who are undocumented, it is easier to slip under the official radar by blending in with the larger black community. Linda Beck, "West African Muslims in America: When Are Muslims Not Muslims?," in Olupona and Gemignani, African Immigrant Religions in America, 197.

71. It should be noted, however, that in her analysis of 2008 American Community Survey data, Jill Wilson found that Africans in general are slightly less likely to live in suburbs than are immigrants from Asia and Europe. However, they are more likely to do so than immigrants from Latin America. Wilson, "Spatial and Demographic Trends."

72. Samantha Friedman, Audrey Singer, Marie Price, and Ivan Cheung, "Race, Immigrants, and Residence: A New Racial Geography of Washington, D.C.," Geographical Review 95, no. 2 (2005): 210–230; Audrey Singer, Susan Hardwick, and Caroline Brettell, eds., Twenty-First Century Gateways: Immigrant Incorporation in Suburban America (Washington, DC: Brookings Institution, 2008); Michele Habecker, "African Immigrants in Washington, D.C.: Seeking Alternative Identities in a Racially Divided City" (doctoral dissertation, Oxford University, 2009).

73. Alex-Assensoh, "African Immigrants and African-Americans," 104–106.

74. See Paul Stoller, *Money Has No Smell: The Africanization of New York City* (Chicago: University of Chicago Press, 2001).
75. Catherine K., interviewed by Violet Johnson, Atlanta, July 9, 2011 (translated from Krio).

NOTES TO CHAPTER 1

1. "The Aims and Objectives of the West African National Secretariat" (London, 1944), National Association for the Advancement of Colored People (NAACP) Papers, group II, box 44, Library of Congress.
2. For more on the history of the ancient empires of the western Sudan, see Mary Quigley, *Ancient West African Kingdoms: Ghana, Mali and Songhai* (Portsmouth, NH: Heinemann, 2002); Robert S. Smith, *Warfare and Diplomacy in Pre-colonial West Africa* (Madison: University of Wisconsin Press, 1989).
3. Mahdi Adamu, *The Hausa Factor in West African History* (New York: Oxford University Press, 1978). For more on the history of the Hausa city-states, see Paul Staudinger, *In the Heart of Hausa States* (Athens: Ohio University Press, 1990); Philip Koslow, *Hausaland: The Fortress Kingdoms* (New York: Chelsea House, 1995); M. G. Smith's series on the history of the Hausa-Fulani states, especially *Government in Kano, 1350–1950* (Boulder, CO: Westview, 1997); for more on Kanem-Bornu, see Augustine Holl, *The Diwan Revisited: Literacy, State Formation and the Rise of Kanuri Domination, AD 1200–1600* (London: Kegan Paul, 2000); Conrad Cairns, *African Knights: The Armies of Sokoto, Bornu and Bagirmi in the Nineteenth Century* (Horsham, UK: Foundry Press, 2006).
4. Cheikh Anta Babou, *Amadu Bamba and the Founding of the Muridiyya of Senegal, 1853–1913* (Athens: Ohio University Press, 2007). For more on the history of Al-hajj Umar and the Tukolor Empire, see David Robinson, "The Impact of Al-Hajj 'Umar on the Historical Traditions of the Fulbe," *Journal of the Folklore Institute* 8, nos. 2–3 (1971): 101–113; Olatunji Oloruntimehin, *The Segu Tukulor Empire* (London: Longman, 1972).
5. Dan Fodio's jihad, known variously as the Hausa jihad, Fulani jihad, or Sokoto jihad, is considered the biggest jihad and the protagonist of the nineteenth-century Islamic Revolution in West Africa. For more on this jihad, see Marilyn Robinson Waldman, "The Fulani Jihad: A Reassessment," *Journal of African History* 6, no. 3 (1965): 333–355; Sule Ahmed Gusau, "Economic Ideas of Shehu Usman Dan Fodio," *Journal of Muslim Minority Affairs* 10, no. 1 (1989): 139–151; Walter E. A. van Beek, "Purity and Statecraft: The Nineteenth Century Fulani Jihad of North Nigeria," in *The Quest for Purity: Dynamics of Puritan Movements*, ed. Walter van Beek (Berlin: Mouton de Gruyter, 1988); Moses Ochonu, "Colonialism within Colonialism: The Hausa-Caliphate Imaginary and the British Colonial Administration of the Nigerian Middle Belt," *African Studies Quarterly* 10, nos. 2–3 (2008).
6. For a history of the Yoruba, see S. Adebanji Akintoye, *A History of the Yoruba People* (Dakar: Amalion, 2010).

7. For more on the history of the Akan, especially the Asante and Fante, see Ivor Wilks, *Forests of Gold: Essays on the Akan and the Kingdom of Asante* (Athens: Ohio University Press, 1995); T. C. McCaskie, *Asante Identities: History and Modernity in an African Village, 1850–1950* (Bloomington: Indiana University Press, 2001).

8. Chinua Achebe, *Things Fall Apart* (1958; repr., New York: Anchor Books, 1994).

9. For a historical analysis of some of what Achebe tackles in the novel, see Elizabeth Isicheri, *The Ibo People and the Europeans: The Genesis of a Relationship to 1906* (London: Faber, 1973).

10. António Carreira, *Cabo Verde: formação e extinção de uma sociedade escravocrata, 1460⬚1878* (Porto: Imprensa Portuguesa, 1972); Marilyn Halter, *Between Race and Ethnicity: Cape Verdean American Immigrants, 1860–1965* (Urbana: University of Illinois Press, 1993).

11. A useful case study of the dispersal of a West African group in the slave trade is Kwasi Konadu, *The Akan Diaspora in the Americas* (New York: Oxford University Press, 2010).

12. *Isaiah Washington: Passport to Sierra Leone* (Comcast Cable Africa Channel, August 1, 2010), a documentary on Washington's visit to Sierra Leone and acceptance of a Sierra Leonean passport and dual citizenship, tackles this important issue of DNA and the African American search for African ancestry.

13. A most useful and vivid study of the confluences of heritages is reputable African historian Ali Mazrui's documentary series *Africans: A Triple Heritage* (PBS, 1986); and a companion to the series, *Africans: A Triple Heritage* (Boston: Little, Brown, 1987).

14. Ali Mazrui, "Francophone Nations and English-Speaking States: Imperial Ethnicity and African Political Formations," in Donald Rothchild and Victor Olorunsola, eds., *State versus Ethnic Claims: African Policy Dilemmas* (Boulder, CO: Westview, 1983), 25–43.

15. David Robinson, *Paths of Accommodation: Muslim Societies and French Colonial Authorities in Senegal and Mauritania, 1880–1920* (Athens: Ohio University Press, 2000), 75.

16. This peculiar episode is related in Jon Woronoff, *West African Wager: Houphouet versus Nkrumah* (Metuchen, NJ: Scarecrow Press, 1972).

17. Brian Catchpole and I. A. Akinjogbin, *A History of West Africa in Maps and Diagrams* (London: Collins, 1984), 5.

18. A. Adu Boahen, *African Perspectives on Colonialism* (Baltimore: Johns Hopkins University Press, 1987).

19. For more on colonial capitalism and the development of towns and cities, see George E. Brooks, "Peanuts and Colonialism: Consequences of the Colonization of Peanuts in West Africa, 1830–1870," *Journal of African History* 16, no. 1 (1975): 29–54; Carolyn Brown, *"We Were All Slaves": African Miners, Culture and Resistance at the Enugu Government Colliery, Nigeria* (Portsmouth, NH: Heinemann, 2003); Ken Swindell, "Serawoollies, Tillibunkas and Strange Farmers:

The Development of Migrant Groundnut Farming Along the Gambia River, 1848–95," *Journal of African History* 21 (1980): 93–104.

20. W. A. Hance, *Population, Migration and Urbanization in Africa* (New York: Columbia University Press, 1970), 269.

21. Max Lock and Partners, *Kaduna, 1917–1967: A Survey and Plan of the Capital Territory for the Government of Northern Nigeria* (London: Faber, 1967), 125–130.

22. Ibid.

23. See Augustine Konneh, "Citizenship at the Margins: Status, Ambiguity, and the Mandingo of Liberia," *African Studies Review* 39, no. 2 (1996): 141–154; Flomo Kokolo, "The Mandingo Question in Liberian History and the Prospect for Peace in Liberia," *Liberian Daily Observer*, April 16, 2010, http://www.liberianobserver.com/node/5778 (accessed August 3, 2010).

24. For more on the Yoruba in Ghana, see J. S. Eades, *Strangers and Traders: Yoruba Migrants, Markets and the State in Northern Ghana* (Trenton, NJ: Africa World Press, 1994).

25. At independence, in Hausaland, northern Nigeria, the Igbo controlled 11 percent of real estate brokerage, 25 percent of the retail trade, 30 percent of the clothing trade, and 79 percent of the department stores. Cited in Amusi Odi, "The Igbo in Diaspora: The Binding Force of Information," *Libraries & Culture* 34, no. 1 (1999): 158–167, 159.

26. For more on the history of the origins of the Creoles of Sierra Leone, see Akintola Wyse, *The Krio of Sierra Leone: An Interpretive History* (Madison: University of Wisconsin Press, 1989); James W. St. G. Walker, *The Black Loyalists: Search for a Promised Land in Nova Scotia and Sierra Leone* (1976; repr., Toronto: University of Toronto Press, 1992).

27. For a case study of Creole elitism, see Abner Cohen, *The Politics of Elite Culture: Explorations in the Dramaturgy of Power in a Modern African Society* (Berkeley: University of California Press, 1981).

28. An excellent case study of the Creole experience in Nigeria is Mac Dixon-Fyle, *A Saro Community in the Niger Delta, 1912–1984: The Potts-Johnsons* (Rochester, NY: University of Rochester Press, 1999).

29. For an overview of Crowther and his legacy, see J. F. Ade Ajayi, *A Patriot to the Core: Bishop Ajayi Crowther* (Ibadan: Spectrum Books, 1996).

30. M. P. Banton, *West African City* (New York: Oxford University Press, 1965), 131.

31. Lillian Trager, *Yoruba Hometowns: Community, Identity, and Development in Nigeria* (Boulder, CO: Lynne Rienner, 2001), 2.

32. For an overview of the Kru diaspora, see Diane Frost, "Diasporan West African Communities: The Kru in Freetown & Liverpool," *Review of African Political Economy* 29, no. 92 (2002): 285–300.

33. Kathleen Sheldon, ed., *Courtyards, Markets, City Streets: Urban Women in Africa* (Boulder, CO: Westview, 1996).

34. Catherine Coles, "Three Generations of Hausa Women in Kaduna, Nigeria, 1925–1985," in Sheldon, *Courtyards, Markets, City Streets*, 73–102. Also useful in

shedding new perspectives on the instrumental role of Hausa women in urban development are articles in the anthology by Catherine Coles and Beverly Mack, eds., *Hausa Women in the Twentieth Century* (Madison: University of Wisconsin Press, 1991).

35. Cyprian Ekwensi, *Jagua Nana* (London: Hutchinson, 1961).

36. D. F. McCall, "Trade and the Role of the Wife in a Modern West African Town," in *Social Change in Modern Africa*, ed. Aidan Southhall (New York: Oxford University Press, 1961), 29.

37. Kenneth Little, *African Women in Towns: An Aspect of Africa's Social Revolution* (Cambridge: Cambridge University Press, 1973), 49.

38. Gracia Clark, "Gender and Profiteering: Ghana's Market Women as Devoted Mothers and 'Human Vampire Bats,'" in *"Wicked" Women and the Reconfiguration of Gender in Africa*, ed. Dorothy Hodgson and Sheryl McCurdy (Portsmouth, NH: Heinemann, 2001), 293–311.

39. Misty Bastian, "'Vultures of the Marketplace': Southeastern Nigerian Women and Discourses of the *Ogu Umunwaanyi* (Women's War) of 1929," in *Women in African Colonial Histories*, ed. Jean Allman, Susan Geiger, and Nakanyike Musisi (Bloomington: University of Indiana Press, 2002), 260–281.

40. The road to independence and the vicissitudes of nationhood constitute a crowded intellectual field. The following are a few examples of accounts and assessments that tackle the many issues: N. C. McClintock, *Kingdoms in the Sand and Sun: An African Path to Independence* (London: I.B. Tauris, 1992); Tony Chafer, *The End of Empire in French West Africa: France's Successful Decolonization?* (London: Berg, 2002); John Dunn, *West African States, Failure and Promise: A Study in Comparative Politics* (Cambridge: Cambridge University Press, 1978); Aristide Zolberg, *Creating Political Order: The Party-States of West Africa* (Skokie, IL: Rand McNally, 1967); Elizabeth Schmidt, *Cold War and Decolonization in Guinea, 1946–1958* (Athens: Ohio University Press, 2007); Anthony Kirk-Greene, ed., *State and Society in Francophone Africa since Independence* (London: A & C Black, 1995).

41. Rothchild and Olorunsola, *State versus Ethnic Claims*, 20.

42. Ibid., 1.

43. There is now a plethora of works on the crisis and the war from diverse perspectives: former generals; Western journalists and volunteer workers; ordinary civilians, especially on the Biafran side; former Nigerian heads of state; novelists; and historians. The following are a few examples: Chief Uche Jom Ojiaku, *Surviving the Iron Curtain: A Microscopic View of What Life Was Like Inside a War-Torn Region* (Frederick, MD: Publish America, 2007); Alfred Uzokwe, *Surviving in Biafra: The Story of the Nigerian Civil War* (iUniverse, 2003); Frederick Forsyth, *The Biafra Story: The Making of an African Legend* (South Yorkshire: Pen and Sword Books, 2007); John Sherman, *War Stories: A Memoir of Nigeria and Biafra* (Indianapolis: Mesa Verde Press, 2002); Ralph Uwechwe, *Reflections on the Nigerian Civil War: Facing the Future* (Bloomington, IN: Trafford, 2006);

General Philip Efiong, *Nigeria and Biafra: My Story* (Elmont, NY: African Tree Press, 2007); and Chimanda Ngozi Adichie, *Half of a Yellow Sun* (New York: Knopf, 2006).

44. From opening remarks given at the conference of the Royal Historical Society, cited in the opening of the published paper, which appears as J. D. Hargreaves, "From Strangers to Minorities in West Africa," *Transactions of the Royal Historical Society* 31 (1981): 95–113.

45. Cyril I. Obi, *The Changing Forms of Identity Politics in Nigeria Under Economic Adjustment: The Case of the Oil Minorities Movement of the Niger Delta* (Nordiska Afrikainstitutet, 2001); E. Osaghae, *Structural Adjustment and Ethnicity in Nigeria* (Uppsala: Nordic Africa Institute, 1995).

46. The plight of the Ogoni people was revealed to the world in the case of Ken Saro-Wiwa and eight other Ogoni rights activists who led the struggle against Shell and the Nigerian government. In 1995, despite pleas and protests from around the world, the Nigerian government hanged them for treason. For more on this case, see Abdul-Rasheed N'Allah, ed., *Ogoni's Agonies: Ken Saro-Wiwa and the Crisis in Nigeria* (Trenton, NJ: Africa World Press, 1998); Ken Saro-Wiwa, *Nigeria: The Brink of Disaster and Genocide in Nigeria* (Saros International, 1991).

47. For overviews on regional cooperation in the nationalist and independence struggles in West Africa, see G. I. C. Eluwa, "Background to the Emergence of the National Congress of British West Africa," *African Studies Review* 14, no. 2 (1971): 205–218; Guy Pfeffermann, "Trade Unions and Politics in French West Africa during the Fourth Republic," *African Affairs* 66, no. 264 (1967): 213–230; Peter Karibe Mendy, "Amilcar Cabral and the Liberation of Guinea Bissau: Context, Challenges and Lessons for Effective African Leadership," *African Identities* 4, no. 1 (2006): 7–21.

48. C. W. Newbury, *The West African Commonwealth* (Durham, NC: Duke University Press, 1964), 5.

49. ECOWAS and ECOMOG, as examples of postcolonial regionalism, have been described and assessed extensively by scholars, especially political scientists. For more, see Kofi Oteng Kufuor, *The Institutional Transformation of the Economic Community of West African States* (Farnham, UK: Ashgate, 2006); and Funmi Olonisakin, *Reinventing Peacekeeping in Africa: Conceptual and Legal Issues in ECOMOG Operations* (New York: Springer, 2000).

50. Quoted at the meeting of the Methodist Boys High School and Methodist Girls High School Alumni Association of Snellville, Georgia, February 21, 2010.

51. For more, see Philip Garigue, "The West African Students' Union: A Study in Culture Contact," *Africa: Journal of the International African Institute* 23, no. 1 (1953): 55–69; Hakim Adi, "West African Students in Britain, 1900–60: The Politics of Exile," *Immigrants and Minorities* 12, no. 3 (1993): 107–128; Gary Wilder, *The French Imperial Nation-State: Negritude and Colonial Humanism Between the Two World Wars* (Chicago: University of Chicago Press, 2005); Brent Hayes

Edwards, *The Practice of Diaspora: Literature, Translation and the Rise of Black Internationalism* (Cambridge, MA: Harvard University Press, 2003).

52. *The Black Docker* (Portsmouth, NH: Heinemann, 1987), by iconic Senegalese writer Semebene Ousmane, is an excellent fictional account of the West African immigrant community of 1950s Marseilles. For more on labor migration from West Africa to France, see Jacques Barou, "In the Aftermath of Colonization: Black African Immigrants in France," in *Migrants in Europe: The Role of Family, Labor and Politics*, ed. Hans Christian Buechler and Judith-Maria Buechler (New York: Greenwood, 1987); and Dominic Thomas, *Black France: Colonialism, Immigration and Transnationalism* (Bloomington, Indiana University Press, 2007).

53. Aderanti Adepoju, "Migration in West Africa" (paper, Policy Analysis and Research Programme of the Global Commission on International Migration), www.gcim.org (accessed August 19, 2010); Blessing Mberu, "Nigeria: Multiple Forms of Mobility in Africa's Demographic Giant" (Migration Information Source, June 2010), http://migrationinformation.net/Profiles/print.cfm?ID=788 (accessed August 19, 2010).

54. One of the first studies of British immigration restrictions is Paul Foot, *Immigration and Race in British Policies* (New York: Penguin, 1965). See also R. Hansen, *Citizenship and Immigration in Post-war Britain: The Institutional Origins of a Multicultural Nation* (New York: Oxford University Press, 2000).

55. Heinz Werner, "Some Current Topics of Labor Migration in Europe," *Intereconomics* 13, no. 3 (1978): 94–97.

56. See, for example, Bruno Riccio, "West African Transnationalisms Compared: Ghanaians and Senegalese in Italy," *Journal of Ethnic and Migration Studies* 34, no. 2 (2008): 217–234; D. M. Carter, *States of Grace: Senegalese in Italy and the New European Immigration* (Minneapolis: University of Minnesota Press, 1997).

57. Figures cited in Mberu, "Nigeria."

58. Mberu, "Nigeria"; IRIN, "West Africa: Migrants Risk all to Cross the Desert," (October 9, 2008), http://www.irinnews.org (accessed August 19, 2010); C. Amalu, "Nigeria: Illegal Migration—59,000 Nigerians in Transit Countries for Europe," *Vanguard*, May 17, 2008.

59. Gordon, "New Diaspora"; Nicholas Van Hear, *New Diasporas: The Mass Exodus, Dispersal and Regrouping of Migrant Communities* (London: UCL Press, 1998); Konadu-Agyemang, Takyi, and Arthur, *New African Diaspora in North America*; Khalid Koser, ed., *The New African Diasporas* (New York: Routledge, 2003); Okpewho and Nzegwu, *New African Diaspora*; Mary Johnson Osirim, "The New African Diaspora: Transnationalism and Transformation in Philadelphia," in *Global Philadelphia: Immigrant Communities Old and New*, ed. Ayumi Takenaka and Mary Johnson Osirim (Philadelphia: Temple University Press, 2010), 226–252.

60. Professor Cyril Patrick Foray, head of the Department of Modern History, Fourah Bay College, University of Sierra Leone, in an address welcoming

students admitted to the History Honours Program, October 11, 1977. He made this statement while explaining the partnership with the U.S. embassy in Freetown for teaching American history, a new addition to the history curriculum in Sierra Leone.

61. Daisie Whaley, "My Experience as a West African Missionary," in *African American Experience in World Mission: A Call beyond Community*, ed. Vaughn T. Watson and Robert J. Stevens (Atlanta: COMINAD, 2002), 113–121, 113.

62. Angela Johnson (née Tuboku-Metzger), interviewed by Violet Johnson, Stone Mountain, GA, March 18, 2009; Lawrence Okafor, *Recent African Immigrants to the U.S.A.: Their Concerns, and How Everyone Can Succeed in the U.S.A.* (Pittsburgh: RoseDog Books, 2003), 2; Violet Showers, "A History of the Methodist Girls School, Freetown, Sierra Leone" (bachelor's dissertation, Fourah Bay College, 1979), 18.

63. Okafor, *Recent African Immigrants*, 3.

64. Quoted in Stephen V. Roberts, *From Every End of the Earth: Thirteen Families and the New Lives They Made in America* (New York: Harper 2009), 61.

65. Kofi K. Apraku, *Outside Looking In: An African Perspective on American Pluralistic Society* (Westport, CT: Praeger, 1996), xv–xvi.

66. Okafor, *Recent African Immigrants*, 3; Apraku, *Outside Looking In*, xv.

67. For more on the 1965 act, see David Reimers, "An Unintended Reform: The 1965 Immigration Act and Third World Immigration to the United States," *Journal of American Ethnic History* 3, no. 1 (1983): 9–28; William McGowan, "The 1965 Immigration Reforms and the *New York Times*: Context, Coverage, and Long-Term Consequences" (Center for Immigration Studies, August 2008), http://www.cis.org/NYT_immigration_coverage (accessed August 26, 2009).

68. Joseph Takougang, "Contemporary African Immigrants to the United States" (2003), http://www.africamigration.com/archive_02/j_takougang.htm (accessed May 17, 2009).

69. Abu Lo, interviewed by Violet Johnson, Atlanta, January 8, 2007; Bruno Riccio, "Disaggregating the Transnational Community: Senegalese Migrants on the Coast of Emilia-Romagna" (working paper series, University of Oxford Transnational Communities, an ESRC Research Programme, 2001), 17.

70. Y. Okegbu, interviewed by Violet Johnson, Macon, GA, May 5, 2008; J. Lomboko, "Reflections on Migration" (Unpublished remarks, Ghanaian Independence Celebration, March 6, 2010, Macon, GA).

71. Sylviane Diouf, quoted in Marieme Daff, "Women Taking Their Place in African Immigration," *Women's eNews*, August 4, 2002, http://womensenews.org (accessed August 19, 2010).

72. For in-depth analyses of the origins and consequences of the civil wars in Liberia and Sierra Leone, see Mark Huband, *The Liberian Civil War* (New York: Routledge, 1998); Stephen Ellis, *The Mask of Anarchy: The Destruction of Liberia and the Religious Dimension of an African Civil War* (New York: New York University Press, 2006); Jeremy Levitt, *The Evolution of Deadly Conflict in Liberia:*

From "Pataltarianism" to State Collapse (Durham, NC: Carolina Academic Press, 2005); Mary Moran, *Liberia: The Violence of Democracy* (Philadelphia: University of Pennsylvania Press, 2008); Ibrahim Abdullah, ed., *Between Democracy and Terror: The Sierra Leone Civil War* (Dakar: Codesria, 2000); Lansana Gberie, *A Dirty War in West Africa: The RUF and the Destruction of Sierra Leone* (Bloomington: Indiana University Press, 2005); Greg Campbell, *Blood Diamonds: Tracing the Deadly Path of the World's Most Precious Stones* (New York: Basic Books, 2004); and for an excellent, poignant personal account, see Ishmael Beah, *A Long Way Gone: Memoirs of a Boy Soldier* (New York: Farrar, Straus and Giroux, 2007).

73. Jeff Drumtra, "West Africa's Refugee Crisis Spills across Many Borders" (Migration Information Source, 2003), http://www.migrationinformation.org (accessed August 19, 2010).

74. For more on the Kassindja landmark case, see Fauziya Kassindja (with Layli Miller Bashir), *Do They Hear You When You Cry?* (New York: Bantam Books, 1998). For examples of other asylum cases around the world since Kassindja's, see "Female Genital Mutilation as Grounds for Asylum," *Forward*, http://www.forwarduk.org (accessed August 25, 2010).

75. From client testimonies from "Just Causes: Transforming Lives through the Law" (City Bar Fund Annual Report, 2002–2003). See also "Hope: 25 Years of Reuniting Families, Providing Dignified Refuge, Opening Doors to Citizenship" (Interfaith Refugee and Immigration Ministries Annual 2007 Report).

76. Arthur, *African Diaspora Identities*, 85.

77. Jacob Sax-Conteh, "So You Won the Diversity Visa Lottery? What Next?," *Cocorioko*, June 18, 2010, http://www.cocorioko.net/old/national/2986 (accessed August 21, 2010).

78. Ibid.; Timothy T. Seaklon, "Liberia: 400 Denied DV Visa," October 1, 2008, http://allafrica.com (accessed August 21, 2010); "Ghana: 'Arranged' Marriages Do Not Help in DV Lottery," November 7, 2007, http://www.myusgreencard.com (accessed August 21, 2010).

79. Enid Schildkrout, "One Family's History: A Microcosmic History of West African Migration" (Introductory remarks, Immigrants: Africans in New York Symposium, April 21, 2006), http://www.africanart.org/uploads/resources/docs/enids_paper (accessed August 7, 2010).

80. Michael Powell and Nina Bernstein, "In Tragedy, Glimpsing Oft-Overlooked Newcomers' Lives," *New York Times*, March 10, 2007.

81. Abdoulaye Kane, "Chain Migration among the Haal Pulaar Community" (paper, African Immigrant Symposium, New York, 2006).

82. Amy Hagopian, Matthew J. Thompson, Meredith Fordyce, Karin E. Johnson, and L. Gary Hart, "The Migration of Physicians from Sub-Saharan Africa to the United States of America: Measures of the African Brain Drain," *Human Resources for Health* 2, no. 17 (2004), http://www.human-resources-health.com (accessed August 25, 2010).

83. Arthur, *African Diaspora Identities*, 51, chap. 2, "Situating Africa's Brian Drain in Global Migrations," is an excellent analysis of this topic.

84. Bernard Bailyn, *The Peopling of British North America* (New York: Vintage Books, 1986), 25–26.

NOTES TO CHAPTER 2

1. Amadu Jacky Kaba, "Educational Attainment, Income Levels and Africans in the United States: The Paradox of Nigerian Immigrants," *West Africa Review* 11 (2009), http://www.africaknowledgeproject.org/index.php/war/article/view/246.

2. Capps, McCabe, and Fix, "New Streams," 12–13.

3. Massey et al., "Black Immigrants and Black Natives"; Pamela Bennett and Amy Lutz, "How African American Is the Net Black Advantage? Differences in College Attendance among Immigrant Blacks, Native Blacks, and Whites," *Sociology of Education* 82 (January 2009): 70–99.

4. "African-Born U.S. Residents Are the Most Highly Educated Group in American Society," *Journal of Blacks in Higher Education* 13 (September 30, 1996): 33; "African Immigrants in the United States Are the Nation's Most Highly Educated Group," *Journal of Blacks in Higher Education* 26 (January 31, 2000): 60.

5. Sara Rimer and Karen Arenson, "Top Colleges Take More Blacks, but Which Ones?," *New York Times*, June 24, 2004; "Roots and Race," *Harvard Magazine*, September–October 2004, 69–70; Clarence Page, "Black Immigrants Collect More Degrees," *Chicago Tribune*, March 18, 2007.

6. Festus E. Obiakor, "Beyond the Equity Rhetoric in America's Teacher Education Programs: An African Immigrant Voice," *Multicultural Learning and Teaching* 5, no. 1 (2010): 22.

7. While the presence of Africans in U.S. higher education has become a subject of discussion, there is very little scholarly work on the subject. One pertinent study deals with Africans in historically black colleges and universities and makes useful references to other institutions: Winnie Edith Ngozi Ochukpue, "A Qualitative Study of African Immigrant Professors in Two Historically Black Institutions in a Southeastern State" (doctoral dissertation, North Carolina State University, 2004).

8. *African Abroad*, April 15, 2007.

9. Ibid.

10. *African Abroad*, June 30, 2007.

11. Capps, McCabe, and Fix, "New Streams," 15.

12. "African Consumer Segment."

13. McCabe, "African Immigrants in the United States."

14. Moses Danquah, interviewed by Violet Johnson, Atlanta, May 5, 2006.

15. Okafor, *Recent African Immigrants*.

16. Capps, McCabe, and Fix, "New Streams," 17. Their research indicates that there is a positive correlation between longer residence in the United States and improved employment options, however.

17. Ayobami Odeyemi, "Illusion versus Reality: An Open Letter to My Brother in America," *U.S. Immigration News*, March 1, 2007.

18. James Brooke, "Foreigners Flock to Slopes to Work, Not Ski," *New York Times*, December 29, 1995.

19. Ibid.

20. Ibid.

21. *Mystery of Birds*, directed and produced by Nnaemeka Andrew Madueke (That Kid Productions, 2011).

22. Chinyere Ojide, "African Legal Secretaries: Messiahs or Judases," *U.S. Immigration News*, May 1, 2006.

23. The term "419 scam" is a colloquialism derived from the specific part on the definitions of and penalties for corruption under Nigerian laws—Section 419 of the Nigeria Penal Code. Examples of American media coverage are "Internet Fleecing Scams Thrive in Nigeria," report by Jeff Koinange of the CNN Lagos Bureau (August 11, 2002); and serialized *20/20* report on "Nigerian Scams" by ABC investigative reporter Brian Ross (December 2006).

24. *U.S. Immigration News*, December 1, 2010. Joseph Rotimi Famuyide had received his law degree from the University of Ife in Nigeria and had practiced law and taught at one of the institutions in Nigeria before immigrating to the United States in 1994.

25. Grace Vanderpue, graduation speech, Atlanta, May 17, 2008.

26. John Powers, "For Obukwelu Brothers, Harvard Football Is Family," *Boston Globe*, November 16, 2012, C1, C10.

27. See Catherine Ceniza Choy, *Empire of Care: Nursing and Migration in Filipino American History* (Durham, NC: Duke University Press, 2003); Mireille Kingma, "Nurses on the Move: A Global Overview," *Health Services Research* 42 (June 2007): 1281–1298; Barbara Brush, Julie Sochalski, and Anne M. Berger, "Imported Care: Recruiting Foreign Nurses to U.S. Health Care Facilities," *Health Affairs* 23, no. 3 (2004): 78–87.

28. Kingma, "Nurses on the Move," 1283.

29. *Gold Star Herald*, May 15, 2006.

30. McCabe, "African Immigrants in the United States.".

31. Senator Judd Gregg (R-NH), cited in *U.S. Immigration News*, July 1, 2007.

32. *U.S. Immigration News*, July 14, 2007.

33. Advertisement on flyer distributed to African ethnic businesses in America and reprinted in some publications in Africa, like the Sierra Leonean *We Yone*, daily newspaper published in Freetown, the capital city.

34. Teresa Cesay, graduation party speech, Jade Banquet Hall, Decatur, GA, May 26, 2005.

35. Fumilayo E. Showers, "'We Are the Real Nurses, They Are Just Opportunists': How African Immigrant Nurses Craft and Manage Professional Identities at Work" (Paper, Eastern Sociological Society, Philadelphia, February 2011).

36. Cited in Showers, "'We Are the Real Nurses.'"

37. Omolara Adeniyi, interviewed by Violet Johnson, Atlanta, May 8, 2011.

38. Rosamond V., interviewed by Violet Johnson, Stone Mountain, GA, May 6, 2008.

39. Ellen W., interviewed by Violet Johnson, Stone Mountain, GA, June 17, 2010.

40. "The Registered Nurse Population: Findings from the National Sample Survey of Registered Nurses" (2004), http://bhpr.hrsa.gov/healthworkforce/rnsurveys/ rnsurvey2004.pdf (accessed June 11, 2012).

41. Cited in Don Anderson, "Man Enough: The 20 X 20 Choose Nursing Campaign," *Minority Nurse*, Summer 2011, http://www.minoritynurse.com/article/ man-enough-20-x-20-choose-nursing-campaign (accessed June 11, 2012).

42. See Vicki Chung, "Men in Nursing," *Minority Nurse*, Summer 2010, http://www. minoritynurse.com/article/men-nursing-0 (accessed June 11, 2012); and Kenny Thompson and Daren Vertein, "Rethinking Gender Stereotypes in Nursing," *Minority Nurse*, Spring 2010, http://www.minoritynurse.com/men-nursing/ rethinking-gender-stereotypes-nursing (accessed June 11, 2012).

43. Anderson, "Man Enough."

44. Gordon Okosumbo, telephone interview by Violet Johnson, June 22, 2009.

45. See, for example, Wallena Gould, "An Open Letter to Historically Black Nursing Schools: Why now is the time to consider starting a nurse anesthesia program," *Minority Nurse*, Fall 2009, http://www.minoritynurse.com/african-american- black-nurses/open-letter-historically-black-nursing-schools (accessed June 11, 2012).

46. See, for example, "Jumoke Ayeni House Warming Ceremony in New Jersey: An Immigrant Success Story Through Nursing," *Africa Abroad*, October 30, 2006.

47. *Awoko*, July 7, 2008.

48. Comments posted on February 9, 2006, to *Nairaland Forum*, http://www.naira- land.com/6602/whyall-africans-studying-nursing (accessed June 4, 2011). Naira is Nigerian currency.

49. *My American Nurse* (Pascal Atuma Productions, 2006).

50. See, for example, Patricia Pessar, "The Dominicans: Women in Households and the Garment Industry," in *New Immigrants in New York*, ed. Nancy Foner (New York: Columbia University Press, 2001); Gaelan Lee Benway, *Gender Migrations: Dominican Women and Men Negotiate Work and Family in Providence, Rhode Island* (Providence: Brown University, 2006).

51. Susan Pearce, *Immigrant Women in the United States: A Demographic Portrait* (Washington, DC: Immigration Policy Center, 2006), 13.

52. Victor Greene, *American Immigrant Leaders, 1800–1910: Marginality and Identity* (Baltimore: Johns Hopkins University Press, 1987).

53. "Why We Formed the Nigerian Nurses Association in America: Interview with Founder of the Nigerian Nurses Association, USA, Dr. (Mrs.) Grace Ogiehon- Enoma," *African Abroad*, October 15, 2010.

54. Ibid.

55. Showers, "'We Are the Real Nurses.'"

56. Schaller Consulting, "The Changing Face of Taxi and Limousine Drivers" (2004), http://www.schallerconsult.com/taxi/taxidriver.pdf (accessed May 17, 2010).

57. Ibid.

58. Dan Q. Tham, "Driving a Cab: The African Immigrant's Signature Underemployment," posted on online newsletter, *Immigrant Connect*, June 2011, http://www.immigrantconnect.org/2011/06/19/driving-a-cab-the-african-immigrants-signature-underemployment/ (accessed July 28, 2011).

59. Alan L. Sitomer, "My Short Drive with a West African Taxi Driver," blog post, June 8, 2011, http://www.alanlawrencestiomer.com (accessed July 26, 2011).

60. Ibid.

61. Nisha Chandran, "America's Promise Drives Nigerian Cab Driver," *Daily Northwestern*, May 20, 2009.

62. Ibid.

63. Kabba, cited by Tham, "Driving a Cab."

64. An account related to Violet Johnson by Barbara Marshall, Chestnut Hill, MA, February 17, 1992.

65. Cited in Anna Boiko-Weyrauch, "Ghanaian Taxi Drivers in America," posted on *Modern Ghana*, April 22, 2009, http://modernghana.com (accessed July 20, 2011).

66. A series of discussions on the earning power of West African, especially Nigerian drivers, that went on for months on http://www.nairaland.com/nigeria/topic-418471.0html (accessed July 26, 2011).

67. Posted by Omega25red, March 25, 2010, http://www.nairaland.com/nigeria/topic-418471.0html.

68. Sierra Leonean taxi driver Joseph Kamara, interviewed by Violet Johnson, Conyers, GA, May 17, 2011. Kamara, a Fourah Bay College and University of Sierra Leone graduate, worked in one of the main banks in Sierra Leone, where he rose to B Signatory, which by the standards there is an accomplished and prestigious position.

69. For more on the protest, see Brain Tierney, "The War on DC Taxi Drivers," *Washington Post*, July 1, 2011.

70. It is sometimes difficult to determine if some of these businesses are "West African," because, while they are often listed as "small, black-owned," the specific ethnicity of the owner or owners is not highlighted or, as may be the case, partnerships are forged across African regions, as is the case of a small Lithonia, Georgia, cab company owned by a Ghanaian and an Eritrean.

71. Christine Haughney, "An African Chief in Cabby's Clothing," *New York Times*, August 12, 2011.

72. Ibid.

73. Dame Babou, cited in Peter Noel, "Africans Are Dying, Too: The Forgotten Victims of the Livery Cabbie Murders," *Village Voice*, April 18, 2000.

74. See Richard Marosi, "One of the Most Dangerous Jobs in New York: Gypsy Cab Driver," Columbia University News Services, http://www.taxi-library.org/marosi.htm (accessed July 17, 2001).

75. The documentary titled *Stop Killing Taxi Drivers* was shown at the Philadelphia Festival of World Cinema as part of a collection called *Distant Cultures*, April 10, 2002.

76. Cited in Noel, "Africans Are Dying, Too."

77. Ibid.

78. Blog conversations on Destee.Com Alive, July 15, 2005 (accessed February 6, 2006).

79. Blog post by Karen on Considermyview.com, January 28, 2009, http://www.considermyview.com (accessed May 17, 2009).

80. Blog post on Destee.com Alive, July 15, 2005.

81. Manning Marable used this experience to illustrate the workings of the new racism in the twenty-first century in a talk titled "Structural Racism and the Challenge of Black Leadership: The Challenge of Youth Leadership," delivered at Bowdoin College, March 2004. See summary by Ashley Harvard, "Whiteness Is on Its Way Out," *Bowdoin Orient*, April 4, 2004.

82. Cornel West, *Race Matters* (New York: Vintage, 1994).

83. Cited in Noel, "Africans Are Dying, Too."

84. Naomi Ishisaka, "Minority-on-Minority Racism: Where Are We Today?," http://www.naomiishisaka.com/writing/minority-on-minority-racism-where-are-we-today (accessed July 28, 2011).

85. Cited in "Ghanaian Fatally Shot in New York, Ex-con Held," *African Abroad*, April 30, 2006.

86. Ibid.

87. Cited in "Ex-con Killed Ghanaian Cab Driver," *Diasporian News*, April 23, 2006, http://www.ghanaweb.com/GhanaHomePage/diaspora/artikel.php?ID=103074 (accessed July 20, 2011)

88. Allieu Kamara, interviewed by Violet Johnson, Lithonia, GA, May 17, 2012.

89. David Sarpong, interviewed by Violet Johnson, Stone Mountain, GA, January 15, 2009.

90. *Diasporian News*, November 14, 2008, http://www.ghanaweb.com (accessed July 20, 2011).

91. *Chicago Dispatcher*, September 1, 2005.

92. Ibid.

93. Modernghana.com, November 24, 2009.

94. David Sarpong, interviewed by Violet Johnson, Clarkson, GA, February 17, 2004.

95. "Ghanaian Broke His Back Driving a Taxi," *African Abroad*, July 15, 2006.

96. Joseph Ajayi, cited in "Working in America," *Nigerian Bubble*, September 17, 2004.

97. Pastor Hezekiah Adeyemi, "Julius Cesar or God Almighty?," sermon delivered at Christ's Church of Salvation, Stone Mountain, GA, January 14, 1994.

98. Reverend Gerald Timity at the funeral of A. Lewis, Lithonia, GA, May 17, 1998.

99. Alpha/Imam Abu King at the party celebrating the recovery of H. Caulker and a fund-raiser for cancer awareness and cure, Decatur, GA, July 16, 2005.

100. Rudolph Okonkwo, "Why Are Africans Dying Young in the USA?," *African Abroad*, March 15, 2011.

101. Ibid.

102. Funmi Adepitan, "Lust for Dollar = Early Grave?," *African Abroad*, February 15, 2007.

103. Ibid.

104. Ibid.

105. Adebayo Olusanya, interviewed by Violet Johnson, Bowie, MD, August 12, 2012.

NOTES TO CHAPTER 3

1. "Atlanta Is Becoming the New Gold Coast," *African Star News Magazine*, February 2008.

2. Stoller, *Money Has No Smell*.

3. In addition to *Money Has No Smell*, for more on Mouridism and its tenets regarding business, see Ousmane Oumar Kane, *The Homeland Is the Arena: Religion, Transnationalism, and the Integration of Senegalese Immigrants in America* (New York: Oxford University Press, 2010); and Cheikh Anta Babou, "The Murid Ethos and the Political Economy of the Muridiyya: Work and Its Meaning in Ahmadu Bamba's Thought," *A Special Publication of the Murid Islamic Community in America* 1 (2001): 21–24. The specific case of women as Mouride entrepreneurs is tackled in Victoria Ebin, "Senegalese Women Migrants in America: A New Autonomy?" (paper, Seminar on Women and Demographic Change in Sub-Saharan Africa, Dakar, Senegal, March 3–6, 1993).

4. "African Consumer Segment," 30.

5. Quoted in interview by Gina Gerdel, "Ghanaian Entrepreneur Shares Story of Success at Africa Week 2010," in Jane Kani Edward, "The White Paper on African Immigration to the Bronx," Bronx African American History Project (BAAHP), 55, http://www.fordham.edu/images/academics/programs/baahp/white_paper_on_african_immigration_to_bronx.pdf (accessed October 14, 2011).

6. John Arthur found that approximately 20 percent of those who participated in his study of African health care professionals living abroad were involved with some kind of related entrepreneurial venture in their home countries. *African Diaspora Identities*, 54.

7. Joel Millman, "Nigerian Pharmacists Fill a Need," *Wall Street Journal*, October 2, 2010, http://online.wsj.com/article/SB10001424052748704789404575523930830427048.html.

8. Ibid.

9. "Nigerian Pharmacists Congregate in Dallas," *Houston Punch*, November 3, 2010.

10. Millman, "Nigerian Pharmacists Fill a Need."

11. "African Food to Cost More in America," *Africa Abroad*, June 15, 2007.

12. Seth Kugel, "Neighborhood Report: Concourse; Little Africa Flourishes, Fufu Flour and All," *New York Times*, February 17, 2002.

13. Leticia Jones, interviewed by Marilyn Halter and Violet Johnson, Cheverly, MD, April 21, 2006.

14. *African Abroad*, April 15, 2007.

15. *African Abroad*, September 30, 2010.

16. Natalie Southwick, "Marie-Claude Mendy Brings African Cuisine—and Art and Hospitality—to Teranga in Boston's South End," *Boston Globe*, August 18, 2010, http://www.boston.com/lifestyle/food/articles/2010/08/18/teranga_serves_up_a_taste_of_senegal/.

17. "Like Mama's Old Pot," *African Star*, January 2008.

18. Ibid.

19. Daff, "Women Taking Their Place."

20. Lamine Sawadogo, interviewed by Boston University African Immigrant Voices Project, November 26, 2006.

21. Abdullah, *Black Mecca*, 197.

22. See, for example, Roy Sleber and Frank Hereman, eds., *Hair in African Art and Culture* (New York: Museum of Fine Art, 2000).

23. Cheikh A. Babou, "Migration and Cultural Change: Money, 'Caste,' Gender, and Social Status among Senegalese Female Hair Braiders in the United States," *Africa Today* 55, no. 2 (2008): 3–22.

24. Sylviane Diouf-Kamara, "Senegalese in New York: A Model Minority?," *Black Renaissance/Renaissance Noire* 1, no. 2 (1997): 92.

25. Babou, "Migration and Cultural Change," 9.

26. In earlier research on this population, Babou found that the divorce rate among Senegalese couples living in North America was as high as 50 percent. See Cheikh Anta Babou, "Brotherhood Solidarity, Education and Migration: The Role of the *Dahiras* among the Murid Muslim Community of New York," *African Affairs* 101, no. 403 (2002): 151–170. Studies of other recent immigrant populations have shown that such shifts in traditional roles for foreign-born men and women have led to similar levels of family dysfunction and conflict. Marital strife among newcomers often stems directly from the male partner's inability to adjust to the woman's greater autonomy and a more egalitarian model of marriage in this country than was the norm in their countries of origin. See Sherri Grasmuck and Patricia Pessar, *Between Two Islands: Dominican Migration* (Berkeley: University of California Press, 1991); Silvia Pedraza, "Women and Migration: The Social Consequences of Gender," *Annual Review of Sociology* 17 (1991): 303–325. Similarly, as recent female immigrants get organized within the larger feminist community, often their very first initiatives

revolve around programs and shelters for battered women staffed by coethnic counselors.

27. Daff, "Women Taking Their Place."

28. See Noliwe M. Rooks, *Hair Raising: Beauty, Culture, and African American Women* (New Brunswick, NJ: Rutgers University Press, 1996); and Ingrid Banks, *Hair Matters: Beauty, Power and Black Women's Consciousness* (New York: New York University Press, 2000).

29. Sherri Day, "New Yorkers & Co.; Braiders Out of Africa With a World of Woes," *New York Times*, March 18, 2001; Monte Williams, "Bargain Braiders Battle for Heads; Hair Stylists from Africa Arrive, Driving Down Prices," *New York Times*, May 19, 2001.

30. Tracey P., interviewed by Violet Johnson, Atlanta, February 17, 2003.

31. "Braids with an African Twist," *Gold Star Herald*, May 15, 2006.

32. Ivan Moreno, "Hair Braider Wins Lawsuit Challenging Utah Rules," Associated Press, August 11, 2012, http://thegrio.com/2012/08/11/hair-braider-wins-lawsuit-challenging-utah-rules/#.

33. "The Seamstress in Western Pennsylvania," *Diasporian News*, March 16, 2003, http://www.ghanaweb.com/GhanaHomePage/NewsArchive/artikel.php?ID=34121 (accessed January 23, 2004).

34. "Dora Okrah's Village Boutique Brings the Beauty of Africa to Atlanta," *African Star*, January 2010.

35. "As Immigration Grows in Michigan, So Do African Businesses," *Diasporian News*, http://www.ghanaweb.com/GhanaHomePage/diaspora/artikel.php?ID=37100 (accessed January 23, 2004).

36. Mojibola Ogunlade, interviewed by Violet Johnson, Atlanta, October 16, 2010.

37. *African Abroad*, March 30, 2007.

38. Yinka M., interviewed by Violet Johnson, Atlanta, January 15, 2007.

39. Noted in Akinyele E. Diaro, "Wealth Creation: Entrepreneurship II—Starting a Business," *U.S. Immigration News*, May 1, 2007.

40. He points to his educational and occupational path to explain why he is an opportunity entrepreneur. He came to Florida from Abijan in the mid-1980s for higher education. Seeing the business opportunities created by the 1996 Olympics, he relocated to Atlanta. By the end of the decade he had moved from selling jeans and T-shirts to the taxi and limousine business. With the increase in immigrants purchasing homes in the early 2000s, he moved to real estate. And in 2008, responding to the rising appetite for homeland foods, he added tropical food retail to his business ventures.

41. "The Rise of Atlanta's Young African Entrepreneurs," *African Star*, February 2008.

42. Sam Dolnick, "For African Immigrants, Bronx Culture Clash Turns Violent," *New York Times*, October 20, 2009.

43. "Why We Don't Patronize Our Businesses," *African Star*, June 2009.

44. "Taking Care of Business: Ghanaian Women in Atlanta," *African Star*, September 2009.

45. For example, Sawaneh Imports in Atlanta, owned by Gambian Mohammed Sawaneh and his African American wife, Mia.

46. Kroger supermarkets in College Station, a Texas university town whose African population of students and professors is growing, carry garri, palm oil, and black soap, all West African staples.

47. For more on the conversation of Chinese neocolonialism, see Richard Dowden, *Africa: Altered States, Ordinary Miracles* (New York: Public Affairs, 2009), esp. chap. 17, "New Colonists or Old Friends? Asia in Africa," 484–508.

48. For more on the "Chinese invasion," see David Garner, "1.3 Billion Dollar Chinese Agriculture Investment in Sierra Leone," *DGC Asset Management*, January 19, 2012, http://dgcassetmanagement.com/Billion-Dollar-Chinese-Agriculture-Investment-in-Sierra-Leone (accessed June 17, 2012); "The Chinese in Africa: Are They Taking Over?," *African Star*, June 2012.

49. "As Immigration Grows in Michigan."

NOTES TO CHAPTER 4

1. Linda Basch, Nina Glick Schiller, and Cristina Blanc-Szanton, *Nations Unbound: Transnational Projects, Postcolonial Predicaments and Deterritorialized Nation-States* (Langhorne, PA: Gordon and Breach, 1994); Alejandro Portes, Luis E. Guarnizo, and Patricia Landdolt, "The Study of Transnationalism: Pitfalls and Promises of an Emergent Social Field," *Ethnic and Racial Studies* 22, no. 2 (1999): 217–236; Nancy Foner, "What's New about Transnationalism? New York Immigrants Today and at the Turn of the Century," *Diaspora* 6 (1997): 355–376; Peggy Levitt, *The Transnational Villagers* (Berkeley: University of California Press, 2001).

2. See esp. Peter Kivisto, "Theorizing Transnational Immigration: A Critical Review of Current Efforts," *Ethnic and Racial Studies* 24, no. 4 (July 2001): 549–577.

3. Basch, Glick Schiller, and Blanc-Szanton, *Nations Unbound*, 7.

4. Berlin, *Making of African America*, 209.

5. Pedro Góis, "Low Intensity Transnationalism: The Cape Verdian Case," *Vienna Journal of African Studies* 8 (2005): 270.

6. Dror Manning, Liberian speech delivered to the Clifton Community Association, January 3, 2004.

7. Quoted in Alexis Okeowo, "In a Pageant: A Borough's New Face," *New York Times*, August 4, 2011.

8. Outdooring in this instance refers to the ritual of bringing a newborn outside right after the baby is named, usually one week after birth.

9. Quoted in Lynne Christy Anderson, *Breaking Bread: Recipes and Stories from Immigrant Kitchens* (Berkeley: University of California Press, 2010), 27.

10. From a flyer announcing an Anambara Association meeting scheduled for February 4, 2007.

11. *Africa Abroad*, August 15, 2011.

12. Announcement of the United Nigerian Foundation—USA Inc., May 15, 2006.

13. *African Star*, May 2011.

14. Orde Coombes, "West Indians in New York: Moving beyond the Limbo Pole," *New York* 3, no. 28 (1970); David Hellwig, "Black Meets Black: Afro-American Reactions to West Indian Immigrants in the 1920s," *Southern Atlantic Quarterly* 77 (Spring 1978): 373–385; Dennis Forsythe, "West Indian Radicalism in America: An Assessment of Ideology," in *Ethnicity in the Americas*, ed. Frances Henry (The Hague: Morton, 1976).

15. *Africa Abroad*, September 30, 2010.

16. Paul T. Adujie, "Nigeria's National Independence Day Celebrations, New York," *African Abroad*, October 6, 2005.

17. *African Abroad*, September 15, 2006.

18. Adujie, "Nigeria's National Independence Day Celebrations."

19. Because in most cases it takes five years after attaining legal permanent residence (LPR) status before immigrants are eligible to apply for citizenship, length of newcomers' residence in the United States usually translates to increased levels of naturalization. Increases in citizenship rates for African immigrants began to be noticeable starting in 2004 with those from Anglophone African countries tending to become citizens at higher rates than other African groups. In 2007 the overall African immigrant citizenship rate was relatively low (26 percent compared to 32 percent of all immigrants), but by 2009 a significant increase had occurred whereby 43.7 percent of African immigrants were naturalized U.S. citizens, about the same share as the overall immigrant population. Of the West African groups, Sierra Leoneans, at 54.7 percent, had the highest rate. Capps, McCabe, and Fix, "New Streams"; McCabe, "African Immigrants in the United States."

20. *Gold Star Herald*, March 31, 2008.

21. *African Abroad*, January 15, 2010.

22. Kane, *Homeland Is the Arena*, 9.

23. "Cape Verdeans Expert Sailors," *Evening Bulletin* (Providence), May 29 , 1929; *Providence Sunday Journal*, November 6, 1949, 4.

24. Halter, *Between Race and Ethnicity*, 40; for more on the packet trade, see esp. chap. 2, "From Archipelago to America: A Sentimental Geography."

25. Kane, *Homeland Is the Arena*, 89; see also Steven Vertovec, *Transnationalism* (New York: Routledge, 2009).

26. Statement by Bright Boateng, *Gold Star*, September 30, 2007.

27. Migration Policy Institute, "Remittances Profile: Nigeria," http://www.migrationinformation.org/datahub/remittances/Nigeria.pdf (accessed December 18, 2012); Georgiana Pop, "Cape Verde," in *Remittance Markets in Africa*, ed. Dilip Ratha and Sanket Mohapatra (Washington, DC: World Bank, 2011), 91–92.

28. Togbga Pyne, interviewed by Violet Johnson, Stone Mountain, GA, May 17, 2008.

29. Cited and translated into English in Ayokunle Olumuyiwa Omobowale, Mofey-isara Oluwatoyin Omobowale, and Olawale Olufolahan Ajami, "Emigration and the Social Value of Remittances in Nigeria," in *Across the Atlantic: African Immigrants in the United States Diaspora*, ed. Emmanuel Yewah and 'Dimeji Togunde (Champaign, IL: Common Ground, 2010), 131.

30. David Njie, interviewed by Violet Johnson, Alpharetta, GA, July 17, 2006.

31. Valentina Mazzucato, Mirjam Kabki, and Lothar Smith, "Transnational Migration and the Economy of Funerals: Changing Practices in Ghana," *Development and Change* 37, no. 5 (September 2006): 1047–1072.

32. See, for example, Omobowale, Omobowale, and Ajami, "Emigration and the Social Value of Remittances," and Giles Mohan and Alfred Zack-Williams, "Globalization from Below: Conceptualizing the Role of the African Diasporas in Africa's Development," *Review of African Political Economy* 29, no. 92 (2002): 211–236.

33. Mariama Kamara, interviewed by Violet Johnson, Freetown, Sierra Leone, July 27, 2008.

34. Philip Emegwali in keynote speech at the 2004 Pan-African International Conference, cited in *Africa Abroad*, June 30, 2007.

35. *Diasporian News*, April 19, 2011, http://www.ghanaweb.com/GhanaHomePage/NewsArchive/artkel.php?ID=207192 (accessed October 3, 2012).

36. We arrived at this approximate figure from numerous oral interviews, advertisements on local radio shows and websites, and an array of community printed materials, including flyers and ethnic newspapers.

37. *African Abroad*, February 28, 2007.

38. *African Abroad*, December 30, 2003.

39. *Daily Independent*, December 12, 2003.

40. *Diaspora News*, February 17, 2012, http://www.ghanaweb.com/GhanaHomePage/diaspora (accessed August 11, 2012).

41. See, for example, Senate Banking, Housing and Urban Affairs Committee hearing on remittances, February 28, 2002, http://www.fairus.org (accessed July 27, 2006).

42. *African Abroad*, June 30, 2006.

43. Bright Boateng, "Money Systems Cash Transfer Debuts in Georgia," *Gold Star*, September 30, 2007.

44. *Gold Star*, September 30, 2007.

45. The ad ran in several West African immigrant publications alongside those of Western Union.

46. Theodora Johnson, interviewed by Violet Johnson, Freetown, Sierra Leone, February 20, 2007.

47. From *Accra Bubble*, May 17, 2005; excerpts reprinted in *African Abroad*, July 30, 2005.

48. From the description of the funeral of Pastor Dr. Adegoke Oyedeji, *African Abroad*, August 29, 2011.

49. From advertisement in *African Abroad*, April 30, 2007.

50. For more on Angelou's account of the African American immigrant community that grew around W. E. B. Du Bois in Accra, Ghana, see Maya Angelou, *All God's Children Need Traveling Shoes* (New York: Vintage, 1991).

51. *African Abroad*, May 30, 2006.

52. *Sierra Leone 365*, December 2002, http://sierraleone365.com (accessed May 15, 2011).

NOTES TO CHAPTER 5

1. Patrick A. Grant, "Coming to America with Eyes Wide Shut," in *Foreign-Born African Americans: Silenced Voices in the Discourse on Race*, ed. Festus E. Obiakor and Patrick A. Grant (New York: Nova, 2005).

2. Booker T. Washington, *The Story of the Negro: The Rise of the Race from Slavery*, vol. 1 (1909; repr., New York: Negro University Press, 1969), 33–34.

3. Other scholars of the new African diaspora have also addressed some of these dynamics. See especially Arthur in *African Diaspora Identities* and Phillipe Wamba in *Kinship: A Family's Journey in Africa and America* (New York: Plume, 1999).

4. In her study of African immigrants in Washington, D.C., Habecker found an exception to the usual contours of the discourse on blackness among the East African populations of Amharic- and Tigrinya-speaking Ethiopians and Eritreans who have tried to sidestep being racialized as black altogether by, instead, creating an alternative that connotes Semitic origins known as Habasha identity. See Shelly Habecker, "Not Black, but Habasha: Ethiopian and Eritrean Immigrants in American Society," *Ethnic and Racial Studies* 35, no. 7 (2012): 1200–1219.

5. Meri Nana-Ama Danquah, "Life as an Alien," in *Half and Half: Writers on Growing Up Biracial and Bicultural*, ed. Claudine Chiawei O'Hearn (New York: Pantheon Books, 1998), 105.

6. Beck, "West African Muslims in America," 198.

7. Ann Simmons, "A Common Ground in African Heritage: Little Ethiopia Event Aims to Bring Black Americans and Immigrants Together," *Los Angeles Times*, November 24, 2003, B1.

8. Akwasi Assensoh, "Conflict or Cooperation? Africans and African Americans in Multiracial America," in *Black and Multiracial Politics in America*, ed. Yvette M. Alex-Assensoh and Lawrence Hanks (New York: New York University Press, 2000), 126.

9. Dan Austin, "A Nigerian-American Runs for United States Congress," *Transatlantic Times*, African Edition 1 (June 2004): 7.

10. See especially the discussion of these dynamics in Harlem in Abdullah, *Black Mecca*, 52.

11. Rob Carson, "Black and African: As Different as Black and White," *News Tribune*, April 27, 2004, http://invisionfree.com/forums/TheRapUp/ar/t1586.htm (accessed June 9, 2012).

12. Oscar Johnson, "Chilly Coexistence: African and African-Americas in the Bronx" (2000), http://www.columbia.edu/itc/journalism/gissler/anthology/Chill-Johnson.html; Jennifer Jackson and Mary Cothran, "Black versus Black: The Relationships among African, African American, and African Caribbean Persons," *Journal of Black Studies* 33, no. 5 (2003): 576–604.

13. "African Consumer Segment."

14. Robinson, *Disintegration*, 176.

15. "Remembering Martin Luther King, Jr.," *Africans Abroad*, January 15, 2007.

16. John H. McWhorter, "Why I'm Black, Not African American," *Los Angeles Times*, September 8, 2004.

17. Rachel Swarns, "African-American Becomes a Term for Debate," *New York Times*, August, 29, 2004.

18. Mukoma W. Ngugi, "African in America or African American?," *Guardian*, January 14, 2011, http://www.guardian.co.uk/commentisfree/cifamerica/2011/jan/13/race-kenya (accessed June 20, 2011).

19. Kane, *Homeland Is the Arena*, 151.

20. Zain Abdullah, "Sufis on Parade: The Performance of Black, African, and Muslim Identities," *Journal of the American Academy of Religion* 77, no. 2 (2009): 1–39; Abdullah, *Black Mecca*, 107–127; Monika Salzbrunn, "The Occupation of Public Space through Religious and Political Events: How Senegalese Migrants Became a Part of Harlem, New York," *Journal of Religion in Africa* 34, no. 4 (2004): 468–492; Ayesha Attah, "Mourides Celebrate 19 Years in North America," *African webzine*, July 30, 2007, http://www.africanmag.com/ARTICLE-504-design001 (accessed June 15, 2008).

21. Abdullah, *Black Mecca*, 111.

22. Ibid., 112.

23. Kane, *Homeland Is the Arena*, 153.

24. Ibid., 154.

25. Abdullah, *Black Mecca*, 127.

26. Beck, "West African Muslims in America," 182–206.

27. Kane, *Homeland Is the Arena*, 138–139.

28. Diallo and Wolff, *My Heart Will Cross This Ocean*, 4–5.

29. John Logan and Glenn Deane, "Black Diversity in Metropolitan America" (Lewis Mumford Center for Comparative Urban and Regional Research, University at Albany, 2003), http://mumford1.dyndns.org/cen2000/report.html.

30. Johnnie Cochran, *A Lawyer's Life* (New York: Thomas Dunne Books, 2002), 176–177.

31. Diallo and Wolff, *My Heart Will Cross This Ocean*, 238.

32. Mike Flugennock, "We Own the Night: 365 Days of Marching—The Amadou Diallo Story" (video, 360 Media), http://www.youtube.com/watch?v=xfVIOUph. Ro.

33. Dan Barry, "Daily Protesters in Handcuffs Keep Focus on Diallo Killing," *New York Times*, March 19, 1999.
34. Ginger Thompson, "'1,000 Rally to Condemn Shooting of Unarmed Man by Police," *New York Times*, February 8, 1999.
35. Frankie Edozien, "Remembering Amadou Diallo," *The African*, February 2002.
36. Ibid.
37. Olubode A., interviewed by Violet Johnson, Atlanta, May 17, 2003.
38. Diallo and Wolff, *My Heart Will Cross This Ocean*, 233.
39. Amy Waldman, "Shooting in the Bronx: The Immigrants; Killing Heightens in the Unease Felt by Africans in New York," *New York Times*, February 14, 1999.
40. Bethlehem Ababaiya, interviewed by Binta Njie, Washington, DC, June 17, 2003.
41. Ida Njie, interviewed by Binta Njie, Houston, May 22, 2003.
42. Frank Bruni, "Invisible, and in Anguish: A Slain Driver's Service Brings Attention to Senegalese," *New York Times*, November 18, 1997.
43. Susan Sachs, "Guineans Still See Opportunity in U.S.," *New York Times*, February 21, 1999.
44. Waldman, "Shooting in the Bronx."
45. Ibid.
46. Mojubaolu Olufunke Okome, "Amadou Diallo: Some Observations by Another African Immigrant," *Africa Resource*, http://www.africaresource.com (accessed November 23, 2005).
47. Manthia Diawara, *We Won't Budge: An African Exile in the World* (New York: Basic Civitas Books, 2003), vii–ix.
48. Diallo and Wolff, *My Heart Will Cross This Ocean*, 194.
49. Elizabeth Alexander, "Can You Be Black and Look at This? Reading the Rodney King Video(s)," in *The Black Public Sphere: A Public Culture Book* (Chicago: Black Public Sphere Collective, 1995), 82.
50. Emmet Till was an African American teenager from Chicago who, on a visit to Mississippi in 1955, was brutally murdered for allegedly insulting a white woman. His death is now acknowledged as one of the catalysts for the modern civil rights movement.
51. Cochran, *Lawyer's Life*, 180–183.
52. Ted Conover, "Kadi Diallo's Trial," *New York Times Magazine*, January 9, 2000.
53. Ibid.
54. Ibid.
55. Reuel R. Rogers, "Race-Based Coalitions among Minority Groups: Afro-Caribbean Immigrants and African-Americans in New York City," *Urban Affairs Review* 39, no. 3 (2004): 283–317.
56. The National Summit itself was held in February 2000, with every state in the United States represented, and in 2002 the National Summit on Africa became the Africa Society, an ongoing think tank and organization for public education. Jill Humphries, "Resisting 'Race': Organizing African Transnational Identities in the United States," in Okpewho and Nzegwu, *New African Diaspora*, 271–299.

57. Alex-Assensoh, "African Immigrants and African-Americans," 107–110, table 1.
58. Quoted in Crary, "African Immigrants Find Opportunity."
59. Diawara, *We Won't Budge*, ix.
60. Stefano Valentino, "Local African Leaders Seek a Common Mission," January 9, 2010, http://missionlocal.org/2010/01/local-african-leaders-seek-a-common-mission/ (accessed April 19, 2010).
61. Berlin, *Making of African America*, 299.
62. Deon Brown, "Black Immigrants Rally for Justice on Capitol Hill," *Gleaner*, April 4, 2013, http://jamaica-gleaner.com/extra/article.php?id=2293 (accessed April 13, 2013).
63. Kobina Aidoo, "Why the Neo African Americans?," June 4, 2009, http://neoafricanamericans.wordpress.com/.
64. Brent Staples, "Decoding the Debate over the Blackness of Barack Obama," *New York Times*, February 11, 2007.
65. Oralandar Brand-Williams, "Africans Find Home in Detroit," *Detroit News*, May 29, 2003.
66. Marcus Samuelsson, *Yes, Chef: A Memoir* (New York: Random House, 2012), 264.
67. Quoted in Brandt Williams, "Problems of Assimilation" (Minnesota Public Radio, February 4, 2002), http://news.minnesota.publicradio.org/features/200202/04_williamsb_africans/assimilation.shtml.
68. Quoted in Habecker, "Not Black, but Habasha," 222.
69. Sarah Manyika, "Oyinbo," in Hintzen and Rahier, *Problematizing Blackness*, 66.
70. Quoted in Susan Sachs, "In Harlem's Fabric: Bright Threads of Senegal," *New York Times*, July 28, 2003, http://www.nytimes.com/2003/07/28/nyregion/in-harlem-s-fabric-bright-threads-of-senegal.html?pagewanted=all&src=pm.

NOTES TO CHAPTER 6
1. Apraku, *Outside Looking In*, xiii, xvii.
2. Michael Bowman, "From Colonial Times, Immigrants Have Changed, Invigorated the United States" (Voice of American Radio, May 3, 2005), www.voanews.com.
3. Savella Ogbode, "Africans at Home and Abroad" (March 21, 2005), www.nigeriansinamerica.com.
4. The term "1.5 generation," originally coined by sociologist Rubén Rumbaut in his 1991 essay "The Agony of Exile: A Study of the Migration and Adaptation of Indochinese Refugee Adults and Children," in *Refugee Children: Theory, Research, and Services*, ed. F. Ahearn, Jr. and H. Athey (Baltimore: Johns Hopkins University Press), 53–91, refers to those who migrate as children, from newborns to adolescents. Rumbaut later refined this notion, differentiating three cohorts of what R. S. Oropesa and Nancy Landale labeled "decimal" generations: (1) those who arrive as teenagers (ages thirteen to seventeen) who thus spend most of their formative years in their native country are considered

to be the 1.25 generation, (2) those who migrate at primary school age (ages six to twelve) are the classic 1.5 group, and (3) the 1.75 generation consists of those who come as very young children (ages zero to five) and are almost entirely socialized in the United States. Straddling the old world and the new, the younger cohort tends to follow similar cultural and developmental experiences as those known as the second generation (usually defined as children born in the United States to at least one immigrant parent), while those in the older group may more closely resemble their immigrant parents in the adaptation process. See Rumbaut, "Ties That Bind: Immigration and Immigrant Families in the U.S.," in *Immigration and the Family: Research and Policy on U.S. Immigrants*, ed. Alan Booth, Ann Crouter, and Nancy Landale (Mahwah, NJ: Lawrence Erlbaum, 1997), 3–45; and R. S. Oropesa and Nancy Landale, "In Search of the New Second Generation: Alternative Strategies for Identifying Second Generation Children and Understanding Their Acquisition of English," *Sociological Perspectives* 40, no. 3 (1997): 429–455.

5. Nigerians in America call themselves "Naija."
6. Olufunke A., interviewed by Violet Johnson, Stone Mountain, GA, September 10, 2006.
7. Halter, *Between Race and Ethnicity.*
8. Kwame Nkrumah, *Ghana: The Autobiography of Kwame Nkrumah* (New York: Thomas Nelson, 1957); and Nnamdi Azikiwe, *My Odyssey* (London: C. Hurst and Co., 1971).
9. Adama K., interviewed by Violet Johnson, Atlanta, September 14, 2006.
10. Logan and Deane, "Black Diversity in Metropolitan America,"; "African Immigrants in the United States Are the Nation's Most Highly Educated Group," 60; Darryl Fears, "Disparity Marks Black Ethnic Groups, Report Says African Americans Trail Immigrants in Income, Education," *Washington Post*, March 13, 2003.
11. Bennett and Lutz, "How African American Is the Net Black Advantage?"; Massey et al., "Black Immigrants and Black Natives."
12. Massey et al., "Black Immigrants and Black Natives," 250–251.
13. Interview with Ehiedu Iweriebor, "Nigerian Community in America Part II" (documentary, October 27, 2010), http://www.youtube.com/watch?v=dPmQYP9 UGno&feature=youtu.be (accessed June 25, 2011).
14. Robert O. Owolabi, *An African's View of the American Society: An Eyewitness Account of 15 Years of Living, Studying and Working in the United States of America* (Chapel Hill, NC: Professional Press, 1996), 95.
15. Philip Kasinitz, John Mollenkopf, Mary Waters, and Jennifer Holdaway, *Inheriting the City: The Children of Immigrants Come of Age* (Cambridge, MA: Harvard University Press, 2008). The focus of the research, carried out from 1998 to 2003, was on several immigrant populations—Dominicans, South Americans (from Colombia, Ecuador, and Peru), English-speaking West Indians, Chinese, and Russian Jews—as well as three native-born comparative populations—native whites, native blacks, and Puerto Ricans.

16. See Herbert J. Gans, "Second Generation Decline: Scenarios for the Economic and Ethnic Futures of the Post-1965 American Immigrants," *Ethnic and Racial Studies* 15, no. 2 (1992): 173–192; Alejandro Portes and Min Zhou, "The New Second Generation: Segmented Assimilation and Its Variants," *Annals of the American Academy of Political and Social Science* 530 (1993): 74–96; Alejandro Portes, Patricia Fernández-Kelly, and William Haller, "Segmented Assimilation on the Ground: The New Second Generation in Early Adulthood," *Ethnic and Racial Studies* 28, no. 6 (2005): 1000–1040.

17. Kasinitz et al., *Inheriting the City*, 358–359.

18. Bennett and Lutz, "How African American Is the Net Black Advantage?," 77, 89.

19. Monique Walker, "Safety Help: Patriots' Ihedigbo Follows Parents' Example with His Education Foundation," *Boston Globe*, October 16, 2011, C1, C12.

20. Ngozi A., interviewed by Violet Johnson, Decatur, GA, March 1995.

21. Habecker, "Not Black, but Habasha," 275–276.

22. Onoso Imoagene, "Identity Choices and the Mechanisms of Identity Formation among 1.5 to Second Generation Adult Nigerian Immigrants in the United Kingdom" (paper, Harvard Migration and Immigrant Incorporation Workshop, Harvard University, March 10, 2009).

23. Msia Kibona Clark, "Questions of Identity among African Immigrants in America," in Okpewho and Nzegwu, *New African Diaspora*, 261–262.

24. Quoted in Jason B. Johnson, "Shades of Gray in Black Enrollment," *San Francisco Chronicle*, February 22, 2005.

25. Among Sierra Leoneans, even individuals who came in technically as refugees may still be from middle-class backgrounds and would likely have had the opportunity to attend private schools and may even have taken European exams like the London GCSE before coming to the United States.

26. See Mojúbàolú Olúfúnké Okome, "Emergent African Immigrant Philanthropy in New York City," *Research in Urban Sociology* 7: 179–191; Stoller, *Money Has No Smell*; Cheikh Anta Babou, "Brotherhood Solidarity, Education and Migration: The Role of the *Dahiras* among the Murid Muslim Community of New York," *African Affairs* 101, no. 403 (2002): 151–170; Diouf-Kamara, "Senegalese in New York"; Mamadou Diouf, "The Senegalese Murid Trade Diaspora and the Making of a Vernacular Cosmopolitanism," trans. Steven Rendall, *Public Culture* 12, no. 3 (2000): 679–702.

27. Instituto Nacional de Estatistica (INE), *Educacão: Censo* (Praia, Cape Verde: INE, 2000).

28. Chad Leith, "First-Generation Immigrant Adolescents from Cape Verde: Ethnic Identities, Socioeconomic Backgrounds, and Educational Outcomes" (unpublished paper, 2007).

29. Kadiatou K., interviewed by Violet Johnson, Clarkson, GA, October 3, 2006.

30. See Prudence Carter, *Keepin' It Real: School Success Beyond Black and White* (New York: Oxford University Press, 2005); Xue Lan Rong and Frank Brown, "The Effects of Immigrant Generation and Ethnicity on Educational Attainment among Young African and Caribbean Blacks in the United States," *Harvard Educational*

Review 71, no. 3 (2001): 536–565; Marcelo Suárez-Orozco, "Immigrant Adaptation to Schooling: A Hispanic Case," 37–61, and John Ogbu, "Low School Performance as an Adaptation: the Case of Blacks in Stockton, California," 249–286, both in *Minority Status and Schooling: A Comparative Study of Immigrant and Involuntary Minorities*, ed. M. Gibson and J. Ogbu (New York: Garland, 1991).

31. Samuel Obi, *Readings for Amerigerian Igbo: Culture, History Language and Legacy* (2010), http://www.authorhouse.com/Bookstore/BookDetail.aspx?BookId=SKU-000411589 (accessed July 25, 2011).

32. Crystal S., interviewed by Violet Johnson, Snellville, GA, October 15, 2006.

33. Nazli Kibria, *Family Tightrope: The Changing Lives of Vietnamese Americans* (Princeton, NJ: Princeton University Press, 1993); Min Zhou and Carl Bankston, *Growing Up American: The Adaptation of Vietnamese Adolescents in the United States* (New York: Russell Sage Foundation, 1998).

34. Rubén Rumbaut, "The Crucible Within: Ethnic Identity, Self-esteem and Segmented Assimilation among Children of Immigrants," *International Migration Review* 28, no. 4 (1994): 748–794; Min Zhou, "Growing Up American: The Challenge Confronting Immigrant Children and Children of Immigrants," *Annual Review of Sociology* 23 (1997): 63–95.

35. Alejandro Portes and Patricia Fernández-Kelly," No Margin for Error: Educational and Occupational Achievement among Disadvantaged Children of Immigrants," *Annals of the American Academy of Political and Social Science* 620, no. 1 (2008): 12–36.

36. Richard De Gourville, "Social and Academic Experiences of Liberian Students: Adapting their Cultural Literacies to a U.S. Urban High School: A Critical Inquiry" (doctoral dissertation, Pennsylvania State University, 2002), 318, 294–295.

37. Conversations with Mator Kpangbai, director, Adelaide Avenue School, Providence, RI, by Marilyn Halter, July 2006–January 2007.

38. De Gourville, "Social and Academic Experiences," 258–261.

39. Sam Ross, interviewed by Cara Bernard for "US Born: From Africa to America" (radio feature, UJW Online Student Voices of the Urban Journalism Workshop), http://www.ujwonline.org/?p=1205 (accessed June 13, 2011).

40. Efua C., interviewed by Violet Johnson, Stone Mountain, GA, March 25, 2007.

41. Laurie Olsen, *Made in America: Immigrant Students in Our Public Schools* (New York: New Press, 1997).

42. Maxzine Kennedy, interviewed by Marilyn Halter, Providence, RI, December 17, 2006.

43. Nancy C. Lopez, *Hopeful Girls, Troubled Boys* (New York: Routledge, 2002); Robert C. Smith, *Mexican New York: Transnational Lives of New Immigrants* (Berkeley: University of California Press, 2005).

44. Lynette Clemetson, "For Schooling a Reverse Emigration to Africa," *New York Times*, September 4, 2003, A21.

45. The interviews conducted by Kasinitz et al., *Inheriting the City*, of those who had been sent for an interlude to their parent's homeland revealed varying

responses; some felt it was a hindrance, while others reported very positively about the experience.

46. Quoted in Veronica Savory McComb, "The Bonds of Faith: Religion and Community among Nigerian Immigrants to the U.S., 1965–Present" (doctoral dissertation, Boston University, 2010), 206.

47. Larry Mayer, "Trip to Nigeria an Emotional One for Ogunleye," *Chicago Bears News*, May 15, 2006, http://www.chicagobears.com/news/article-1/Trip-to-Nigeria-an-emotional-one-for-Ogunleye/5CA64248-BEDF-4C15-8BF6-175ECCF2ED73(accessed February 20, 2010). Fifteen years later, in 2008, Ogunleye returned with several other NFL players of Nigerian descent to provide aid in the form of scholarships to young students and to assist in clean water initiatives.

48. Alex Kabba, "Immigrants' Children Gone Wild! The Difficulty of Raising Black Children in the USA," *African Abroad*, March 30, 2007, 34, 39.

49. Abimbola Ishola, moderator, "Episode 40: Nollywood Film 'Tobi' Debuts in NYC" (*Culture Shock: Nigerians in America*, June 10, 2011), http://cultureshock-nigerians.com/shows/episode-40-nollywood-film-tobi-debuts-in-nyc/ (accessed June 18, 2011).

50. Mary C. Waters, *Black Identities: West Indian Immigrant Dreams and American Realities* (New York: Russell Sage, 1999), chap. 8 is particularly useful; Milton Vickerman, *Crosscurrents: West Indian Immigrants and Race* (New York: Oxford University Press, 1999).

51. Benjamin Bailey, "Dominican-American Ethnic/Racial Identities and United States Social Categories," *International Migration Review* 35, no. 3 (2001): 677–708.

52. Ruben Hadzide, address delivered at the banquet to celebrate the fiftieth anniversary of independence of the Republic of Ghana, Hyatt Regency, Chicago, March 10, 2007, http://ghanaweb.com.

53. Remi Aluko and Diana Sherblom, "Passing Culture on to the Next Generation: African Immigrant Language and Culture Schools in Washington, D.C.," in *Articles from the 1997 Festival of American Folklife Program Book* (Washington, DC: African Immigrant Folklife Project, 1997).

54. Ibid.

55. Leigh Swigart, *Extended Lives: The African Immigrant Experience in Philadelphia* (Philadelphia: Balch Institute for Ethnic Studies, 2001), 4.

56. Danquah, "Life as an Alien," 105.

57. Waters, *Black Identities*, 285.

58. Rodney D. Coates, "Talking Affirmative Action: Race, Opportunity, and Everyday Ideology," *Contemporary Sociology* 36, no. 4 (2007): 334–335.

59. Rimer and Arenson, "Top Colleges Take More Blacks"; "Roots and Race."

60. Kasinitz et al., *Inheriting the City*, 303, 331–333.

61. McCene H., interviewed by Marilyn Halter, Providence, RI, December 13, 2006.

62. Andree G., interviewed by Marcy DePina, Newark, NJ, July 28, 2006.

63. Ross, interviewed by Bernard for "US Born."

64. Dympna Ugwu-Oju, *What Will My Mother Say: A Tribal African Girl Comes of Age in America* (Chicago: Bonus Books, 1995), 281.

65. Maria A., interviewed by Marilyn Halter, Fairhaven, MA, June 25, 2004.

66. Isabel S., interviewed by Marilyn Halter, Boston, April 6, 2011.

67. Paul De Barros, quoted in Johnny Diaz and Scott Greenberger, "Not White, Not Black, Not Hispanic—Boston's Cape Verdeans Have Long Been Misunderstood," *Boston Globe*, February 15, 2004, B1.

68. Adonis F., interviewed by Marilyn Halter, Fairhaven, MA, May 18, 2004.

69. Gina Sánchez, "Contested Identities: Negotiating Race and Culture in a Cape Verdean Diaspora Community" (doctoral dissertation, University of Texas at Austin, 1999).

70. Rudolf Ogoo Okonkwo, "The Challenges in Raising African Boys in America," *African Abroad*, July 30, 2010, 28.

71. Rose V., interviewed by Violet Johnson, Lithonia, GA, June 4, 2011.

72. "Minnesota Killings Tied to Somali Gangs," Associated Press, July 20, 2009, http://www.msnbc.msn.com/id/32010471/ns/us_news-crime_and_courts/ (accessed July 28, 2009); Vanessa Ho, "Kids' Troubles Shake Seattle's East Africans," *Seattle Post-Intelligencer*, April 12, 2006. Habecker did not find any evidence of organized gangs among African youth in Washington, D.C.

73. Quoted in Habecker, "Not Black, but Habasha," 274–275.

74. Kasinitz et al., *Inheriting the City*, 242.

75. Christina Hickman, "The Sound of Cultural Harmony: Music of Candida Rose Fuses American, Cape Verdean Traditions," *The Standard Times*, June 30, 2011: A2.

76. See http://www.fufuandoreos.com/index.html. Audiences have reported that after the show, when she's present, Obehi's mother serves up her homemade fufu for those in attendance.

77. Kasinitz et al., *Inheriting the City*, found a similar pattern of ethnic pride among the subjects of their study.

78. Emily Wax, "Trading Up: Swathing the World in African fashion," *Washington Post*, July 1, 2011, C7.

79. Ibid. The Afropolitan fashion website is mybennucafe.com.

80. Yolanda Sangweni, "Generation Next: Meet the Afropolitans, Africa's Transcontinental Children," *Arise Magazine*, March 2011, 96–101, http://www.arisemagazine.net/articles/generation-next/87396/ (accessed July 12, 2011).

81. Temistocles F., interviewed by Marilyn Halter, Fairhaven, MA, January 22, 2005.

82. See MySpace.com/ladymada.

83. Nelson George, *Hip Hop America* (New York: Penguin, 1998), 121–127.

84. Berlin, *Making of African America*, 227.

85. Russell Contreras, "Musician Hooked on W. African, Hip-Hop Blend," *Boston Globe*, October 19, 2006.

86. See MySpace.com/ladymada; CVMusicWorld.com.

87. Beah, *Long Way Gone*, 192.
88. Danquah, "Life as an Alien," 106–107.
89. Ibid., 107.
90. Winston S., interviewed by Marilyn Halter, Providence, RI, November 13, 2006.
91. Denise G., interviewed by Marilyn Halter, Providence, RI, December 1, 2006; Leith, "First-Generation Immigrant Adolescents," 18.
92. McCene H., interviewed by Marilyn Halter, Providence, RI, December 13, 2006.
93. Natasha K., interviewed by Marilyn Halter, Providence, RI, December 1, 2006.
94. Malik A., interviewed by Marcy DePina, Newark, NJ, October 8, 2006.
95. Karin Brulliard, "To Africa, for Culture and Credits," *Washington Post*, September 23, 2007, C01.
96. Joy Roberts, interviewed by Violet Johnson, Lithonia, GA, September 20.
97. Petra Cahill, "Bridging the Gap in Harlem: African Immigrants, Black Teens Discuss Differences," December 10, 2004, http://www.nbcnews.com/id/6531471/#.Ut1CESk07cs (accessed July 10, 2009)
98. Eliott McLaughlin, "Continental Divide Separates Africans, African-Americans," Blacks in America 2, CNN, July 15, 2009, http://www.cnn.com/2009/US/07/14/africans.in.america/index.html#cnnSTCText (accessed June 15, 2011).
99. Celestine Alipui, interviewed by Marilyn Halter and Violet Johnson, Houston, February 27, 2007.
100. Rosemary Luckens Traoré, "Colonialism Continued: African Students in an Urban High School in America," *Journal of Black Studies* 34 (2004): 360–361.
101. Ibid., 354.
102. Robert Moran, Gaiutra Bahadur, and Susan Snyder, "Residents Say Beating Fits Widespread Pattern," *Philadelphia Inquirer*, November 3, 2005; Elmer Smith, "'Normal' at Tilden Middle School Is Different," *Philadelphia Inquirer*, November 4, 2005.
103. A. T., interviewed by Violet Johnson, Lilburn, GA, October 17, 2006.

NOTES TO THE CONCLUSION

1. John H. McWhorter, "Why I'm Black."
2. See esp. Kathleen Conzen, David A. Gerber, Ewa Morawska, George E. Pozzetta, and Rudolph J. Vecoli, "The Invention of Ethnicity: A Perspective from the U.S.A.," *Journal of American Ethnic History* 12, no. 1 (1992): 3–41.
3. Arthur, *Invisible Sojourners*.
4. In addition to Ahmadou Diallo, the other West African–born candidates were Nigerian Americans Abiodun Bello and Bola Omotosho. Second-generation Naaimat Muhammad, whose parents are from Ghana and Togo, was included in the "West African contingent," which signified the remarkable heightened African presence. See Elly W. Yu, "African Immigrants in Bronx Vying for City Council Seat Traditionally Held by African Americans," *New York Daily News*, March 1, 2013.

Abdullah, Ibrahim, ed. 2000. *Between Democracy and Terror: The Sierra Leone Civil War*. Dakar: Codesria.

Abdullah, Zain. 2001. "West Africans." In *Encyclopedia of American Immigration*, ed. James Ciment. Armonk, NY: M.E. Sharpe: 1070–1078.

———. 2008. "Negotiating Identities: A History of Islamization in Black West Africa." *Journal of Islamic Law and Culture* 10 (1): 5–18.

———. 2009. "African 'Soul Brothers' in the 'Hood: Immigration, Islam, and the Black Encounter." *Anthropological Quarterly* 82 (1): 37–62.

———. 2009. "Sufis on Parade: The Performance of Black, African, and Muslim Identities." *Journal of the American Academy of Religion* 77 (2): 199–237.

———. 2010. *Black Mecca: The African Muslims of Harlem*. New York: Oxford University Press.

Abusharaf, Rogaia Mustafa. 2002. *Wanderings: Sudanese Migrants and Exiles in North America*. Ithaca, NY: Cornell University Press.

Achebe, Chinua. 1958, reprinted 1994. *Things Fall Apart*. New York: Anchor Books.

Adamu, Mhadi. 1978. *The Hausa Factor in West African History*. New York: Oxford University Press.

Adelman, Howard and John Sorenson, eds. 1994. *African Refugees: Development Aid and Repatriation*. Boulder, CO: Westview.

Adepitan, Funmi. 2007. "Lust for Dollar = Early Grave?" *African Abroad*. February 15.

Adepoju, Aderanti. 2004. "Changing Configurations of Migration in Africa." Migration Information Source. September 1. http://www.migrationinformation.org/Feature/display.cfm?ID=251#top.

———. 2005. "Migration in West Africa." Paper prepared for the Policy Analysis and Research Programme of the Global Commission on International Migration. www.gcim.org.

Adi, Hakim. 1993. "West African Students in Britain, 1900–60: The Politics of Exile." *Immigrants and Minorities* 12 (3): 107–128.

Adichie, Chimamanda Ngozi. 2003. *Purple Hibiscus*. New York: Anchor Books.

———. 2004. "The Line of No Return." *New York Times*. November 29.

———. 2006. *Half of a Yellow Sun*. New York: Knopf.

———. 2008. "The Color of an Awkward Conversation." *Washington Post*. June 8: B07.

———. 2013. *Americanah*. New York: Knopf.

Adujie, Paul T. 2005. "Nigeria's National Independence Day Celebrations, New York." *African Abroad.* October 6.

Afolayan, Michael. 2002. "The Impact of United States Diversity Visa Lottery on Elite Migrants." In *Nigeria in the Twentieth Century*, ed. Toyin Falola. Durham, NC: Carolina Academic Press: 743–756.

"African-Born U.S. Residents Are the Most Highly Educated Group in American Society." 1996. *Journal of Blacks in Higher Education* 13 (September 30): 33–34.

"The African Consumer Segment." 2009. Los Angeles: New American Dimensions. April 27. http://www.newamericandimensions.com/.

"African Immigrants in the United States Are the Nation's Most Highly Educated Group." 2000. *Journal of Blacks in Higher Education* 26 (January 31): 60.

Ajayi, J. F. Ade. 1996. *A Patriot to the Core: Bishop Ajayi Crowther.* Ibadan: Spectrum Books.

Ajrouch, Kristine J. and Abdi M. Kusow. 2007. "Racial and Religious Contexts: Situational Identities among Lebanese and Somali Muslim Immigrants." *Ethnic and Racial Studies* 30 (1): 72–94.

Akintoye, S. Adebanji. 2010. *A History of the Yoruba People.* Dakar: Amalion.

Alexander, Elizabeth. 1995. "Can You Be Black and Look at This? Reading the Rodney King Video(s)." In *The Black Public Sphere: A Public Culture Book.* Chicago: Black Public Sphere Collective: 81–98.

Alex-Assensoh, Yvette. 2009. "African Immigrants and African-Americans: An Analysis of Voluntary African Immigration and the Evolution of Black Ethnic Politics in America." *African and Asian Studies* 8 (1–2): 89–124.

Aluko, Remi and Diana Sherblom. 1997. "Passing Culture on to the Next Generation: African Immigrant Language and Culture Schools in Washington, D.C." In *Articles from the 1997 Festival of American Folklife Program Book.* Washington, DC: African Immigrant Folklife Project. http://www.folklife.si.edu/resources/festival1997/language.htm.

Amalu, C. 2008. "Nigeria: Illegal Migration—59,000 Nigerians in Transit Countries for Europe." *Vanguard.* May 17.

Anderson, Don. 2011. "Man Enough: The 20 X 20 Choose Nursing Campaign." *Minority Nurse.* Summer. http://www.minoritynurse.com/nursing-associations/man-enough-20-x20-choose-nursing-campaign.

Anderson, Lynne Christy. 2010. *Breaking Bread: Recipes and Stories from Immigrant Kitchens.* Berkeley: University of California Press.

Angelou, Maya. 1991. *All God's Children Need Traveling Shoes.* New York: Vintage.

Anigbo, Chike Alex. 1995. "The African New-Diaspora: Dynamics of Prospects for Afrocentrism and Counterpenetration: A Case Study of the Nigerian Community in the United States." Doctoral dissertation, Howard University.

Apraku, Kofi K. 1991. *African Émigrés in the United States: A Missing Link in Africa's Social and Economic Development.* Westport, CT: Praeger.

———. 1996. *Outside Looking In: An African Perspective on American Pluralistic Society.* Westport, CT: Praeger.

Arnarfi, John, Stephen Kwankye, et al. 2003. "Migration from and to Ghana: A Background Paper." Working paper, Development Research Centre on Migration, Globalisation and Poverty.

Arthur, John A. 2000. *Invisible Sojourners: African Immigrant Diaspora in the United States*. Westport, CT: Praeger.

———. 2008. *The African Diaspora in the United States and Europe: The Ghanaian Experience*. Burlington, VT: Ashgate.

———. 2009. *African Women Immigrants in the United States: Crossing Transnational Borders*. New York: Palgrave Macmillan.

———. 2010. *African Diaspora Identities: Negotiating Culture in Transnational Migration*. Lanham, MD: Lexington Books.

Asgedom, Mawi. 2002. *Of Beetles and Angels: A Boy's Remarkable Journey from a Refugee Camp to Harvard*. Boston: Little, Brown.

Ashabranner, Brent. 1999. *The New African Americans*. North Haven, CT: Linnet.

Assensoh, Akwasi. 2000. "Conflict or Cooperation? Africans and African Americans in Multiracial America." In *Black and Multiracial Politics in America*, ed. Yvette M. Alex-Assensoh and Lawrence Hanks. New York: New York University Press: 113–132.

Associated Press. 2009. "Minnesota Killings Tied to Somali Gangs." July 20. http://www.msnbc.msn.com/id/32010471/ns/us_news-crime_and_courts/.

Attah, Ayesha. 2007. "Mourides Celebrate 19 Years in North America." *African webzine*. July 30.http://www.africanmag.com/ARTICLE-504-design001.

Attah-Poku, Agyemang. 1996. *The Socio-cultural Adjustment Question: The Role of Ghanaian Immigrant Ethnic Associations in America*. Brookfield, VT: Ashgate.

Austin, Dan. 2004. "A Nigerian-American Runs for United States Congress." *Transatlantic Times*, African Edition 1 (June): 7.

Awokoya, Janet. 2012. "Reconciling Multiple Black Identities: The Case of 1.5 and 2.0 Nigerian Immigrants." In *Africans in Global Migration: Searching for Promised Lands*, ed. John Arthur, Joseph Takougang, and Thomas Owusu. Lanham, MD: Lexington Books: 97–116.

Azikiwe, Nnamdi. *My Odyssey*. London: C. Hurst, 1971.

Babou, Cheikh Anta. 2001. "The Murid Ethos and the Political Economy of the Muridiyya: Work and Its Meaning in Ahmadu Bamba's Thought." *Murid Dahiras, Evolutions and Perspectives: A Special Publication of the Murid Islamic Community in America* 1: 21–24.

———. 2002. "Brotherhood Solidarity, Education and Migration: The Role of the Dahiras among the Murid Muslim Community of New York." *African Affairs* 101 (403): 151–170.

———. 2007. *Amadu Bamba and the Founding of the Muridiyya of Senegal, 1853–1913*. Athens: Ohio University Press.

———. 2008. "Migration and Cultural Change: Money, 'Caste,' Gender, and Social Status among Senegalese Female Hair Braiders in the United States." *Africa Today* 55 (2): 3–22.

Bagley, Cherie and Elaine Copeland. 1994. "African and African American Graduate Students' Racial Identity and Personal Problem-Solving." *Journal of Counseling and Development* 73 (2): 167–172.

Bailey, Benjamin. 2001. "Dominican-American Ethnic/Racial Identities and United States Social Categories." *International Migration Review* 35 (3): 677–708.

Bailyn, Bernard. 1986. *The Peopling of British North America*. New York: Vintage Books.

Banks, Ingrid. 2000. *Hair Matters: Beauty, Power and Black Women's Consciousness*. New York: New York University Press.

Banton, M. P. 1965. *West African City*. New York: Oxford University Press.

Barou, Jacques. 1987. "In the Aftermath of Colonization: Black African Immigrants in France." In *Migrants in Europe: The Role of Family, Labor and Politics*, ed. Hans Christian Buechler and Judith-Maria Buechler. New York: Greenwood.

Barry, Dan. 1999. "Daily Protesters in Handcuffs Keep Focus on Diallo Killing." *New York Times*. March 19.

Basch, Linda, Nina Glick Schiller, and Cristina Blanc-Szanton. 1994. *Nations Unbound: Transnational Projects, Postcolonial Predicaments and Deterritorialized Nation-States*. Langhorne, PA: Gordon and Breach.

Bastian, Misty. 1999. "Nationalism in a Virtual Space: Immigrant Nigerians on the Internet." *West Africa Review* 1 (1). http://www.westafricareview.com/vol1.1/bastian.html.

———. 2002. "'Vultures of the Marketplace': Southeastern Nigerian Women and Discourses of the *Ogu Umunwaanyi* (Women's War) of 1929." In *Women in African Colonial Histories*, ed. Jean Allman, Susan Geiger, and Nakanyike Musisi. Bloomington: University of Indiana Press: 260–281.

Batalha, Luís and Jorgen Carling, eds. 2008. *Transnational Archipelago: Perspectives on Cape Verdean Migration and Diaspora*. Amsterdam: University of Amsterdam Press.

Beah, Ishmael. 2007. *A Long Way Gone: Memoirs of a Boy Soldier*. New York: Farrar, Straus and Giroux.

Beck, Linda. 2007. "West African Muslims in America: When Are Muslims Not Muslims?" In Olupona and Gemignani, *African Immigrant Religions in America*, 182–206.

Bennett, Pamela R. and Amy Lutz. 2009. "How African American Is the Net Black Advantage? Differences in College Attendance among Immigrant Blacks, Native Blacks, and Whites." *Sociology of Education* 82 (1): 70–99.

Benway, Gaelan Lee. 2006. *Gender Migrations: Dominican Women and Men Negotiate Work and Family in Providence, Rhode Island*. Providence: Brown University.

Berlin, Ira. 2010. *The Making of African America: The Four Great Migrations*. New York: Viking.

Biney, Moses. 2011. *From Africa to America: Religion and Adaptation among Ghanaian Immigrants in New York*. New York: New York University Press.

Bixler, Mark. 2005. *The Lost Boys of Sudan: An American Story of the Refugee Experience*. Athens: University of Georgia Press.

Boahen, A. Adu. 1987. *African Perspectives on Colonialism*. Baltimore: Johns Hopkins University Press.

Boiko-Weyrauch, Anna. 2009. "Ghanaian Taxi Drivers in America." *Modern Ghana.* April 22. http://modernghana.com.

Brand-Williams, Oralandar. 2003. "Africans Find Home in Detroit." *Detroit News.* May 29.

Brettell, Caroline. 2008. "'Big D': Incorporating New Immigrants in a Sunbelt Suburban Metropolis." In *Twenty-First Century Immigrant Gateways: Immigrant Incorporation in Suburban America*, ed. Audrey Singer, Caroline Brettell, and Susan Hardwick. Washington, DC: Brookings Institution Press: 53–86.

Brinkerhoff, Jennifer. 2009. *Digital Diasporas: Identity and Transnational Engagement.* New York: Cambridge University Press.

Brooke, James. 1995. "Foreigners Flock to Slopes to Work, Not Ski." *New York Times.* December 29.

Brooks, George E. 1975. "Peanuts and Colonialism: Consequences of the Colonization of Peanuts in West Africa, 1830–1870." *Journal of African History* 16 (1): 29–54.

Brown, Carolyn. 2003. *"We Were All Slaves": African Miners, Culture and Resistance at the Enugu Government Colliery, Nigeria.* Portsmouth, NH: Heinemann.

Brown, Deon. 2013. "Black Immigrants Rally for Justice on Capitol Hill." *Gleaner.* April 4. http://jamaica-gleaner.com/extra/article.php?id=2293.

Brown, Jacqueline Nassy. 1998. "Black Liverpool, Black America and the Gendering of Diasporic Space." *Cultural Anthropology* 13 (2): 291–325.

———. 2005. *Dropping Anchor Setting Sail: Geographies of Race in Black Liverpool.* Princeton, NJ: Princeton University Press.

Brulliard, Karin. 2007. "To Africa, for Culture and Credits." *Washington Post.* September 23: C01.

Bruni, Frank. 1997. "Invisible, and in Anguish: A Slain Driver's Service Brings Attention to Senegalese." *New York Times.* November 18.

Brush, Barbara, Julie Sochalski, and Anne M. Berger. 2004. "Imported Care: Recruiting Foreign Nurses to U.S. Health Care Facilities." *Health Affairs* 23 (3): 78–87.

Byfield, Judith. 2000. "Introduction: Rethinking the African Diaspora." *African Studies Review* 43 (1): 1–9.

Cairns, Conrad. 2006. *African Knights: The Armies of Sokoto, Bornu and Bagirmi in the Nineteenth Century.* Horsham, UK: Foundry Press.

Campbell, Greg. 2004. *Blood Diamonds: Tracing the Deadly Path of the World's Most Precious Stones.* New York: Basic Books.

Capps, Randy and Michael Fix, eds. 2012. *Young Children of Black Immigrants in America: Changing Flows, Changing Faces.* Washington, DC: Migration Policy Institute.

Capps, Randy, Kristen McCabe, and Michael Fix. 2011. "New Streams: Black African Migration to the United States." Washington, DC: Migration Policy Institute. http://www.migrationpolicy.org/pubs/AfricanMigrationUS.pdf.

Carling, Jorgen. 2002. "Migration in the Age of Involuntary Immobility: Theoretical Reflections and Cape Verdean Experiences." *Journal of Ethnic and Migration Studies* 28 (1): 5–42.

——. 2004. "Emigration, Return and Development in Cape Verde: The Impact of Closing Borders." *Population, Space and Place* 10 (2): 113–132.

Carling, Jorgen and Lisa Åkesson. 2009. "Mobility at the Heart of a Nation: Patterns and Meanings of Cape Verdean Migration." *International Migration* 47 (3): 123–155.

Carreira António. 1972. *Cabo Verde: Formação e extinção de uma sociedade escravocrata, 1460–1878*. Porto: Imprensa Portuguesa.

Carson, Rob. 2004. "Black and African: As Different as Black and White." *News Tribune*. April 27. http://invisionfree.com/forums/TheRapUp/ar/t1586.htm.

Carter, D. M. 2007. *States of Grace: Senegalese in Italy and the New European Immigration*. Minneapolis: University of Minnesota Press.

Carter, Prudence. 2005. *Keepin' It Real: School Success beyond Black and White*. New York: Oxford University Press.

Catchpole, Brian and I. A. Akinjogbin. 1984. *A History of West Africa in Maps and Diagrams*. London: Collins.

Chacko, Elizabeth. 2003. "Ethiopian Ethos and the Making of Ethnic Places in the Washington Metropolitan Area." *Journal of Cultural Geography* 20 (2): 21–42.

——. 2004. "Identity and Assimilation among Young Ethiopian Immigrants." *Geographical Review* 93 (4): 491–506.

Chacko, Elizabeth and Ivan Cheung. 2006. "The Formation of a Contemporary Ethnic Enclave: The Case of 'Little Ethiopia' in Los Angeles." In *Race, Ethnicity and Place in a Changing America*, ed. John Frazier and Eugene Tettey-Fio. Binghamton, NY: Global: 131–139.

Chafer, Tony. 2002. *The End of Empire in French West Africa: France's Successful Decolonization?* London: Berg.

Chandran, Nisha. 2009. "America's Promise Drives Nigerian Cab Driver." *Daily Northwestern*. May 20.

Choy, Catherine Ceniza. 2003. *Empire of Care: Nursing and Migration in Filipino American History*. Durham, NC: Duke University Press.

Chude-Sokei, Louis. 2007. "Redefining 'Black.'" *Los Angeles Times*. February 18. http://www.latimes.com/news/opinion.

Chung, Vicki. 2010. "Men in Nursing." *Minority Nurse*. Summer. http://www.minoritynurse.com/article/men-nursing-0.

Clark, Gracia. 2001. "Gender and Profiteering: Ghana's Market Women as Devoted Mothers and 'Human Vampire Bats.'" In *"Wicked" Women and the Reconfiguration of Gender in Africa*, ed. Dorothy Hodgson and Sheryl McCurdy. Portsmouth, NH: Heinemann: 293–311.

Clark, Msia Kibona. 2008. "Identity among First and Second Generation African Immigrants in the United States." *African Identities* 6 (2): 169–181.

——. 2009. "Questions of Identity among African Immigrants in America." In Okpewho and Nzegwu, *New African Diaspora*, 255–270.

Clegg, Claude A., III. 2004. *The Price of Liberty: African Americans and the Making of Liberia*. Chapel Hill: University of North Carolina Press.

Clemetson, Lynette. 2003. "For Schooling a Reverse Emigration to Africa." *New York Times.* September 4: A21.

Coates, Rodney D. 2007. "Talking Affirmative Action: Race, Opportunity, and Everyday Ideology." *Contemporary Sociology* 36 (4): 334–335.

Cochran, Johnnie. 2002. *A Lawyer's Life.* New York: Thomas Dunne Books.

Cohen, Abner. 1981. *The Politics of Elite Culture: Explorations in the Dramaturgy of Power in a Modern African Society.* Berkeley: University of California Press.

Coles, Catherine. 1996. "Three Generations of Hausa Women in Kaduna, Nigeria, 1925–1985." In Sheldon, *Courtyards, Markets, City Streets,* 73–102.

Coles, Catherine and Beverly Mack, eds. 1991. *Hausa Women in the Twentieth Century.* Madison: University of Wisconsin Press.

Conley, Ellen. 2004. *The Chosen Shore: Stories of Immigrants.* Berkeley: University of California Press.

Conover, Ted. 2000. "Kadi Diallo's Trial." *New York Times Magazine.* January 9.

Contreras, Russell. 2006. "Musician Hooked on W. African, Hip-Hop Blend." *Boston Globe.* October 19.

Conzen, Kathleen, David A. Gerber, Ewa Morawska, George E. Pozzetta, and Rudolph J. Vecoli. 1992. "The Invention of Ethnicity: A Perspective from the U.S.A." *Journal of American Ethnic History* 12 (1): 3–41.

Coombes, Orde. 1970. "West Indians in New York: Moving beyond the Limbo Pole." *New York Magazine.* July 13: 28–32.

Cooper, Helene. 2008. *The House at Sugar Beach: In Search of a Lost African Childhood.* New York: Simon & Schuster.

Copeland-Carson, Jacqueline. 2004. *Creating Africa in America: Translocal Identity in an Emerging World City.* Philadelphia: University of Pennsylvania Press.

Crary, David. 2007. "African Immigrants Find Opportunity." *Seattle Post-Intelligencer.* July 16.

Creese, Gillian. 2010. "Erasing English Language Competency: African Migrants in Vancouver, Canada." *Journal of International Migration and Integration* 11 (3): 295–313.

Cunningham, Jennifer. 2005. "Tensions between African and African Americans surface Again." *New York Amsterdam News.* February 3: 4. http://connection.ebscohost.com/c/articles/16074522/tensions-between-africans-african-americans-surface-again.

Daff, Marieme. 2002. "Women Taking Their Place in African Immigration." *Women's eNews.* August 8. http://www.womenenews.org/article.cfm/dyn/aid/993/context/cover.

Daley, Patricia. 1998. "Black Africans in Great Britain: Spatial Concentration and Segregation." *Urban Studies* 35 (10): 1703–1724.

D'Alisera, JoAnn. 2001. "I Love Islam: Popular Religious Commodities, Sites of Inscription, and Transnational Sierra Leonean Identity." *Journal of Material Culture* 6 (1): 91–110.

————. 2004. *An Imagined Geography: Sierra Leonean Muslims in America*. Philadelphia: University of Pennsylvania Press.

————. 2009. "Images of a Wounded Homeland: Sierra Leonean Children and the New Heart of Darkness." In *Across Generations: Immigrant Families in America*, ed. Nancy Foner. New York: New York University Press: 114–134.

Danquah, Meri Nana-Ama. 1998. "Life as an Alien." In *Half and Half: Writers on Growing Up Biracial and Bicultural*, ed. Claudine Chiawei O'Hearn. New York: Pantheon Books: 99–111.

Davies, Amy Z. 2008. "Characteristics of Adolescent Sierra Leonean Refugees in Public Schools in New York City." *Education and Urban Society* 40 (3): 361–371.

Day, Sherri. 2001. "New Yorkers & Co.; Braiders Out of Africa With a World of Woes." *New York Times*. March 18.

De Gourville, Richard. 2002. "Social and Academic Experiences of Liberian Students: Adapting Their Cultural Literacies to a U.S. Urban High School: A Critical Inquiry." Doctoral dissertation, Pennsylvania State University.

Diallo, Kadiatou and Craig Wolff. 2003. *My Heart Will Cross This Ocean: My Story, My Son, Amadou*. New York: One World.

Diaro, Akinyele E. 2007. "Wealth Creation: Entrepreneurship II—Starting a Business." *U.S. Immigration News*. May 1.

Diawara, Manthia. 2003. *We Won't Budge: An African Exile in the World*. New York: Basic Civatas Books.

Diaz, Johnny and Scott Greenberger. 2004. "Not White, Not Black, Not Hispanic— Boston's Cape Verdeans Have Long Been Misunderstood." *Boston Globe*. February 15: B1.

Diouf, Mamadou. 2000. "The Senegalese Murid Trade Diaspora and the Making of a Vernacular Cosmopolitanism." Translated by Steven Rendall. *Public Culture* 12 (3): 679–702.

Diouf-Kamara, Sylviane. 1997. "Senegalese in New York: A Model Minority?" *Black Renaissance/Renaissance Noire* 1 (2): 92.

Dixon, David. 2006. "Characteristics of the African Born in the United States." Migration Policy Institute. http://migrationinformation.org/USfocus/display. cfm?ID=366.

Dixon-Fyle, Mac. 1999. *A Saro Community in the Niger Delta, 1912–1984: The Potts-Johnsons*. Rochester, NY: University of Rochester Press.

Djamba, Yanki K. 1999. "African Immigrants to the United States: A Socio-demographic Profile in Comparison to Native Blacks." *Journal of Asian and African Studies* 34 (2): 210–215.

Dodoo, F. Nii-Amoo. 1997. "Assimilation Difference among Africans in America." *Social Forces* 76 (2): 527–546.

Dodoo, F. Nii-Amoo and Baffour E. Takyi. 2002. "Africans in the Diaspora: Black-White Earnings Differences among America's Africans." *Ethnic and Racial Studies* 25 (6): 913–941.

Dodoo, F. Nii-Amoo, Baffour E. Takyi, and Jesse Mann. 2006. "On the Brain Drain of Africans to America: Some Methodological Observations." *Perspectives on Global Development & Technology* 5 (3): 155–162.

Dodson, Howard and Sylviane A. Diouf. 2004. *In Motion: The African American Migration Experience*. New York: Schomburg Center for Research in Black Culture.

Dolnick, Sam. 2009. "For African Immigrants, Bronx Culture Clash Turns Violent." *New York Times*. October 20.

Donnelly, John. 2006. "Americans Adopting More African Children." *Boston Globe*. May 19.

Dosi, Mohamed A. M., Leonce Rushubirwa, and Garth A. Myers. 2007. "Tanzanians in the Land of Oz: Diaspora and Transnationality in Wichita, Kansas." *Social & Cultural Geography* 8 (5): 657–671.

Dowden, Richard. 2009. *Africa: Altered States, Ordinary Miracles*. New York: Public Affairs.

Drumtra, Jeff. 2003. "West Africa's Refugee Crisis Spills across Many Borders." Migration Information Source. http://www.migrationinformation.org/feature/display. cfm?ID=148.

Dunn, John. 1978. *West African States, Failure and Promise: A Study in Comparative Politics*. Cambridge: Cambridge University Press.

Dunn-Marcos, Robin, Konia Kollehlon, Bernard Ngovo, and Emily Russ. 2005. *Liberians: An Introduction to Their History and Culture*. Washington, DC: Center for Applied Linguistics.

Eades, J. S. 1994. *Strangers and Traders: Yoruba Migrants, Markets and the State in Northern Ghana*. Trenton, NJ: Africa World Press.

Ebin, Victoria. 1993. "Senegalese Women Migrants in America: A New Autonomy?" Paper presented at the Seminar on Women and Demographic Change in Sub-Saharan Africa, Dakar, Senegal, March 3–6.

Edozien, Frankie. 2002. "Remembering Amadou Diallo." *The African*. February.

Edwards, Brent Hayes. 2003. *The Practice of Diaspora: Literature, Translation and the Rise of Black Internationalism*. Cambridge, MA: Harvard University Press.

Efiong, General Philip. 2007. *Nigeria and Biafra: My Story*. Elmont, NY: Africa Tree Press.

Eggers, Dave. 2006. *What Is the What*. San Francisco: McSweeney's.

Einolf, Christopher. 2001. *The Mercy Factory: Refugees and the American Asylum System*. Chicago: Ivan R. Dee.

Eissa, Salih Omar. 2005. "Diversity and Transformation: African Americans and African Immigration in the United States." Immigration Policy Center. http://www. americanimmigrationcouncil.org/sites/default/files/docs/Diversity%20and%20 Transformation%20March%202005.pdf.

Ekwensi, Cyprian. 1961. *Jagua Nana*. London: Hutchinson.

El-Khawas, Mohamed. 2004. "Brain Drain: Putting Africa between a Rock and a Hard Place." *Mediterranean Quarterly* 15 (4): 37–56.

Ellis, Stephen. 2006. *The Mask of Anarchy: The Destruction of Liberia and the Religious Dimension of an African Civil War*. New York: New York University Press.

Eluwa, G. I. C. 1971. "Background to the Emergence of the National Congress of British West Africa." *African Studies Review* 14 (2): 205–218.

Ette, Ezekiel Umo. 2011. *Nigerian Immigrants in the United States: Race, Identity, and Acculturation*. Lanham, MD: Lexington Books.

Eze, Evans. 2002. "Africans in the Diaspora: Contrasting International Immigration. A Study of West African Immigrants in the Baltimore/Washington Area." Doctoral dissertation, American University.

Falola, Toyin and Niyi Afolabi, eds. 2007. *African Minorities in the New World*. New York: Routledge.

———, eds. 2009. *The Human Cost of African Migration*. New York: Routledge.

Farr, James. 1983. "A Slow Boat to Nowhere: The Multi-racial Crews of the American Whaling Industry." *Journal of Negro History* 68 (2): 159–170.

Fears, Darryl. 2003. "Disparity Marks Black Ethnic Groups, Report Says African Americans Trail Immigrants in Income, Education." *Washington Post*. March 13.

Feliciano, Cynthia. 2009. "Education and Identity Formation among Children of Latin American and Caribbean Immigrants." *Sociological Perspectives* 52 (2): 135–158.

Fikes, Kesha. 2006. "Emigration and the Spatial Production of Difference from Cape Verde." In *Globalization and Race: Transformations in the Cultural Production of Blackness*, ed. Kamari Maxine Clarke and Deborah Thomas. Durham, NC: Duke University Press: 154–170.

———. 2009. *Managing African Portugal: The Citizen-Migrant*. Durham, NC: Duke University Press.

Fix, Michael and Jeanne Batalova. 2008. *Uneven Progress: The Employment Pathways of Skilled Immigrants to the United States*. Washington, DC: Migration Policy Institute.

Foley, Michael and Dean Hoge. 2007. *Religion and the New Immigrants: How Faith Communities Form Our Newest Citizens*. New York: Oxford University Press.

Foner, Nancy. 1997. "What's New about Transnationalism? New York Immigrants Today and at the Turn of the Century." *Diaspora* 6: 355–376.

Foot, Paul. 1965. *Immigration and Race in British Policies*. New York: Penguin.

Forsyth, Frederick. 2007. *The Biafra Story: The Making of an African Legend*. South Yorkshire: Pen and Sword Books.

Forsythe, Dennis. 1976. "West Indian Radicalism in America: An Assessment of Ideology." In *Ethnicity in the Americas*, ed. Frances Henry. The Hague: Morton: 301–332.

Friedman, Samantha, Audrey Singer, Marie Price, and Ivan Cheung. 2005. "Race, Immigrants, and Residence: A New Racial Geography of Washington, D.C." *Geographical Review* 95 (2): 210–230.

Frost, Diane. 2002. "Diasporan West African Communities: The Kru in Freetown & Liverpool." *Review of African Political Economy* 29 (92): 285–300.

Gans, Herbert J. 1992. "Second Generation Decline: Scenarios for the Economic and Ethnic Futures of the Post-1965 American Immigrants." *Ethnic and Racial Studies* 15 (2): 173–192.

Garigue, Philip. 1953. "The West African Students' Union: A Study in Culture Contact." *Africa: Journal of the International African Institute* 23 (1): 55–69.

Garner, David. 2012. "1.3 Billion Dollar Chinese Agriculture Investment in Sierra Leone." *DGC Asset Management.* January 19. http://dgcassetmanagement.com/ Billion-Dollar-Chinese-Agriculture-Investment-in-Sierra-Leone.

Gberie, Lansana. 2005. *A Dirty War in West Africa: The RUF and the Destruction of Sierra Leone.* Bloomington: Indiana University Press.

George, Nelson. 1998. *Hip Hop America.* New York: Penguin.

Getabun, Solomon Addis. 2007. *The History of Ethiopian Immigrants and Refugees in America, 1900–2000: Patterns of Migration, Survival and Adjustment.* New York: LFB.

Gibau, Gina Sánchez. 2005. "Contested Identities: Narratives of Race and Ethnicity in the Cape Verdean Diaspora," *Identities: Global Studies in Culture and Power* 12 (3): 405–438.

———. 2005. "Diasporic Identity Formation among Cape Verdeans in Boston." *Western Journal of Black Studies* 29 (2): 532–529.

———. 2010. "Cyber CVs: Online Conversations on Cape Verdean Diaspora Identities." In *Diasporas in the New Media Age: Identity, Politics, and Community,* ed. Andoni Alonso and Pedro Oiarzabal. Reno: University of Nevada Press: 110–121.

Gibson, M. and J. Ogbu, eds. *Minority Status and Schooling: A Comparative Study of Immigrant and Involuntary Minorities.* New York: Garland, 1991.

Gilroy, Paul. 1993. *The Black Atlantic: Modernity and Double Consciousness.* Cambridge, MA: Harvard University Press.

Góis, Pedro. 2005. "Low Intensity Transnationalism: The Cape Verdian Case." *Vienna Journal of African Studies* 8: 255–276.

Goldin, Ian, Geoffrey Cameron, and Meera Balarajan. 2011. *Exceptional People: How Migration Shaped Our World and Will Define Our Future.* Princeton, NJ: Princeton University Press.

Gordon, April. 1998. "The New Diaspora—African Immigration to the United States." *Journal of Third World Studies* 15 (1): 79–103.

Gould, Wallena. 2009. "An Open Letter to Historically Black Nursing Schools: Why Now Is the Time to Consider Starting a Nurse Anesthesia Program." *Minority Nurse.* Fall. http://www.minoritynurse.com/african-american-black-nurses/ open-letter-historically-black-nursing-schools.

Grant, Patrick A. "Coming to America with Eyes Wide Shut." In Obiakor and Grant, *Foreign-Born African Americans: Silenced Voices in the Discourse on Race,* 63–70.

Grasmuck, Sherri and Patricia Pessar. 1991. *Between Two Islands: Dominican Migration.* Berkeley: University of California Press.

Green, Susan. 2003. "'We Hear It Is Raining in Willmar': Mexican and Somali Immigrants to West Central Minnesota." *Amerikastudien* 48: 79–95.

Greenbaum, Susan. 2002. *More Than Black: Afro-Cubans in Tampa.* Gainesville: University Press of Florida.

Greene, Daniel and Tracy Poe. 2003. "Global and Local Sources of Arab and African Immigrants: How to Define New Immigrant Groups." *Amerikastudien* 48: 97–113.

Greene, Victor. 1987. *American Immigrant Leaders, 1800–1910: Marginality and Identity.* Baltimore: Johns Hopkins University Press.

Grieco, Elizabeth. 2010. "Race and Hispanic Origin of the Foreign-Born Population in the United States." U.S. Census American Community Survey Report. January.

Gusau, Sule Ahmed. 1989. "Economic Ideas of Shehu Usman Dan Fodio." *Journal of Muslim Minority Affairs* 10 (1): 139–151.

Habecker, Michele. 2009. "African Immigrants in Washington, D.C.: Seeking Alternative Identities in a Racially Divided City." Doctoral dissertation, Oxford University.

Habecker, Shelly. 2012. "Not Black, but Habasha: Ethiopian and Eritrean Immigrants in American Society." *Ethnic and Racial Studies* 35 (7): 1200–1219.

Hagopian, Amy, Matthew J. Thompson, Meredith Fordyce, Karin E. Johnson, and L. Gary Hart. 2004. "The Migration of Physicians from Sub-Saharan Africa to the United States of America: Measures of the African Brain Drain." *Human Resources for Health* 2 (17). http://www.human-resources-health.com.

Halter, Marilyn. 1993. *Between Race and Ethnicity: Cape Verdean American Immigrants, 1860–1965.* Urbana: University of Illinois Press.

———. 2000. *Shopping for Identity: The Marketing of Ethnicity.* New York: Schocken Books.

———. 2004. "Cape Verdeans in the United States." In the *Encyclopedia of Diasporas: Immigrant and Refugee Cultures Around the World*, vol. 2, ed. Melvin Ember, Carole Ember, and Ian Skoggard. New York: Kluwer: 615–623.

———. 2007. "West Africans." In *The New Americans: A Handbook to Immigration since 1965*, ed. Mary Waters and Reed Ueda. Cambridge, MA: Harvard University Press: 283–294.

———. 2009. "Diasporic Generations: Distinctions of Race, Nationality and Identity in the Cape Verdean Community, Past and Present." In *Community, Culture and the Makings of Identity: Portuguese-Americans along the Eastern Seaboard*, ed. Kimberly DaCosta Holton and Andrea Klimt. Dartmouth, MA: Center for Portuguese Studies and Culture: 525–553.

Hance, W. A. 1970. *Population, Migration and Urbanization in Africa.* New York: Columbia University Press.

Hansen, R. 2000. *Citizenship and Immigration in Post-war Britain: The Institutional Origins of a Multicultural Nation.* New York: Oxford University Press.

Hargreaves, J. D. 1981. "From Strangers to Minorities in West Africa." *Transactions of the Royal Historical Society* 31: 95–113.

Harris, Hermione. 2006. *Yoruba in Diaspora: An African Church in London.* New York: Palgrave Macmillan.

Harvard, Ashley. 2004. "Whiteness Is on Its Way Out." *Bowdoin Orient.* April 4.

Hatton, Thomas and Jeffrey Williamson. 2003. "Demographic and Economic Pressure on Emigration out of Africa." *Scandinavian Journal of Economics* 105 (3): 465–486.

Haughney, Christine. 2011. "An African Chief in Cabby's Clothing." *New York Times.* August 12.

Hellwig, David. 1978. "Black Meets Black: Afro-American Reactions to West Indian Immigrants in the 1920s." *Southern Atlantic Quarterly* 77 (Spring): 373–385.

Heywood, Linda and John Thornton. 2011. "African Ethnicities and Their Origins." *Root.* October 1. http://www.theroot.com/buzz/african-ethnicities-and-their-origins.

———. 2011. "Pinpointing DNA Ancestry in Africa." *Root.* October 1. http://www.theroot.com/views/tracing-dna-not-just-africa-one-tribe?page=0,1.

Hickman, Christina. 2011. "The Sound of Cultural Harmony: Music of Candida Rose Fuses American, Cape Verdean Traditions." *Standard Times.* June 30: A2.

Hintzen, Percy Claude and Jean Muteba Rahier, eds. 2003. *Problematizing Blackness: Self-Ethnographies by Black Immigrants to the United States.* New York: Routledge.

Ho, Vanessa. 2006. "Kids' Troubles Shake Seattle's East Africans." *Seattle Post-Intelligencer.* April 12.

Holl, Augustine. 2000. *The Diwan Revisited: Literacy, State Formation and the Rise of Kanuri Domination, AD 1200–1600.* London: Kegan Paul.

Hollist, Pede. 2012. *So the Past Does Not Die.* Barmenda, Cameroon: Langaa RPCIG.

Holtzman, Jon. 2000. "Dialing 911 in Nuer: Gender Transformations and Domestic Violence in a Midwestern Sudanese Refugee Community." In *Immigration Research for a New Century: Multidisciplinary Perspectives,* ed. Nancy Foner, Ruben G. Rumbaut, and Steven J. Gold. New York: Russell Sage Foundation: 390-408.

———. 2000. *Nuer Journeys, Nuer Lives: Sudanese Refugees in Minnesota.* Boston: Allyn & Bacon.

Horowitz, Rachael. 2010. "Eat, Stay, Love." *Imprint.* January 30. http://archives.jrn.columbia.edu/2010-2011/imprintmag.org/2010/01/30/west-africa-in-harlem/index.html.

Huband, Mark. 1998. *The Liberian Civil War.* New York: Routledge.

Huisman, Kimberly, Mazie Hough, Kristen Langellier, and Carol Nordstrom Toner. 2011. *Somalis in Maine: Crossing Cultural Currents.* Berkeley, CA: North Atlantic Books.

Humphries, Jill 2009. "Resisting 'Race': Organizing African Transnational Identities in the United States." In Okpewho and Nzegwu, *New African Diaspora,* 271–299.

Ibrahim, A. E. K. M. 1999. "Becoming Black: Rap and Hip-Hop, Race, Gender, Identity, and the Politics of ESL Learning." *TESOL Quarterly* 33 (3): 349–369.

Imoagene, Onoso. 2009. "Identity Choices and the Mechanisms of Identity Formation among 1.5 to Second Generation Adult Nigerian Immigrants in the United Kingdom." Paper presented at the Harvard Migration and Immigrant Incorporation Workshop, Harvard University, March 10.

IRIN. 2008. "West Africa: Migrants Risk all to Cross the Desert." October 9. http://www.irinnews.org.

Isicheri, Elizabeth. 1973. *The Ibo People and the Europeans: The Genesis of a Relationship to 1906.* London: Faber.

Jackson, Jennifer and Mary Cothran. 2003. "Black versus Black: The Relationships among African, African American, and African Caribbean Persons." *Journal of Black Studies* 33 (5): 576–604.

Jensen, John, Adrien Ngudiankama, and Melissa Filippi-Franz. 2005. "Religious Healing among War-Traumatized African Immigrants." In *Religion and Healing in America*, ed. Linda Barnes and Susan Sered. New York: Oxford University Press: 159–172.

Johnson, Jason B. 2005. "Shades of Gray in Black Enrollment." *San Francisco Chronicle*. February 22.

Johnson, Oscar. 2000. "Chilly Coexistence: African and African-Americas in the Bronx." http://www.columbia.edu/itc/journalism/gissler/anthology/Chill-Johnson.html.

Johnson, Violet Showers. 2008. "'What, Then, Is the African American?' African and Afro-Caribbean Identities in Black America." *Journal of American Ethnic History* 28 (1): 77–103.

———. 2006. *The Other Black Bostonians: West Indians in Boston, 1900-1950*. Bloomington: Indiana University Press.

———. 2009. "Recreating Sustainable Communities in Exile: Leadership Roles of Sierra Leonean Refugee and Internally Displaced Women in Freetown, London, and Atlanta." *International Journal of Environmental, Cultural, Economic and Social Sustainability* 5 (5): 287–300.

Kaba, Amadu Jacky. 2009. "Educational Attainment, Income Levels and Africans in the United States: The Paradox of Nigerian Immigrants." *West Africa Review* 11. http://www.africaknowledgeproject.org/index.php/war/article/view/246.

Kabba, Alex. 2007. "Immigrants' Children Gone Wild! The Difficulty of Raising Black Children in the USA." *African Abroad*. March 30: 34, 39.

Kamya, Hugo. 1997. "African Immigrants in the United States: The Challenge for Research and Practice." *Social Work* 42 (2): 154–165.

Kanam, Nana. 2007. "Uptown, Africa Toujours." *New York Times*. July 22. http://www.nytimes.com/2007/07/22/nyregion/thecity/22harl.html?_r=1.

Kane, Abdoulaye. 2006. "Chain Migration among the Haal Pulaar Community." Paper presented at the African Immigrant Symposium, New York.

Kane, Ousmane Oumar. 2010. *The Homeland Is the Arena: Religion, Transnationalism, and the Integration of Senegalese Immigrants in America*. New York: Oxford University Press.

Kanu, Kingsley, Jr. 2008. "Reaching African Immigrants in America: Why This Emerging Group Could Represent a Promising Consumer Market for Major Companies." *Black Enterprise*. August 1. http://www.highbeam.com/doc/1G1-204894073.html.

Kase, Aaron and F. H. Rubino. 2010. "Refugees Settling in Philadelphia." *Philadelphia Weekly*. March 2. http://www.philadelphiaweekly.com/news-and-opinion/cover-story/Refugees-settling-in-Philadelphia.html?page=1&comments=1&showAll=.

Kasinitz, Philip, John Mollenkopf, Mary Waters, and Jennifer Holdaway. 2008. *Inheriting the City: The Children of Immigrants Come of Age*. Cambridge, MA: Harvard University Press.

Kassindja, Fauziya (with Layli Miller Bashir). 1998. *Do They Hear You When You Cry?* New York: Bantam Books.

Kent, Mary Mederios. 2007. "Immigration and America's Black Population." *Population Bulletin* 62 (4): 1–16.

Kibria, Nazli. 1993. *Family Tightrope: The Changing Lives of Vietnamese Americans.* Princeton, NJ: Princeton University Press.

Kingma, Mireille. 2007. "Nurses on the Move: A Global Overview." *Health Services Research* 42 (June): 1281–1298.

Kirk-Greene, Anthony, ed. 1995. *State and Society in Francophone Africa since Independence.* London: A & C Black.

Kivisto, Peter. 2001. "Theorizing Transnational Immigration: A Critical Review of Current Efforts." *Ethnic and Racial Studies* 24 (4): 549–577.

Kokolo, Flomo. 2010. "The Mandingo Question in Liberian History and the Prospect for Peace in Liberia." *Liberian Daily Observer.* April 16. http://www.liberianobserver.com/node/5778.

Kollehlon, Konia and Edward Eule. 2003. "The Socioeconomic Attainment Patterns of Africans in the United States." *International Migration Review* 37 (4): 1163–1190.

Konadu, Kwasi. 2010. *The Akan Diaspora in the Americas.* New York: Oxford University Press.

Konadu-Agyemang, Kwado. 1999. "Characteristics and Migration Experiences of Africans in Canada with Specific Reference to Ghanaians in Greater Toronto." *Canadian Geographer* 43 (4): 400–414.

Konadu-Agyemang, Kwado and Baffour Takyi. 2001. "African Immigrants in the USA: Some Reflection on the Their Pre- and Post-migration Experiences." *Arab World Geographer/Le Géographe du monde arabe* 4 (1): 31–47.

———. 2006. "An Overview of African Immigration to U.S. and Canada." In Konadu-Agyemang, Takyi, and Arthur, *New African Diaspora in North America,* 2–12.

Konadu-Agyemang, Kwado, Baffour Takyi, and John Arthur, eds. 2006. *The New African Diaspora in North America: Trends, Community Building, and Adaptation.* Lanham, MD: Lexington Books.

Konneh, Augustine. 1996. "Citizenship at the Margins: Status, Ambiguity, and the Mandingo of Liberia." *African Studies Review* 39 (2): 141–154.

Koser, Khalid, ed. 2003. *The New African Diasporas.* New York: Routledge.

Koslow, Philip. 1995. *Hausaland: The Fortress Kingdoms.* New York: Chelsea House.

Kposowa, Augustine. 2002. "Human Capital and the Performance of African Immigrants in the U.S. Labor Market." *Western Journal of Black Studies* 26 (3): 175–183.

Kufuor, Kofi Oteng. 2006. *The Institutional Transformation of the Economic Community of West African States.* Farnham, UK: Ashgate, 2006.

Kugel, Seth. 2002. "Neighborhood Report: Concourse; Little Africa Flourishes, Fufu Flour and All." *New York Times.* February 17.

Kusow, Abdi. 2006. "Migration and Racial Formations among Somali Immigrants in North America." *Journal of Ethnic and Migration Studies* 32 (3): 533–551.

Langmia, Kehumba and Eric Durham. 2007. "Bridging the Gap: African and African-American Communication on Historically Black Colleges and Universities." *Journal of Black Studies* 37 (6): 805–826.

Laporte, Laurie. 2007. "The Continuities of Modernity: Cape Verdean Identity and Emigration." Doctoral dissertation, Boston University.

Leith, Chad. 2007. "First-Generation Immigrant Adolescents from Cape Verde: Ethnic Identities, Socioeconomic Backgrounds, and Educational Outcomes." Unpublished paper.

Lenoir, Gerald and Nunu Kidane. 2007. "African Americans and Immigrants: Shall We Hang Together or Hang Separately?" *Black Scholar* 37 (1): 50–52.

Levitt, Jeremy. 2005. *The Evolution of Deadly Conflict in Liberia: From "Pataltarianism" to State Collapse*. Durham, NC: Carolina Academic Press.

Levitt, Peggy. 2001. *The Transnational Villagers*. Berkeley: University of California Press.

Little, Kenneth. 1973. *African Women in Towns: An Aspect of Africa's Social Revolution*. Cambridge: Cambridge University Press.

Lobo, Arun. 2001. "US Diversity Visas Are Attracting Africa's Best and Brightest." *Population Today* 29 (5): 1–2.

Lock, Max and Partners. 1967. *Kaduna, 1917–1967: A Survey and Plan of the Capital Territory for the Government of Northern Nigeria*. London: Faber.

Logan, Bernard. 1987. "The Reverse Transfer of Technology from Sub-Saharan Africa to the United States." *Journal of Modern African Studies* 25 (4): 597–612.

Logan, John. 2007. "Who Are the Other African Americans? Contemporary African and Caribbean Immigrants in the United States." In Shaw-Taylor and Tuch, *Other African Americans*, 49–67.

Logan, John and Glenn Deane. 2003. "Black Diversity in Metropolitan America." Lewis Mumford Center for Comparative Urban and Regional Research, University at Albany. http://mumford.albany.edu/census/BlackWhite/BlackDiversityReport/Black_Diversity_final.pdf.

Lopez, Nancy C. 2002. *Hopeful Girls, Troubled Boys*. New York: Routledge.

Louise, Princess Marie. 1926. *Letters from the Gold Coast*. London: Methuen.

Lubkemann, Stephen. 2004. "Diasporas and Their Discontents: Return without Homecoming in the Forging of Liberian and African American Identity." *Diaspora* 13 (1): 123–128.

Madibbo, A. I. 2004. "Minority within a Minority: Black Francophones of Ontario and the Dynamics of Power and Resistance." Doctoral dissertation, University of Toronto.

Manyika, Sarah. "Oyinbo." In Hintzen and Rahier, *Problematizing Blackness*, 65–84.

Mason, Patrick L. 2009. "Culture Matters: America's African Diaspora and Labor Market Outcomes." May 25. http://works.bepress.com/cgi/viewcontent.cgi?article=1010&context=patrick_l_mason.

Massey, Douglas, Margarita Mooney, Kimberly Torres, and Camille Charles. 2007. "Black Immigrants and Black Natives Attending Selective Colleges and Universities in the United States." *American Journal of Education* 113 (February): 243–271.

Mayer, Larry. 2006. "Trip to Nigeria an Emotional One for Ogunleye." *Chicago Bears News*. May 15. http://www.chicagobears.com/news/NewsStory.asp?story_id=2091.

Mazrui, Ali. 1983. "Francophone Nations and English-Speaking States: Imperial Ethnicity and African Political Formations." In Rothchild and Olorunsola, *State versus Ethnic Claims*, 25–43.

———. 1986. *Africans: A Triple Heritage*. Documentary series. PBS.

———. 1987. *Africans: A Triple Heritage*. Boston: Little, Brown.

Mazzucato, Valentina, Mirjam Kabki, and Lothar Smith. 2006. "Transnational Migration and the Economy of Funerals: Changing Practices in Ghana." *Development and Change* 37 (5): 1047–1072.

Mberu, Blessing. 2010. "Nigeria: Multiple Forms of Mobility in Africa's Demographic Giant." Migration Information Source. June. http://www.migrationinformation.org/Profiles/display.cfm?ID=788.

McCabe, Kristen. 2011. "African Immigrants in the United States." Migration Policy Institute. July 21. http://www.migrationinformation.org/USfocus/display.cfm?id=847.

McCall, D. F. 1961. "Trade and the Role of the Wife in a Modern West African Town." In *Social Change in Modern Africa*, ed. Aidan Southhall. New York: Oxford University Press: 286–299.

McCaskie, T. C. 2001. *Asante Identities: History and Modernity in an African Village, 1850–1950*. Bloomington: Indiana University Press.

McClintock, N. C. 1992. *Kingdoms in the Sand and Sun: An African Path to Independence* . London: I.B. Tauris.

McComb, Veronica Savory. 2010. "The Bonds of Faith: Religion and Community among Nigerian Immigrants to the U.S., 1965–present." Doctoral dissertation, Boston University.

McGowan, William. 2008. "The 1965 Immigration Reforms and the *New York Times*: Context, Coverage, and Long-Term Consequences." Center for Immigration Studies. August. http://www.cis.org/NYT_immigration_coverage.

McLaughlin, Eliott. 2009. "Continental Divide Separates Africans, African-Americans." Blacks in America 2. CNN. July 15. http://www.cnn.com/2009/US/07/14/africans.in.america/index.html#cnnSTCText.

McSpadden, Lucia Ann. 1987. "Ethiopian Refugee Resettlement in the Western United States: Social Context and Psychological Well-Being." *International Migration Review* 21 (3): 796–819.

McWhorter, John H. 2004. "Why I'm Black, Not African American." *Los Angeles Times*. September 8.

Medoff, Peter and Holly Sklar. 1994. *Streets of Hope: The Fall and Rise of an Urban Neighborhood*. Boston: South End Press.

Meintel, Deirdre. 2002. "Cape Verdean Transnationalism, Old and New." *Anthropologica* 44: 25–42.

Mendy, Peter Karibe. 2006. "Amilcar Cabral and the Liberation of Guinea Bissau: Context, Challenges and Lessons for Effective African Leadership." *African Identities* 4 (1): 7–21.

Mengestu, Dinaw. 2007. *The Beautiful Things That Heaven Bears.* New York: Riverhead.

Millman, Joel. 1994. "From Dakar to Detroit." *Forbes* 154 (7): 86–87.

———. 1997. *Other Americans: How Immigrants Renew Our Country, Our Economy, and Our Values.* New York: Viking.

———. 2010. "Nigerian Pharmacists Fill a Need." *Wall Street Journal.* October 2. http://online.wsj.com/article/SB10001424052748704789404575523930830427048.html.

Mohan, Giles and Alfred Zack-Williams. 2002. "Globalization from Below: Conceptualizing the Role of the African Diasporas in Africa's Development." *Review of African Political Economy* 29 (92): 211–236.

Moran, Mary. 2008. *Liberia: The Violence of Democracy.* Philadelphia: University of Pennsylvania Press.

Moran, Robert, Gaiutra Bahadur, and Susan Snyder. 2005. "Residents Say Beating Fits Widespread Pattern." *Philadelphia Inquirer.* November 3.

Moreno, Ivan. 2012. "Hair Braider Wins Lawsuit Challenging Utah Rules." Associated Press. August 11. http://thegrio.com/2012/08/11/hair-braider-wins-lawsuit-challenging-utah-rules/#.

Mudede, Charles. 2001. "Out of Africa: Young African Immigrants Must Choose between Being African or African American." *Stranger.* July 12–18. www.thestranger.com.

Mwakikagile, Godfrey. 2006. *Relations between Africans and African Americans: Misconceptions, Myths and Realities.* Grand Rapids, MI: Pan-African Books.

N'Allah, Abdul-Rasheed, ed. 1998. *Ogoni's Agonies: Ken Saro-Wiwa and the Crisis in Nigeria.* Trenton, NJ: Africa World Press.

Newbury, C. W. 1964. *The West African Commonwealth.* Durham, NC: Duke University Press.

Ngugi, Mukoma W. 2011. "African in America or African American?" *Guardian.* January 14. http://www.guardian.co.uk/commentisfree/cifamerica/2011/jan/13/race-kenya.

Njue, John Gitaari. 2004. "Schooling and the Ethnicity of Race: Newcomer African Immigrant Children in a Predominantly Minority Urban High School (Minnesota)." Doctoral dissertation, University of Iowa.

Nkrumah, Kwame. 1957. *Ghana: The Autobiography of Kwame Nkrumah.* New York: Thomas Nelson.

Noel, Peter. 2000. "Africans Are Dying, Too: The Forgotten Victims of the Livery Cabbie Murders." *Village Voice.* April 18.

Nwoye, Augustine. 2009. "Understanding and Treating African Immigrant Families: New Questions and Strategies." *Psychotherapy and Politics International* 7 (2): 95–107.

Nyang, Sulayman. 1998. "The African Immigrant Family in the United States of America: Challenges and Opportunities." Paper presented at the Centre for African Peace and Conflict Resolution of California State University, Sacramento. http://connection.ebscohost.com/c/articles/90540562/african-immigrant-family-united-states-america-challenges-opportunities.

Obama, Barack. 2004. *Dreams of My Father: A Story of Race and Inheritance*. New York: Three Rivers Press.

Obi, Cyril I. 2001. *The Changing Forms of Identity Politics in Nigeria under Economic Adjustment: The Case of the Oil Minorities Movement of the Niger Delta*. Uppsala, Sweden: Nordic Africa Institute.

Obi, Samuel. 2010. *Readings for Amerigerian Igbo: Culture, History Language and Legacy*. http://www.authorhouse.com/Bookstore/BookDetail. aspx?BookId=SKU-000411589.

Obiakor, Festus E. 2010. "Beyond the Equity Rhetoric in America's Teacher Education Programs: An African Immigrant Voice." *Multicultural Learning and Teaching* 5 (1): 22–33.

Obiakor, Festus E. and Patrick A Grant, eds. 2002. *Foreign-Born African Americans: Silenced Voices in the Discourse on Race*. New York: Nova.

Ochonu, Moses. 2008. "Colonialism within Colonialism: The Hausa-Caliphate Imaginary and the British Colonial Administration of the Nigerian Middle Belt." *African Studies Quarterly* 10 (2–3). http://go.galegroup.com.ezproxy.bu.edu/ps/i.do?ty=as&v =2.1&lm=TX~Ochonu&u=mlin_b_bumml&it=search&s=DA-SORT&p=AONE&st =T002&dblist=AONE&qt=PU~%22African+Studies+Quarterly%22&sw=w.

Ochukpue, Winnie Edith Ngozi. 2004. "A Qualitative Study of African Immigrant Professors in Two Historically Black Institutions in a Southeastern State." Doctoral dissertation, North Carolina State University.

Odeyemi, Ayobami. 2007. "Illusion versus Reality: An Open Letter to My Brother in America." *U.S. Immigration News*. March 1.

Odi, Amusi. 1999. "The Igbo in Diaspora: The Binding Force of Information." *Libraries & Culture* 34 (1): 158–167.

Offoha, Marcellina. 1989. "Educated Nigerian Professionals in the United States: The Phenomenon of Brain Drain." Doctoral dissertation, Temple University.

Ogbaa, Kalu. 2003. *The Nigerian Americans*. Westport, CT: Greenwood.

Ogbu, John. 1991. "Low School Performance as an Adaptation: The Case of Blacks in Stockton, California." In Gibson and Ogbu, *Minority Status and Schooling*, 249–286.

Ojiaku, Chief Uche Jom. 2007. *Surviving the Iron Curtain: A Microscopic View of What Life Was Like Inside a War-Torn Region*. Frederick, MD: Publish America.

Ojide, Chinyere. 2006. "African Legal Secretaries: Messiahs or Judases." *U.S. Immigration News*. May 1.

Okafor, Lawrence. 2003. *Recent African Immigrants to the U.S.A.: Their Concerns, and How Everyone Can Succeed in the U.S.A.* Pittsburgh: RoseDog Books.

Okeowo, Alexis. 2011. "In a Pageant: A Borough's New Face." *New York Times*. August 4.

Okome, Mojúbàolú Olúfúnké. 2002. "The Antinomies of Globalization: Causes of Contemporary African Immigration to the United States of America." *Ìrìnkèrindò: A Journal of African Migration* 1 (1): 1–34.

———. 2004. "Emergent African Immigrant Philanthropy in New York City." *Research in Urban Sociology* 7: 179–191.

———. 2005. "Amadou Diallo: Some Observations by Another African Immigrant."
     Africa Resource. http://www.africaresource.com.
Okonkwo, Rudolf Ogoo. 2010. "The Challenges in Raising African Boys in America."
     African Abroad. July 30: 28.
———. 2011. "Why Are Africans Dying Young in the USA?" *African Abroad*. March 15.
Okpewho, Isidore and Nkiru Nzegwu, eds. 2009. *The New African Diaspora*. Bloom-
     ington: Indiana University Press.
Okwu, Michael. 2005. "Family Tree Project Helps Trace Deep History." *Today*.
     November 18. http://today.msnbc.msn.com/id/10095659/ns/today/t/
     family-tree-project-helps-trace-deep-history/.
Olagoke, Ezekiel. 2003. "Religion and Globalization: African Christians in the United
     States." Paper presented at the annual meeting of the Association for the Sociology
     of Religion, Atlanta, GA. http://hirr.hartsem.edu/sociology/olagoke.html.
Olonisakin, Funmi. 2000. *Reinventing Peacekeeping in Africa: Conceptual and Legal
     Issues in ECOMOG Operations*. New York: Springer.
Oloruntimehin, Olatunji. 1972. *The Segu Tukulor Empire*: London: Longman.
Olsen, Laurie. 1997. *Made in America: Immigrant Students in Our Public Schools*. New
     York: New Press.
Olumba, Ann Nosiri and Diane N'Diaye. 1997. "Local Radio and Local Populations:
     African Immigrants in Washington, D.C." *Cultural Survival Quarterly* 20 (4): 51.
Olupona, Jacob. 2007. "Communities of Believers: Exploring African Immigrant Reli-
     gion in the United States." In Olupona and Gemignani, *African Immigrant Religions
     in America*, 27–46.
Olupona, Jacob and Regina Gemignani, eds. 2007. *African Immigrant Religions in
     America*. New York: New York University Press.
Omobowale, Ayokunle Olumuyiwa, Mofeyisara Oluwatoyin Omobowale, and Olawale
     Olufolahan Ajami. 2010. "Emigration and the Social Value of Remittances in Nige-
     ria." In Yewah and Togunde, *Across the Atlantic*, 127–136.
Oropesa, R. S. and Nancy Landale. 1997. "In Search of the New Second Generation:
     Alternative Strategies for Identifying Second Generation Children and Understand-
     ing Their Acquisition of English." *Sociological Perspectives* 40 (3): 429–455.
Osaghae, E. 1995. *Structural Adjustment and Ethnicity in Nigeria*. Uppsala: Nordic
     Africa Institute.
Osirim, Mary Johnson. 2010. "The New African Diaspora: Transnationalism and
     Transformation in Philadelphia." In *Global Philadelphia: Immigrant Communities
     Old and New*, ed. Ayumi Takenaka and Mary Johnson Osirim. Philadelphia: Temple
     University Press: 226–252.
Ousmane, Semebene. 1987. *The Black Docker*. Portsmouth, NH: Heinemann.
Owolabi, Robert O. 1996. *An African's View of the American Society: An Eyewitness
     Account of 15 Years of Living, Studying and Working in the United States of America*.
     Chapel Hill, NC: Professional Press.
Owusu, Thomas. 1999. "Residential Patterns and Housing Choices of Ghanaian Immi-
     grants in Toronto, Canada." *Housing Studies* 14 (1): 77–97.

———. 2000. "The Role of Ghanaian Immigrant Associations in Toronto, Canada." *International Migration Review* 34 (4): 1155–1181.

Page, Clarence. 2007. "Black Immigrants Collect More Degrees." *Chicago Tribune.* March 18.

Palk, Susannah Palk. 2010. "Kase Lawal: Not Your Average Oil Baron," *CNN.* May 18. http://www.cnn.com/2010/WORLD/africa/05/18/kase.lukman.lawal/index.html.

Pearce, Susan. 2006. *Immigrant Women in the United States: A Demographic Portrait.* Washington, DC: Immigration Policy Center.

Pedraza, Silvia. 1991. "Women and Migration: The Social Consequences of Gender." *Annual Review of Sociology* 17: 303–325.

Peil, Margaret. 1995. "Ghanaians Abroad." *African Affairs* 94 (376): 345–367.

Perry, Donna L. 1997. "Rural Ideologies and Urban Imaginings: Wolof Immigrants in New York City." *Africa Today* 44 (2): 229–259.

Pessar, Patricia. 2001. "The Dominicans: Women in Households and the Garment Industry." In *New Immigrants in New York*, ed. Nancy Foner. New York: Columbia University Press: 251–274.

Pfeffermann, Guy. 1967. "Trade Unions and Politics in French West Africa during the Fourth Republic." *African Affairs* 66 (264): 213–230.

Pop, Georgiana. 2011. "Cape Verde." In *Remittance Markets in Africa*, ed. Dilip Ratha and Sanket Mohapatra. Washington, DC: World Bank: 91–111.

Portes, Alejandro and Patricia Fernández-Kelly. 2008. "No Margin for Error: Educational and Occupational Achievement among Disadvantaged Children of Immigrants." *Annals of the American Academy of Political and Social Science* 620 (1): 12–36.

Portes, Alejandro, Patricia Fernández-Kelly, and William Haller. 2005. "Segmented Assimilation on the Ground: The New Second Generation in Early Adulthood." *Ethnic and Racial Studies* 28 (6): 1000–1040.

Portes, Alejandro, Luis E. Guarnizo, and Patricia Landdolt. 1999. "The Study of Transnationalism: Pitfalls and Promises of an Emergent Social Field." *Ethnic and Racial Studies* 22 (2): 217–236.

Portes, Alejandro and Min Zhou. 1993. "The New Second Generation: Segmented Assimilation and Its Variants." *Annals of the American Academy of Political and Social Science* 530: 74–96.

Powell, Michael and Nina Bernstein. 2007. "In Tragedy, Glimpsing Oft-Overlooked Newcomers' Lives." *New York Times.* March 10.

Powers, John. 2012. "For Obukwelu Brothers, Harvard Football Is Family." *Boston Globe.* November 16: C1, C10.

Quart, Alissa. 2007. "The Child Soldiers of Staten Island." *Mother Jones.* June 30. http://www.motherjones.com/commentary/columns/2007/07/witness.html.

Quigley, Mary. 2002. *Ancient West African Kingdoms: Ghana, Mali and Songhai.* Portsmouth, NH: Heinemann.

Ratha, Dilip, Sanket Mohapatra, Caglar Ozden, Sonia Plaza, William Shaw, and Abebe Shimeles. 2011. *Leveraging Migration for Africa: Remittances, Skills and Investments.* Washington, DC: World Bank. http://siteresources.worldbank.org/

EXTDECPROSPECTS/Resources/476882-1157133580628/AfricaStudyEntireBook. pdf.

Reimers, David. 1983. "An Unintended Reform: The 1965 Immigration Act and Third World Immigration to the United States." *Journal of American Ethnic History* 3 (1): 9–28.

———. 2005. *Other Immigrants: Global Origins of the American People.* New York: New York University Press.

Reynolds, Rachel R. 2002. "An African Brain Drain: Igbo Decisions to Immigrate to the US." *Review of African Political Economy* 92: 273–294.

Riccio, Bruno. 2001. "Disaggregating the Transnational Community: Senegalese Migrants on the Coast of Emilia-Romagna." Working paper series, University of Oxford Transnational Communities, an ESRC Research Programme.

———. 2008. "West African Transnationalisms Compared: Ghanaians and Senegalese in Italy." *Journal of Ethnic and Migration Studies* 34 (2): 217–234.

Rimer, Sara and Karen Arenson. 2004. "Top Colleges Take More Blacks, but Which Ones?" *New York Times.* June 24.

Roberts, Stephen V. 2009. *From Every End of the Earth: Thirteen Families and the New Lives They Made in America.* New York: Harper.

Robinson, David. 1971. "The Impact of Al-Hajj 'Umar on the Historical Traditions of the Fulbe." *Journal of the Folklore Institute* 8 (2–3): 101–113.

———. 2000. *Paths of Accommodation: Muslim Societies and French Colonial Authorities in Senegal and Mauritania, 1880–1920.* Athens: Ohio University Press.

Robinson, Eugene. 2010. *Disintegration: The Splintering of Black America.* New York: Doubleday.

Robinson, Lori. 2006. "Black Like Whom?" *Crisis* 113 (1): 24–30.

Rocklin, Jeremy. 2007. *Dollars and Dreams: West Africans in New York.* Film. Watertown, MA: Documentary Educational Resources.

Rogers, Reuel. 2001. "'Black Like Who?' Afro-Caribbean Immigrants, African Americans, and the Politics of Group Identity." In *Islands in the City: West Indian Migration to New York,* ed. Nancy Foner. Berkeley: University of California Press: 163–192.

———. 2004. "Race-Based Coalitions among Minority Groups: Afro-Caribbean Immigrants and African-Americans in New York City." *Urban Affairs Review* 39 (3): 283–317.

Romero, Patricia, ed. 1992. *Women's Voices on Africa: A Century of Travel Writing.* Princeton, NJ: Marcus Wiener.

Rong, Xue Lan and Frank Brown. 2001. "The Effects of Immigrant Generation and Ethnicity on Educational Attainment among Young African and Caribbean Blacks in the United States." *Harvard Educational Review* 71 (3): 536–565.

———. 2002. "Socialization, Culture, and Identities of Black Immigrant Children: What Educators Need to Know and Do." *Education and Urban Society* 34 (2): 247–273.

Rooks, Noliwe M. 1996. *Hair Raising: Beauty, Culture, and African American Women.* New Brunswick, NJ: Rutgers University Press.

"Roots and Race." 2004. *Harvard Magazine.* September–October: 69–70.

Rothchild, Donald and Victor Olorunsola, eds. 1983. *State versus Ethnic Claims: African Policy Dilemmas*. Boulder, CO: Westview.

Rozhon, Tracie. 2000, "TURF; Grit and Glory in South Harlem." *New York Times*. March 16.

Rumbaut, Rubén. 1991. "The Agony of Exile: A Study of the Migration and Adaptation of Indochinese Refugee Adults and Children." In *Refugee Children: Theory, Research, and Services*, ed. F. Ahearn, Jr. and H. Athey. Baltimore: Johns Hopkins University Press: 53–91.

———. 1994. "The Crucible Within: Ethnic Identity, Self-esteem and Segmented Assimilation among Children of Immigrants." *International Migration Review* 28 (4): 748–794.

———. 1997. "Ties That Bind: Immigration and Immigrant Families in the U.S." In *Immigration and the Family: Research and Policy on U.S. Immigrants*, ed. Alan Booth, Ann Crouter, and Nancy Landale. Mahwah, NJ: Lawrence Erlbaum: 3–45.

———. 2004. "Ages, Life Stages and Generational Cohorts: Decomposing the Immigrant First and Second Generations in the United States." *International Migration Review* 38 (3): 1160–1205.

Sachs, Susan. 1999. "Guineans Still See Opportunity in U.S." *New York Times*. February 21.

———. 2003. "In Harlem's Fabric: Bright Threads of Senegal." *New York Times*. July 28. http://www.nytimes.com/2003/07/28/nyregion/in-harlem-s-fabric-bright-threads-of-senegal.html?pagewanted=all&src=pm.

Salzbrunn, Monika. 2004. "The Occupation of Public Space through Religious and Political Events: How Senegalese Migrants Became a Part of Harlem, New York." *Journal of Religion in Africa* 34 (4): 468–492.

Samuelsson, Marcus. 2006. *The Soul of a New Cuisine: The Discovery of the Foods and Flavors of Africa*. Hoboken, NJ: John Wiley.

———. 2012. *Yes, Chef: A Memoir*. New York: Random House.

Sánchez, Gina. "Contested Identities: Negotiating Race and Culture in a Cape Verdean Diaspora Community." Doctoral dissertation, University of Texas at Austin, 1999.

Sangweni, Yolanda. 2011. "Generation Next: Meet the Afropolitans, Africa's Transcontinental Children." *Arise Magazine*. March: 96–101. http://www.arisemagazine.net/articles/generation-next/87396/.

Saro-Wiwa, Ken. 1991. *Nigeria: The Brink of Disaster and Genocide in Nigeria*. Port Harcourt, Nigeria: Saros International.

Sax-Conteh, Jacob. 2010. "So You Won the Diversity Visa Lottery? What Next?" *Cocorioko*. June 18. http://www.cocorioko.net/old/national/2986.

Schaller Consulting. 2004. "The Changing Face of Taxi and Limousine Drivers." http://www.schallerconsult.com/taxi/taxidriver.pdf.

Schildkrout, Enid. 2006. "One Family's History: A Microcosmic History of West African Migration." Introductory remarks at the Immigrants: Africans in New York Symposium. April 21. http://www.africanart.org/uploads/resources/docs/enids_paper.

Schmidt, Elizabeth. 2007. *Cold War and Decolonization in Guinea, 1946–1958*. Athens: Ohio University Press.

Schmidt, Susan. 2005. "Liberian Refugees: Cultural Considerations for Social Service Providers." Baltimore: Lutheran Immigration & Refugee Services and U.S. Conference of Catholic Bishops Migration and Refugee Services.

Seaklon, Timothy T. 2008. "Liberia: 400 Denied DV Visa." October 1. http://allafrica.com.

Selasi, Taiye. 2013. *Ghana Must Go*. New York: Penguin.

Selassie, Bereket. 1996. "Washington's New African Immigrants." In *Washington Odyssey: A Multicultural History of the Nation's Capital*, ed. Francine Curro Cary. Washington, DC: Smithsonian Books: 264–275.

Shaw-Taylor, Yoku. 2007. "The Intersection of Assimilation, Race, Presentation of Self, and Transnationalism in America. In Shaw-Taylor and Tuch, *Other African Americans*, 1–47.

Shaw-Taylor, Yoku and Stephen Tuch, eds. 2007. *The Other African Americans: Contemporary African and Caribbean Immigrants in the United States*. Lanham, MD: Rowman & Littlefield.

Sheldon, Kathleen, ed. 1996. *Courtyards, Markets, City Streets: Urban Women in Africa*. Boulder, CO: Westview.

Sherman, John. 2002. *War Stories: A Memoir of Nigeria and Biafra*. Indianapolis: Mesa Verde Press.

Showers, Fumilayo E. 2011. "'We Are the Real Nurses, They Are Just Opportunists': How African Immigrant Nurses Craft and Manage Professional Identities at Work." Paper presented at the Eastern Sociological Society meeting, Philadelphia, February.

Showers, Violet. 1979. "A History of the Methodist Girls School, Freetown, Sierra Leone." Bachelor's dissertation, Fourah Bay College.

Sieber, Tim. 2005. "Popular Music and Cultural Identity in the Cape Verdean Post-Colonial Diaspora." *Etnográfica* 9 (1): 123–148.

Simmons, Ann. 2003. "A Common Ground in African Heritage: Little Ethiopia Event Aims to Bring Black Americans and Immigrants Together." *Los Angeles Times*. November 24: B1.

Sinduhije, Alexis. 1998. "Welcome to America." *Transition* 0 (78): 4–23.

Singer, Audrey. 2004. "The Rise of New Immigrant Gateways." Brookings Institution Living Cities Census Series. February. http://www.brookings.edu/reports/2004/02demographics_singer.aspx.

Singer, Audrey, Susan Hardwick, and Caroline Brettell, eds. 2008. *Twenty-First Century Gateways: Immigrant Incorporation in Suburban America*. Washington, DC: Brookings Institution.

Sleber, Roy and Frank Hereman, eds. 2000. *Hair in African Art and Culture*. New York: Museum of Fine Art.

Smith, Elmer. 2005. "'Normal' at Tilden Middle School Is Different." *Philadelphia Inquirer*. November 4.

Smith, M. G. 1997. *Government in Kano, 1350–1950*. Boulder, CO: Westview.

Smith, Robert C. 2005. *Mexican New York: Transnational Lives of New Immigrants*. Berkeley: University of California Press.

Smith, Robert S. 1989. *Warfare and Diplomacy in Pre-colonial West Africa*. Madison: University of Wisconsin Press.

Southwick, Natalie. 2010. "Marie-Claude Mendy Brings African Cuisine—and Art and Hospitality—to Teranga in Boston's South End." *Boston Globe*. August 18. http://www.boston.com/lifestyle/food/articles/2010/08/18/teranga_serves_up_a_taste_of_senegal/.

Staples, Brent. 2007. "Decoding the Debate over the Blackness of Barack Obama." *New York Times*. February 11.

Staudinger, Paul. 1990. *In the Heart of Hausa States*. Athens: Ohio University Press.

Stevens, W. David. 2004. "Spreading the Word: Religious Beliefs and the Evolution of Immigrant Congregations." *Sociology of Religion* 65 (2): 121–138.

Stoller, Paul. 1996. "Spaces, Places, and Fields: The Politics of West African Trading in New York City's Informal Economy." *American Anthropologist* 98 (4): 776–788.

———. 2002. *Money Has No Smell: The Africanization of New York City*. Chicago: University of Chicago Press.

———. 2003. "Marketing Afrocentricity: West African Trade Networks in North America." In Koser, *New African Diasporas*, 71–94.

Suárez-Orozco, Marcelo. 1991. "Immigrant Adaptation to Schooling: A Hispanic Case." In Gibson and Ogbu, *Minority Status and Schooling*, 37–61.

Swarns, Rachel. 2004. "African-American Becomes a Term for Debate." *New York Times*. August 29.

Swigart, Leigh. 2001. *Extended Lives: The African Immigrant Experience in Philadelphia*. Philadelphia: Balch Institute for Ethnic Studies.

Swindell, Ken. 1980. "Serawoollies, Tillibunkas and Strange Farmers: The Development of Migrant Groundnut Farming along the Gambia River, 1848–95." *Journal of African History* 21: 93–104.

Táíwò, Olúfémi. 2003. "This Prison Called My Skin: On Being Black in America." In Hintzen and Rahier, *Problematizing Blackness*, 41–42, 47–48.

Takougang, Joseph. 1995. "Recent African Immigrants to the United States: A Historical Perspective." *Western Journal of Black Studies* 19 (1): 50–57.

———. 2003. "Contemporary African Immigrants to the United States." http://www.africamigration.com/archive_02/j_takougang.htm.

Takyi, Baffour. 2002. "The Making of the Second Diaspora: On the Recent African Immigrant Community in the United States of America." *Western Journal of Black Studies* 26 (1): 32–43.

———. 2009. "Africans Abroad: Comparative Perspectives on America's Postcolonial West Africans." In Okpewho and Nzegwu, *New African Diaspora*, 236–254.

Terrazas, Aaron. 2009. "African Immigrants in the United States." Migration Policy Institute. http://www.migrationinformation.org/USfocus/display.cfm?id=719.

Tetty, Wisdom and Korbla Puplampu, eds. 2005. *The African Diaspora in Canada: Negotiating Identity and Belonging*. Calgary: University of Calgary Press.

Tham, Dan Q. 2011. "Driving a Cab: The African Immigrant's Signature Underemployment." *Immigrant Connect*. June. http://www.immigrantconnect.org/2011/06/19/driving-a-cab-the-african-immigrants-signature-underemplyment.

Thomas, Dominic. 2007. *Black France: Colonialism, Immigration and Transnationalism*. Bloomington: Indiana University Press.

Thomas, Kevin. 2011. "What Explains the Increasing Trend in African Emigration to the U.S.?" *International Migration Review* 45 (1): 3–28.

Thompson, Ginger. 1999. "1,000 Rally to Condemn Shooting of Unarmed Man by Police," *New York Times*. February 8.

Thompson, Kenny and Daren Vertein. 2010. "Rethinking Gender Stereotypes in Nursing." *Minority Nurse*. Spring. http://www.minoritynurse.com/men-nursing/rethinking-gender-stereotypes-nursing.

Tierney, Brain. 2011. "The War on DC Taxi Drivers." *Washington Post*. July 1.

Togunde, 'Dimeji and Jacob Rinkinen. 2009. "Agents of Change: Differences in Migration Intentions among University Undergraduates in Nigeria." *International Journal of Interdisciplinary Social Sciences* 4 (2): 175–190.

Trager, Lillian. 2001. *Yoruba Hometowns: Community, Identity, and Development in Nigeria*. Boulder, CO: Lynne Rienner.

Traoré, Rosemary Luckens. 2004. "Colonialism Continued: African Students in an Urban High School in America." *Journal of Black Studies* 34: 348–369.

Ugwu-Oju, Dympna. 1995. *What Will My Mother Say: A Tribal African Girl Comes of Age in America*. Chicago: Bonus Books.

Ungar, Sanford. 1995. *Fresh Blood: The New American Immigrants*. New York: Simon & Schuster.

Uwechwe, Ralph. 2006. *Reflections on the Nigerian Civil War: Facing the Future*. Bloomington, IN: Trafford.

Uzoigwe, Godfrey. 2008. "A Matter of Identity. Africa and Its Diaspora in America since 1900, Continuity and Change." *African and Asian Studies* 7 (2–3): 259–288.

Uzokwe, Alfred. 2003. *Surviving in Biafra: The Story of the Nigerian Civil War*. Bloomington, IN: iUniverse.

van Beek, Walter. 1988. "Purity and Statecraft: The Nineteenth Century Fulani Jihad of North Nigeria." in *The Quest for Purity: Dynamics of Puritan Movements*, ed. Walter van Beek. Berlin: Mouton de Gruyter: 149–182.

van Dalen, Hendrik, George Groenewold, and Jeannette Schoorl. 2005. "Out of Africa: What Drives the Pressure to Emigrate?" *Journal of Population Economics* 18 (4): 741–778.

Van Hear, Nicholas. 1998. *New Diasporas: The Mass Exodus, Dispersal and Regrouping of Migrant Communities*. London: UCL Press.

Veney, Cassandra R. 2009. "The Effects of Immigration and Refugee Policies on Africans in the United States: From the Civil Rights Movement to the War on Terrorism." In Okpewho and Nzegwu, *New African Diaspora*, 196–214.

Vertovec, Steven. 2009. *Transnationalism*. New York: Routledge.

Vickerman, Milton. 1999. *Crosscurrents: West Indian Immigrants and Race*. New York: Oxford University Press.

Waldman, Amy. 1999. "Shooting in the Bronx: The Immigrants; Killing Heightens in the Unease Felt by Africans in New York." *New York Times*. February 14.

Waldman, Marilyn Robinson. 1965. "The Fulani Jihad: A Reassessment." *Journal of African History* 6 (3): 333–355.

Walker, James W. St. G. 1976, reprinted 1992. *The Black Loyalists: Search for a Promised Land in Nova Scotia and Sierra Leone*. Toronto: University of Toronto Press.

Walker, Monique. 2011. "Safety Help: Patriots' Ihedigbo Follows Parents' Example with His Education Foundation." *Boston Globe*. October 16: C1, C12.

Wamba, Philippe. 1999. *Kinship: A Family's Journey in Africa and America*. New York: Plume.

Washington, Booker T. 1909, reprinted 1969. *The Story of the Negro: The Rise of the Race from Slavery*. Vol. 1. New York: Negro University Press.

Waters, Mary C. 1999. *Black Identities: West Indian Immigrant Dreams and American Realities*. New York: Russell Sage.

Wax, Emily. 2011. "Trading Up: Swathing the World in African Fashion." *Washington Post*. July 1: C1, C7.

Werner, Heinz. 1978. "Some Current Topics of Labor Migration in Europe." *Intereconomics* 13 (3): 94–97.

West, Cornel. *Race Matters*. New York: Vintage, 1994.

Whaley, Daisy. 2002. "My Experience as a West African Missionary." In *African American Experience in World Mission: A Call beyond Community*, ed. Vaughn T. Watson and Robert J. Stevens. Atlanta: COMINAD: 113–121.

Wilder, Gary. 2005. *The French Imperial Nation-State: Negritude and Colonial Humanism between the Two World Wars*. Chicago: University of Chicago Press.

Wilks, Ivor. 1995. *Forests of Gold: Essays on the Akan and the Kingdom of Asante*. Athens: Ohio University Press.

Williams, Brandt. 2002. "Problems of Assimilation." Minnesota Public Radio. February 4. http://news.minnesota.publicradio.org/features/200202/04_williamsb_africans/assimilation.shtml.

Williams, Monte. 2001. "Bargain Braiders Battle for Heads; Hair Stylists from Africa Arrive, Driving Down Prices." *New York Times*. May 19.

Williams, Zachery, Robert Samuel Smith, Seneca Vaught and, Babacar M'Baye. 2008. "A History of Black Immigration into the United States through the Lens of the African Civil Rights and Human Rights Movement." In *Immigrant Rights in the Shadow of Citizenship*, ed. Rachael Ida Buff. New York: New York University Press: 159–178.

Wilson, Jill. 2003. "African-Born Residents of the United States." Washington, DC: Migration Policy Institute. http://www.migrationinformation.org/USfocus/display.cfm?id=147.

———. 2003. "African Immigrants in Metropolitan Washington: A Demographic Overview." Washington, DC: Brookings Institution. http://www.brookings.edu/es/urban/speeches/20031118_wilson.htm.

———. 2003. "Africans on the Move: A Descriptive Geography of African Immigration to the United States with a Focus on Metropolitan Washington, D.C." Master's thesis, George Washington University.

———. 2010. "Spatial and Demographic Trends in African Immigration to the U.S." Paper presented at the Colloquium on New Americans from Africa and the Immigrant Experience in the United States, George Washington University, May 19.

Wilson, Jill and Shelly Habecker. 2008. "The Lure of the Capital City: An Anthro-geographical Analysis of Recent African Immigration to Washington, D.C." *Population, Space and Place* 14 (5): 433–448.

Woronoff, Jon. 1972. *West African Wager: Houphouet Versus Nkrumah*. Metuchen, NJ: Scarecrow Press.

Wyse, Akintola. 1989. *The Krio of Sierra Leone: An Interpretive History*. Madison: University of Wisconsin Press.

Yeboah, Ian. 2008. *Black African Neo-Diaspora: Ghanaian Immigrant Experiences in the Greater Cincinnati, Ohio, Area*. Lanham, MD: Lexington Books.

Yenika-Agbaw, Vivian. 2009. "African Child Rearing in the Diaspora: A Mother's Perspective." *Journal of Pan African Studies* 3 (4): 3–13.

Yewah, Emmanuel and 'Dimeji Togunde, eds. 2010. *Across the Atlantic: African Immigrants in the United States Diaspora*. Champaign, IL: Common Ground.

Yu, Elly W. 2013. "African Immigrants in Bronx Vying for City Council Seat Traditionally Held by African Americans." *New York Daily News*. March 1.

Zehr, Mary Ann. 2001. "Out of Africa." *Education Week* 20 (27): 30–36.

Zeleza, Paul Tiyambe. 2004. "The African Academic Diaspora in the United States and Africa: The Challenges of Productive Engagement." *Comparative Studies of South Asia, Africa, and the Middle East* 24 (1): 265–278.

Zhou, Min. 1997. "Growing Up American: The Challenge Confronting Immigrant Children and Children of Immigrants." *Annual Review of Sociology* 23: 63–95.

Zhou, Min and Carl Bankston. 1998. *Growing Up American: The Adaptation of Vietnamese Adolescents in the United States*. New York: Russell Sage Foundation.

Zolberg, Aristede. 1967. *Creating Political Order: The Party-States of West Africa*. Skokie, IL: Rand McNally.

INDEX

Marilyn Halter is Professor of History and American Studies at Boston University, where she is also a Research Associate at the Institute on Culture, Religion and World Affairs. Her books include *Between Race and Ethnicity: Cape Verdean American Immigrants, 1860–1965* and *Shopping for Identity: The Marketing of Ethnicity.*

Violet Showers Johnson is Professor of History and Director of Africana Studies at Texas A&M University. Her publications include *The Other Black Bostonians: West Indians in Boston, 1900–1950.*